Post-Keynesian Views of the Crisis and its Remedies

At the end of the twentieth century, mainstream economics was based on theories which viewed capitalism as a self-regulating system, whereby crises come about due to external shocks and would be automatically corrected by the price mechanism if it was flexible enough. Post-Keynesian economists, however, consider that the business cycle and the crises are endogenously generated. They recommend active policies as a response, though the remedies may be worse than the illness if they are not applied at the right moment and in the right proportions.

The first great recession of the twenty-first century offers post-Keynesian economists an opportunity to prove the realism of their models. It is also a chance to make theoretical improvements, to abandon some hypotheses and to introduce new ones.

This book, from a top group of international economists, analyses the causes, consequences and evolution of the crisis from a variety of post-Keynesian perspectives. It then presents a case for realistic and essential remedies. The book is both theoretical and applied, with a global reach and a particular focus on the European debt crisis.

Óscar Dejuán is Professor of Economics and Head of the Department of Economics and Finance at University of Castilla-La Mancha, Spain

Eladio Febrero is a lecturer at University of Castilla-La Mancha, Spain

Jorge Uxó is a lecturer at University of Castilla-La Mancha, Spain

Routledge critical studies in finance and stability

Edited by Jan Toporowski

School of Oriental and African Studies, University of London, UK

The 2007–8 Banking Crash has induced a major and wide-ranging discussion on the subject of financial (in)stability and a need to revaluate theory and policy. The response of policy-makers to the crisis has been to refocus fiscal and monetary policy on financial stabilisation and reconstruction. However, this has been done with only vague ideas of bank recapitalisation and 'Keynesian' reflation aroused by the exigencies of the crisis, rather than the application of any systematic theory or theories of financial instability.

Routledge Critical Studies in Finance and Stability covers a range of issues in the area of finance including instability, systemic failure, financial macroeconomics in the vein of Hyman P. Minsky, Ben Bernanke and Mark Gertler, central bank operations, financial regulation, developing countries and financial crises, new portfolio theory and New International Monetary and Financial Architecture.

1 **Banking Systems in the Crisis**
The faces of Liberal capitalism
Edited by Sue Konzelmann and Marc Fovargue-Davies

2 **Post-Keynesian Views of the Crisis and its Remedies**
Edited by Óscar Dejuán, Eladio Febrero and Jorge Uxó

Post-Keynesian Views of the Crisis and its Remedies

Edited by Óscar Dejuán, Eladio Febrero and Jorge Uxó

Routledge
Taylor & Francis Group
LONDON AND NEW YORK

First published 2013
by Routledge
2 Park Square, Milton Park, Abingdon, Oxon OX14 4RN

Simultaneously published in the USA and Canada
by Routledge
711 Third Avenue, New York, NY 10017

Routledge is an imprint of the Taylor & Francis Group, an informa business

British Library Cataloguing in Publication Data
A catalogue record for this book is available from the British Library

Library of Congress Cataloging in Publication Data
Post-Keynesian views of the crisis and its remedies/edited by Óscar Dejuán, Eladio Febrero and Jorge Uxó.
pages cm
1. Global Financial Crisis, 2008–2009. 2. Recessions. 3. Financial crises–Government policy. 4. International finance. 5. Economic policy. 6. Keynesian economics. I. Dejuán, Óscar. II. Febrero, Eladio. III. Uxó González, Jorge.
HB37172008.P67 2013
330.9′0511–dc23 2012041707

ISBN: 978-0-415-82276-3 (hbk)
ISBN: 978-0-203-52854-9 (ebk)

Typeset in Times New Roman
by Wearset Ltd, Boldon, Tyne and Wear

Contents

Figures

Tables

Contributors

Nigel F.B. Allington, Ecole de Management, Grenoble, France; and Centre for Economic and Public Policy and Downing College, University of Cambridge, United Kingdom.

Fabián Amico, University of Luján, Argentina.

Philip Arestis, University of Cambridge, United Kingdom; and University of the Basque Country, Spain.

Alberto Bagnai, Università 'Gabriele D'Annunzio', Italy.

Fernando Bermejo, University of Castilla-La Mancha, Spain.

Sergio Cesaratto, University of Siena, Italy.

Óscar Dejuán, University of Castilla-La Mancha, Spain.

Steven M. Fazzari, Weidenbaum Center on the Economy, Government and Public Policy, Washington University in St. Louis, United States of America.

Eladio Febrero, University of Castilla-La Mancha, Spain.

Alejandro Fiorito, University of Luján, Argentina.

Ana-Rosa González, University of the Basque Country, Spain.

Eckhard Hein, Berlin School of Economics and Law and Institute for International Political Economy (IPE) Berlin, Germany.

Richard C. Koo, Nomura Research Institute, Tokyo, Japan.

Kazimierz Laski, Vienna Institute for International Economic Studies, Austria.

John S.L. McCombie, Centre for Economic and Public Policy and Downing College, University of Cambridge, United Kingdom.

Jesús Paúl, CEU-San Pablo University, Spain.

Maureen Pike, Centre for Economic and Public Policy, University of Cambridge, United Kingdom.

Leon Podkaminer, Vienna Institute for International Economic Studies, Austria.

Jorge Uxó, University of Castilla-La Mancha, Spain.

Introduction

Óscar Dejuán, Eladio Febrero and Jorge Uxó

Another book on the crisis? Value added of this book

The Great Depression of 1929 not only shook the foundations of the economy but also those of economics as a science. At that time Keynes was finishing the *Treatise of Money*, a work that proposed some changes in the traditional interpretation of the business cycle. While the book was in press, he realized that instead of amending the paradigm he had better shift to a different one. In a letter to George Bernard Shaw, dated 1935, Keynes wrote:

> you have to know that I believe myself to be writing a book on economic theory which will largely revolutionize – not, I suppose, at once but in the course of the next ten years – the way the world thinks about economic problems.

A new economic paradigm certainly emerged from the dashes of the Great Depression. Yet, Keynes's novel ideas were soon absorbed by mainstream economics. Only a few of Keynes's and Kalecki's disciples tried to deploy its revolutionary content. We are thinking of people like Roy Harrod, Richard Kahn, Joan Robinson or Nicholas Kaldor. This is the origin of the post-Keynesian school. A group that, despite its small size, has generally had a say in the major economic debates of the second half of the twentieth century. This is an advantage of being near the loudspeaker of economics.

The Great Recession of 2008 is comparable in depth and length to that of 1929. Can it be interpreted and solved by the neoclassical paradigm that continues to be the dominant one? Are the old Keynesian ideas a better alternative or should they be redefined to adapt to new circumstances? Would new economic ideas and new institutions emerge from the current crisis to define a brand new paradigm?

In a previous book (Dejuán *et al.*, 2011) we asked economists from different streams of thought to reflect on the causes of the first Great Recession of the twenty-first century. "Competing views on the crisis" was its subtitle. We realized how difficult it is for human nature to recognize its own mistakes and to be open to new ways of thinking. In this book we focus on a single school: post-Keynesianism. Since economic crises are embedded in the post-Keynesian model, one might expect that it would be better equipped to deal with them. But this is something that has still to be proved in books like this.

Most of the contributions came from special sessions on the crisis organized at the traditional post-Keynesian meeting points (Cambridge, Bilbao, Berlin, to be more precise). All in all there are 12 chapters, written by 18 authors, affiliated to 11 universities and research centres located in nine different countries. The focus lies on the Eurozone, which is at the epicentre of the crisis right now. Yet the book contains relevant exponents from the US where the crisis started in 2007–2008, from Japan which, 18 years earlier, experienced a major financial crash, and from Latin America whose economies have suffered recurrently from financial shocks. All of the contributors have made an effort to think about the kind of policies that will get us out of the crisis and the type of institutions that may prevent similar crises in the future. Nonetheless, we should not expect a systematic treatment of the topics. Repetitions and contradictions are unavoidable in a project like this. It's for the reader to judge whether the book conveys a coherent understanding of the crisis and its remedies.

Special features of post-Keynesian economics on which this book relies

So far we have assumed the existence of a post-Keynesian school of thought. The sceptical reader will raise, at least, two questions. Are there enough common elements among post-Keynesian economists to build a paradigm? Are these elements different from the ones that built the Great Neoclassical Synthesis, the neo-Keynesian school of macroeconomic thought, and other groups that fancy themselves as "Keynesian"?

One should admit that post-Keynesianism is an ongoing work that has as many facets as the schools involved in the deployment of the Keynesian revolution over the years (for a complete history of post-Keynesianism see King, 2002). To begin with, the post-Keynesian tree has two independent but complementary roots: Keynes and Kalecki. As a matter of fact, Kalecki was the most influential in the early Cambridge group, which tried to generalize and dynamize the *General Theory* by introducing distributive variables and growth. (Harrod, 1939; Kaldor, 1955–1956; Kaldor, 1957; Robinson, 1962). After 1960, Sraffian economists suggested blending the Keynesian theory of output and money with the classical theory of value and distribution (Sraffa, 1960; Garegnani, 1962; Pasinetti, 1974). In the US, radical Keynesians were more interested in the financial messages of the *General Theory*. Minsky (1975), Davidson (1978), and Kregel (1985) emphasized the problem of fundamental uncertainty that led the economy into recurrent liquidity and debt traps. Fundamental or radical uncertainty has given rise to continuing methodological debates (Dow, 1996[1985]). The post-Keynesian paradigm was also enriched (at the cost of more diversification) with the contributions of relevant institutionalists (from Galbraith (1967) till Hodgson (2004)) and evolutionary economists inspired by Schumpeter (1912/1934).

In a recent monographic number of ROPE (King, 2012) four alternative ways to relate with neoclassical economics are described: to ignore, to fight, to cooperate, or to compete. Mainstream economics can ignore post-Keynesianism altogether. Post-Keynesian economists cannot. If the latter want to be heard they have to demonstrate the inconsistencies of neoclassical theory and praxis. The criticisms of people like Arestis and Sawyer of the new Macroeconomic Consensus is a good example of this strategy (Arestis and Sawyer, 2004). At the same time, post-Keynesian economists have to prove that they are better equipped to deal with the real problems of the economy. One of the aims of this book is to show that they can provide a better explanation of the causes and remedies of the current crisis.

Despite these differences within the post-Keynesian school, one can find a theoretical and methodological core that defines a proper paradigm able to deal with most economic problems (Fontana and Stterfield, 2009; Lavoie, 2006). In this section we shall review the specific features of post-Keynesianism separating the real side from the financial side, and reserving a special section for balance of payment disequilibria. Policy prescriptions and institutional reforms also deserve their own section. This way of thinking has helped the editors to organize this book and, hopefully, will provide non-specialist readers with the necessary background.

The real side of the economy

The *principle of effective demand* constitutes the main novelty introduced by Keynes in the *General Theory* (Keynes, 1936). A simpler version was advanced by Kalecki in the early 1930s (Kalecki, 1971). According to this principle, the level of output and employment at a given moment of time does not depend on the available supply of labour and capital but on expected demand at "normal" prices. This principle may be stated in a simpler and more compelling way by means of the multiplier. The level of output and employment at a given moment will be a multiple of the expected autonomous demand which includes exports, public expenditure, and private investment. The multiplier reflects the adjustment through quantities as an alternative to the neoclassical adjustment via prices (which includes the real wage and the real rate of interest). The value of the multiplier depends on the propensity to consume. Keynes defines it as a psychological variable. Kalecki relates it to the distribution of income. A redistribution of income in favour of profits would depress the value of the multiplier and render the system more unstable.

Most Keynesian economists (integrated in the neoclassical synthesis) accept that demand may create isolated problems in the short run and require the types of stabilization policies suggested by Keynes. In the long run, however, the only conceivable equilibrium for them is the one corresponding to full employment. Real output will eventually grow at its natural rate given by demographical and technological trends. Post-Keynesian economists, on the contrary, apply the principle of effective demand both in the short and long run, both in a static context and a dynamic one. In a given year, output is a multiple of the expected level of autonomous demand. In the long run, the rate of growth of output will be a multiple of the expected growth of autonomous demand. Growth expectations constitute the key independent variable of the Keynesian system (Eatwell, 1983).

Yet these expectations change from time to time due to objective factors (let's say the saturation of the markets for the goods that were driving the economy so far) or subjective ones (a liquidity preference burst, for instance). Through the acceleration mechanism and induced technical change, autonomous demand triggers cumulative processes on income. This is the basis of the Kardor–Verdoorn growth model that is the starting point of some chapters.

Booms and busts are checked by the disequilibria they help to create. Inflation is the first one. They refer to a cost-push inflation depicted by the Phillips curve. In recent years, due to the globalization of the economy, the curve has flattened. Right now, the price of assets is a major matter of concern. The external deficit is a second disequilibrium and a bottleneck of growth as we are going to see.

The financial side

The relevance of money and finance constitutes the second cornerstone of the *General Theory*. Keynes made fun of mainstream economics that described capitalism as a barter economy where money is neutral. In a "monetary production economy", Keynes concluded, money is not neutral. "Money matters, Wall Street matters", became a typical post-Keynesian dictum. As we have already seen, Keynes and his first American followers emphasized the financial and economic problems derived from a sudden preference for liquidity in a world dominated by fundamental uncertainty. Over time, post-Keynesian economics have developed new categories of analysis that will appear in several chapters of our book: (1) endogeneity of money; (2) financial fragility; (3) stock-flow consistent models; (4) financialization.

"Money is credit driven and demand determined". This is another catchphrase of the school (Moore, 1988; Wray, 1998). The *endogeneity of credit-money* grants banks a central role in the circuit of income. They create the means of payment that allows the deployment of effective demand. After 1996, in an epoch when central banks opted for low interest rates, commercial banks tried to keep profitability high by multiplying the credit granted to households and firms. Yet, credit implies debt. At any given moment, the deflationary effect of the repayment of debt may be stronger than the impulse given by new credits. The theoreticians of the *monetary circuit* refer to the "efflux" and "refflux" movements of money and demand (Graziani, 2003). The *stock-flow consistent models* allow us to compute, more precisely, the deflationary impact of the stock of debt on the flows of disposable income and aggregate demand (Godley and Lavoie, 2006).

The financial fragility hypothesis highlights the tendency towards higher and riskier debt structures in times of prosperity, when banks compete for borrowers.

Fragility becomes dangerous when a significant part of all new loans are directed towards speculative purposes (Minsky, 1975, 2004). Keynes had already warned about this danger:

> Speculators may do no harm as bubbles on a steady stream of enterprise. But the position is serious when enterprise becomes the bubble on a whirlpool of speculation. When the capital development of a country becomes a by-product of the activities of a casino, the job is likely to be ill-done.
>
> (1936, p. 142)

The expansion of credit after 1996, and even more so after 2002, facilitated the creation of bubbles in the real estate and the stock exchange markets. The burst of these bubbles after 2007 heralded September 2008's financial crash.

The "financialization" of capitalist economies starts in the early twentieth century, as Hilferding aptly explained (1910/1981). At the beginning of the twenty-first century we can think in terms of a finance-dominated capitalism (Hein, 2012). Its dominance can be traced in the following facts that have played a role in the current financial crisis and its transmission to the real economy: (1) a higher weight of the value added of financial institutions; (2) a higher weight of property rents (interest payments and capital gains) over entrepreneurial profits and wages; (3) a higher indebtedness of all agents measured by the "debt/primary (or disposable) income" ratio; (4) continuous innovations to exploit new forms of speculation and to figure out new products that disguise the increasing risks of modern finance.

The balance of payments constraint

The real and financial side of economic relations go hand in hand with the balance of payments constraint. Post-Keynesian economists had stressed its significance in relation to growth (McCombie and Thirlwall, 1994). Developing countries are well aware that a persistent deficit aborts the growth process and may trigger an exchange rate crisis with long term consequences. In the future these countries will be obliged to pay a risk premium to borrow in international markets (Priewe and Herr, 2005). The external constraint was less binding for developed countries. The creation of a common European currency, led some economists to think that countries within the Eurozone could draw deficits forever since they could finance them at very low interest rates. The Euro has certainly stretched the limits of deficits and external debt burden. But the constraints have not disappeared and some countries have finally reached them. The interest payments on their huge external debt are causing a deflationary effect that delays the recovery of deficit countries. The amount of current account deficit and external debt also influences the risk premium on sovereign debt. Otherwise it would be impossible to explain the high risk premium that some European governments are paying despite their relatively low "sovereign debt/GDP" ratio.

Several chapters in this book remind us of a meaningful accounting identity: deficit and surplus are the two sides of the same coin. Persistent external deficits in Southern Europe reflect persistent surpluses in Northern Europe; China's permanent surplus would not be possible without the permanent deficit in the US; and so on. Keynes was aware that the balance of payments constraint was the international reflection of the problem of effective demand. His proposal at the Bretton Wood conference (a proposal that was dismissed in favour of White's plan) included the penalization of persistent surpluses. Far from reducing external trade, the goal was to encourage competitive countries to increase their own expenditure abroad.

Institutional reforms and economic policy

Keynes, Kalecki, and their post-Keynesian followers were conscious of the advantages of free-market economies. But they were no less conscious that they are unstable and prone to crises. A crisis may derive from economic disequilibria (inflation, current account deficits…) or from financial ones (hoarding, over-indebtedness, speculative bubbles, financial panics…). Under certain circumstances, the interplay between economic and financial variables may create a cumulative process that transforms a particular disequilibrium into a general crisis. For sure, certain economic mechanisms act in a countercyclical way. Yet there is no warranty that they will overcome the cyclical ones. It goes without saying that they cannot return the economy to a full employment path of growth whose very existence is denied by post-Keynesian economists.

Wise institutions are required to anchor expectations and smooth economic cycles. The International Clearing System proposed by Keynes at the Bretton Wood Conference, already mentioned, should be reconsidered, as some authors of this book actually have. It would prevent countries falling into the mercantilist temptation of running continuous surpluses in order to accumulate gold, foreign currencies, or financial assets. Another repeated conclusion is that central banks should play the role of "lenders of last resort" to sustain confidence in a world based on fiat money. They may create moral hazard problems. But the crisis has shown that unregulated financial institutions have also created a lot of them. Future reforms of the financial system should take care of ensuring the economic accountability of public and private decision makers.

Once the economy has fallen into a recession, governments should deploy an active economic policy to reactivate the economy as soon as possible. Most of the chapters in this book condemn the austerity policies implemented in the EU after mid 2010. If their goal was to balance the public budget they have been a complete and utter failure. After depressing demand and income, tax collection was bound to fall. Of course, fiscal policy has to be implemented at the right level (usually at the international one). And it should be reinforced by appropriate monetary measures. Otherwise the risk premium of sovereign debt may rise, as has been the case from mid 2010.

Monetary policy became somewhat downgraded after Keynes stated that liquidity traps make it useless, especially when it was more necessary (in recessions). Some post-Keynesian economists try to recover the prominence of monetary policy in a broader financial perspective. The goals of this policy should also be broadened. In the current global economy, inflation of produced goods and services (the only ones that enter into the CPI) is less of a problem than asset inflation. Both the central bank (CB) (through capital requirements) and the Treasury (via taxes on capital gains) should penalize loans devoted to speculative purposes. During the boom prior to the crisis, these loans pumped bubbles into the real estate market and into the stock exchange. When these bubbles burst in 2007, the way was paved for the financial crash of September 2008.

The reader should not expect full agreement on policy prescriptions, since they are influenced by ideological parameters. Post-Keynesian economists consider that capitalism is a rather unstable system, but they do not always recommend the same stabilization measures and they do not attach the same effectiveness to them. Some authors conclude their contributions with the warning that the suggested remedies could have disturbing effects in the long run.

Structure and content of the book

The authors of the 12 chapters of this book were asked to analyse the causes and remedies of the crisis from a post-Keynesian standpoint. Although all of them offer a thorough analysis of the crisis it is possible to group the chapters according to their analytical focus. The outline presented in the previous section may be useful for this task, although we'd better alter the order. The first part of the book gathers together the chapters which emphasize the financial problems that triggered off the crisis. Chapters in the second part focus on the balance of payments disequilibria that some contributors locate in the roots of the Eurozone debt crisis. This is common knowledge in developing countries that the expansion of China has disguised for the time being. In the third part we include chapters that stress the problems of the real economy and the performance of variables like investment, distribution, and so on. All of them highlight the failure of austerity policies implemented after 2010 and propose alternative ones.

Part I – The financial side: the burden of debt and the loss of confidence

1 *Eckhard Hein – Finance-dominated capitalism, re-distribution and the financial and economic crises: a European perspective.* In this chapter the euro crisis is viewed as the most recent episode of the crisis of finance-dominated capitalism. It is shown that the economic policy reactions of European governments and institutions, narrowly interpreting the crisis as a sovereign debt crisis caused by the irresponsible behaviour of some member country governments, are misguided and will lead to deflationary stagnation and an increasing risk of disintegration of the Euro area. For

this reason, an alternative macroeconomic policy approach, tackling the basic contradictions of finance-dominated capitalism and the deficiencies of European economic policy institutions and economic policy strategies, is outlined.

2 *Richard C. Koo – The world in balance sheet recession: causes, cures and politics.* Western economies head towards a Japan-like lost decade. The key difference with an ordinary recession, is that in a balance-sheet recession the private sector minimizes debt, following the bursting of a nationwide asset price bubble, and this can produce a lost decade. When a debt-financed bubble bursts, asset prices collapse while liabilities remain, leaving millions of private sector balance sheets underwater. Households and businesses are forced to repair their balance sheets by increasing savings or paying down debt and this act of deleveraging reduces aggregate demand and throws the economy into a very special type of recession. Today private sectors in the US, the UK, Spain, and Ireland are undergoing massive deleveraging in spite of record low interest rates. This means these countries are all in serious balance sheet recessions. Policy makers, spooked by the events in Greece, have pushed strongly to cut budget deficits, but nothing is worse than fiscal consolidation when a sick private sector is minimizing debt.

3 *Nigel F.B. Allington, John S.L. McCombie, and Maureen Pike – All lucky breaks come to an end: the shortcomings of macroeconomic models following the financial crisis and the contribution of behavioural economics to the reconfiguration of macroeconomics.* The subprime crisis raised some fundamental questions about the usefulness of mainstream economics. This chapter considers the shortcomings of the New Neoclassical Synthesis and the New Macroeconomic Consensus in analysing the causes and consequences of the crisis. It demonstrates that the major problem was the assumption that the future could be modelled in terms of Knightian risk (as in the rational expectations and efficient markets hypotheses). It is shown that the near collapse of the banking system in the advanced countries was due to a rapid increase in radical uncertainty. Suggestions are made for the future development of financial macroeconomics using the insights from behavioural economics.

4 *Óscar Dejuán – The debt trap.* A debt trap can be compared with quicksand. Both share the same fate: whatever you do, you become more and more trapped. Both in quicksand and debt traps salvation is supposed to come from outside and requires, to start with, the "draining" of the land/balance sheets. This chapter analyses how a handful of advanced countries fell into a debt trap and the difficulties in escaping from it despite serious efforts to cut off consumption and investment. It concludes that the EU and the European central bank (ECB) should help in the restructuring of debt. The chapter uses a post-Keynesian model where economic flows and financial stocks are interrelated. Consumption and the income multiplier depend on the indebtedness ratio.

Part II – The balance of payments constraint: trade deficits as a source of risky debt

5 *Sergio Cesaratto – Controversial and novel features of the Eurozone crisis as a balance of payments crisis.* This contribution examines alternative conventional and heterodox explanations of the Eurozone foreign imbalances. On the one hand, those provided both by neoclassical and by influential mainstream German economists; on the other, those who interpret the crisis as a classical Balance of Payments (BoP) crisis and relate it to German mercantilism. While the chapter favours the interpretation of the crisis as a BoP crisis, it also points out some novel features of the Eurozone crisis compared to previous experiences. These original tracts look at the role of the Eurosystem (ECB plus national central banks) in refinancing the BoP deficits of peripheral countries.

6 *Alberto Bagnai – Unhappy families are all alike: Minskyan cycles, Kaldorian growth, and the Eurozone peripheral crises.* Most analyses of the causes of the Eurozone crisis seem to have reached a consensus about one point, namely, that every peripheral country is in crisis in its own way. This chapter states that, on the contrary, insisting on analogies could prove more useful and it permits the highlighting of the role of the Eurozone core in the build-up of the crisis. This is certainly not the first time that a country or a group of countries are being crushed under the weight of too heavy a currency, and the author shows that these crises "are all alike": they reproduce, in their essence, the main features of the Mynskyan "boom and bust" cycle. This approach allows the author to identify the common roots of the apparently different crises and to define common management or exit strategies. In this respect, his analysis shows that as far as the two major peripheral countries are concerned (Italy and Spain), the "market-driven destabilization" mechanism has interacted with another well-known tenet of post-Keynesian economics, the Verdoorn–Kaldor model of cumulative growth.

7 *Jesús Paúl and Jorge Uxó – The adjustment of current account imbalances within the European Monetary Union since the beginning of the Great Recession: some strengths and many weaknesses.* Current account imbalances within the Eurozone are at the roots of its economic crisis. This chapter argues, first, that the official view about the causes of the external imbalances and their relationship with the roots of the crisis is inadequate. Second, it shows that the Great Recession has led to a reversal in the divergent trend in current accounts within the EMU as a result of its effect on unit labour costs, real exchange rates, or domestic demand. Nevertheless, the adjustment is limited, it is having strong recessionary effects, and the underlying problems that led to current account imbalances are not solved.

8 *Fabián Amico and Alejandro Fiorito – The effects of the great recession of 2008 on the neo-Keynesian development experiences: the cases of Argentina and Brazil.* The emergence of China as a major trading power was at the centre of global economic changes, affecting the main features of the new pattern of international growth. This circumstance has brought better

economic opportunities for many peripheral countries. Brazil and Argentina benefited from the strong demand for commodities. This allowed an unprecedented combination of high economic growth, current account surpluses and a remarkable reduction of external debt. In this context, both countries have been experiencing a "neo-Keynesian" new pattern of growth where improvements are achieved without substantive policies aimed at changing patterns of trade specialization. The authors apply the early vision of Lewis (1980) to the rise of China as the new engine of growth after 2000. Some policy implications and some potential dilemmas for the future growth of these countries will be discussed briefly.

Part III – The real side of the economy: the problem of effective demand and the failure of austerity policies

9 *Kazimierz Laski and Leon Podkaminer – Net private savings in relation to the government's financial balance: some basic principles of macroeconomics disregarded by the European Union's economic policy makers.* It is demonstrated – through the restatement of the essential identities of macroeconomics – that the elimination of public sector deficits is incompatible with the private sector preference for the accumulation of net financial wealth. Moreover, public sector deficits are essential for positive profits in the business sector. Concluding, it is argued that the fiscal policy orientation of the European Union (epitomized by the Maastricht Treaty, and its recent variants) lacks a proper economic rationale. As such this orientation may be seen as co-responsible for the weak long term performance of the EU as well as contributing to its recent crises.

10 *Ana-Rosa González, Philip Arestis and Óscar Dejuán – Business investment, growth and crisis.* The current economic crisis was accompanied by a collapse in business investment. The recovery won't happen until a massive wave of investment occurs. There is nothing new in these assertions. Economic downturns and upturns coincide with the deceleration and acceleration of business investment. But is investment the cause or the consequence of the cycle and the major crises? This is the first question addressed in this chapter. The second consists in identifying the complete set of determinants of investment. This knowledge will help us to find the best economic policies to overcome the first great recession of the twenty-first century.

11 *Steven M. Fazzari – Does the effectiveness of fiscal stimulus depend on economic context?* Does the effectiveness of fiscal policy in stabilizing an economy depend on the underlying economic context in which the policy is implemented? The answer must certainly be yes, but it differs across various dimensions of "context", three of which are considered here: first, the state of economic activity relative to some measure of the economy's potential; second, the openness of the economy; third, the level of government debt. The discussion that follows is largely based on the US economy, where default on sovereign debt obligation is not a concern. This US-based

analysis does not apply, however, to countries that borrow in a foreign currency or to countries that must maintain a fixed exchange rate, which takes its most extreme form for countries that are part of a currency union. The author argues that to develop an effective institutional framework for a currency union like the one based on the Euro, the designers must begin from the principles analysed here.

12 *Eladio Febrero and Fernando Bermejo – Spain during the Great Recession: teetering on the brink of collapse.* The aim of this chapter is threefold. First, it provides an explanation of the main causes of Spain's economic crisis. Second, it makes some recommendations for bringing its economy back to pre-downturn figures, mostly consisting in expansive fiscal policies-cum-inflation in trade surplus countries and outright purchases of public debt by the ECB. Third, it reviews what is actually being done, essentially fiscal austerity measures and liberalizing reforms in the labour market. The authors conclude that austerity policies will drive the Spanish economy to a protracted state of recession, making it impossible to reach fiscal balance goals because of falling tax revenue.

References

Arestis, P., and Sawyer, M. (2004). *Re-examining Monetary and Fiscal Policies in the 21st Century*. Cheltenham, UK: Edward Elgar.

Davidson, P. (1978). *Money and the Real World*. London: Macmillan.

Dejuán, Ó., Febrero, E., and Marcuzzo, M. C. (2011). *The First Great Recession of the 21st Century*. Cheltenham, UK: Edward Elgar.

Dow, S. C. (1996[1985]). *The Methodology of Macroeconomic Thought: A Conceputal Analysis of Schools of Thought in Economics*. Aldershot, UK: Edward Elgar.

Eatwell, J. (1983). The Long Period Theory of Employment. *Cambridge Journal of Economics, 7*, 269–285.

Fontana, G., and Stterfield, M. (Eds). (2009). *Macroeconomic Theory and Macroeconomic Pedagogy*. New York: Palgrave Macmillan.

Galbraith, J. K. (1967). *The New Industrial State*. Boston, MA: Houghton Mifflin.

Garegnani, P. (1962). *Il Problema de la Domanda Effettiva nello Sviluppo Economico Italiano*. Rome: SVIMEZ.

Godley, W., and Lavoie, M. (2006). *Monetary Economics: An Integrated Approach to Credit, Money, Income, Production and Wealth*. New York: Palgrave.

Graziani, A. (2003). *The Monetary Theory of Production*. New York: Cambridge University Press.

Harrod, R. F. (1939). An Essay in Dynamic Theory. *Economic Journal, 49*, 14–33.

Hein, E. (2012). *The Macroeconomics of Finance-Dominated Capitalism: And its Critics*. Cheltenham, UK: Edward Elgar.

Hilferding, R. (1910/1981). *Finance Capital: A Study of the Latest Phase of Capitalist Development*. London: Routledge.

Hodgson, G. M. (2004). *The Evolution of Institutional Economics: Agency, Structure and Darwinism in American Institutionalism*. London and New York: Routledge.

Kaldor, N. (1955–56). Alternative Theories of Distribution. *Review of Economic Studies, 23*, 63–100.

Kaldor, N. (1957). A model of economic growth. *Economic Journal, 64*, 591–624.

Kalecki, M. (1971). *Selected Essays in the Dynamics of the Capitalist Economy (1933–1970)*. Cambridge, UK: Cambridge University Press.

Keynes, J. M. (1936). *The General Theory of Employment, Interest and Money*. London and New York: Harcourt Brace Jovanovich.

King, J. E. (2002). *A History of Post-Keynesian Economics since 1936*. Cheltenham, UK: Edward Elgar.

King, J. E. (2012). Post Keynesian and Others. *Review of Political Economy, 24*, 305–319.

Kregel, J. A. (1985). Hamlet without the Prince: Cambridge Macroeconomics without Money. *American Economic Review, 72*, 133–139.

Lavoie, M. (2006). *Introduction to Post-Keynesian Economics*. London: Palgrave Macmillan.

McCombie, J. S. L., and Thirlwall, A. P. (1994). *Economic Growh and the Balance-of-Payments Constraint*. New York: St Martin Press.

Minsky, H. P. (1975). *John Maynard Keynes*. New York: Columbia University Press.

Minsky, H. P. (2004). *Induced Investment and Business Cycles*. Cheltenham, UK: Edward Elgar.

Moore, B. J. (1988). *Horizontalist and Verticalist: The Macroeconomics of Credit Money*. Cambridge, UK: Cambridge University Press.

Pasinetti, L. (1974). *Growth and Income Distribution: Essays in Economic Theory*. Cambridge, UK: Cambridge University Press.

Priewe, J., and Herr, H. (2005). *The Macroeconomics of Development and Poverty Reduction*. Baden-Baden, Germany: Nomos.

Robinson, J. (1962). *Essays on the Theory of Economic Growth*. London: Macmillan.

Schumpeter, J. (1912/1934). *The Theory of Economic Development*. Cambridge, MA: Harvard University Press.

Sraffa, P. (1960). *Production of Commodities by Means of Commodities: Prelude to a Critique of Economic Theory*. Cambridge, UK: Cambridge University Press.

Wray, L. R. (1998). *Understanding Modern Money*. Cheltenham, UK: Edward Elgar.

Part I

The financial side

The burden of debt and the loss of confidence

1 Finance-dominated capitalism, re-distribution and the financial and economic crises

A European perspective[1]

Eckhard Hein

Introduction

The financial and economic crises in Europe have occurred against the background of the long-run developments imposed by finance-dominated capitalism and neo-liberalism since the early 1980s. These developments have been characterised by de-regulation of national and international goods, labour and financial markets, in particular, re-distribution of income at the expense of (low) wages, and rising imbalances of current accounts at the global level and at regional levels, in particular within the European Monetary Union since its inception in 1999. The financial and economic crises, which started with the collapse of the subprime mortgage market in the US in 2007, which gained momentum by the breakdown of Lehmann Brothers in 2008, and which led to a serious recession at the world scale with a decline in real GDP in many advanced capitalist economies not seen for generations in 2008/09, has turned into a currency crisis, the euro crisis since 2010. This crisis is threatening the further existence of the euro because of the specific institutional conditions for economic policy making in the Euro area. First, the explicit guarantee of public debt of member countries by the monetary authority of the currency union, the European Central Bank (ECB), is excluded from the treaties and regulations of the EU. Therefore, member country governments issue debt in a common currency, the euro, but not in their own currency, in the sense that their own central bank would guarantee the monetisation of this debt if required. Second, fiscal transfers among member countries have also been ruled out by the treaties, so that government debt of a single member country is not guaranteed by the community of member country governments as a whole. Third, there have been no efficient mechanisms to prevent the building up of internal and external macroeconomic imbalances across the Euro area countries, which in the crisis contributed to the rapid increases in government deficits and debt and to the massive doubts regarding the creditworthiness of some member countries, given the first two deficiencies.

In this chapter we interpret the euro crisis as the most recent episode of the crisis of finance-dominated capitalism. Therefore, we will first analyse the dimensions of increasing inequality for the major European countries during the period of finance-dominated capitalism. Our analysis will focus on the Euro area member countries Austria, Belgium, France, Germany, Greece, Ireland, Italy, the Netherlands, Portugal, and Spain. Having analysed the trends towards increasing inequality, we will then deal with the current account imbalances within the Euro area which have developed in the business cycle prior to the crisis and distinguish two extreme types of development, the debt-led consumption boom type and the export-led mercantilist type. Against this background we will then examine the euro crisis and the misguided economic policy reactions by European governments and European institutions. Since the dysfunctional economic policy institutions and misguided economic policy making are threatening the further existence of the euro as a currency, we will finally draft an alternative macroeconomic policy approach overcoming these deficiencies. The final section will sum up and conclude.

Rising inequality in the period of finance-dominated capitalism and neo-liberalism – the European case

The neo-liberal period since the early 1980s and the emergence of finance-dominated capitalism have been associated with considerable redistribution of income in major European countries.[2] With respect to functional income distribution we observe a massive redistribution at the expense of labour and in favour of broad capital income. The labour income share, as a measure taken from the national accounts and corrected for the changes in the composition of employment regarding employees and self-employed, has shown a falling trend in most of the Euro area member countries considered here since the early 1980s, with cyclical fluctuations due to the well-known counter-cyclical properties of the labour income share. In order to eliminate cyclical fluctuations of the labour income share, we have calculated cyclical averages for the three business cycles from the early 1980s until 2008 (Table 1.1). On average over the cycle the labour income share has fallen in all countries in our data set except Portugal, from the first cycle (early 1980s to the early 1990s) to the third cycle (early 2000s until 2008). The fall has been most substantial in Austria and Ireland with more than ten percentage points of GDP at factor costs, and in Greece, Italy, France and Spain with more than five percentage points of GDP. In Belgium, Germany and the Netherlands the labour income share has fallen by less than five percentage points of GDP at factor costs.

Three main channels through which financialisation and neo-liberalism have negatively affected the share of direct labour in national income can be identified (Hein 2011b, 2012, ch. 2). First, the sectoral composition of the economy has changed in favour of the high profit share financial corporations and at the expense of the non-financial corporate sector and the government sector with lower or zero profit shares. Second, overhead costs, in particular top management salaries and interest payments, and profit claims imposed on the corporate sector by shareholders have increased. This has caused the mark-up on direct unit labour costs in pricing of firms in incompletely competitive markets to rise and the share of labour income to fall, because the mark-up has to cover overhead costs and

Table 1.1 Labour income share as percentage of GDP at current factor costs, average values over the trade cycle, early 1980s to 2008

	1. Early 1980s to early 1990s	*2. Early 1990s to early 2000s*	*3. Early 2000s to 2008*	*Change (3. – 1.), percentage points*
Austria	75.66	70.74	65.20	–10.46
Belgium	70.63	70.74	69.16	–1.47
France	71.44	66.88	65.91	–5.53
Germany	67.11	66.04	63.34	–3.77
Greece[a]	67.26	62.00	60.60	–6.66
Ireland	70.34	60.90	55.72	–14.61
Italy	68.31	63.25	62.37	–5.95
Netherlands	68.74	67.21	65.57	–3.17
Portugal	65.73	70.60	71.10	5.37
Spain	68.32	66.13	62.41	–5.91

Source: European Commission (2010), author's calculations.

Notes

The labour income share is given by the compensation per employee divided by GDP at factor costs per person employed. The beginning of a trade cycle is given by a local minimum of annual real GDP growth in the respective country.

a Adjusted to fit in three-cycle pattern.

profit claims. Third, the bargaining power of workers and trade unions has been weakened, triggered by shareholder value orientation and short-termism of management, increasing relevance of the financial sector with weak trade unions relative to the non-financial and the government sector with stronger trade unions, the threat-effect of liberalisation and globalisation of finance and trade, deregulation of the labour market, and downsizing or abandoning government demand management policies.

With respect to personal income distribution increasing inequality can be observed in many of the European countries in our data set from the mid 1980s until the mid 2000s. Taking the Gini coefficient as an indicator, this is true for the distribution of market income, with France and the Netherlands being exceptions (Table 1.2). In Germany, Italy and Portugal the Gini coefficient has risen considerably. If we include redistribution via taxes and social policies by the state, Belgium, France, Greece, Ireland and Spain have not seen an increase in their Gini coefficients, with considerable declines in Spain, France and Greece. The other countries, however, have also experienced an increasing inequality in disposable income in the period of neo-liberalism and finance-dominated capitalism. This increase was particularly pronounced in Austria, Germany, Italy and Portugal. Although tax and social policies have reduced income inequality in all the countries under investigation, in many countries this has not prevented an increase in inequality over time. This is also the conclusion the OECD (2008) draws for a broader set of countries and from the application of other measures of income inequality.

Table 1.2 Gini coefficient before and after taxes

Gini coefficient after taxes

	Mid 1970s	*Mid 1980s*	*Around 1990*	*Mid 1990s*	*Around 2000*	*Mid 2000s*	*Change from mid 1980s to mid 2000s*
Austria	–	–	–	–	–	0.43	–
Belgium	–	0.45	–	0.47	0.46	0.49	0.04
France	–	0.52	0.51	0.48	0.50	0.48	–0.04
Germany	–	0.44	0.42	0.46	0.48	0.51	0.07
Greece	–	–	–	–	–	–	–
Ireland	–	–	–	–	0.43	0.42	–
Italy	–	0.42	0.44	0.51	0.52	0.56	0.14
Netherlands	0.42	0.47	0.47	0.48	0.42	0.42	–0.05
Portugal	0.46	–	0.44	0.49	0.48	0.54	0.08[a]
Spain	–	–	–	–	–	–	–

Gini coefficient after taxes

	Mid 1970s	*Mid 1980s*	*Around 1990*	*Mid 1990s*	*Around 2000*	*Mid 2000s*	*Change from mid 1980s to mid 2000s*
Austria	–	0.24	–	0.24	0.25	0.27	0.03
Belgium	–	0.27	–	0.29	0.29	0.27	0.00
France	–	0.31	0.30	0.28	0.28	0.28	–0.03
Germany	–	0.26	0.26	0.27	0.27	0.30	0.04
Greece	0.41	0.34	–	0.34	0.34	0.32	–0.02
Ireland	–	0.33	–	0.32	0.30	0.33	0.00
Italy	–	0.31	0.30	0.35	0.34	0.35	0.04
Netherlands	0.25	0.26	0.28	0.28	0.28	0.27	0.01
Portugal	0.35	–	0.33	0.36	0.36	0.38	0.03[a]
Spain	–	0.37	0.34	0.34	0.34	0.32	–0.05

Source: OECD (2010), author's calculations.

Notes

Data refer to cash income of households and are broken down to individuals. The income attributed to each individual is adjusted for household size, but does not distinguish between adults and children.

a Change from mid 1970s to mid 2000s.

Imbalances in the Euro area

Against the background of rising inequality in personal income distribution in many countries and falling labour income shares associated with financialisation and neo-liberalism since the early 1980s, different 'types of capitalism under financialisation' have developed,[3] which are complementary and which have fed rising current account imbalances in the world economy, but also at regional levels, and in particular so in the Euro area. The current account of the Euro area has been roughly balanced on average over the cycle from the early 2000s to 2008 (European Commission 2010), so that in the aggregate current account surplus member countries have their respective deficit counterparts within the Euro area. Of course, individual Euro member states also have surpluses or deficits vis-à-vis the non-Euro area rest of the world. But these roughly cancel out for the Euro area in the aggregate.

Distinguishing the 'types of capitalism under financialisation', first, we have the 'debt-led consumption boom' type; second, there has developed a counterpart, the 'export-led mercantilist' type; and third, in between these two extremes we have the 'domestic demand-led' type. In the 'debt-led consumption boom' type it is debt-financed consumption demand which allows for flourishing aggregate demand and the realisation of rising profits against the background of redistribution at the expense of (low) labour incomes and stagnating real investment, which is another feature of finance-dominated capitalism.[4] In the 'export-led mercantilist' type it is export surpluses which stabilise aggregate demand and take care of the realisation of profits.[5] The third type, the 'domestic demand-led' type, can neither rely on export surpluses, which distinguishes it from the second type, nor on flourishing debt-financed consumption, which distinguishes it from the first type.

Since the intra Euro area current account imbalances have exploded in particular since the early 2000s (Figure 1.1), in the course of recovery from the burst of the new economy boom of the late 1990s, we take cyclical average data for the business cycle of the early 2000s until the 2008/2009 crisis to distinguish these types and allocate the countries examined in this chapter to them.

In the cycle of the early 2000s, the 'debt-led consumption boom' type can be found in Greece, Ireland and Spain (Table 1.3.a). All these economies have seen considerable increases in residential property prices and/or in wealth–income ratios in the period considered here (Table 1.4, Figure 1.2.b). This increase in notional wealth, together with liberalised financial markets and weakened conditions of creditworthiness, was conducive to soaring consumption demand and hence considerable growth contributions of private consumption and domestic demand. Relatively high real GDP growth as compared to the 'export-led mercantilist' countries, but negative financial balances (as a share of nominal GDP) of the private household sector and thus increasing private household debt were the consequences. This also translated into negative balances of the private sector as a whole – with the corporate sector being in surplus in all countries of this group except Spain. The public sector contributed to the negative domestic

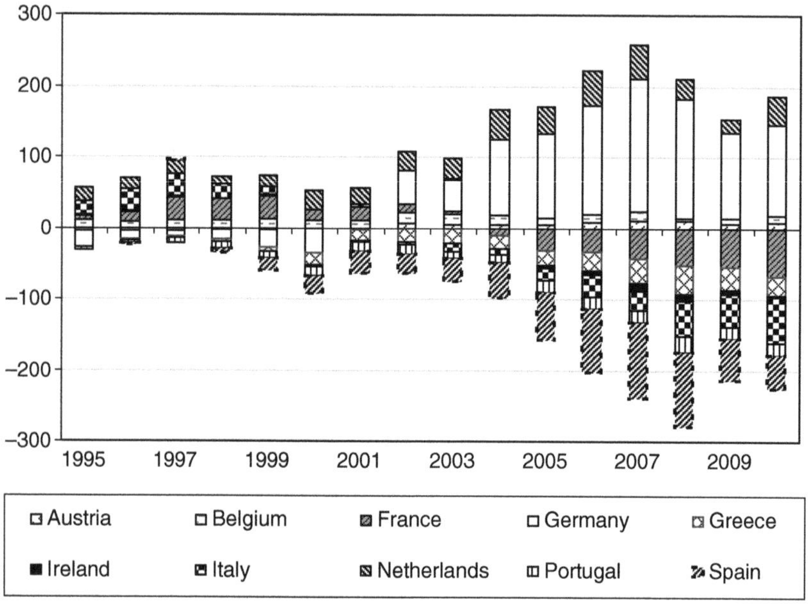

Figure 1.1 Current account in billions ECU/euro, selected Euro area countries, 1995–2010 (source: European Commission (2011a), author's representation).

financial balance in all the countries, but to a different degree – considerably in Greece, but only marginally in Ireland and Spain. We will come back to this in more detail in the next section. Since aggregate domestic expenditures exceeded national income, these countries had to run current account deficits, i.e. the financial balances of the external sector were positive for each of the countries pursuing the 'debt-led consumption boom' type of development. In particular Greece and Spain had to rely on the inflow of foreign financial resources. Strong domestic demand growth in the 'debt-led consumption boom countries' was accompanied by negative growth contributions of the balance of goods and services in these countries but Ireland, where the growth contribution of external demand was positive, too.[6] For these countries, above Euro area average unit labour cost growth and inflation accompanied by nominal appreciation of the euro, and thus a loss of competitiveness of domestic producers (positive rates of change in the effective exchange rate), have contributed to the deficits in the balance of goods and services and in the current account. The 'debt-led consumption boom' economies were the Euro area demand engines of the cycle from the early 2000s to 2008.

The counterparts to the 'debt-led consumption boom' economies at the Euro area level were the 'export-led mercantilist' economies. This group consists of Austria, Belgium, Germany and the Netherlands (Table 1.3.b). These economies were characterised by surpluses in their balances of goods and services and in

Table 1.3a Key macroeconomic variables for 'debt-led consumption boom' economies: average values for the trade cycle from the early 2000s to 2008

	Greece	*Ireland*	*Spain*
Financial balances of external sector as a share of nominal GDP, %	12.49	2.88	7.10
Financial balances of public sector as share of nominal GDP, %	–5.74	–0.13	–0.03
Financial balance of private sector as a share of nominal GDP, %	–6.75	–2.74	–7.07
Financial balance of private household sector as a share of nominal GDP, %	–11.44	–6.29	–1.54
Financial balance of the corporate sector as a share of nominal GDP, %	4.69	3.55	–5.53
Real GDP growth, %	3.89	3.92	3.02
Growth contribution of domestic demand including stocks, percentage points	4.10	3.26	3.82
Growth contribution of private consumption, percentage points	2.79	1.87	1.74
Growth contribution of public consumption, percentage points	0.49	0.59	0.93
Growth contribution of gross fixed capital formation, percentage points	0.79	0.79	1.14
Growth contribution of the balance of goods and services, percentage points	–0.20	0.66	–0.81
Net exports of goods and services as a share of nominal GDP, %	–10.97	12.23	–4.69
Change in labour income share, as percentage of GDP at current factor costs, from previous cycle, percentage points	–1.40	–5.17	–3.71
Growth rate of nominal unit labour costs, %	3.47	3.95	3.31
Inflation (HCPI growth rate), %	3.41	3.50	3.33
Growth rate of nominal effective exchange rates (relative to 23 countries), %	1.60	2.81	1.53
Growth rate of real effective exchange rates (relative to 23 countries), %	2.91	4.97	2.82

Source: European Commission (2010), author's calculations.

Note
The beginning of a trade cycle is given by a local minimum of annual real GDP growth in the respective country.

their current accounts, i.e. the financial balances of the respective external sectors were in deficit. Although some of these countries (Belgium, the Netherlands) had seen considerable increases in wealth–income ratios and/or in residential property prices, whereas others had not (Austria, Germany) (Table 1.4, Figures 1.2.a, b), financial balances of private households (as a share of nominal GDP) remained in surplus. The financial balances of the private sectors were strongly positive in each of these countries. Growth contributions of private consumption and domestic demand were moderate, as for Austria, Belgium and the

Netherlands, or very weak, as in the case of Germany, and these countries relied considerably on the positive growth contributions of the balance of goods and services. Only in Belgium was the growth contribution of external demand rather small. The basis for external surpluses were thus weak domestic demand, on the one hand, but also low unit labour cost growth and low inflation, on the other hand. For 'export-led mercantilist' countries the real effective exchange rate relative to 23 industrial economies increased to a lesser extent than in the 'debt-led consumption

Table 1.3.b Key macroeconomic variables for 'export-led mercantilist' economies: average values for the trade cycle from the early 2000s to 2008

	Austria	*Belgium*	*Germany*	*Netherlands*
Financial balances of external sector as a share of nominal GDP, %	–2.26	–3.90	–5.55	–7.15
Financial balances of public sector as share of nominal GDP, %	–1.45	–0.56	–2.09	–0.85
Financial balance of private sector as a share of nominal GDP, %	3.70	4.46	7.64	8.00
Financial balance of private household sector as a share of nominal GDP, %	4.68	4.25	5.90	0.16
Financial balance of the corporate sector as a share of nominal GDP, %	–0.98	0.21	1.74	7.84
Real GDP growth, %	2.13	1.84	1.44	1.96
Growth contribution of domestic demand including stocks, percentage points	1.26	1.70	0.85	1.43
Growth contribution of private consumption, percentage points	0.76	0.63	0.18	0.37
Growth contribution of public consumption, percentage points	0.28	0.45	0.16	0.75
Growth contribution of gross fixed capital formation, percentage points	0.19	0.62	0.49	0.35
Growth contribution of the balance of goods and services, percentage points	0.77	0.14	0.58	0.52
Net exports of goods and services as a share of nominal GDP, %	4.35	4.02	5.56	7.63
Change in labour income share, as percentage of GDP at current factor costs, from previous cycle, percentage points	–5.54	–1.58	–2.71	–1.64
Growth rate of nominal unit labour costs, %	1.05	2.02	0.17	1.88
Inflation (HCPI growth rate), %	2.12	2.34	1.78	1.94
Growth rate of nominal effective exchange rates (relative to 23 countries), %	1.21	1.48	2.09	1.37
Growth rate of real effective exchange rates (relative to 23 countries), %	0.55	1.58	0.14	1.56

Source: European Commission (2010), author's calculations.

Note
The beginning of a trade cycle is given by a local minimum of annual real GDP growth in the respective country.

boom' countries, implying an increase in price competitiveness of the former relative to the latter. The 'export-led mercantilist' countries have thus benefitted from regional demand being driven by the 'debt-led consumption boom' countries. However, following this model came at a price: GDP growth in the export-led countries remained well below GDP growth in the debt-led economies, and in particular the more closed large economy of Germany performed even worse than the more open and smaller economies of Austria, Belgium and the Netherlands.

Table 1.3.c Key macroeconomic variables for 'domestic demand-led' economies, average values for the trade cycle from the early 2000s to 2008

	France	*Italy*	*Portugal*
Financial balances of external sector as a share of nominal GDP, %	1.25	1.59	9.40
Financial balances of public sector as share of nominal GDP, %	–3.18	–3.16	–3.65
Financial balance of private sector as a share of nominal GDP, %	1.93	1.57	–5.75
Financial balance of private household sector as a share of nominal GDP, %	3.80	3.91	1.54
Financial balance of the corporate sector as a share of nominal GDP, %	–1.87	–2.34	–7.29
Real GDP growth, %	1.64	0.73	0.82
Growth contribution of domestic demand including stocks, percentage points	2.13	0.81	1.04
Growth contribution of private consumption, percentage points	1.24	0.44	1.05
Growth contribution of public consumption, percentage points	0.38	0.27	0.20
Growth contribution of gross fixed capital formation, percentage points	0.56	0.08	–0.25
Growth contribution of the balance of goods and services, percentage points	–0.50	–0.08	–0.19
Net exports of goods and services as a share of nominal GDP, %	–0.52	–0.07	–8.08
Change in labour income share, as percentage of GDP at current factor costs, from previous cycle, percentage points	–0.97	–0.88	0.49
Growth rate of nominal unit labour costs, %	2.01	2.95	2.41
Inflation (HCPI growth rate), %	1.98	2.36	2.68
Growth rate of nominal effective exchange rates (relative to 23 countries), %	1.84	1.92	1.26
Growth rate of real effective exchange rates (relative to 23 countries), %	1.98	3.12	1.59

Source: European Commission (2010), author's calculations.

Note

The beginning of a trade cycle is given by a local minimum of annual real GDP growth in the respective country.

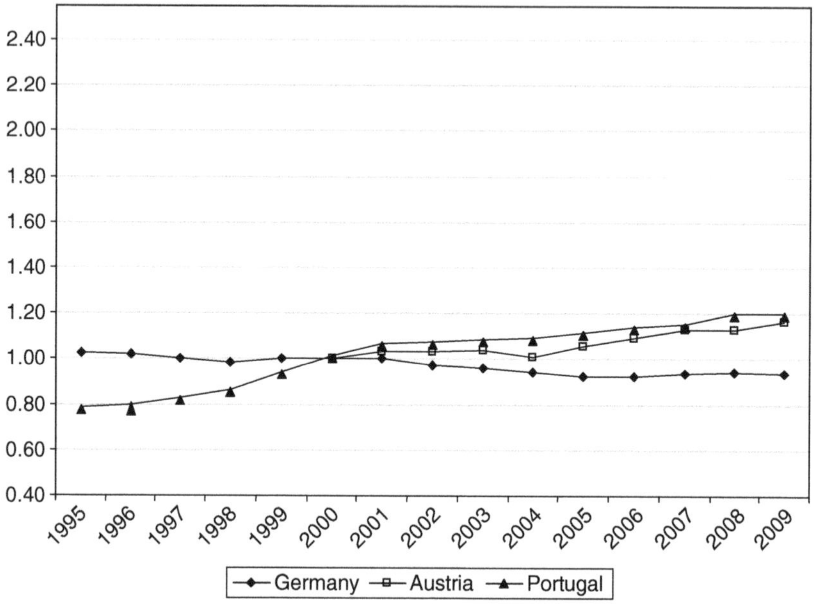

Figure 1.2.a Residential property prices for Austria, Germany and Portugal, 1995–2009 (source: BIS (2010), author's calculations).

Note
Index 2000 = 1.

In the cycle of the early 2000s to 2008, France, Italy and Portugal can neither be considered to have been 'debt-led consumption boom' economies nor 'export-led mercantilist' economies. Growth was rather domestic demand led. Although France and Italy saw significant increases in net wealth–income ratios and in residential property prices (Table 1.4, Figure 1.2.a), whereas Portugal did not (Figure 1.2.b), financial balances of private households remained positive in all of the three countries. The corporate sector had negative balances in these countries and together with negative public sector balances this meant current account deficits, which were considerable particularly in Portugal.

Although not experiencing a debt-led consumption boom, growth was driven by domestic demand in the face of rising (Portugal) or only weakly declining (France, Italy) labour income shares and considerable public deficits in each of the countries. The balances of goods and services were negative and so were the growth contributions of external demand. The loss of price competitiveness with respect to the 'export-led mercantilist' Euro area countries, i.e. higher unit labour cost growth and higher inflation than in these countries, may have contributed to the external deficit. GDP growth remained particularly weak in Portugal and Italy, whereas France had higher growth than the stagnating mercantilist economy of Germany, but lower growth than the rest of the countries in the other two groups.

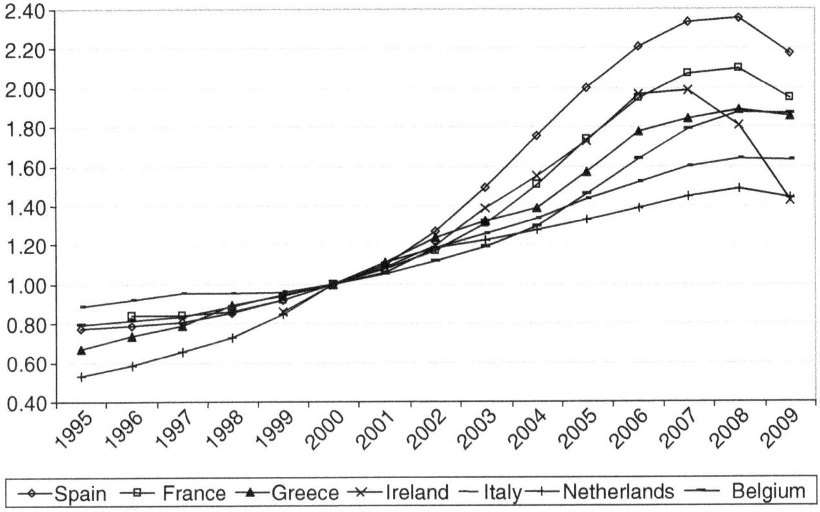

Figure 1.2.b Residential property prices for Belgium, France, Greece, Italy, Ireland, Netherlands and Spain, 1995–2009 (source: BIS (2010), author's calculations).

Note
Index 200 = 1.

Table 1.4 Household gross debt and net wealth, % of annual disposable income

	Gross debt			*Net wealth*		
	1995	*2000*	*2005*	*1995*	*2000*	*2005*
Austria	34	–	88[a]	–	–	–
Belgium	57	–	75[a]	–	–	–
France	66	78	89	461	547	752
Germany	97	111	107	541	575	578[a]
Greece	–	–	–	–	–	–
Ireland	48	82	141	–	618	775
Italy	32	46	59	702	820	936[a]
Netherlands	113	175	246	369	528	515
Portugal	54	–	125[a]	–	–	–
Spain	59	83	107[b]	540	646	935[b]

Source: Girourard *et al.* (2007, p. 9), Goodbody Stockbrokers (2009, p. 30).

Notes
a 2006.
b 2004.
Debt refers to total liabilities outstanding at the end of the period. Net wealth is defined as non-financial and financial assets minus liabilities. Data is from national statistics.

Euro crises and misguided policy reactions

When the crisis hit the European economies in 2008/2009, the three 'types of capitalism under financialisation' outlined in the previous sections were affected and real GDP declined in all of the countries in our data set, in some of them considerably, without any clear pattern regarding the intensity of the crisis (European Commission 2011a). In the course of the crisis government deficits increased in order to stabilise the private real and financial sectors and government debt to GDP ratios jumped up (Figures 1.3 and 1.4). This seems to be the reason why the current euro crisis is considered as a crisis of government deficits and debt by many observers – above all by the dominating economic policy makers in Germany, the European Commission and the European Council.[7] A first look at the developments might even seem to confirm this view. Since the start of the global financial crisis in 2007 the, up to that point in time, almost negligible spreads of government bond yields of Euro area member states relative to the benchmark German bonds increased, most notably for Greece, Ireland, Portugal and Spain (GIPS) (see Figure 1.5). This development continued, especially for Ireland and Greece and particularly so in mid 2009. In spring 2010, the development escalated dramatically again in the Greek case.

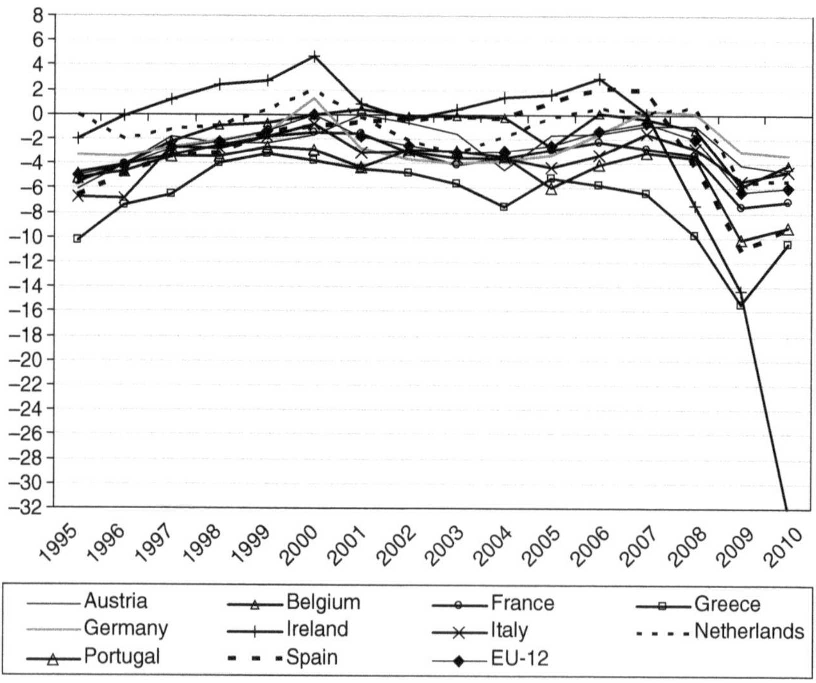

Figure 1.3 General government financial balance relative to GDP, selected Euro area countries, 1995–2010, % (source: European Commission (2011a), author's calculations).

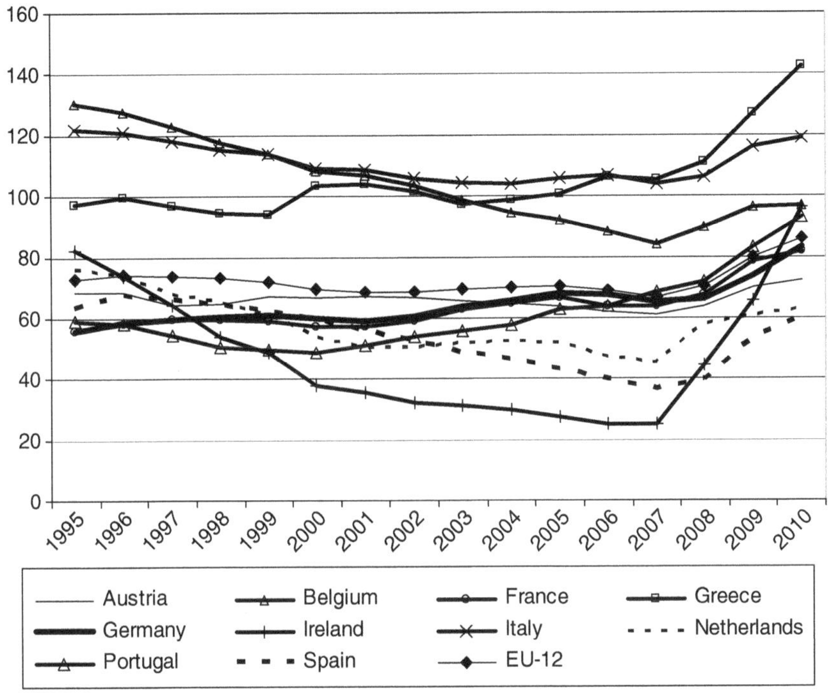

Figure 1.4 General government gross consolidated debt relative to GDP, selected Euro area countries, 1995–2010, % (source: European Commission (2011a), author's calculations).

Emergency measures had to be taken in order to prevent a Greek government default. The relief provided by the rescue package for Greece (€110 billion) by the Euro area countries and the IMF, and by the European Financial Stability Mechanism (EFSM) and the European Financial Stability Facility (EFSF) set up subsequently to prevent further problems for other governments proved to be very short lived.[8] In October 2010 spreads for Irish government bond yields increased dramatically again so that in November of the same year, the Irish government finally decided to request assistance by the EFSM, the EFSF and the IMF (€85 billion). In spring 2011, the Portuguese government had to do the same (€78 billion). And in the course of 2011 the Greek government debt problem worsened again, such that in late 2011 a more than 50 per cent voluntary loss of private holdings of Greek government and an increase and extension of the rescue package were agreed, using the EFSF as a financing vehicle.

Since mainstream economics and economic policy debates see the high and rising government debts as the main reason for the crisis, the failure of the Stability and Growth Pact (SGP) to contain government deficits and debt is therefore considered to be the most important problem to be tackled in the Euro area. From that point of view the main threat for the euro is caused by

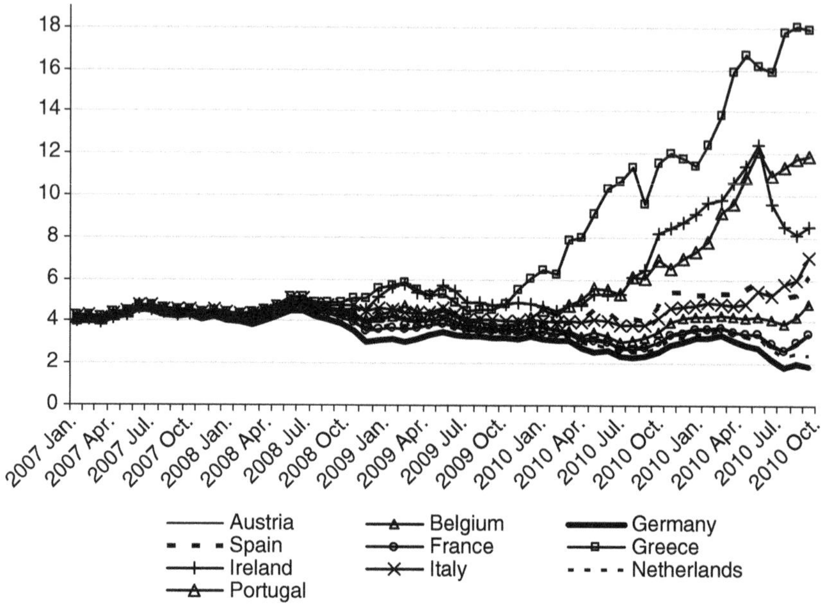

Figure 1.5 Ten-year government bond yields, selected Euro area countries, January 2007 to November 2011, % (source: ECB (2011a), author's representation).

governments, which have run irresponsibly high deficits leading public finances to the brink of default. The current debate over and the reforms of the economic policy framework in the European Union (EU) and the Euro area is therefore still dominated by the paradigm that has led to the crisis.

However, some important urgency measures have been taken to stabilise financial markets and prevent government defaults. These are, first, the introduction of the EFSF as well as the EFSM and of the European Stability Mechanism (ESM), which has assumed the role of providing external financial assistance to Euro area member states in trouble, originally scheduled for June 2013, already in July 2012, and also the extensions of the stabilization tools for the EFSM and ESM agreed at the meeting of the heads of state or government of the Euro area and EU institutions in July 2011 (Council of the EU 2011b). The latter includes allowing the EFSF and the ESM to finance recapitalisation of financial institutions through loans to governments and to intervene into secondary government bond markets under certain conditions. Second, and maybe more importantly, the interventions of the ECB into secondary government bonds markets, buying government debt of those countries which are in trouble, have so far prevented a collapse of these markets and have provided some relief for the countries under attack.[9]

But these measures are far from solving the major institutional deficiencies, i.e. the lack of an explicit guarantee of public debt of member countries by the ECB.

The meeting of the European Council (2011b) in December 2011 did not even consider the proposal of Eurobonds (or Stability Bonds) put forward by the European Commission (2011b) which could have been a first step towards the remedy of the problems. And there is no general political support – to say the least – for the interventions of the ECB into government bonds markets aimed at stabilising these markets and dampening the upwards pressure on interest rates on government debt.

The rescue measures for the financial sector, furthermore, have been combined with the requirements of restrictive fiscal and wage policies as conditions to get access to the EFSF and the ESM, a tighter SGP, a new 'Euro Plus Pact', and a 'New Fiscal Compact' among Euro area member countries, which will impose deflationary pressures on major parts of the Euro area and will thus prevent stabilisation (or reduction) of public debt–GDP ratios.[10]

In March 2011, for example, the European Council (2011a, p. 2) 'endorsed the priorities for fiscal consolidation and structural reform. It underscored the need to give priority to restoring sound budgets and fiscal sustainability, reducing unemployment through labour market reforms and making new efforts to enhance growth'. In particular, the European Council (2011a, p. 2) required reductions of the structural budget deficits of 'well above 0.5 per cent of GDP' for 2012 in most countries, in order to restore 'confidence'.[11] The 'Euro Plus Pact' agreed upon at that meeting is mainly targeted at improving competitiveness by means of monitoring wage setting, in particular in the public sector, at labour market reforms increasing 'flexicurity', promoting life-long learning and reducing taxes on low-paid labour, and at improving sustainability of public finances by means of extending effective retirement ages, reducing early retirement and implementing fiscal rules (i.e. 'debt brakes') into national legislation. These commitments in the 'Euro Plus Pact' are to be reflected in the annual National Reform and the Stability Programmes, which are assessed by the Commission, the Council and the Eurogroup in the context of the so-called European Semester, and will thus have a major impact on European economic policies in the years to come.

This approach was underlined by the agreement of the Euro area heads of state and governments in December 2011 (European Council 2011b). The 'New Fiscal Compact' reinforced the target of balanced or in surplus government budgets, i.e. structural deficits should not exceed 0.5 per cent of GDP. This target is to be introduced into the national legal systems at a constitutional level. Furthermore, deviations from this target are to trigger automatic correction mechanisms. Such automatism, including sanctions imposed by the European Commission, shall also be applied if a country breaches the 3 per cent of GDP limit for its government deficit, unless a qualified majority of the Euro area member states is opposed. Furthermore, it was agreed to reduce government debt exceeding the 60 per cent of GDP threshold by one-twentieth per year, irrespective of the macroeconomic constellation.

Taking a look at the data, many doubts regarding the interpretation of mainstream European policy advisers and makers regarding the origin of the euro crisis are raised (Figure 1.3). For Greece, of course, the picture seems clear, as the budget deficit was very large over the whole period since the mid 1990s. For Portugal, however, the picture is less clear, as the budget deficit was not larger than that of Germany for a long period of time. And, most strikingly, both Ireland and Spain looked perfectly in order before the crisis as they seemed to follow the SGP in an almost ideal manner. Ireland ran a budget surplus of 3 per cent of GDP in 2006 and Spain had a surplus of 1.9 per cent in 2007. Turning to gross government debt in relation to GDP (Figure 1.4), the evidence for the purely fiscal view of the crisis becomes even weaker: Portugal used to have a considerably smaller debt burden than Germany. And in 2007 gross government debt in relation to GDP was only 25 per cent in Ireland and 36 per cent in Spain, far below the 60 per cent threshold of the SGP.

In the data we observe a more complex picture, which against the background of the aforementioned institutional and economic policy deficiencies helps to explain the current euro crisis,[12] if we take into account the interconnection of public, private and foreign deficits and surpluses:

$$\begin{aligned}&\text{Public sector financial balance}\\&+\text{Private sector financial balance}\\&+\text{Foreign sector financial balance}\\&=0\end{aligned} \tag{1.1}$$

The dynamic debt-led consumption boom development before the crisis in Ireland (Figure 1.6.f) and Spain (Figure 1.6.j) was associated with huge deficits of the private sector and (relatively small) surpluses in the government balances and to a much larger extent with current account deficits against the rest of the world, i.e. surpluses of the respective external sectors. When the crisis hit, the private sector balances quickly turned into surplus and governments stabilising the economy had to accept dramatic increases in government deficits. Therefore, the 'unsustainable' government deficit turns out to be a consequence of unsustainable private and external sector balances before the crisis in the first place.

For the two other economies currently included in the rescue packages, Greece (Figure 1.6.e), a debt-led consumption boom type, and Portugal (Figure 1.6.i), a domestic demand-led type of economy before the crisis, both the private sector and the government sector continuously ran deficits after the introduction of the euro. Before the crisis, those deficits had to be financed by capital inflows and hence current account deficits of about 12 per cent of GDP in the case of Greece, and about 10 per cent of GDP in the case of Portugal. In the course of the financial and economic crises, in both countries the government stepped in to prevent the economy from collapsing when the private sector reduced deficits or began to run surpluses again, leading to rising public deficits.

Therefore, it seems that the current euro crisis is rooted in earlier private deficits and current account imbalances and has not been caused by excessive public deficits. In the four countries outlined above, the private sector obviously tended to spend more than its income. This was associated with government surpluses

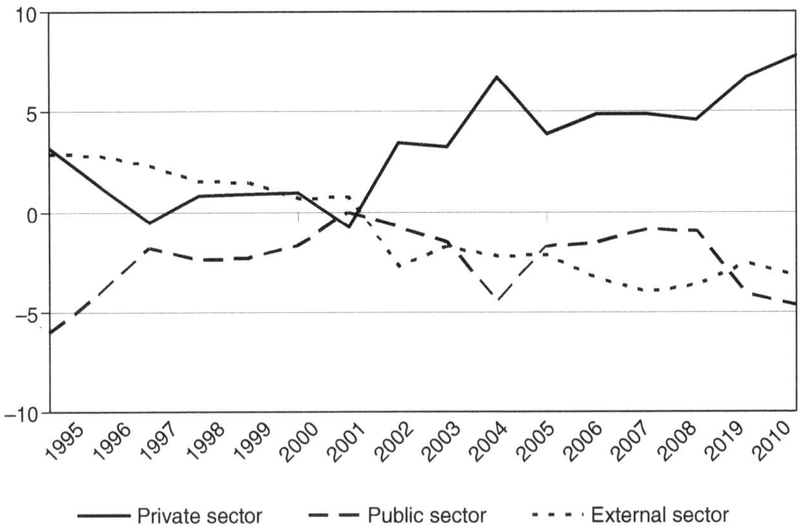

(a) Austria

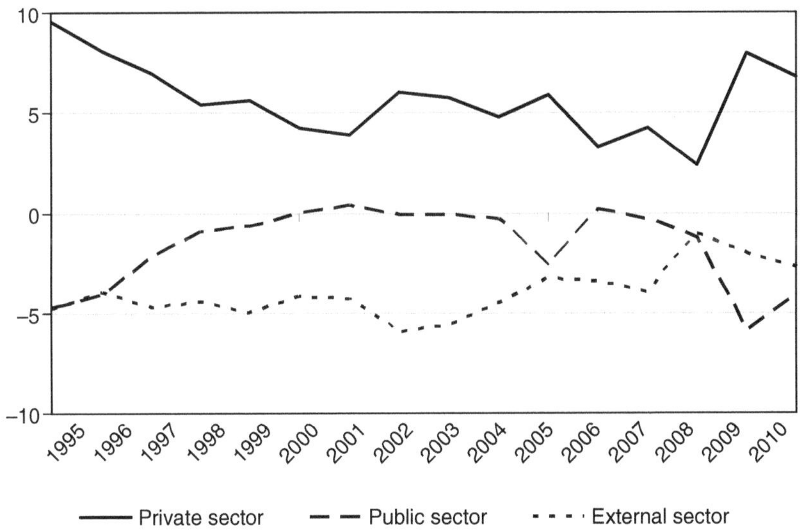

(b) Belgium

Figure 1.6 Sectoral financial balances as a percentage share of nominal GDP, selected Euro area countries, 1995–2010 (source: European Commission (2011a), author's calculations).

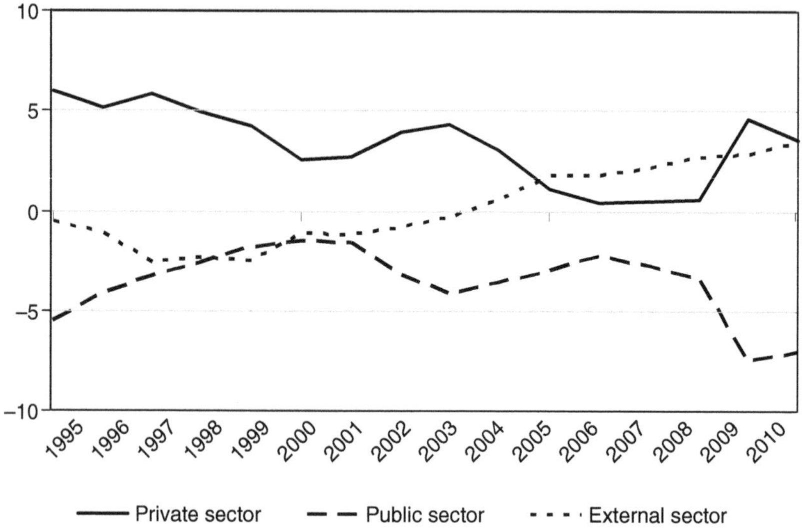

(c) France

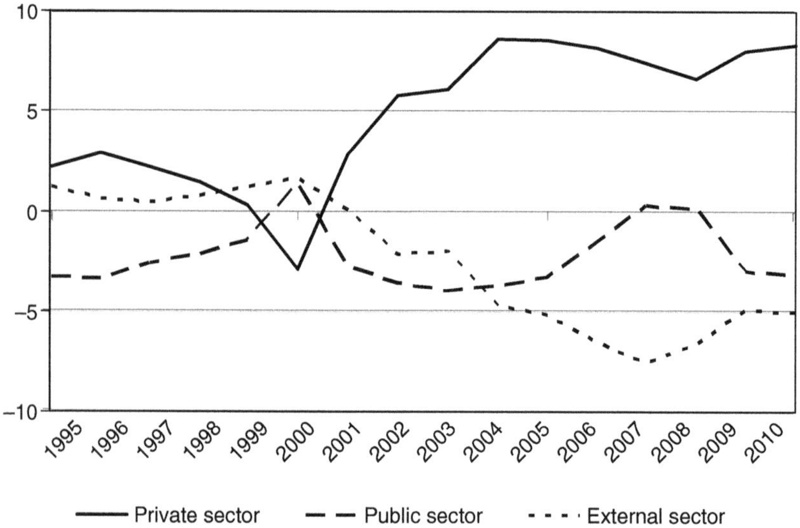

(d) Germany

Figure 1.6 Continued

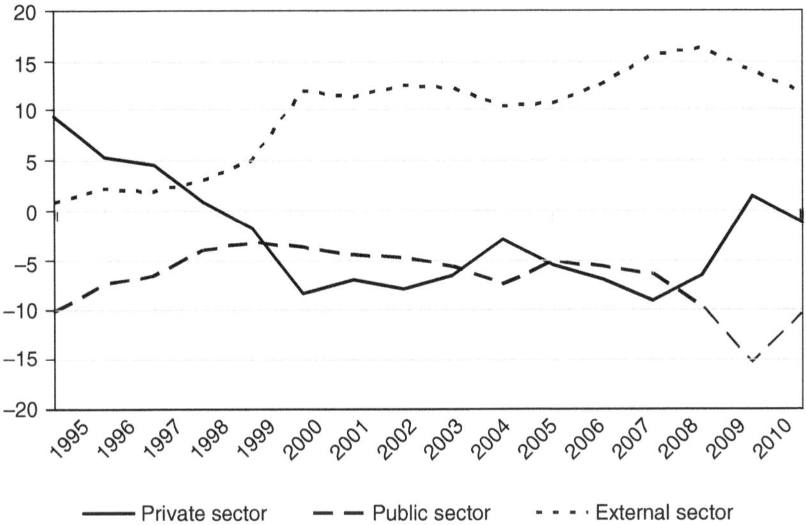

(e) Greece

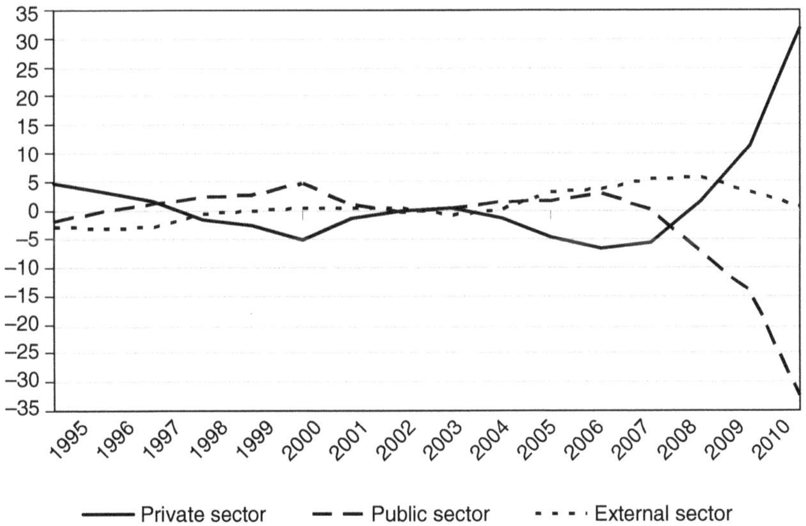

(f) Ireland

Figure 1.6 Continued

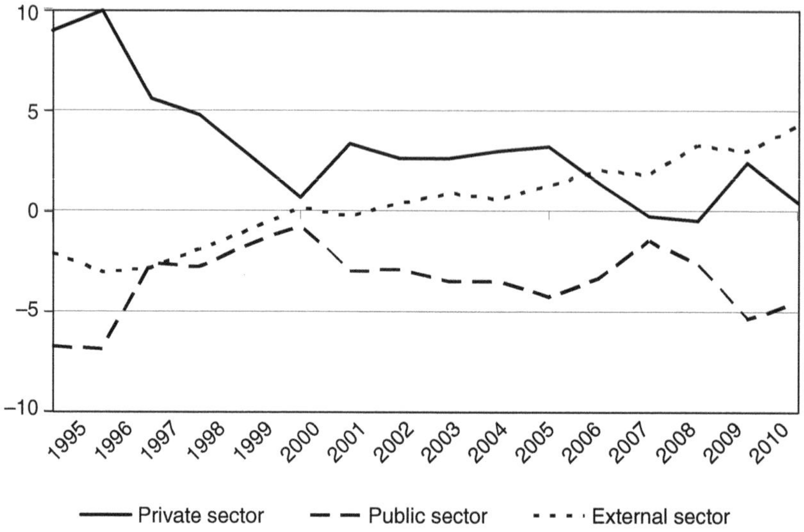

(g) Italy

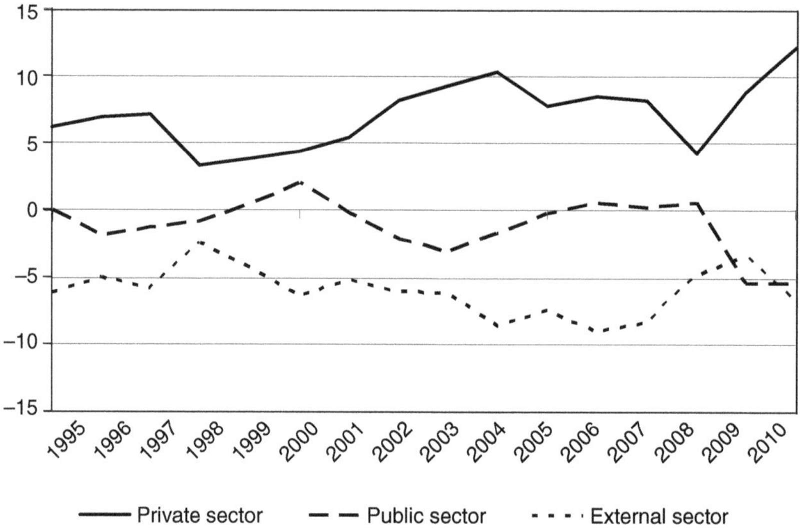

(h) The Netherlands

Figure 1.6 Continued

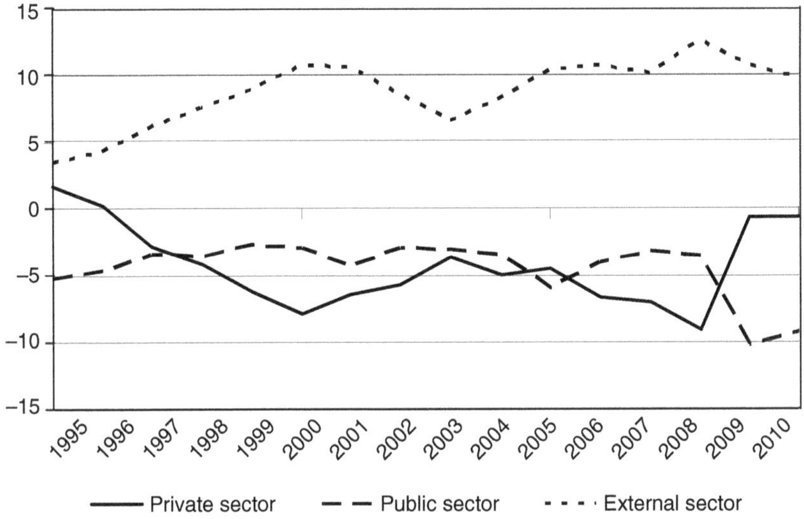

(i) Portugal

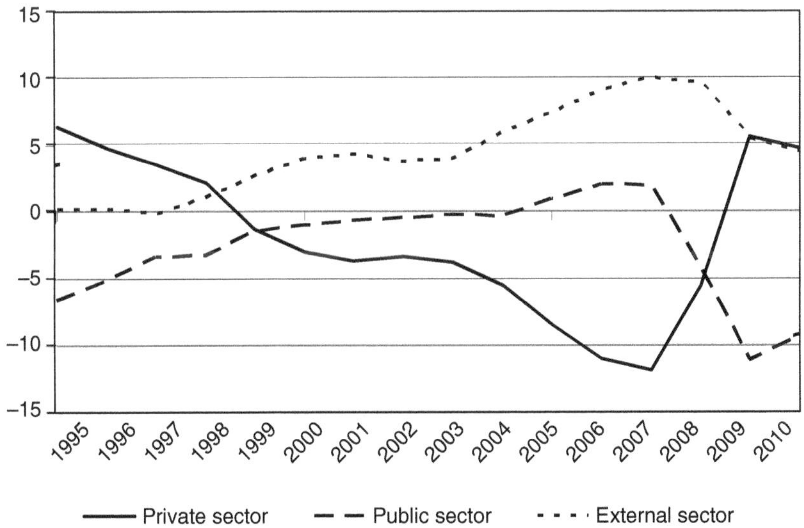

(j) Spain

Figure 1.6 Continued

(Ireland, Spain) or amplified by government deficits (Portugal, Greece), which led to very high and rising current account deficits in the four countries.

For Italy, a domestic demand-led economy before the crisis, the picture is less clear (Figure 1.6.g). In this country the private sector balance was consistently positive. Therefore the government deficit could be financed partly by the private sector surplus and partly by the capital inflows associated with the moderate, but continuously rising, current account deficit. When the crisis hit, the improvement in the private sector balance was compensated mostly by an increase in the government deficit. A similar pattern can be observed for France (Figure 1.6.c), another domestic demand-led economy in the Euro area. What is worrisome in both cases is the continuous improvement of the external sector balances in both countries, i.e. the continuous deterioration of the respective current accounts.

Since the current account of the Euro area as a whole was roughly balanced in the period before the crisis, there must have been other countries within the Euro area in which the private sector consistently ran surpluses. If in such cases the government is not willing (or is prevented by the SGP) to run a correspondingly high deficit, then this will imply a deficit of the respective foreign sectors, i.e. current account surpluses. It does not come as a surprise that these characteristics hold for the export-led mercantilist countries of the Euro area Germany (Figure 1.6.d), the Netherlands (Figure 1.6.h), Austria (Figure 1.6.a) and Belgium (Figure 1.6.b), with Germany as the largest Euro area country being the most important mercantilist economy.[13]

So far we have argued that in order to explain the euro crisis we should not focus on the government financial balances only, but should take into account the financial balances of all three macroeconomic sectors. This has again brought to the fore the current account imbalances among Euro area member countries which have escalated since the introduction of the euro. As we have outlined in the third section of this chapter, these imbalances have been the outcome of the two extreme 'types of development of capitalism under financialisation', i.e. the 'debt-led consumption boom' type, on the one hand, and the 'export-led mercantilist' type, on the other hand, which have also been observed in the Euro area in the face of financial deregulation and re-distribution at the expense of (low) labour incomes. In the course of the crisis of finance-dominated capitalism these imbalances triggered rising public deficit– and debt–GDP ratios which then, given the institutional lack of a convincing guarantee of public sector debt in the Euro area, provided the grounds for the euro crisis.

Getting out of the crisis

Getting out of the euro crisis requires addressing the long-run developments of finance-dominated capitalism which have caused the crisis of this type of capitalism, i.e. the inefficient regulation of financial markets, the increased inequality in income distribution and the imbalances in the current accounts at the global and the European level, on the one hand. In Hein and Truger (2011) we have proposed a 'Keynesian New Deal at the Global and the European Level' in order to tackle these roots of the crisis.[14] This policy package should include, first, the re-regulation of the financial sector in order to prevent future financial excesses and financial crises, second, the re-orientation of macroeconomic policies towards stimulating and stabilising domestic demand, in particular in the current account surplus countries and, third, the re-construction of international macro-economic policy coordination and a new world financial order, in order to rebalance the world and the regional economies. Within this broader framework, on the other hand, the EU and the Euro area will have to overcome the specific institutional and economic policy failures which have made the financial and economic crises a euro crisis.[15]

In what follows we will focus on the requirements to overcome the euro crisis, and we will base our arguments on the Post-Keynesian approach to macroeconomics and macroeconomic policies developed in Hein and Stockhammer (2010) as an alternative to the now discredited New Consensus macro-economics, on which much of the existing economic policy framework in the Euro area was built.[16] In order to improve the growth rate of the Euro area as a whole and to provide the conditions and incentives for each country to grow at a rate consistent with roughly balanced current accounts, major institutional reforms in the EU and the Euro area are required.[17]

First, the institutional setting of the ECB and its monetary policy strategy have to be modified so that the ECB is forced to take into account the long-run distribution, employment and growth effects of its policies, and to pursue a monetary policy targeting low real interest rates. In a first step, an adjustment towards the objectives of the US Federal Reserve might be helpful, which include stable prices, maximum employment and moderate long-term interest rates on an equal footing (Meyer 2001). In its monetary policy strategy the ECB should refrain from fine tuning the economy in real or nominal terms and should rather target low interest rates, such that long-term real interest rates remain below Euro area average productivity growth in the medium run. This should be conducive to real investment and growth in the Euro area as a whole. The ECB, moreover, ought to focus on financial market stability. Instead of the blunt instrument of the interest rate it should introduce those instruments which are appropriate to contain bubbles in specific asset markets in specific countries or regions, i.e. credit controls or asset-based reserve requirements (Palley 2010). Furthermore, the ECB should act as a lender of last resort to the banking system, and it should guarantee public debt of the Euro area member countries, allowing these countries to issue debt in their 'own currency'. This would immediately reduce the pressure imposed by 'financial markets' on those countries presently in crisis and would provide the conditions for a long-run oriented solution to the current account imbalances within the Euro area.

Second, the orientation of labour market and social policies towards deregulation and flexibilisation, still prevalent in the EU and the Euro area, will have to be abandoned in favour of re-organising labour markets, stabilising labour unions and employer associations, and adopting Euro area-wide minimum wage legislation.[18] This could provide the institutional requirements for the effective implementation of stabilising nominal wage policies. Nominal wages should rise according to the sum of long-run average growth of labour productivity in the national economy plus the target rate of inflation for the Euro area as a whole. This would contribute to roughly equal inflation rates across the Euro area, and it would prevent mercantilist strategies based on nominal wage moderation.

Third, the SGP at the European level has to be abandoned and needs to be replaced by a means of coordination of national fiscal policies at the Euro area level which allows for the short- and long-run stabilising role of fiscal policies. Hein and Truger (2007) have suggested the coordination of long-run expenditure paths for non-cyclical government spending, i.e. those components of spending which are under control of the government. Such expenditure paths could be geared towards stabilising aggregate demand in the Euro area at full employment levels, and automatic stabilisers plus discretionary counter-cyclical fiscal policies could be applied to fight demand shocks. In order to avoid current account imbalances within the Euro area, these expenditure paths would have to make sure of the following: on average over the cycle and the average tax rate in each member country given, as a first approximation, the government deficits in single countries, i.e. government spending (G) minus taxes (T), would have to be roughly equal to the excess of private saving (S) over private investment (I) in the respective country, such that the current accounts are roughly balanced at a high level of aggregate demand and employment ($S-I=G-T$),[19] and GDP growth is close to the balance of payments constrained growth rate of the individual country.

As we have shown in the third and fourth sections of this chapter, the basic problem underlying the present euro crisis, apart from the absence of a convincing guarantee of Euro area member country public debt by the ECB, are the massive current account imbalances which have developed within the Euro area. Whereas on average over the pre-crisis period, GDP growth in Greece, Ireland, Spain and Portugal has exceeded their respective balance of payments constrained growth rates, GDP growth in Austria, Belgium, Germany and the Netherlands has fallen short of the respective balance of payments constrained growth rates. From this, it follows that the immediate task for the member countries is to adjust actual growth to the respective balance of payments constrained growth rates. This orientation is important in order to rebalance economic development in the Euro area, even if the ECB would guarantee public debt of Euro area member countries and thus contribute to stabilising the markets for public sector debt. However, we will conditionally relax this requirement below.

For the current account surplus countries this means that they should use expansive fiscal policies to increase domestic demand and adjust actual growth towards their balance of payments constrained growth rates. This provides the conditions for the current account deficit countries to reduce their deficits. For a transitional period, the current account surplus countries should also increase their rates of inflation relative to the rates of inflation in the current account deficit countries, in order to rebalance price competitiveness among Euro area member countries. Nominal wage growth should therefore exceed the wage norm mentioned above, i.e. the sum of national productivity growth plus the Euro area inflation target, during the adjustment process.

The major task for the current account deficit countries, with the exception of Ireland,[20] will be to improve their balance of payments constrained growth rates. This means, on the one hand, to contribute to a reduction of the inflation differentials with respect to the surplus countries, by means of nominal wage growth below the sum of national productivity growth plus the inflation target. In order to prevent the risk of deflation in these countries during the process of adjustment, the Euro area inflation target should be increased above the rather ambitious present target of 'below, but close to 2 per cent' for the harmonised index of consumer prices (HICP). On the other hand, current account deficit countries have to increase the income elasticity of demand for their exports and to reduce the income elasticity of demand for imports by means of industrial, structural and regional policies; this means they have to improve their non-price competitiveness.[21]

Even if these adjustment processes of actual and balance of payments constrained growth rates in each of the Euro area member countries take place, we would not expect complete adjustment in the short or medium run. Growth rates of member countries will differ due to productivity catch-up processes and it is hard to imagine that these differences in growth rates will be matched by reverse differentials in inflation rates or by inverse relative income elasticities of demand for exports and imports. In other words, it is not very likely that the more rapidly growing catching up countries will have lower inflation, higher income elasticities of demand for their exports and lower income elasticities of demand for imports than the slowly growing more advanced economies, so that actual growth differentials will be matched exactly by balance of payments constrained growth differentials. Therefore, current account surpluses and deficits will arise due to these differentials.

Coordinating fiscal policies and government deficits at the Euro area level should therefore take tolerable current account deficits associated with catch-up processes into account in the short and medium run. As shown in Hein *et al.* (2012),[22] in a currency union with a balanced current account with the rest of the world and therefore with a (close to) zero net foreign assets/liabilities position, a constant net foreign liabilities–GDP ratio of the current account deficit member countries will be associated with a rising net foreign assets–GDP ratio of the current account surplus member countries, provided that GDP growth in the deficit countries exceeds growth in the surplus countries. Alternatively, a constant net foreign assets–GDP ratio of the surplus countries will be accompanied by falling net foreign liabilities–GDP ratios of the deficit countries, or net foreign assets–GDP ratios of surplus countries will be rising and net foreign liabilities–GDP ratios of deficit countries will be falling. Sustainably higher growth than that of the surplus countries on Euro area average should therefore be the ultimate criterion for tolerable current account deficits in the coordination process of fiscal policies within the Euro area. Current account deficits of countries with a below surplus country average GDP growth rate, and the related current account surpluses of the surplus countries, should not be tolerated and should be tackled symmetrically, i.e. by both deficit and surplus countries, with the measures outlined above.

Current account deficits will have to be financed by capital imports. Appropriate financial regulations, avoiding asset price inflation and credit bubbles, are key prerequisites for sustainable growth and for the stability of productivity growth catch-up processes and the related current account deficits and net foreign liabilities position. Long-term capital flows as a means of finance of acceptable current account deficits are therefore most important. Long-term direct investment may be the most stable and beneficial, but structural effects (and also the outflow of profits) have to be taken into account, as the example of Ireland in the recent past has taught us. If capital inflows are financed by credit, the focus should be on long-term credit.

Therefore, the EU and the Euro area will have to develop institutions which take care of the transfer of the current account surpluses of the more slowly growing mature member countries to the catching-up less developed economies. First, the ECB will have to explicitly guarantee public debt of all member countries and thus stabilise financial markets and keep interest rates on government debt below the long-run nominal GDP growth rate of the respective country. Second, fiscal policies among the Euro area member countries will have to be coordinated along the lines developed above: on average over the cycle and the average tax rate in each member country given, the government deficits would have to be roughly equal to the excess of private saving over private investment in the respective country, taking into account acceptable current account deficits or surpluses given by catch-up processes and thus differential long-run growth rates. Third, the European Investment Bank, together with the European regional and structural funds and the government institutions of the recipient countries, should be involved in directing private capital flows into appropriate sectors and areas of the current account deficit countries which facilitate real catch-up processes and avoid bubbles in certain sectors (i.e. in housing or financial sectors).

Conclusions

In this chapter we have interpreted the euro crisis in a broader context as the latest episode of the crisis of finance-dominated capitalism. We have analysed major features of finance-dominated capitalism, specifically the increasing inequality of income distribution and the rising imbalances of current accounts, for a set of major Euro area countries. Against this background we have then examined the euro crisis and the economic policy reactions of European governments and institutions. Since these policy makers narrowly interpret the crisis as a sovereign debt crisis caused by irresponsible behaviour of some member country governments, their policy reactions and recommendations focusing on constraining government deficits and debt by means of tighter rules and deflationary policies are doomed to fail and will increase the risk of deflationary stagnation and finally disintegration of the Euro area as a whole. Therefore, we have outlined an alternative macroeconomic policy approach tackling the basic contradictions of finance-dominated capitalism and the deficiencies of European economic policy institutions and economic policy strategies. What is urgently required in order to prevent a worsening of the crisis in the Euro area is, on the one hand, a central bank which convincingly guarantees public debt of Euro area member countries. On the other hand, an expansionary macroeconomic policy approach, in particular in the current account surplus countries of the Euro area, needs to be applied in order to improve income distribution and to overcome the imbalances which have arisen in the past and which are at the roots of the crisis.

Notes

1 The main arguments put forward in this chapter are based on my forthcoming book *The Macroeconomics of Finance-dominated Capitalism – and its Crisis* (Hein 2012) and on the research results which have gone into that book. For a more detailed elaboration on the macroeconomic theory of finance-dominated capitalism, in particular, see the respective chapters in that book. For most valuable research assistance regarding the subject of the present chapter I would like to thank Nina Dodig and Matthias Mundt. I am also most grateful for helpful comments to Trevor Evans and Milka Kazandziska.

2 For similar analysis for a broader set of countries see Hein (2011a, 2011b, 2012) and Hein and Mundt (2012).

3 For similar analyses for the global scale see van Treeck *et al.* (2007), Bibow (2008), Fitoussi and Stiglitz (2009), UNCTAD (2009), van Treeck (2009), Wade (2009), Hein and Truger (2011), Stockhammer (2010a, 2010b) and Hein and Mundt (2012).

4 On the depressing effects of finance-dominated capitalism, or ‘financialisation’, on investment in real capital stock see Hein (2012, ch. 3) and the references provided there.

5 Note that from national accounting we obtain: Gross profits net of taxes=Gross investment+Export surplus+Government budget deficit−Workers’ saving+Capitalists’ consumption (Kalecki 1971, p. 82).

6 In the case of Ireland, the current account deficit (and the positive financial balance of the external sector) was not due to a deficit in external trade but rather a deficit in the flows of primary incomes. Although the balance of goods and services in Ireland was positive, we have not included it into the ‘export-led mercantilist’ group of countries discussed below, because Ireland, as the other ‘debt-led consumption boom’ countries, showed a negative balance of the private sector and of the domestic sectors as a whole. Surpluses in the balance of goods and services were thus required in order to meet the payment commitments associated with the negative balance of primary incomes and to avoid an even larger deficit in the current account.

7 See for example the argument of the German Federal Ministry of Finance (2011) in the German Stability Programme submitted to the European Commission and the European Council (2011a) in its proposal for the ‘Euro Plus Pact’.

8 See European Commission (2012a) for information on the Greek Loan Facility and European Commission (2012b) for information on the EFSM, the EFSF and the rescue packages provided for Ireland and Portugal.

9 For information on these interventions see ECB (2011b).

10 See the agreements of the meeting of the Economic and Financial Affairs Council (ECOFIN) on 15 March 2011 (Council of the EU 2011a), the conclusions of the meeting of the European Council (2011a) on 24/25 March 2011, the statement by the heads of state or government of the Euro area and EU institutions on 21 July 2011 (Council of the EU 2011b) and the statement by the Euro area heads of state and governments on 9 December 2011 (European Council 2011b).

11 See also the agreement the ECOFIN regarding the reform of the SGP and the surveillances of economic policies (Council of the EU 2011a).
12 For similar explanations see Uxó *et al.* (2011) and Stockhammer (2011).
13 For a more detailed analysis and critique of the mercantilist macroeconomic policy strategy in Germany and its implications for the imbalances in the Euro area see Hein and Truger (2007, 2009, 2010) and Cesaratto and Stirati (2010).
14 See also Hein (2012, ch. 7).
15 On the 'design faults' of the European Monetary and Economic Union see more extensively Arestis and Sawyer (2011), however, without establishing any relationship of the euro crisis with the crisis of finance-dominated capitalism.
16 For the NCM see Goodfriend and King (1997), Clarida *et al.* (1999) and Woodford (2003), and for detailed critiques of the NCM and its application in economic policy making, see Arestis (2009, 2011a, 2011b), Arestis and Sawyer (2004a), and Hein and Stockhammer (2010).
17 On the determinants of the balance of payments constrained growth rate see Thirlwall (1979, 2002) and on the application of this concept to the analysis of the imbalances within a currency area, i.e. the euro area, see Hein *et al.* (2012) and Hein (2012, ch. 8).
18 Of course, this does not imply the same minimum wage rate for the whole Euro area, but country-specific minimum wages, which, however, should be set according to some Euro area wide rule.
19 This is, of course, the functional finance approach proposed by Lerner (1943) and more recently again by Arestis and Sawyer (2004b).
20 In the case of Ireland, the current account deficit was not due to a deficit in external trade but rather a deficit in the flows of primary incomes.
21 Following Thirlwall (2002, p. 78), 'The only sure and long-term solution to raising a country's growth rate consistent with balance of payments equilibrium on current account is structural change to raise ε and to reduce π'. The variable ε is the income elasticity of the demand for exports and π is the income elasticity of the demand for imports.
22 See also Hein (2012, ch. 8).

References

Arestis, P. (2009) 'New Consensus macroeconomics and Keynesian critique', in E. Hein, T. Niechoj and E. Stockhammer (eds), *Macroeconomic Policies on Shaky Foundations: Whither Mainstream Economics?* (Marburg: Metropolis).

Arestis, P. (2011a) 'Keynesian economics and the New Consensus in macroeconomics', in E. Hein and E. Stockhammer (eds), *A Modern Guide to Keynesian Macroeconomics and Economic Policies* (Cheltenham: Edward Elgar).

Arestis, P. (2011b) 'European Economic and Monetary Union policies from a Keynesian perspective', in E. Hein and E. Stockhammer (eds), *A Modern Guide to Keynesian Macroeconomics and Economic Policies* (Cheltenham: Edward Elgar).

Arestis, P. and Sawyer, M. (2004a) *Re-examining Monetary and Fiscal Policy for the 21st Century* (Cheltenham: Edward Elgar).

Arestis, P. and Sawyer, M. (2004b) 'On fiscal policy and budget deficits', *Intervention. Journal of Economics*, 1 (2): 61–74.

Arestis, P. and Sawyer, M. (2011) 'The design faults of the Economic and Monetary Union', *Journal of Contemporary European Studies*, 19 (1): 21–32.

Bibow, J. (2008) 'The international monetary (non-) order and the "global capital flows paradox"', in E. Hein, T. Niechoj, P. Spahn and A. Truger (eds), *Finance-led Capitalism? Macroeconomic Effects of Changes in the Financial Sector* (Marburg: Metropolis).

Cesaratto, S. and Stirati, A. (2010) 'Germany and the European and global crises', *International Journal of Political Economy*, 39 (4): 56–86.

BIS (2010) *Bank for International Settlements: Property Price Statistics*, www.bis.org/statistics/pp.htm.

Clarida, R., Gali, J. and Gertler, M. (1999) 'The science of monetary policy: a New Keynesian perspective', *Journal of Economic Literature*, 37: 1661–1707.

Council of the EU (2011a) *Council Reaches Agreement on Measures to Strengthen Economic Governance*, Brussels, 15 March, 7681/11, PRESSE 63.

Council of the EU (2011b) *Statement by the Heads of State or Government of the Euro Area and EU Institutions*, Brussels, 21 July.

ECB (2011a) *Long Term Interest Rate Statistics*, December, www.ecb.int/stats/money/long/html/index.en.html.

ECB (2011b) *Weekly Financial Statements*, www.ecb.int/press/pr/wfs/2011/html/index.en.html.

European Commission (2010) *AMECO Database*, Spring, http://ec.europa.eu/economy_finance/db_indicators/ameco/index_en.htm.

European Commission (2011a) *AMECO Database*, Spring, http://ec.europa.eu/economy_finance/db_indicators/ameco/index_en.htm.

European Commission (2011b) *Green Paper on the Feasibility of Introducing Stability Bonds*, Brussels, 23 November, COM(2011) 818 final.

European Commission (2012a) *The Greek Loan Facility*, http://ec.europa.eu/economy_finance/eu_borrower/greek_loan_facility/index_en.htm.

European Commission (2012b) *European Financial Stability Mechanism (EFSM)*, http://ec.europa.eu/economy_finance/eu_borrower/efsm/index_en.htm.

European Council (2011a) *Conclusions*, 24/25 March, EUCO 10/11.

European Council (2011b) *Statement by the Euro Area Heads of State or Government*, Brussels, 9 December.

Fitoussi, J.-P. and Stiglitz, J. (2009) 'The ways out of the crisis and the building of a more cohesive world', OFCE Document de Travail, No. 2009-17 (Paris: OFCE).

German Federal Ministry of Finance (2011) *German Stability Programme 2011 Update*, Berlin.

Girouard, N., Kennedy, M. and Andre, C. (2007) 'Has the rise in debt made households more vulnerable?' OECD Economics Working Paper, No. 535, ECO/WKP(2006)63 (Paris: OECD).

Goodbody Stockbrokers (2009) *Irish Economic Commentary*, 15 October (Dublin: Goodbody Stockbrokers).

Goodfriend, M. and King, R.G. (1997) 'The New Neoclassical Synthesis and the role of monetary policy', in B.S. Bernanke and J.J. Rotemberg (eds), *NBER Macroeconomics Annual: 1997* (Cambridge, MA: MIT Press).

Hein, E. (2011a) 'Redistribution, global imbalances and the financial and economic crisis: the case for a Keynesian New Deal', *International Journal of Labour Research*, 3 (1): 51–73.

Hein, E. (2011b) 'Financialisation, re-distribution, and the financial and economic crisis: a Kaleckian perspective', in T. Niechoj, Ö. Onaran, E. Stockhammer, A. Truger and T. van Treeck (eds), *Stabilising an Unequal Economy? Public Debt, Financial Regulation, and Income Distribution* (Marburg: Metropolis).

Hein, E. (2012) *The Macroeconomics of Finance-dominated Capitalism – and its Crisis* (Cheltenham: Edward Elgar).

Hein, E. and Mundt, M. (2012) *Financialisation and the Requirements and Potentials for Wage-led Recovery: A Review Focussing on the G20*, Conditions of Work and Employment Series No. 37 (Geneva: International Labour Organization).

Hein, E. and Stockhammer, E. (2010) 'Macroeconomic policy mix, employment and inflation in a Post-Keynesian alternative to the New Consensus model', *Review of Political Economy*, 22: 317–354.

Hein, E. and Truger, A. (2007) 'Germany's post-2000 stagnation in the European context: a lesson in macroeconomic mismanagement', in P. Arestis, E. Hein and E. Le Heron (eds), *Aspects of Modern Monetary and Macroeconomic Policies* (Basingstoke: Palgrave Macmillan).

Hein, E. and Truger, A. (2009) 'How to fight (or not to fight) a slowdown', *Challenge. The Magazine of Economic Affairs*, 52 (3): 52–75.

Hein, E. and Truger, A. (2010) 'Financial crisis, global recession and macroeconomic policy reactions: the case of Germany', in S. Dullien, E. Hein, A. Truger and T. van Treeck (eds), *The World Economy in Crisis: The Return of Keynesianism?* (Marburg: Metropolis).

Hein, E. and Truger, A. (2011) 'Finance-dominated capitalism in crisis: the case for a Keynesian New Deal at the European and the global level', in P. Arestis and M. Sawyer (eds), *New Economics as Mainstream Economics, International Papers in Political Economy* (Basingstoke: Palgrave Macmillan).

Hein, E., Truger, A. and van Treeck, T. (2012) 'The European financial and economic crisis: alternative solutions from a (Post-)Keynesian perspective', in P. Arestis and M. Sawyer (eds), *The Euro Crisis, International Papers in Political Economy* (Basingstoke: Palgrave Macmillan).

Kalecki, M. (1971) *Selected Essays on the Dynamics of the Capitalist Economy, 1933–1970* (Cambridge: Cambridge University Press).

Lerner, A. (1943) 'Functional finance and federal debt', *Social Research*, 10: 38–51.

Meyer, L.H. (2001) 'Inflation targets and inflation targeting', *Federal Reserve Bank of St. Louis Review*, 83 (6): 1–13.

OECD (2008) *Growing Unequal? Income Distribution and Poverty in OECD Countries* (Paris: OECD).

OECD (2010) *OECD.StatExtracts*, http://stats.oecd.org/Index.aspx.

Palley, T. (2010) 'Asset price bubbles and counter-cyclical monetary policy: why central banks have been wrong and what should be done', *Intervention. European Journal of Economics and Economic Policies*, 7 (1): 91–107.

Stockhammer, E. (2010a) 'Income distribution, the finance-dominated accumulation regime, and the present crisis', in S. Dullien, E. Hein, A. Truger and T. van Treeck (eds), *The World Economy in Crisis: The Return of Keynesianism?* (Marburg: Metropolis).

Stockhammer, E. (2010b) 'Neoliberalism, income distribution and the causes of the crisis', Research on Money and Finance, Discussion Paper No. 19 (London: Department of Economics, SOAS).

Stockhammer, E. (2011) 'Peripheral Europe's debt and German wages: the role of wage policy in the Euro area', Research on Money and Finance, Discussion Paper No. 29 (London: Department of Economics, SOAS).

Thirlwall, A.P. (1979) 'The balance of payments constraint as an explanation of international growth differences', *Banca Nazionale del Lavoro Quarterly Review*, 128: 45–53.

Thirlwall, A.P. (2002) *The Nature of Economic Growth* (Cheltenham: Edward Elgar).

UNCTAD (2009) *The Global Economic Crisis: Systemic Failures and Multilateral Remedies* (New York and Geneva: UNCTAD).

Uxó, J., Paul, J. and Febrero, E. (2011) 'Current account imbalances in the Monetary Union and the Great Recession: causes and policies', *Panoeconomicus*, 58 (5): 571–592.

Van Treeck, T. (2009) 'The political economy debate on 'financialisation': a macro-economic perspective', *Review of International Political Economy*, 16: 907–944.
Van Treeck, T., Hein, E. and Dünhaupt, P. (2007) *Finanzsystem und wirtschaftliche Entwicklung: neuere Tendenzen in den USA und in Deutschland*, IMK Studies 5/2007 (Duesseldorf: Macroeconomic Policy Institute (IMK) at Hans Boeckler Foundation).
Wade, R. (2009) 'From global imbalances to global reorganisations', *Cambridge Journal of Economics*, 33 (4): 539–562.
Woodford, M. (2003) *Interest and Prices: Foundations of a Theory of Monetary Policy Princeton* (Princeton, NJ: Princeton University Press).

2 The world in balance sheet recession

Causes, cures and politics

Richard C. Koo

A recurring concern in the Western economies today is that they may be headed toward a Japan-like lost decade. Remarkable similarities between house price movements in the United States this time and in Japan 15 years ago, illustrated in Figure 2.1, suggest that the two countries have indeed contracted a similar disease. The post-1990 Japanese experience, however, also demonstrated that the nation's recession was no ordinary recession.

Recession driven by deleveraging leads to prolonged slump

The key difference between an ordinary recession and one that can produce a lost decade is that in the latter, a large portion of the private sector is actually

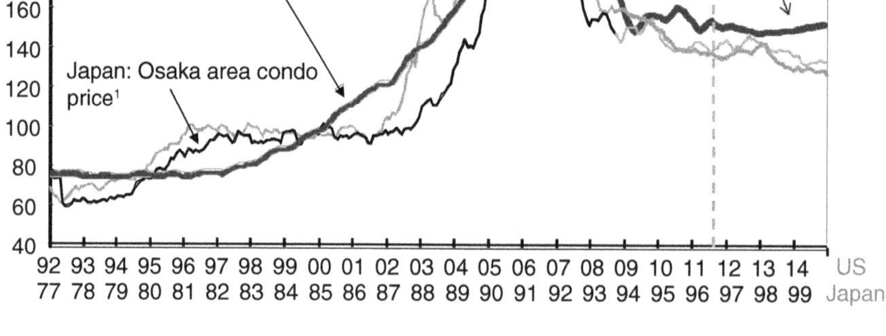

Figure 2.1 US housing prices mirror Japan's experience (sources: Bloomberg; Real Estate Economic Institute, Japan; S&P, S&P/Case-Shiller Home Price Indices, as of October 5, 2011).

Note

1 Per m^2, five-month moving average.

minimizing debt instead of maximizing profits following the bursting of a nation-wide asset price bubble. When a debt-financed bubble bursts, asset prices collapse while liabilities remain, leaving millions of private sector balance sheets underwater. In order to regain their financial health and credit ratings, households and businesses are forced to repair their balance sheets by increasing savings or paying down debt. This act of deleveraging reduces aggregate demand and throws the economy into a very special type of recession.

The first casualty of this shift to debt minimization is monetary policy, the traditional remedy for recessions, because people with negative equity are not interested in increasing borrowing at any interest rate. Nor will there be many willing lenders for those with impaired balance sheets, especially when the lenders themselves have balance sheet problems. Moreover, the money supply, which consists mostly of bank deposits, contracts when the private sector collectively draws down bank deposits to repay debt. Although the central bank can inject liquidity into the banking system, it will be hard-pressed to reverse the shrinkage of bank deposits when there are no borrowers and the money multiplier is zero or negative at the margin.

As shown in Figures 2.2 and 2.3, massive injections of liquidity by both the Federal Reserve in the US and the Bank of England in the UK not only failed to prevent contractions in credit available to the private sector, but also produced only miniscule increases in the money supply. This is exactly what happened to Japan after the bursting of its bubble in 1990, as shown in Figure 2.4.

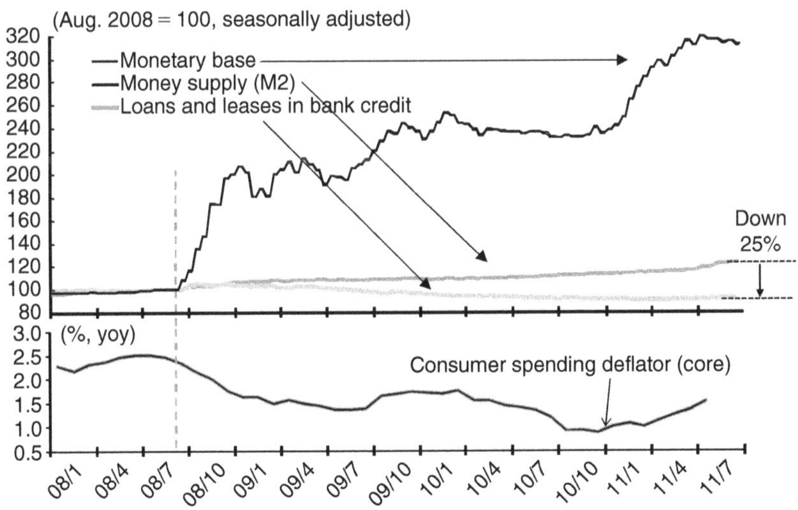

Figure 2.2 Drastic liquidity injection failed to increase money supply (I): US (sources: Board of Governors of the Federal Reserve System, US Department of Commerce).

Note
Commercial bank loans and leases, adjustments for discontinuities made by Nomura Research Institute.

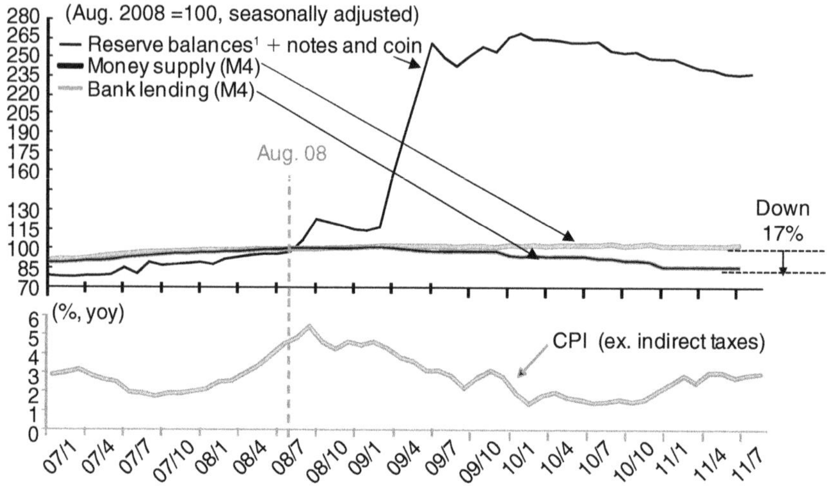

Figure 2.3 Drastic liquidity injection failed to increase money supply (II): UK (sources: Bank of England, Office for National Statistics, UK).

Note
Reserve Balances data are seasonally unadjusted. Money supply and bank lending data exclude intermediate financial institutions.

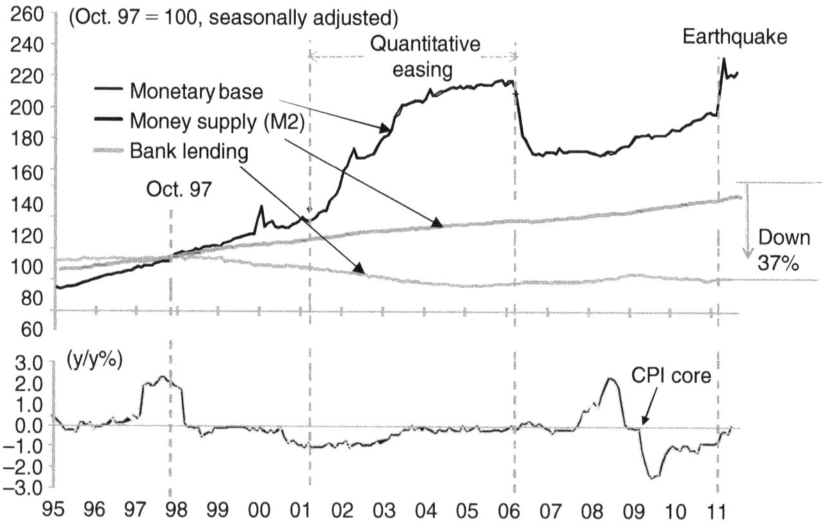

Figure 2.4 Drastic liquidity injection failed to increase money supply (III): Japan (source: Bank of Japan).

Note
Bank lending is seasonally adjusted by Nomura Research.

Nor is there any reason why bringing back inflation or inflation targeting should work, because people are paying down debt in response to the fall in *asset* prices, not consumer prices. And with the money multiplier negative at the margin, the central bank does not have the means to produce the money supply growth needed to increase the inflation rate.

More importantly, when the private sector deleverages in spite of zero interest rates, the economy enters a deflationary spiral because, in the absence of people borrowing and spending money, the economy *continuously* loses demand equal to the sum of savings and net debt repayments. This process will continue until either private sector balance sheets are repaired or the private sector has become too poor to save (i.e., the economy enters a depression).

To see this, consider a world where a household has an income of $1,000 and a savings rate of 10 percent. This household would then spend $900 and save $100. In the usual or textbook world, the saved $100 will be taken up by the financial sector and lent to a borrower who can best use the money. When that borrower spends the $100, aggregate expenditure totals $1,000 ($900 plus $100) against original income of $1,000, and the economy moves on. When demand for the $100 in savings is insufficient, interest rates are lowered, which usually prompts a borrower to take up the remaining sum. When demand is excessive, interest rates are raised, prompting some borrowers to drop out.

In the world where the private sector is minimizing debt, however, there are no borrowers for the saved $100 even with interest rates at zero, leaving only $900 in expenditures. That $900 represents someone's income, and if that person also saves 10 percent, only $810 will be spent. Since repairing balance sheets after a major bubble bursts typically takes many years—15 years in the case of Japan—the saved $90 will go un-borrowed again, and the economy will shrink to $810, and then $730 and so on.

This is exactly what happened during the Great Depression, when everyone was paying down debt and no one was borrowing and spending. From 1929 to 1933, the United States lost 46 percent of its GDP mostly because of this debt-repayment-induced deflationary spiral. It was also largely for this reason that the US money supply shrank by nearly 30 percent during the four-year period.

The discussion above suggests that there are at least two types of recessions: those triggered by the usual business cycle and those triggered by private sector deleveraging or debt minimization. Since the economics profession never considered the latter type of recession, there is no name for it in the literature. In order to distinguish this type of recession from ordinary recessions, it is referred to here as a *balance sheet recession.* Like nationwide debt-financed bubbles, balance sheet recessions are rare and, left untreated, will ultimately develop into a depression.

Significance of Japanese experience

Japan faced a balance sheet recession following the bursting of its bubble in 1990 as commercial real estate prices fell 87 percent nationwide. The resulting loss of national wealth in shares and real estate alone was equivalent to three years of 1989 GDP. In comparison, the United States lost national wealth equivalent to one year of 1929 GDP during the Great Depression. Japan's corporate sector responded by shifting from its traditional role as a large borrower of funds to a massive re-payer of debt, as shown in Figure 2.5. The net debt repayment of the corporate sector increased to more than 6 percent of GDP a year. And this was on top of household savings of over 4 percent of GDP a year, all with interest rates at zero. In other words, Japan could have lost 10 percent of GDP every year, just as the US did during the Great Depression.

Japan managed to avoid a depression, however, because the government borrowed and spent the aforementioned $100 every year, thereby keeping the economy's expenditures at $1,000 ($900 in household spending plus $100 in government spending). In spite of a massive loss of wealth and private sector deleveraging reaching over 10 percent of GDP per year, Japan managed to keep its GDP above the bubble peak throughout the post-1990 era (Figure 2.6), and the unemployment rate never climbed above 5.5 percent.

This government action maintained incomes in the private sector and allowed businesses and households to pay down debt. By 2005 the private sector had completed its balance sheet repairs.

Although this fiscal action increased government debt by 460 trillion yen or 92 percent of GDP during the 1990–2005 period, the amount of GDP preserved by fiscal action compared with a depression scenario was far greater. For example, if we assume, rather optimistically, that without government action Japanese GDP would have returned to the pre-bubble level of 1985, the difference between this hypothetical GDP and actual GDP would be over 2,000

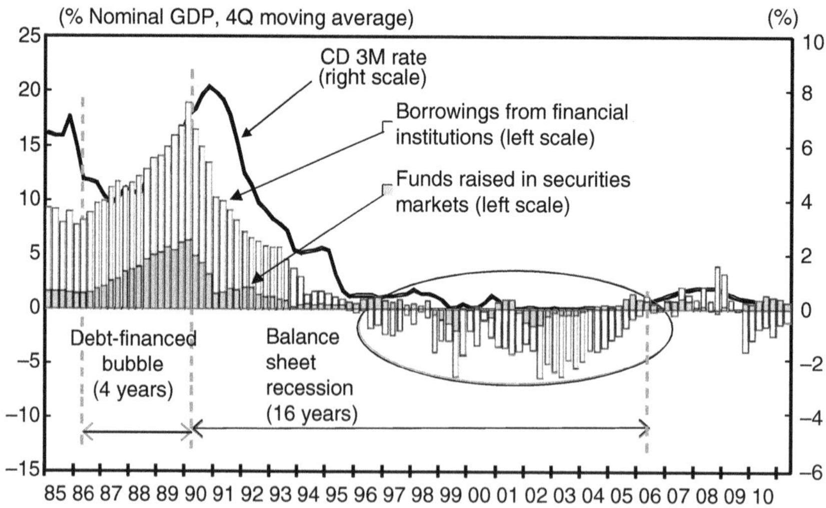

Figure 2.5 Japan's deleveraging under zero interest rates lasted for ten years (sources: Bank of Japan, Cabinet Office, Japan).

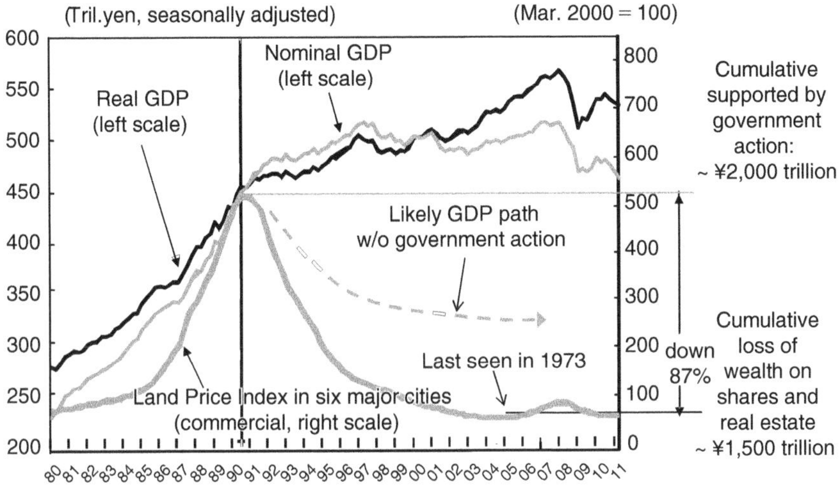

Figure 2.6 Japan's GDP grew despite massive loss of wealth and private sector deleveraging (sources: Cabinet Office, Japan Real Estate Institute).

trillion yen for the 15-year period. In other words, Japan spent 460 trillion yen to buy 2,000 trillion yen of GDP, making it a tremendous bargain. And because the private sector was deleveraging, the government's fiscal actions did not lead to crowding out, inflation or skyrocketing interest rates.

Post-1990 Japan also managed to keep its money supply from falling in spite of private sector deleveraging because government borrowing took the place of private sector borrowing and prevented a contraction of banks' assets. This is shown in Figure 2.7. The post-1933 US money supply also stabilized and started growing again because the Roosevelt administration began borrowing money aggressively for its New Deal programs, as shown in Figure 2.8.

Many authors have argued that it was monetary policy that led to the post-1933 US recovery, but they all failed to look at the asset side of banks' balance sheets. From 1933 to 1936, only lending to the government increased, while lending to the private sector did not increase at all. And lending to the government increased because the government had to finance the New Deal programs. Both of the examples above indicate that fiscal stimulus is essential in keeping both GDP *and* the money supply from contracting during a balance sheet recession.

The world in balance sheet recession

Today private sectors in the US, the UK, Spain and Ireland (but not Greece) are undergoing massive deleveraging in spite of record low interest rates. This means these countries are all in serious balance sheet recessions. The private sectors in Japan and Germany are not borrowing, either. With borrowers

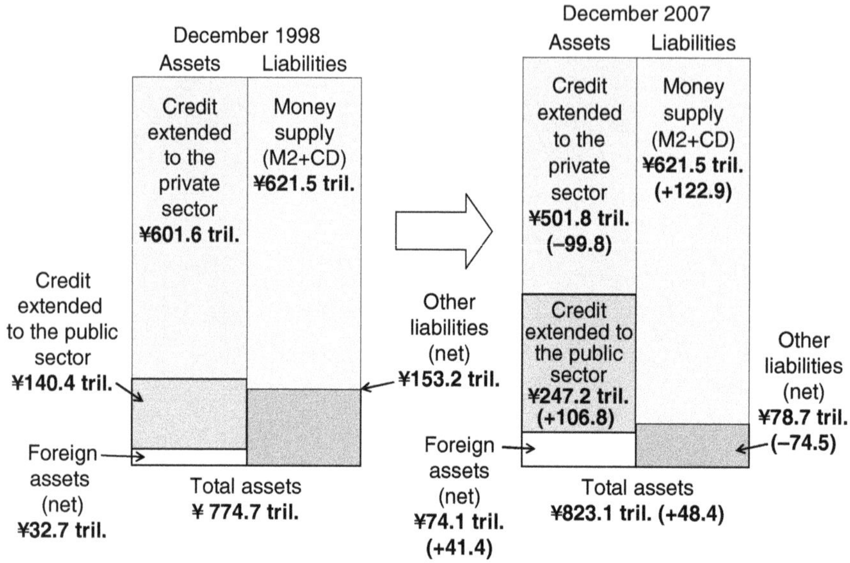

Figure 2.7 Japan's money supply has been sustained by government borrowings (source: Bank of Japan "Monetary Survey").

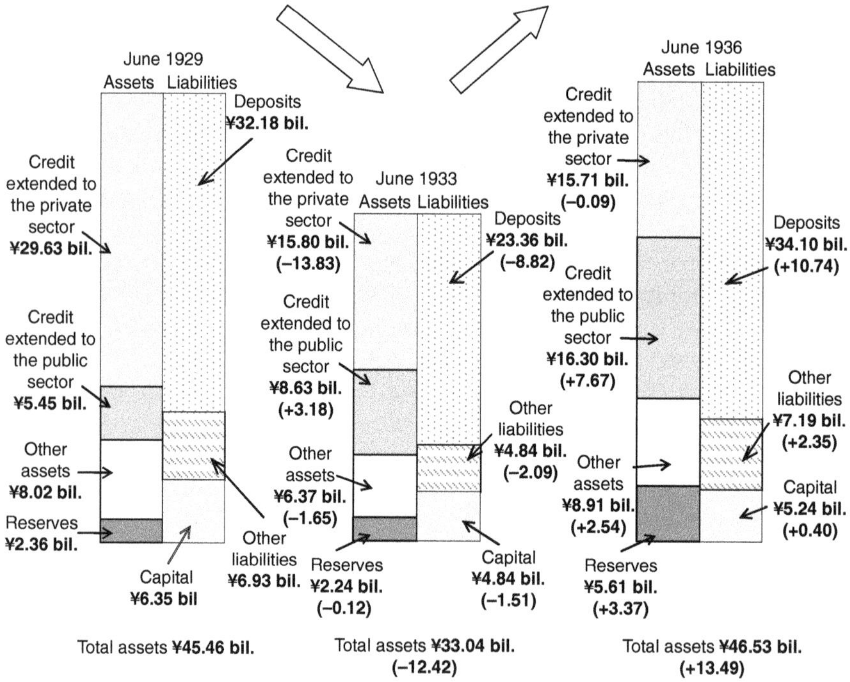

Figure 2.8 Post-1933 US money supply growth was also made possible by government borrowings (source: Board of Governors of the Federal Reserve System (1976) *Banking and Monetary Statistics 1914–1941*, pp. 72–79).

disappearing and banks reluctant to lend, it is no wonder that, after nearly three years of record low interest rates and massive liquidity injections, industrial economies are still doing so poorly.

Flow of funds data for the US (Figure 2.9) show a massive shift away from borrowing to savings by the private sector since the housing bubble burst in 2007. The shift for the private sector as a whole represents over 9 percent of US GDP at a time of zero interest rates. Moreover, this increase in private sector savings exceeds the increase in government borrowings (5.8 percent of GDP), which suggests that the government is not doing enough to offset private sector deleveraging.

Flow of funds data for the UK (Figure 2.10) tell the same story, with the growth in private savings (7.7 percent of GDP) exceeding the increase in government deficit (7.0 percent of GDP). Once again, this means the UK government is not doing enough to stabilize the economy by offsetting private sector deleveraging.

Yet policymakers in both countries, spooked by the events in Greece, have pushed strongly to cut budget deficits, with the UK pushing harder than the US. Although shunning fiscal profligacy is the right approach when the private sector is healthy and is maximizing profits, nothing is worse than fiscal consolidation when a sick private sector is minimizing debt. Removing government support in the midst of private sector deleveraging is equivalent to removing the aforementioned $100 from the economy's income stream, and that will trigger a deflationary spiral as the economy shrinks from $1,000 to $900 to $810.

Unfortunately, the proponents of fiscal consolidation are only looking at the growth in the fiscal deficit while ignoring even bigger increases in private sector

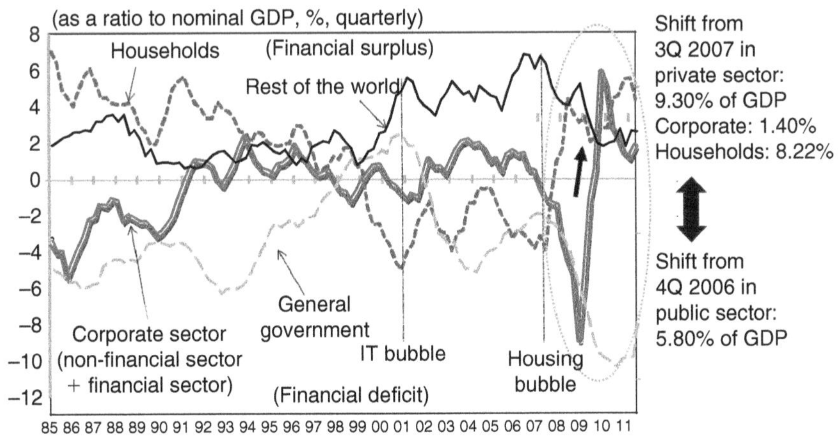

Figure 2.9 US in balance sheet recession: US private sector increased savings massively after the bubble (sources: FRB, US Department of Commerce).

Note

For figures, four-quarter averages ending with Q/11 are used.

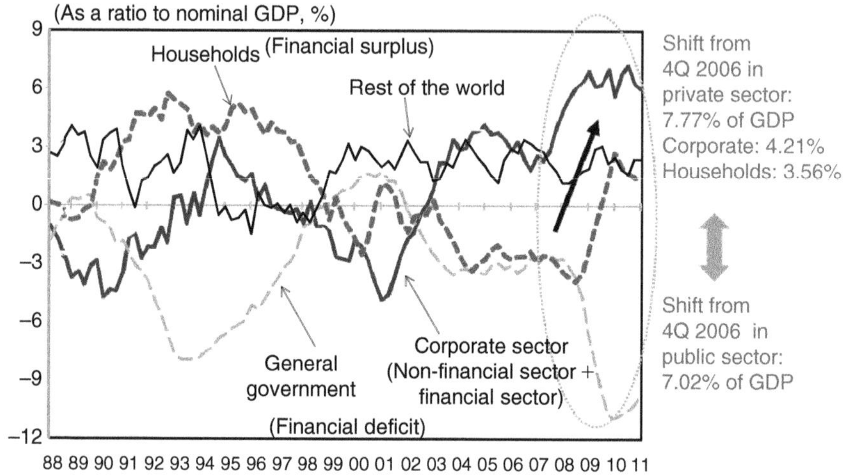

Figure 2.10 UK in balance sheet recession: massive increase in private savings after the bubble (source: Office for National Statistics, UK).

Note
For figures, four-quarter averages ending with 1Q/11 are used.

savings. Indeed these governments are repeating the Japanese mistake of premature fiscal consolidation in 1997 and 2001, which in both cases triggered a deflationary spiral and ultimately *increased* the deficit (Figure 2.11).

The mistake in 1997, for example, resulted in five quarters of negative growth and increased the deficit by 68 percent, from 22 trillion yen in 1996 to 38 trillion yen in 1999. It took Japan ten years to climb out of the hole created by this policy error. Japan would have come out of its balance sheet recession much faster and at a significantly lower cost than the 460 trillion yen noted above had it not implemented austerity measures on those two occasions. The US made the same mistake of premature fiscal consolidation in 1937, with equally devastating results.

Except for certain countries in the Eurozone which will be discussed below, there is no reason why a government should face financing problems during a balance sheet recession. The amount of money it must borrow and spend to avert a deflationary spiral is exactly equal to the un-borrowed and un-invested savings in the private sector (the $100 mentioned above) that is sitting somewhere in the financial system.

With very few viable borrowers left in the private sector, fund managers who must invest in fixed income assets without foreign exchange risk have no choice but to lend to the government, which is the last borrower standing. Although deficit hawks pushing for fiscal consolidation often talk about "bond market vigilantes," the fact that ten-year bond yields in the US and UK today are only around 2 percent—unthinkably low given fiscal deficits of nearly 10 percent of GDP—indicates that bond market participants are aware of the nature and

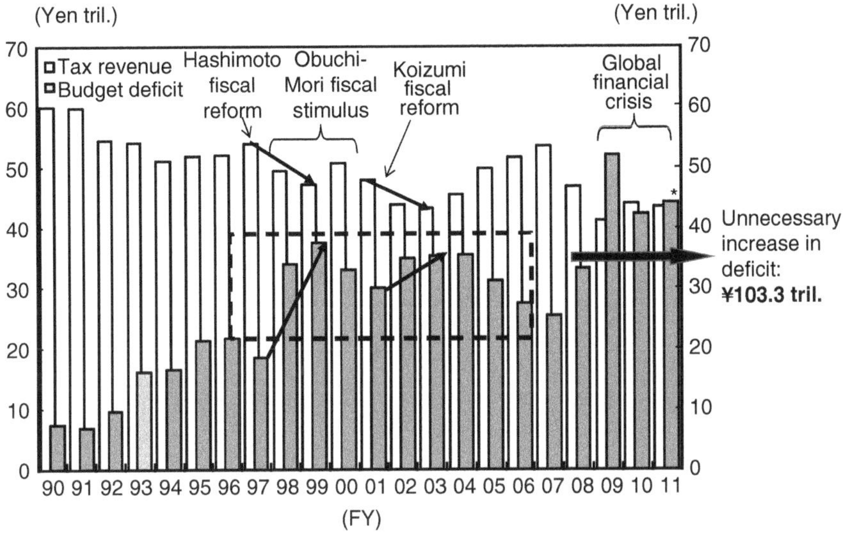

Figure 2.11 Premature fiscal reforms in 1997 and 2001 weakened economy, reduced tax revenue and increased deficit (source: Ministry of Finance, Japan).

Note
* estimated by MOF.

dynamics of balance sheet recessions. Indeed bond yields in the US and UK today are equivalent to Japanese bond yields in 1997.

Reason for Eurozone debt crisis

While Western economies experience balance sheet recessions and most government bond yields fall to historic lows, investors continue to demand high yields to hold the debt of Eurozone countries like Spain and Ireland. The reason behind this phenomenon is a factor unique to the Eurozone: fixed-income fund managers can buy government bonds issued by *other* Eurozone countries without taking on any exchange rate risk. If they grow worried about their own government's fiscal position, they can simply buy other government's debt.

Spain and Ireland, for instance, are both in serious balance sheet recessions, with private sector deleveraging reaching 17 percent of GDP in Spain (Figure 2.12) and a whopping 21 percent of GDP (Figure 2.13) in Ireland, all under record low interest rates. Indeed the entire Eurozone is in a balance sheet recession (Figure 2.14). Even though this means there is huge pool of private sector savings available in these countries, Spanish and Irish pension fund managers who do not like their own countries' debt can easily buy German government bonds. That leaves the governments of both Spain and Ireland unable to tap their own private savings surpluses to fight the balance sheet recessions.

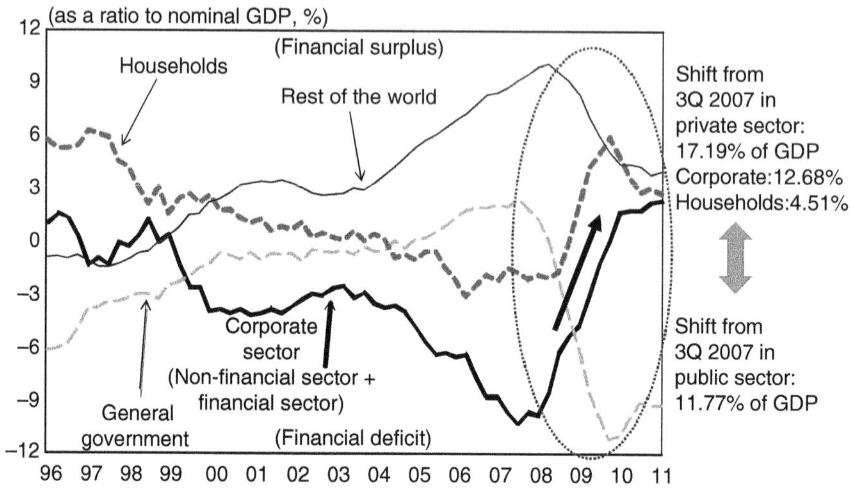

Figure 2.12 Spain in balance sheet recession: massive increase in private savings after the bubble (source: Banco de España).

Note
For figures, four-quarter averages ending with 1Q/11 are used.

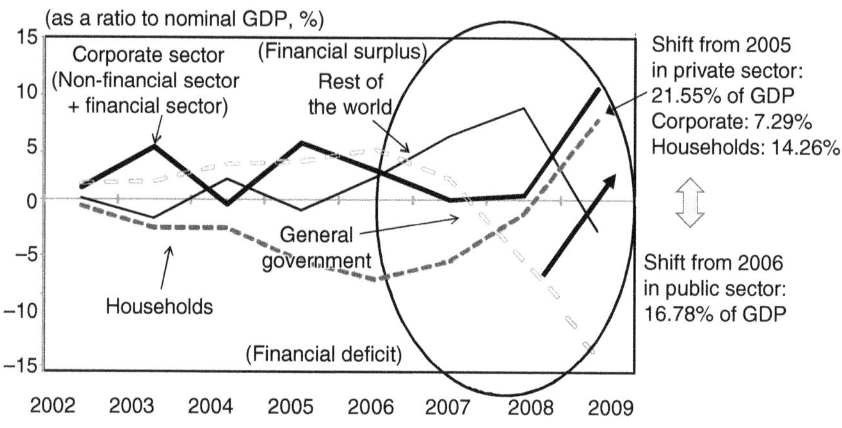

Figure 2.13 Ireland in balance sheet recession: massive increase in private savings after the bubble (sources: Eurostat, Central Statistics Office, Ireland).

If the governments of countries like Germany and the Netherlands actively borrow and spend the money flowing in from Spain and Ireland, that will sustain economic activity in the broader Eurozone economy and have a positive impact on Spain and Ireland as well. Unfortunately, the governments of Germany and the Netherlands are focused entirely on deficit-reduction efforts in a bid to

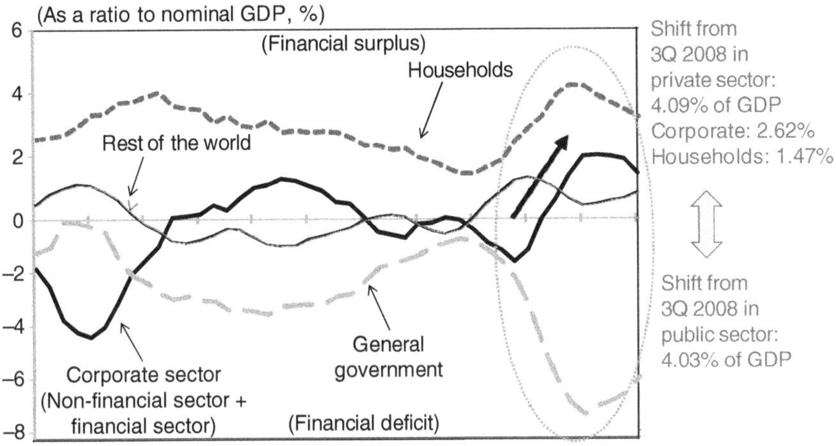

Figure 2.14 Eurozone in balance sheet recession: massive increase in private savings after the bubble (source: ECB).

Note
For figures, four-quarter averages ending with 1Q/11 are used.

observe the 3 per cent ceiling on budget deficits prescribed by the Maastricht Treaty.

Countries in balance sheet recessions such as Spain are desperately in need of fiscal stimulus but are unable to take advantage of the rapid increase in domestic savings and are therefore forced to engage in fiscal consolidation of their own. That causes the aforementioned $100 to be removed from the income steam, prompting a deflationary spiral. And since the countries receiving those savings are not borrowing and spending them, the broader Eurozone economy is rapidly weakening. It is no wonder that the Spanish unemployment rate is over 21 percent and Irish GDP has fallen more than 10 percent from its peak.

Fund flows within the Eurozone were following the opposite pattern until just a few years ago. Banks in Germany, which had fallen into a balance sheet recession after the telecom bubble collapsed in 2000, aggressively bought the debt of southern European nations, which were denominated in the same currency but offered higher yields than domestic debt. The resulting capital inflows from Germany poured further fuel on to the fire of housing bubbles in these countries.

There is thus a tendency within the Eurozone for fund flows to go to extremes. When times are good, funds flow into booming economies in search of higher returns, thereby exacerbating the bubbles. When the bubbles finally burst, the funds shift suddenly to the countries least affected by the boom.

The problem with these shifts is that they are pro-cyclical, tending to amplify swings in the economy. Countries that are in the midst of a bubble and do not need or want additional funds experience massive inflows. Meanwhile, countries facing balance sheet recessions and in need of funds can only watch as money flows abroad, preventing their governments from implementing the fiscal stimulus needed to stabilize the economy.

Solution for Euro: allow only nationals to buy government bonds

One way to solve this Eurozone-specific problem of capital shifts would be to prohibit member nations from selling government bonds to investors from other countries. Allowing only the citizens of a nation to hold that government's debt would, for example, prevent the investment of Spanish savings in German government debt. Most of the Spanish savings that have been used to buy other countries' government debt would therefore return to Spain. This would push Spanish government bond yields down to the levels observed in the US and the UK, thereby helping the Spanish government implement the fiscal stimulus required during a balance sheet recession.

The Maastricht Treaty with its rigid 3 percent GDP limit on budget deficits made no provision for balance sheet recessions. This is understandable given that the concept of balance sheet recessions did not exist when the Treaty was being negotiated in the 1990s. In contrast, the proposed new rule would allow individual governments to pursue autonomous fiscal policies within its constraint. In effect, governments could run larger deficits as long as they could persuade citizens to hold their debt. This would both instill discipline and provide flexibility to individual governments. By internalizing fiscal issues, the new rule would also free the European Central Bank from having to worry about fiscal issues in individual countries and allow it to focus its efforts on managing monetary policy.

In order to maximize efficiency gains in the single market, the new restriction should apply only to holdings of government bonds. German banks should still be allowed to buy Greek private sector debt, and Spanish banks should still be allowed to buy Dutch shares.

In retrospect, this rule should have been in place since the beginning of the euro. If that were the case, none of the problems the Eurozone now faces would have materialized. Unfortunately, the euro was allowed to run for more than ten years without the rule, accumulating massive imbalances along the way. It may take many years to undo the damage.

In the meantime, it will be necessary to continue financing certain countries with bonds issued jointly by a body like the European Financial Stability Facility (EFSF). But compared with the present situation, where there is no end-game, the declaration of an end to member state sales of government bonds to other nationals five or ten years from now should help restore confidence in the euro. This is because none of the problems that have plagued the euro up to now would be repeated if the new rule were adopted.

Ending the Eurozone's crisis will require a two-pronged approach. First, international bodies like the EU and ECB need to declare that member countries experiencing balance sheet recessions must implement and maintain fiscal stimulus to support the economy until private sector balance sheets are repaired. Second, Eurozone member nations must declare that in ten years they will prohibit the sale of government debt to anyone other than their own nationals.

The first prescription would provide the international organizations' seal of approval for the fiscal stimulus needed to stabilize economies afflicted by balance sheet recessions, while the second would prohibit savings in countries like Spain from being invested in German government bonds. Without these two "game changers," forcing Eurozone nations in balance sheet recessions to engage in fiscal consolidation will simply make the problem worse.

Unfortunately, both ECB President Jean-Claude Trichet and BOE Chairman Mervyn King are still pushing for additional fiscal retrenchment. Among international organizations, only the IMF appears to have recognized the need for fiscal stimulus in countries facing balance sheet recessions.

Difficulty of maintaining fiscal stimulus in democracies

Federal Reserve Chairman Ben Bernanke understands the risk of balance sheet recessions and has been warning since early 2010 that now is not the time to engage in fiscal consolidation. Given that he was once a believer in the omnipotence of monetary policy, this represents a dramatic change of heart. Unfortunately, he and National Economic Council Chairman Gene Sperling are the only two officials openly pushing for fiscal stimulus: everyone else, including President Obama himself at times, seems to be in favor of fiscal consolidation. But with the US private sector still deleveraging massively in spite of zero interest rates, nothing is potentially more dangerous for the US economy than premature fiscal consolidation.

More broadly, recent developments in Washington, London, Madrid and other Western capitals have proven that it is extremely difficult to maintain fiscal stimulus in a democracy during peacetime. This is a crucial problem during a balance sheet recession because fiscal stimulus must be maintained for the duration of the private sector deleveraging process in order to minimize both the length and the final fiscal cost of the recession. Unfortunately, in most democracies fiscal hawks are out in numbers demanding an end to fiscal stimulus as soon as the economy shows the first signs of life.

For example, many on both sides of the Atlantic have grown complacent after seeing certain economic and market indicators improve from their trough in the first half of 2009. The stock market, for example, was up nearly 60 percent at one point. Industrial production, which fell back to the level of 1998 in the US and to the level of 1997 in the Eurozone following the Lehman collapse, climbed back to the level of 2005 on both sides of the Atlantic, although it remains far below the peak levels of 2007.

This "recovery" has prompted a huge backlash from the Republican and Tea Party opposition in the US seeking immediate fiscal consolidation. They argue that big government is bad government and that pork-barrel fiscal stimulus is costing future generations billions if not trillions. In the UK, the Brown government, which implemented fiscal stimulus in 2009, was promptly voted out of office and replaced with the fiscal hawks of the Cameron government. In the Eurozone, fiscal consolidation is now the only game in town. Even in Japan, the new DPJ government is pushing for a tax hike to pay for reconstruction work in the wake of the March 11 earthquake–tsunami–nuclear power plant disaster.

As a result of this backlash from fiscal hawks, the fiscal stimuli implemented by these countries in response to the Lehman-induced financial crisis are being allowed to expire. Private sector deleveraging, on the other hand, continues unabated at alarmingly high levels in all of these countries. Consequently, all of these economies are decelerating if not contracting altogether.

If the contraction appears serious and painful enough, the governments are likely to implement further fiscal stimulus, only to be forced back into fiscal consolidation once the stimulus breathes life back into the economy. This pattern of on-again, off-again fiscal stimulus is the reason why it took Japan 15 years to climb out of its own balance sheet recession. As shown in Figure 2.11, this policy zigzag, especially the austerity initiatives in 1997 and 2001, prolonged the recession by at least five years if not longer and added at least $1 trillion to the public debt unnecessarily. This policy zigzag also caused the disastrous collapse of the US economy in 1937.

Something else that slows down the implementation of fiscal stimulus in a democracy is the issue of how the money should be spent. As the previous example of 460 trillion yen in fiscal stimulus buying 2,000 trillion yen in Japanese GDP during the 1990–2005 period demonstrates, how the money is spent is largely irrelevant during a balance sheet recession: the important thing is *that* the money be spent.

In a democracy, however, where most people see only the trees and not the forest, even those few political leaders who understand the need for stimulus end up arguing endlessly about which projects the money should be spent on. In the meantime, the economy continues to shrink in the $1,000-to-$900-to-$810 deflationary spiral described above. Only during wartime, when it is obvious where the money should be spent, can democracies implement and sustain the kind of fiscal stimulus needed to overcome a balance sheet recession in the shortest possible time.

Even those who manage to prevent an economic meltdown by implementing necessary fiscal stimulus *before* the crisis are likely to be bashed instead of praised by the public. This is because the general public typically cannot envision what might have happened in the absence of fiscal stimulus. Seeing only a large deficit and no crisis, they assume the money must have been wasted on useless projects. That is exactly what happened to Liberal Democratic politicians in Japan, President Barack Obama in the US and former Prime Minister Gordon Brown in the UK. Although their actions saved their economies from devastating deflationary spirals, they were bashed because the public is unable to contemplate the counterfactual scenario. The man or woman who prevents a crisis never becomes a hero. For a hero to emerge we must first have a crisis, as Hollywood movies will attest.

It has also become popular in some circles to talk about medium-term fiscal consolidation while pushing for a short-term fiscal stimulus. Although this sounds responsible at one level, it is totally irresponsible at another. When the private sector is deleveraging in spite of zero interest rates, a condition that has never been anticipated in the economics or business literature, it is safe to assume that the private sector is very sick. Talking about medium-term consolidation in this environment is like asking a seriously injured person just admitted to an intensive care unit whether she can afford the expensive treatment needed. If asked this question enough times, the patient may become so depressed and discouraged that her condition will actually worsen, ultimately resulting in an even larger medical bill.

It has become commonplace to talk about the so-called policy duration effect of monetary policy. The July 2011 announcement by the Fed that it will not raise interest rates until well into 2013 was a prime example of maximizing this effect. For some reason, however, we hear nothing about the policy duration effect of fiscal policy. Talk of medium-term fiscal consolidation effectively *minimizes* the policy duration effect of whatever fiscal stimuli that are still in place, which in a sense is highly irresponsible. Since the patient must be cured somehow, the government should work to maximize the policy duration effect of both monetary and fiscal policies in order to minimize the final cost of treatment. It is never a good idea to depress both the brakes and the accelerator at the same time.

The above reality, together with the recent push for fiscal consolidation in Western capitals, suggests that it is difficult to maintain fiscal stimulus in a democracy during peacetime. Recovering from a balance sheet recession will therefore take a long time in a democracy.

"Exit problem" in balance sheet recessions

The long time required for the economy to pull out of a balance sheet recession means the private sector must spend many painful years paying down debt. That in turn brings about a debt "trauma" of sorts in which the private sector refuses to borrow money even after its balance sheet is fully repaired. This trauma may take years if not decades to overcome. But until the private sector is both willing and able to borrow again, the economy will be operating at less than full potential and may require continued fiscal support from the government to stay afloat. Overcoming this trauma may be called the "exit problem."

In Japan, where the private sector has grown extremely averse to borrowing after its bitter experience of paying down debt from 1990 to 2005, businesses are not borrowing money in spite of willing lenders and the lowest interest rates in human history. As a result, the ten-year government bond is yielding only around 1 percent even though government debt amounts to nearly 200 percent of GDP.

After the US private sector's devastating experience of paying down debt during the Great Depression, the same aversion to borrowing kept interest rates unusually low for a full 30 years, until 1959 (Figure 2.15). The fact that it took the US three decades to bring interest rates back up to 4 percent even with

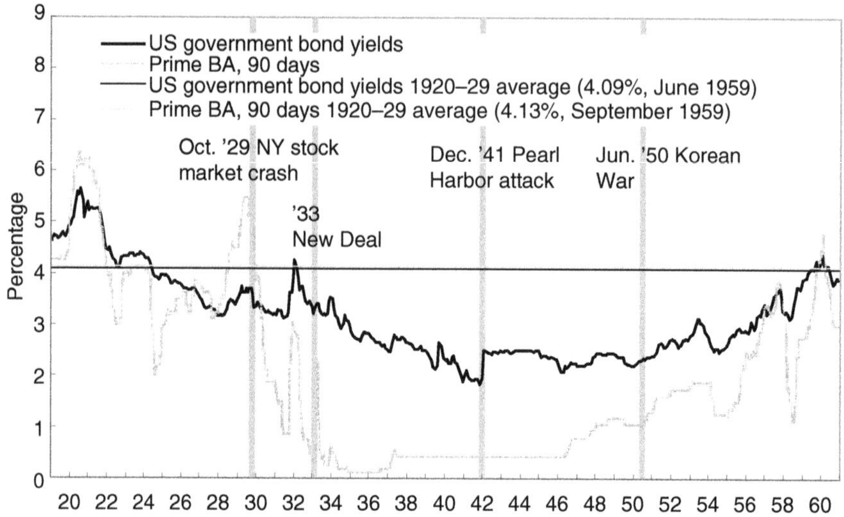

Figure 2.15 Exit problem: US took 30 years to normalize interest rates after 1929 because of aversion to borrowing (source: FRB, *Banking and Monetary Statistics 1914–1970 Vol. 1*, pp. 450–451 and 468–471, *Vol. 2*, pp. 674–676 and 720–727).

massive fiscal stimuli in the form of the New Deal and World War II suggests the severity of the trauma. Indeed many of those Americans forced to pay down debt during the Depression never borrowed again.

The experiences of post-1929 US and post-1990 Japan suggest that interest rates will remain low for a very long time even after private sector balance sheets are repaired. The governments of countries facing exit problems should therefore introduce incentives for businesses to borrow. Such incentives, which may include investment tax credits and accelerated depreciation allowances, should be exceptionally generous in order to attract private sector attention. The sooner the trauma is overcome, the sooner the government can embark on fiscal consolidation. The generosity will more than pay for itself once the private sector trauma is overcome.

Ending panic was the easy part; rebuilding balance sheets is the hard part

A distinction should also be drawn between balance sheet recessions and financial crises, since both are present in the post-Lehman debacle. The former is a borrower's phenomenon, while the latter is a lender's phenomenon. This distinction is important because the economic "recovery" starting in 2009 has been largely limited to a recovery from the policy mistake of allowing Lehman

Brothers to fail. The collapse of Lehman sparked a global financial crisis that weakened the economy far more severely and rapidly than what would have been suggested by balance sheet problems alone.

Unlike balance sheet recessions, in which monetary policy is largely impotent, financial crises can and must be addressed by the monetary authorities. Available tools include liquidity infusions, capital injections, explicit and implicit guarantees, lower interest rates and asset purchases. According to IMF figures, the Federal Reserve, together with governments and central banks around the world, injected some $8.9 trillion in liquidity and guarantees for this purpose in the wake of the Lehman shock.

The Lehman panic was caused by the government's decision not to safeguard the liabilities of a major financial institution when so many institutions had similar problems. Consequently, the panic dissipated when the authorities moved to safeguard those liabilities. That was the "recovery" observed in some quarters since the spring of 2009.

Although the panic has subsided, all the balance sheet problems that existed before the Lehman failure are still in place. If anything, the continuous fall in house prices since then has exacerbated these problems. Balance sheet problems are likely to slow down the recovery or derail it altogether unless the government moves to offset the deflationary pressure coming from private sector deleveraging. In other words, the recovery so far was the easy part—(B) in Figure 2.16. The hard work of repairing millions of impaired private sector balance sheets is just beginning—(A) in Figure 2.16.

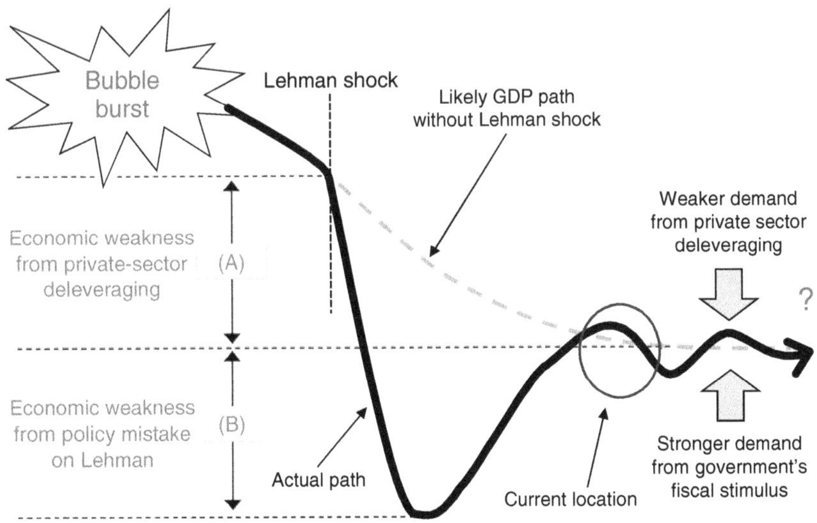

Figure 2.16 Recovery from Lehman shock is *not* recovery from balance sheet recession (source: Nomura Research Institute).

Conclusion

It is laudable for policy makers to shun fiscal profligacy and aim for self-reliance on the part of the private sector. But every several decades, the private sector loses its self-control in a bubble and sustains heavy financial injuries when the bubble bursts. That forces the private sector to pay down debt in spite of zero interest rates, triggering a deflationary spiral. At such times and at such times *only*, the government must borrow and spend the private sector's excess savings, not only because monetary policy is impotent at such times but also because the government cannot tell the private sector *not* to repair its balance sheet.

Although anyone can push for fiscal consolidation in the form of higher taxes and lower spending, whether such efforts actually succeed in reducing the budget deficit is another matter entirely. When the private sector is both willing and able to borrow money, fiscal consolidation efforts by the government will lead to a smaller deficit and higher growth as resources are released to the more efficient private sector. But when the financial health of the private sector is so impaired that it is forced to deleverage even with interest rates at zero, a premature withdrawal of fiscal stimulus will both increase the deficit and weaken the economy. Key differences between the textbook world and the world of balance sheet recessions are summarized in Table 2.1.

With massive private sector deleveraging continuing in the US and in many other countries in spite of historically low interest rates, this is no time to embark on fiscal consolidation. Such measures must wait until it is certain the private sector has finished deleveraging and is ready to borrow and spend the savings that would be left un-borrowed by the government under an austerity program.

Table 2.1 Contrast between profit maximization and debt minimization

Private sector behavior		*Profit maximization*	*Debt minimization*
1 Phenomenon		Textbook economy	Balance sheet recession
2 Fundamental driver		Adam Smith's "invisible hand"	Fallacy of composition
3 Corporate financial condition		Assets > liabilities	Assets < liabilities
4 Outcome		Greatest good for greatest number	Depression if left unattended
5 Monetary policy		Effective	Ineffective (liquidity trap)
6 Fiscal policy		Counterproductive (crowding out)	Effective
7 Prices		Inflationary	Deflationary
8 Interest rates		Normal	Very low
9 Savings		Virtue	Vice (paradox of thrift)
10 Remedy for banking crisis	a Localized	Quick NPL disposal Pursue accountability	Normal NPL disposal Pursue accountability
	b Systemic	Slow NPL disposal	Slow NPL disposal

Source: Richard Koo, *The Holy Grail of Macroeconomics: Lessons from Japan's Great Recession Updated*, John Wiley & Sons, Singapore, 2009, p. 176.

There will be plenty of time to pay down the accumulated public debt because the next balance sheet recession of this magnitude is likely to be generations away, given that those who learned a bitter lesson in the present episode will not make the same mistake again. The next bubble and balance sheet recession of this magnitude will happen only after we are no longer here to remember them.

3 All lucky breaks come to an end

The shortcomings of macroeconomic models following the financial crisis and the contribution of behavioural economics to the reconfiguration of macroeconomics[1]

Nigel F.B. Allington, John S.L. McCombie and Maureen Pike

Introduction

The 2007 subprime crisis continues to generate a large literature, although a consensus is emerging on what factors caused it. Namely: inadequate regulation of financial institutions and instruments; problems connected with the securitisation of disparate revenue streams to create ever riskier financial instruments; the inadequate credit ratings of the various tranches by the three major credit rating agencies where there was a conflict of interests (ratings were purchased by the originators of the instruments and not the investors); principal–agent problems in the banking system leading to excessive risk taking in the context of low interest rates; moral hazard (the belief that banks were 'too big to fail'); contagion effects in Europe and elsewhere; global imbalances attributable to surpluses in China, the Middle Eastern economies and Japan; and the failure of monetary policy that kept interest rates too low and for too long. To this must be added the amplifying effects of the large increase in leverage of the banks that had occurred over the previous two decades (see, for example, Blanchard, 2009; Brunnermeier, 2009; Rajan, 2005, 2010; Roubini and Mihm, 2010). Consequently the crisis *per se* is not examined in any depth, rather the focus of this chapter is on the failure of macroeconomic theory and in particular the rational expectations hypothesis (REH) and the efficient markets hypothesis (EMH). The subprime crisis exposed more than any formal testing could have done the deficiencies in the New Classical macroeconomic paradigm while a jaundiced view of the usefulness of econometrics in altering any economist's *weltanschauung* can be found in Summers (1991).

An uneasy truce had emerged after the acrimonious debates of the 1980s between the Neo-Keynesians and the New Classical economists over the REH and the assumption of market clearing. The New Neoclassical Synthesis emerged based essentially on the New Classical approach, except that it incorporated rational expectations and sticky prices from Neo-Keynesian economics. This, in the view of Goodfriend (2004, 2007) amongst others, supposedly gave macroeconomics sound microfoundations. Apart from some mainstream dissenters like Solow (2008) most macroeconomists outside the post-Keynesian group supported this synthesis. The fragile truce ended, however, with the subprime crisis as the lucky break of the past came to an end. For example, Blanchflower (2009), then a member of the UK's Monetary Policy Committee, dismissed macroeconomic theory as useless in understanding the crisis and providing an appropriate policy response. Buiter (2009), another former member of the Committee concurred. The fundamental foundations of received macroeconomics were questioned by Krugman (2009) and Cochrane (2009) indicating growing divisions over the veracity of the model.

In this chapter, first the development of the New Neoclassical Synthesis (NNS) and the New Macroeconomics Consensus (NMC) based on the former synthesis are examined (the NMC refers to the applied studies and policy implications, most notably inflation targeting). The shortcomings of this approach are then considered in the light of the subprime crisis. In particular, one of the major shortcomings of the NNS, namely that individuals and institutions act in the presence of Knightian uncertainty (in a non-ergodic world) rather than, as assumed by the NNS, being faced by risk given by a well-defined probability distribution. The conclusions look at the methodological way forward, with a discussion of some aspects of behavioural economics and behavioural finance.

From the non-ergodicity of the *General Theory* to the ergodicity of the REH and EMH and back again

The Great Depression led to a paradigm shift with the publication of *The General Theory of Employment, Interest, and Money* (1936) and the development of the 'economics of Keynes' displacing 'the postulates of the classical economics'. The central tenet of the *General Theory* was the role of inadequate effective demand in accounting for unemployment and *not* real or money wage rigidity. Of crucial importance was the role of expectations and how individuals responded to the future (most notably in Chapter 12 of the *General Theory* and in Keynes's (1937) response to his critics). The volatility of capitalist systems both in terms of investment decisions and asset prices depends on how individuals, both singly and collectively, respond to uncertainty. In other words, the economic system is non-ergodic (Davidson, 1982–83) and investor psychology is of crucial importance (De Bondt *et al.*, 2008).

However, in the 1940s and 1950s macroeconomics did not follow Keynes's lead and seek a deeper understanding of 'conventional expectations', that is to say, expectations driven by conventions. (This only occurred several decades later with the development of behavioural economics.) The blame for this 'wrong turning' can be laid squarely at the door of Hicks as he later conceded (Hicks, 1979) and the development of the IS-LM model where, within a general equilibrium framework, uncertainty disappeared. The grafting on to the IS/LM model of the neoclassical labour market analysis led as a matter of logic (what McCombie and Pike (2013) have termed 'paradigmatic determinism') to involuntary unemployment being determined by real wages being too high. The Lucas critique, the need for microfoundations and 'model consistent' or rational expectations and the assumption of market clearing led to the rise of New Classical economics. Here, involuntary unemployment was seen as a theoretically meaningless concept (Lucas, 1978).

In this approach, the representative agent is modelled using an intertemporal expected utility maximising framework. This explains fluctuations in employment, given the individual's expectations of intertemporal exogenous productivity shocks. The role of the rate of interest is to reconcile the intertemporal demand for, and supply of, output. The empirical fact that real wages varied procyclically refuted the neoclassical explanation of real wage rigidity as a cause of unemployment (which implies a countercyclical real wage). Hence, cyclical fluctuations, again as a result of paradigmatic determinism, must be caused by shifts in the demand function for labour due to technological shocks. Thus, the core of this approach is the real business cycle. Even the occurrence of excess capacity is explained as the result of optimising procedures, namely, variations in the intensity with which maintenance is carried out (McCombie and Pike, 2013).

The Neo-Keynesians had been developing models within the same macroeconomic framework with optimising models based on the representative agent, but had introduced optimal reasons for temporary price stickiness, such as menu costs (Calvo pricing). Given the underlying similarity of the conceptual framework, these insights were eventually incorporated into the real business cycle model, but within an imperfectly competitive framework and a mark-up pricing policy. Nevertheless, the rigidities were the result of an optimisation process. It is this that gives a role for monetary policy.

The limitations of the NNS (and its counterpart, the dynamic stochastic general equilibrium (DSGE) models) were well known even before the subprime crisis (McCombie and Pike, 2013). The use of the representative agent, far from being an innocuous assumption, is the *sine qua non* of the whole approach. It does not solve the aggregation problem, but merely assumes it away. For example, the aggregate production function does not exist theoretically, even as an approximation (Fisher, 1992) and it cannot be justified in terms of empirical verification and Friedman's instrumentalist approach (Felipe and McCombie, 2005). Kirman (1992) has shown that the preferences of the representative agent can be totally different from those of all the individuals that the agent is supposed to represent. Thus, 'individual maximisation does not engender collective rationality, nor does the fact that the collectivity exhibits a certain rationality necessarily imply that the individuals act rationally. There is no simple direct relation between individual and collective behaviour' (p. 118).There is also the Sonnenschein–Mantel–Debreu theorem which has serious implications for these models through the existence of multiple equilibria and stability, which has been totally ignored, with one or two notable exceptions (Solow, 2008). Chen (2010), adopting a statistical approach shows that, under quite plausible assumptions, the law of large numbers implies that the relative deviation of macroeconomic indices is between 0.1 and 1 per cent. This implies that the number of 'agents' for the US should be between 6,000 and 200,000. Thus, 'the observed relative fluctuations are at least 20 times larger than could be explained by the microfoundations models in labour or producer models' (p. 58).

The representative agent assumption also rules out any unemployment due to Keynesian demand deficiency and especially that arising from coordination failures. The shortcomings of the DSGE model also revolve around the necessary assumption of the transversality condition. This condition effectively rules out any consideration of bankruptcy or the existence of risk premia (see Buiter, 2009; Goodhart, 2010). Given these shortcomings, attempts are now being made within this paradigm to relax these assumptions by introducing risk premia and explicitly modelling systemic risk. However, it can be legitimately asked, given the other paradigmatic assumptions of the DSGE models, whether this will lead to any greater insights. There is still no need for financial institutions, including banks, or even money in these models (Meyer, 2001). Thus, they cannot provide a theoretical explanation of the effects of the subprime crisis, which arose *endogenously* from the banking system given that an understanding of it requires detailed contextual knowledge of the institutional framework (see below).

The failure of the Taylor rule and the new macroeconomic consensus

The implications of the NNS are twofold. First, it gave confidence to policy makers that the economy was self-stabilising and, indirectly, it led to 'light financial regulation' on both sides of the Atlantic. Second, it provided a theoretical justification for inflation targeting (Meyer, 2001). This raises the question of how useful the NCM is in explaining the causes of the crisis.

The limitations of the NCM were known before the crisis (Arestis, 2009), but were likewise ignored by the central banks. It assumes that the inflation rate to be targeted (core inflation) rises due to excess demand. Consequently it excludes any element of cost-push inflation and real wage resistance which many have plausibly argued was the major cause of inflation in the early 1970s (McCombie, 2010, pp. 119–23). A further shortcoming is that it excludes any role for increased competition from China and India allowing the advanced countries to keep down costs by importing low inflation as an explanation of the Great Moderation. This led to low inflation and consequently low interest rates that fuelled the borrowing binge and inflated the house price bubble in the US and some other developed countries (with the notable exceptions of Canada and Austria).

Within this framework, the only way the house price bubble can be adequately explained is via lax monetary policy, unless it is treated as an exogenous shock (Fama, 2010). The former is the view of Taylor (2007, 2009). He finds that over the period 2002–2006 the actual federal funds rate was substantially below the level predicted by the Taylor rule. According to Taylor, low interest rates generated the housing boom. With the housing boom, delinquency rates and foreclosures fell. But when the house price bubble burst, the last two rose dramatically, triggering the crisis. The implication is that defaults are a rational response: 'when prices are falling, the *incentives* to make payments are much less' (Taylor, 2009, p. 12). These models do not offer much scope for involuntary actions when, for example, households cannot pay their mortgages.

However, this explanation is not convincing. Taylor justifies the argument by showing that the rapid growth in the number of housing starts, which showed a rapid rise over the period from 2000 to 2006, would not have been so fast if interest rates had been higher. Thus, Taylor (2009) comes to the conclusion that: 'this extra-easy [interest rate policy] accelerated the housing boom and thereby led to the bust' (p. 16). Rates fell from 6.5 per cent in late 2000 to 1.75 per cent in December 2001 and to 1 per cent in June 2003.[2] The policy implication is straightforward – the Federal Reserve should have stuck to the Taylor rule and rates over the period 2002 to 2006 should have been 200 basis points higher: see Figure 3.1.

There are a number of problems with this explanation. First, remaining within the NCM framework, Bernanke (2010), drawing on Dokko *et al.*'s (2009) reduced-form vector-autoregressive model, points out that the correct measure of inflation to use in the Taylor rule should be the *forecast* and not the *actual* rate because monetary policy operates with a time lag.[3] When this is used, there is no evidence that interest rates were too low (they are within two standard deviations of the forecast values). (Allington *et al.* (2010) find the same result for the operation of European monetary policy.)

Second, the number of housing starts in the US is very small compared with the total housing stock (only 1.73 per cent in 2001). Moreover, while the growth of housing starts was fast over the period 2001–2006 at 5.16 per cent per annum,

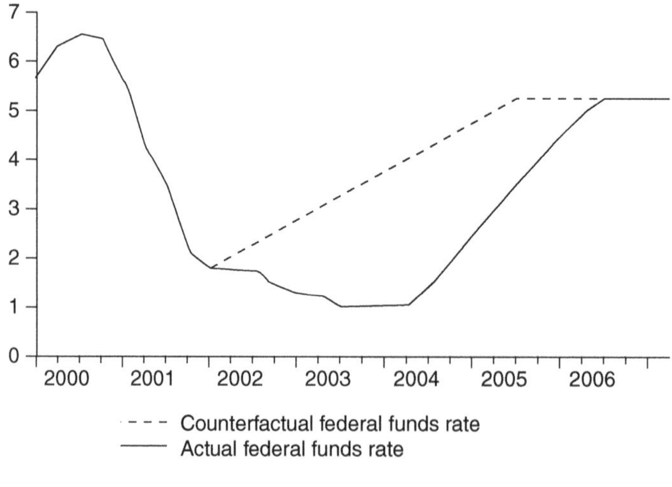

Figure 3.1 US interest rates under the Taylor rule, 2001–2006 (source: Taylor, 2009).

the average rate for the previous ten years was still rapid at 4.62 per cent. It is reasonable to conclude that, if anything, the increased supply of housing would have dampened the rate of increase in house prices, not accelerated it. Furthermore, the evidence suggests that only a small proportion of the rise in house price can be attributed to interest rate policy (Bernanke, 2010, p. 13). Vector analysis suggests that the actual federal funds rate was close to the predicted value whereas the increase in house prices was well outside the predicted range. Hence, Bernanke (2010) concludes: 'when historical relationships are taken into account, it is difficult to ascribe the house price bubble either to monetary policy or to the broader macroeconomic environment' (p. 14).

Clearly, the cause must lie elsewhere and the evidence is that the house price bubble was determined endogenously and was the result of financial innovation. The explosive growth of the securitisation of mortgages, particularly subprime mortgages, and the move to 'originate and distribute' (with the shifting of the risk burden from the banks to investors) was primarily responsible for the start of the boom.[4] Evidence for this is provided by Mian and Sufi (2009 and 2010). Using US county data they first calculate the fraction of mortgage applications that were turned down by banks in 1996. They term this 'latent demand' and find those counties with the higher level of latent demand had the greater growth in mortgages and house prices after 1996. This cannot be attributed to an increase in the overall level of creditworthiness in these counties. In fact, their per capita income was falling. They also found that the rapid increase in the granting of mortgages was associated with securitisation. Those areas where the latent demand was eventually satisfied were the ones that subsequently had proportionally the largest number of defaults. In their opinion, which is shared by many others, the proximate cause of the crisis was moral hazard on behalf of the originators (the banks) of the subprime mortgages who increased the supply of credit (see Rajan, 2005; Keys *et al.*, 2010). But clearly there is more to it than this.

The world is non-ergodic

The key cause was the failure of credit ratings for asset-backed securities that were derived using assumptions based on ergodicity. One of the central tenets of Keynes's explanation of the instability of the capitalist system was the pervasive influence of Knightian uncertainty (Knight, 1921) and animal spirits on both the investment decision and stock market purchases (see again Chapter 12 of the *General Theory* and Keynes, 1937).

Risk is a situation where the individual, using past experience, can form a subjective distribution function about a particular process, say stock returns. That is, it reflects the one that actually exists. Thus, it is possible to assign a numerical probability to an event occurring. Because it is necessary to learn about the probability generating function over time, it is a requirement that this does not change; in other words the world must be ergodic. (Stationarity of the data is a necessary, but not sufficient condition for ergodicity.) Estimates of risk are normally calculated as a function of the standard deviation of returns (Tobin, 1958).

Referring to the stock market, Keynes noted that in a crisis or speculative boom when there is no basis for rational calculations, expectations become 'conventional', by which he meant driven by convention. One important convention in the formation of expectations is the belief that the majority have better information than the individual. If all participants were to take this view, then herd behaviour arises leading to a self-fulfilling prophecy and either 'irrational exuberance' or investor panic. Yet, because these animal spirits are difficult to model (or else lead to nihilistic conclusions) modern macroeconomics had disregarded these important insights of Knight and Keynes at least until the development of behavioural finance.

Indeed, macroeconomics went to the other extreme with the widespread adoption of REH by both the New Classical and Neo-Keynesians in the late 1980s. And although macroeconomics is effectively divorced from the theory of finance, the EMH assumed rational expectations (Fama, 1965). Thus the EMH requires the joint test of the REH and the Capital Asset Pricing Model. The REH assumes that the world is ergodic, a concept first given prominence in economics by Samuelson (1965 and 1973) who utilised the martingale result (see LeRoy 1989). Samuelson argued that the assumption of ergodicity was necessary if economics was to be 'scientific', but he nevertheless warned against attaching too much importance to his result because 'it does not prove that actual competitive markets work well' (p. 48).[5] Hence the strong version of the REH assumes any individual (who, to make the assumption coherent, has to be the representative agent) makes use of *all* available information (past, present and future, both public and private as well as assuming that the model is the correct representation of the world) without making systematic errors. This implies that the individual's subjective probability distribution is the same as the 'true', or objective probability distribution, and can be determined from historical data. In other words, the objective density function must not change (Samuelson's 1965 assumption) or if it does, the individual must be able to ascertain the new distribution in some mechanical way (Frydman and Goldberg, 2008, p. 17).[6] But individuals clearly cannot perform these mental gymnastics from past data. Given therefore that the future is unknowable, the REH and EMH founders on Hume's 'fallacy of induction' principle (1888). More practically, Frydman and Goldberg (2010) argue that the inevitability of structural changes in the probability generating function, occurring over time, empirically undermines the claim that the EMH 'is the best tested proposition in all the social sciences' (Cochrane, 2009, p. 3). If the probability distribution changes over time, then conventional testing techniques are flawed, even if attempts are made to allow for these changes. Moreover, in the case of the Capital Asset Pricing Model, where it did perform well in the 1960s, later examination suggested that it was, in the words of Fama, 'atrocious as an empirical model' (cited by Frydman and Goldberg, 2008, p. 17).

Leamer (2010) has argued that non-ergodicity is about three-valued logic. Suppose, he argues, that it can be deduced from a model that there is a particular probability of an event occurring, p_1 and on that basis a particular decision is taken, say, whether to invest or not. This is an example of Knightian uncertainty.

But suppose that an alternative and equally good model gives a probability of, p_2 this is a 'world of Knightian uncertainty in which expected utility maximisation does not produce a decision' (p. 39). This assumes, of course, that the distribution over the interval p_1 to p_2 is not uniform. Instead, there are epistemic probabilities over the intervals. While the decision-making is two-valued logic, either invest or don't, the state of mind is three valued – invest, do not invest or else I do not know.

The subprime crisis illuminated the failings of the EMH in a way that no econometric test or *a priori* reasoning could have done. While the process of securitisation was not new, it grew rapidly in the mid-2000s.[7] But securitisation was unreservedly welcomed by the former Federal Reserve Chairman, Greenspan and former Treasury Secretary, Summers in the light of the EMH as yet another financial innovation that would led to the more efficient allocation of capital resources through the diversification of risk.[8] Securitisation took an illiquid asset, the flow of payments from subprime mortgages with an assumed probability of default and on this basis constructed a Collateralised Debt Obligation (CDO) that could be sold on to other financial institutions. By dividing the CDOs into tranches, so that the junior tranche bore the first (higher) risk and the senior tranche the least, the latter could be given a credit rating (mostly AAA) which was substantially higher than the rating would have been without that division. Thus investors with different attitudes towards risk could be accommodated. While the junior tranche bore greater risk, it consequently generated a higher return. Then more sophisticated CDOs were created using the junior tranches to create mezzanine CDOs and CDO^2s and this led to further AAA rated tranches.[9] In fact, the number of AAA rated CDOs as a proportion of the total greatly exceeded the number of AAA rated corporate bonds.

The major change was that the banks providing the subprime loans were now engaged in 'originate and distribute' and did not assess the creditworthiness of the individual mortgagees. The risk had been passed on to the investor and was assessed using complex computer algorithms to calculate the likelihood of default. This was based on past data which, it was assumed, followed a Gaussian distribution: one of the crucial assumptions was that past performance was an excellent predictor of future returns. This extrapolation bias caused errors because established trends were assumed to continue irrespective of the size of the sample or any possible mean reversion. And in the US, house prices were thought unlikely to fall across the whole of the nation so that the risk attached to Mortgage Backed Securities (MBSs) and similar derivatives were too low. As Coval *et al.* (2009) have shown, the probabilities on default are extremely sensitive to the exact parameters chosen for the model and the procedures crucially did not take account of the potential for *systemic* failure. Rather, securitisation was assumed to have removed this problem by diversifying the risk.

Indeed Fitch, one of the three major credit ratings agencies, revealed that their ratings were based on the assumption that house prices would increase indefinitely. Asked what would happen if house prices fell by between 1 or 2 per cent for any extended period of time, they replied that their models: 'would break down completely' (cited by Coval *et al.*, 2009). The absurdity of the argument can be judged from Figure 3.2 that shows the probability density estimate for the FT All-Share Index. Here, if the probability distribution during the so-called Golden Decade 1997 to 2007 were true, then the three worst equity returns in UK history, 1720, 1987 and 2007 would have to be regarded as 'once in a lifetime – of the universe – events' (Haldane, 2009, p. 8).

The details of the subprime crisis are well known. With the collapse of the US housing market, the default rate on subprime mortgages rose and the current market value of CDOs became uncertain and the level of risk associated with them could not be determined. Wenli *et al.* (2010) show that changes to the US bankruptcy law in 2005 caused the level of defaults on prime and subprime mortgages to rise, driving house prices down even faster. Consequently, the market for CDOs froze[10] (violating in the process one of the assumptions of the EMH) and the value of all the CDOs plummeted. Those companies such as Lehman Brothers and AIG that had sold Credit Default Swaps (CDSs) acted as insurers against default on CDOs and offered premiums based on a Gaussian distribution assuming the probability of default to be small.[11] They ignored the probability of a systemic collapse in the value of CDOs (the so-called 'fat tail' problem).

The crisis elicited a mixed response from the authorities with Lehman Brothers forced into bankruptcy and AIG bailed out by the US government because of

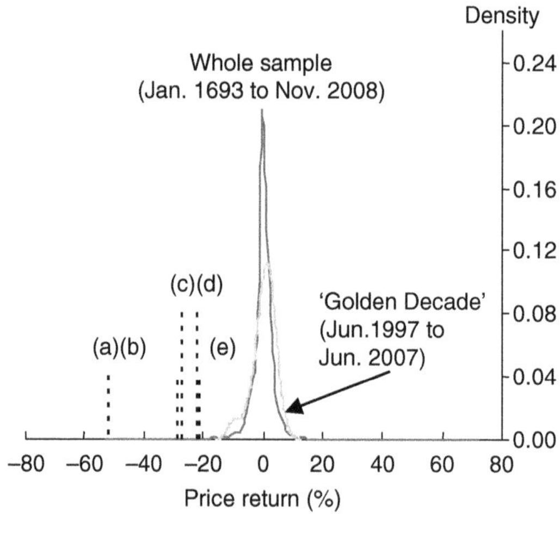

Figure 3.2 Probability density estimate for the FT All-Share Index (source: Haldane, 2009; Global Financial Data).

Notes
a South Sea Bubble (September 1720).
b South Sea Bubble (October 1720).
c Black Monday (October 1987).
d Second World War merchant shipping attacked (July 1940).
e Price/wage controls; unions, etc. (March 1974).

the perceived systemic risk in the US and Europe from its failing. CDOs held by the banks 'off balance sheet', typically in Structured Investment Vehicles, had to be brought back on to the balance sheet. With no 'market maker' to purchase these CDOs and to guarantee a well-organised and orderly resale market, they were virtually worthless under mark-to-market pricing. As a result, the banks' capital base collapsed. As Davidson (2008) pointed out, given the uncertainty over the value of the CDOs and thus the soundness of the banks' capital base, there was a flight to liquidity by the banks. And interbank lending froze given the uncertainty over the ability of any borrowing banks to repay. This had knock-on effects pushing Northern Rock in the UK into bankruptcy: not because it held 'toxic assets', but because it depended on the short-term money market to fund its aggressive expansion strategy. (The government quickly decided to nationalise it.) There was also a simultaneous credit crunch with credit rationed even for seemingly creditworthy firms.[12] The subsequent recession therefore did not hinge on real wages being too high, but resulted from the liquidity problems of firms which, through the multiplier, led to a severe collapse in Keynesian aggregate demand. Bernanke and Blinder (1988) incorporated a model of the credit crunch into the standard IS-LM framework.

Davidson (2008) has convincingly argued that this was not a Minskyian 'Ponzi moment', but rather the result of increased uncertainty and the ultimate insolvency of the counterparties. He is in agreement, therefore, with Taylor (2009) who points to the rapid widening of the LIBOR–OIS spread indicating that the cause of the crisis was uncertainty; the inability of the market to value accurately the capital assets of the banks. If this diagnosis is correct, then simply pumping money into the economy (Quantitative Easing versions I, II or III or Operation Twist) in an attempt to bring down the spread, would prove ineffective. Instead, the banks should be recapitalised so that they can resume their lending activities.

Was the subprime crisis a random shock?

It has been argued by Fama (2010) and Lucas (2009) that because few professional economists or financial journalists saw the crisis coming, this is a justification of the EMH! Lucas, for example, wrote:

> one thing we are not going to have, now or ever, is a set of models that forecast sudden falls in the value of financial assets, like the declines that followed the failure of Lehman Brothers in September 2008. This is nothing new. It has been known for more than 40 years and is one of the main implications of Eugene Fama's 'efficient markets hypothesis'.

As the EMH assumes individuals make use of *all* the available information, then bubbles and their inevitable collapse have to be treated as unforeseen stochastic shocks. Lucas is surely correct when he claims that policy-makers could not predict the exact *timing* or the precise *severity* of the crisis. But the fact is that the endogenous changes through financial innovations in capital markets and the structure of incentives facing traders in the banks were obvious for anyone who had a detailed knowledge of financial institutions to see, particularly the regulators. The NCM and the DSGE are based on the assumption that the functioning of a complex system like an economy can be adequately described and predicted on the basis of linearised relationships between a few macroeconomic variables.[13] Hence, if the model abstracts from the actual behaviour of financial institutions, then by definition information about them is irrelevant under REH. And while the timing of the collapse could not be predicted, it is clear that as Rajan (2005), the then Chief Economist at the IMF pointed out, there was a high probability of a severe banking crisis. The shortcomings of the EMH and its underlying assumptions had also been demonstrated during the collapse of Long-Term Capital Management in 1997, but the lesson had not been learnt. Its collapse also signalled the authorities' disregard for moral hazard where the Federal Reserve organised a collective bailout of the investing banks (Allington *et al.*, 2012).

This complex reality throws into doubt what precisely is meant by the assumption in the REH that agents make use of 'all available information'. The forgoing analysis makes it clear that the subprime crisis was endogenously determined and that only the timing and its depth were exogenous. In a non-ergodic world, where there is institutional change that is path dependent, future and unknowable events cannot all be considered as random and this puts another nail in the coffin that is the REH.[14]

Is behavioural finance the way forward?

The financial crisis has served to point up the weaknesses in the central propositions underlying the NNS model, and in particular the DSGE one used by the Federal Reserve and many other central banks, including the REH and the stronger versions of the EMH. While it is easy to criticise the failings of that model and it may remain as a benchmark from which new departures are made, deciding what to put in its place is rather more difficult. Certainly the crisis demonstrated the impotency of monetary policy and there remains considerable disagreement about the efficacy of fiscal policy. The crisis also highlighted the failure to incorporate financial markets and institutions into the formal models of macroeconomics. For far too many economists, finance was simply a veil that obscured the real economy from view (Mehrling, 2000).

Despite advances in risk management, based on portfolio and option pricing theory, the 2007 financial crisis caused huge damage to many financial institutions simply because the systems in place could not manage the behaviour of individuals within the financial institutions. It is here that behavioural finance offers some important insights that can supplement existing risk management structures. The biggest danger comes from risks that occur infrequently and yet lead to catastrophic losses. These are obviously difficult to anticipate because the available data simply describes past events and cannot predict the future, the more so since the focus is on risk rather than Knightian uncertainty where the probabilities are not known, elsewhere referred to as the 'unknown unknowns'. This 'disaster myopia' typically occurs in a bull market where risk-taking becomes procyclical and analysts follow herd behaviour in the pricing of instruments and in their investment strategies. Put simply, uncertainty cannot be managed by crunching numbers, rather the analysts and investors must excise their judgement.

An early attempt to model bounded rationality was Kahneman and Tversky's (1979) prospect theory that examines decision-making under uncertainty using psychology to derive the now famous S-shaped 'value function'. The insight from prospect theory is that investors are characterised as expected regret utility minimisers with the emphasis on any potential losses from some investment strategy rather than the gains, each measured against a benchmark of the par value or the original purchase price of the asset. Behavioural finance then builds on this by recognising that models have an important influence on decisions and the subsequent behaviour of investors, but that emotion can also have an impact on those decisions. This information will systematically be taken into account in the investment process, but noise will complicate the perception of that information and bias the result. These biases include: regret, what might have been done leading to *post hoc* justification of the actions actually taken and pessimism leading to herd behaviour and panic selling of assets, or, in a bull market, extra risk-taking leading to the phenomenon of buying high and selling low. The level of risk tolerance in turn depends on the capital the institutions have (where risk increases with capital availability). A further bias arises from too much reliance on the predictive skills of analysts using their knowledge and hard data that breeds familiarity where successful investment strategies are internalised and any failures are externalised and attributed to external uncontrollable events.

The theory can be operationalised first, by determining how to frame the choices that face individuals and, second, by examining the effect of bounded 'memories' (Thaler, 2000). This refers to the empirical observation that memory can be selective not just by making it difficult to distinguish between bad decisions and bad outcomes. Further research by Tversky and Wakker (1995) indicates that decision-making under uncertainty is affected by the degree of uncertainty, but also by its source. Individuals therefore react differently depending on whether the uncertainty is due to structural instability (aleatory uncertainty) or lack of clear knowledge (epistemic uncertainty). Their conclusions have clear implications for studying investment decisions in financial markets that up to now have been ignored.

Given the failure of DSGE models some economists have turned to the nascent field of behavioural economics that takes account of individuals' emotions, cognitive errors and any other psychological factors that can have an impact on their decisions. Thaler (1997), defines it as having three characteristics. First, there is rational choice, second, an analysis of actual behaviour based on collecting and processing data and, third, the use of the second feature to 'explain and understand the ways of in which rational theories fail to describe the world we live in' (p. 439). Financial markets should therefore be viewed within an evolutionary framework where markets, policy instruments, institutions and investors interact dynamically in a Darwinian (evolutionary) fashion. Financial agents compete and adapt, although this does not occur in any optimal way, but rather like Schumpeter's entrepreneurs, agents adapt under the destructive powers of capitalism. Instead of maximising utility under rational expectations, individuals seek to maximise their survival. Behaviour evolves through natural selection and what Simon (1955) calls 'satisficing' occurs when individual choices are deemed 'satisfactory' through a process of trial and error, rather than through 'optimising' behaviour. If the environment changes, then behaviour is adapted through a combination of competition, cooperation, market-making behaviour, general equilibrium and disequilibrium dynamics. Experimental work can help to map the effect of these changes and exciting examples are the credibility of monetary policy and individual agents' perceptions of inflation (Yuxiang and Chen, 2010) and simulations of agents' reactions to asymmetric information on the fundamental value of assets (Kirchler, 2010).

The Adaptive Markets Hypothesis (AMH) that encompasses this approach argues that prices reflect information gained from environmental conditions by the relevant market participants in financial markets including market-makers, hedge-fund managers and investors. Financial markets, it is argued, would be more efficient the greater the number of participants and the higher the level of competition. Thus, Lo (2007) argues that 'under the AMH, investment strategies undergo cycles of profitability and loss in response to changing business conditions, the number of competitors entering and exiting the industry, and the type and magnitude of profit opportunities available' (pp. 18–19). This insight can be used to determine 'actual expectations' (AE) where 'agents display various forms of "bounded rationality" using heuristic decision rules and displaying inertia in their reaction to new information. They have also been shown in financial markets to be strongly influenced by emotional and hormonal reactions' (Colander *et al.*, 2009, p. 8). See also Lo *et al.* (2005) and Coates and Herbert (2008).

In addition, the new sub-discipline of neuroeconomics finds compatibility between rational decision-making and emotion. Lo and Repin (2002) show that 'physiological variables associated with the autonomic nervous system are highly correlated with market events even for highly experienced professional securities traders'. And they go on to say

> the ordinary degree of competitiveness of the global financial markets and the outsized rewards that accrue to the 'fittest' traders suggests that Darwinian selection – 'survival of the richest', to be precise – is at work in determining the typical profile of the successful trader.

The authors conclude that even though behavioural economics is still in its infancy, it appears to be able to reconcile the contradictions between the EMH and behavioural reality. Thus the relationship between risk and reward is probably unstable through time depending on individual preferences and institutional factors such as prudential regulation and taxes. The implication of this, in contrast with the view of the EMH, is that the equity risk premium is time-varying and path-dependent. Another important conclusion is that 'of the three fundamental components of any market equilibrium – prices, probabilities and preferences – preferences are clearly the most fundamental and the least understood', so that this remains a pressing area for new research.

One recent attempt to find a new synthesis with behavioural economics was the meeting in 2010 at Virginia (US) of economists and computer scientists from the Federal Reserve, the Bank of England and various policy groups where 'agent-based models' (ABM) were explored. Agents (whether traders, firms or households) are assumed not to be representative of the whole population following some sort of ergodic process. Instead, individual agents are assigned behavioural rules where prices might be based on economic fundamentals, but where empirical evidence based on extrapolating past trends can provide equally valid rules when complemented with external consistency (Colander *et al.*, 2009). Here, if agents can interact directly and ignore pricing, then herd behaviour based on majority opinion becomes highly plausible. Computer simulations are used under different institutional rules to determine what the outcomes of herd behaviour might be and these are found to exhibit large fluctuations with crashes found to be the norm through feedback mechanisms: equilibrium becomes the exception rather than the norm in this process. If these new ABM were mathematised they would not be linear and the outcomes would not be systematically related to the causes. Juselius (2006) has shown that cointegrated VAR models are very useful in identifying robust models in a given data set. Thus, as Colander *et al.* (2009, p. 11) note:

> the 'general-to-specific' empirical approach has a good chance of nesting a multivariate, path-dependent data-generating process and relevant dynamic macroeconomic theories. Unlike approaches in which data are silenced by prior restrictions, the cointegrated VAR model gives the data a rich context in which to speak.

In this résumé of some promising fields for future research, one final important issue is the virtually universal opposition to market regulation given the free-market ideology that accompanies the NNS. Thus, market failures are given less attention than they deserve including externalities, public goods, imperfect competition, asymmetric information combined with adverse selection and, most importantly, moral hazard. The free market focus saw the deregulation of financial markets across the developed world including explicit or implicit removal of Glass-Steagall-type legislation in the US and the UK. Behavioural economics in the view of McDonald (2009) can provide an explanation for the 2007 crisis by focusing on six key features and drawing out the operational policy implications from them.

First, there is present bias or hyperbolic discounting, whereby the present is valued more highly than the future so that individuals may come to regret the decisions they made earlier: their behaviour is time-inconsistent. Second, the self-serving bias which means that assets are frequently priced above their fundamental value creating a bubble, although investors believe that they can sell before the market falls, but subsequently exactly the same errors are made: they are quintessential 'plungers' in Tobin's terms. Third, new mathematical models were developed to calculate the risk associated with particular assets, but extraordinarily these ignored the risk that house prices would fall despite knowledge of their cyclical nature. Akerlof and Shiller (2009) explain this by invoking the concept of the 'new era': in this new era falling asset prices were considered a thing of the past. Fourth, the same authors argue that individuals overestimate the value of the increase in asset prices like house prices – the longer they have owned the house the larger the gain appears to be and the larger the loans they secure against the house. This is money illusion. Fifth, agents also compare the rate of return with an unrealistic benchmark rate and because of 'loss aversion' take excessive risks. Consequently, recent low returns have led to the search for higher yields and greater risk-taking. Finally, sixth, herding would exaggerate all of these tendencies – for example, taking on a subprime mortgage because others are doing so.

McDonald's point is that these facets of the subprime financial crisis provide a convincing argument for regulation, on the basis that individuals need to be protected from their own decisions and to be persuaded to take a longer view. This is in contrast with the NNS model that assumes individuals seek their own self-interest. Given the abject failure of government regulation what insights might behavioural economics offer? The answer might be 'libertarian paternalism' as a default position. Akerlof and Shiller (2009) offer one practical example, where the outstanding balance on a mortgage is adjusted according to changes in contiguous house prices so that the risk from changes in house prices would be shared between the borrower and the lender. This would accord with Kahneman and Tversky's finding of loss aversion investor. More generally, regulation would need to respond to rising markets and the most obvious example is countercyclical capital requirements for banks. They would need to hold more capital in a period of boom and lend less and hold less capital in a recession and lend more. This accords with Minsky's view and will be part of Basel III. Any regulation, of course, must take into account the costs and the benefits.

Conclusions

Alan Greenspan conceded before Congress on 23 October 2008 that 'the modern risk paradigm [based on an ergodic view of the world] had held sway for decades. The whole intellectual edifice, however, has collapsed'. This chapter has shown that macroeconomics had travelled a long way from the non-ergodic world of Keynes to its very antithesis in the REH and EMH, but that the subject is now moving back again. The way forward, therefore, may be to include the operational insights of behavioural economics where experimental work is generating insights into the formation of expectations in different markets including many financial markets. The data collected can then be incorporated into cointegrated VAR models. These behavioural economists also believe that in a non-ergodic world government policy interventions to shape institutions are necessary to improve the economic performance of markets by a system of floors and ceilings (Davidson, 1882–1883). In a review of the subject, Akerlof (2001) has argued that 'in the spirit of Keynes' *General Theory*, behavioural macroeconomists are rebuilding the microfoundations that were sacked by the New Classical economists' (pp. 367–8). The so-called Behavioural Market Hypothesis offers enormous potential that is only now beginning to be tapped, but it has already provided the beginnings of a new microfoundation for macroeconomics. While there have been individual studies of the financial markets and agents' behaviour incorporating AE, a fully worked out macroeconomic model remains some way off.

Frydman and Goldberg (2007, 2008, 2010) have attempted to provide an alternative approach to the REH, although based on a microeconomic (or individualistic) approach to macroeconomics. They call this the Conditional Expectations Hypothesis. Under what they term 'Imperfect Knowledge Economics', the formation of forecasts or expectations is subject to learning and is contextual and subject to change. They develop a theory where learning occurs and there are qualitative constraints, meaning there is no unique set of expectations. For example, bulls and bears can be modelled so that their expectations about the possibility of a price changes move in different directions. There is not space to discuss this approach further, but it is another possibility for developing a formalisation of Keynesian conventional expectations.

Notes

1 An earlier version of this article was published as an article entitled 'The Failure of the New Macroeconomic Consensus and Rise of Behavioural Economics: From Non-Ergodicity to the Efficient Markets Hypothesis and Back Stock Market Prices and the Conduct of Monetary Policy under the New Monetary Consensus' in the *International Journal of Public Policy*, Vol. 7, Nos 1/2/3, 2011.
2 Bernanke (2010, p. 3) makes the point that the FOMC also provided 'forward guidance' that policy was likely to remain 'accommodative for a "considerable period"'.
3 The choice of the measure of inflation is also crucial. Taylor (1993) used the GDP deflator, Taylor (2009) the CPI measure, whereas the US's Federal Open Market Committee (FOMC) uses the index for personal consumption expenditures (PCE). Each measure provides a different signal to policy-makers who also have to judge whether the changes in inflation are temporary or longer lasting. This requires judgement not rules.
4 Seventy-five per cent of subprime loans were securitised in 2006 and 20 per cent of all mortgages were subprime in that year.
5 Samuelson noted that in the short run markets can be micro efficient with regard to individual instruments, but macro inefficient with respect to the whole market (see Shefrin, 2008).
6 See also Hendry and Mizon (2010) for a discussion of the econometric problems that arise when there are unanticipated changes. Because almost no time series is found to be stationary, DSGE models 'are intrinsically non-structural and must fail the Lucas critique since their derivation depends upon constant expectations distributions' (p. 13).

7 Securitisation of mortgages was partly responsible for a minor credit crunch in 1990 and Bernanke and Lown (1991, p. 217) could conceive of no good economic reason for securitisation.
8 During the 1990s, Greenspan and Summers actively opposed further regulation of the financial markets. This was on the grounds that self-regulation was perfectly adequate and any regulation would reduce the competitiveness of the US finance industry. Summers had been instrumental in the eventual repeal of the Glass-Steagall Act in 1999 that separated deposit banks from investment banks.
9 Mezzanine asset and mortgage-backed securities are mainly backed by BBB or even lower-rated mortgage bonds. In 2006 $200 billion of these were issued (with 70 per cent exposed to subprime bonds) representing 40 per cent of all CDOs issued that year.
10 See Davidson (2008) for a discussion of the absence of a market-maker in the subprime crisis.
11 On that basis they held no capital assets to meet possible 'insurance' claims.
12 This occurred on a much smaller scale in 1990 in the US as a result of a fall in the banks' holdings of real estate assets which were part of their capital adequacy ratio. See Bernanke and Lown (1991). Monetary policy was assumed to be able to cope with the credit crunch, except where the banks refused to lend (i.e. there is credit rationing) and there was a liquidity trap. Thus the 2007 crisis was a very much more severe rerun of the 1990 credit crunch.
13 Chen (2010) argues that these liberalised relationships merely conceal complex nonlinear relationships that should be analysed using complexity analysis.
14 North (1999) provides an economic historian's view of non-ergodicity.

References

Akerlof, G.A. (2001) 'Behavioural Macroeconomics and Macroeconomic Behaviour', Prize Lecture, 8 December.

Akerlof, G.A. and Shiller, R.J. (2009) *Animal Spirits: How Human Psychology Drives the Economy, and Why it Matters for Global Capitalism*, Princeton, NJ: Princeton University Press.

Allington, N.F.B., McCombie, J.S.L. and Halford, M. (2010) 'The Taylor Rule and European Monetary Policy, 1999–2009', Cambridge Centre for Economic and Public Policy, University of Cambridge, mimeo.

Allington, N.F.B., McCombie, J.S.L. and Pike, M. (2012) 'Lessons not Learned: From the Collapse of Long-Term Credit Management to the Subprime Crisis', *Journal of Post Keynesian Economics*, Vol. 34, No. 4, pp. 555–82.

Arestis, P. (2009), 'New Consensus Macroeconomics and Keynesian Critique', in E Hein, T. Niechoji and E. Stockhammer (eds), *Macroeconomic Policies on Shaky Foundations: Wither Mainstream Macroeconomics?* Marburg: Metropolois-Verlage.

Bernanke, B.S. (2010) 'Monetary Policy and the Housing Bubble', paper presented at the Annual Meeting of the American Economic Association at Atlanta, Georgia, 3 January.

Bernanke, B.S. and Blinder, A.S. (1988) 'Credit, Money, and Aggregate Demand', *American Economic Review Papers and Proceedings*, Vol. 78, No. 2, pp. 435–9.

Bernanke, B.S. and Lown, C.S. (1991) 'The Credit Crunch', *Brookings Papers on Economic Activity*, Vol. 2, pp. 205–39.

Blanchard, O. (2009) 'The Crisis: Basic Mechanisms and Appropriate Policies', IMF Working Papers 09/80, Washington: International Monetary Fund.

Blanchflower, D. (2009) 'The Future of Monetary Policy', Lecture given at Cardiff University, 24 March.

Brunnermeier, M. (2009) 'Deciphering the Liquidity and Credit Crunch, 2007–2008', *Journal of Economic Perspectives*, Vol. 23, No. 1, pp. 77–100.

Buiter, W. (2009) 'The Unfortunate Uselessness of Most "State of the Art" Academic Monetary Economics', *Financial Times*, 3 March: http://blogs.ft.com/maverecon/2009/03/the-unfortunate-uselessness-of-most-state-of-the-art-academic-monetary-economics/ (accessed 24 January 2013).

Chen, P. (2010) 'Evolutionary Economic Dynamics: Persistent Cycles, Disruptive Technology, and the Trade-off between Stability and Complexity', in P. Chen (ed.), *Economic Complexity and Equilibrium Illusion: Essays on Market Instability and Macro Vitality*, Abingdon: Routledge.

Coates, J.M. and Herbert, J. (2008) 'Endogenous Steroids and Financial Risk Taking on a London Trading Floor', Proceeding of the National Academy of Sciences, pp. 6167–72.

Cochrane, J.H. (2009) 'How did Paul Krugman get it so Wrong?' 16 September: http://faculty.chicagobooth.edu/john.cochrane/research/Papers/krugman_response.htm (accessed 24 January 2013).

Colander, D., Föllmer, H., Hass, A., Goldberg, M., Juselius, K., Kirman, A., Lux, T. and Sloth, B. (2009) 'The Financial Crisis and the Systematic Failure of Academic Economics', Kiel Institute for the World Economy, Kiel Working Paper No. 1489, February.

Coval, J.D., Jurek, J. and Stafford, E. (2009) 'The Economics of Structured Finance', *Journal of Economic Perspectives*, Vol. 23, No. 1, pp. 3–26.

Davidson, P. (1982–83) 'Rational Expectations: A Fallacious Foundation for Studying Crucial Decision-Making Processes', *Journal of Post Keynesian Economics*, Vol. 5, No. 2, pp. 182–98.

Davidson, P. (2008) 'Is the Current Financial Distress Caused by the Subprime Mortgage Crisis a Minsky Moment? Or is it the Result of Attempting to Securitise Illiquid Non-Commercial Mortgage Loans?' *Journal of Post Keynesian Economics*, Vol. 30, No. 4, pp. 669–76.

De Bondt, W., Muradoglu, G., Shefrin, H. and Staikouras, S.K. (2008) 'Behavioural Finance: Quo Vadis', *Journal of Applied Finance*, Vol. 18, No. 2, pp. 1–15.

Dokko, J., Doyle, B., Kiley, M.T., Kim, J., Sherlund, S., Sim, J. and Van Den Heuval, S. (2009) 'Monetary Policy and the Housing Bubble', Finance and Economics Discussion Series 2009-49, Washington, Board of Governors of the Federal System, December.

Fama, E.F. (1965) 'The Behaviour of Stock-Market Prices', *Journal of Business*, Vol. 38, No. 1, pp. 34–105.

Fama, E.F. (2010) 'Rational Irrationality: Interview with Eugene Fama', *New Yorker*, 13 January.

Felipe, J. and McCombie, J.S.L. (2005) 'How Sound are the Foundations of the Aggregate Production Function?' *Eastern Economic Journal*, Vol. 31, No. 3, pp. 467–88.

Fisher, F.M. (1992) 'Aggregation', in J. Monz (ed.), *Aggregate Production Functions and Related Topics*, London: Harvester Wheatsheaf.

Frydman, R. and Goldberg, M.D. (2007) *Imperfect Knowledge Economics: Exchange Rates and Risk*, Princeton, NJ: Princeton University Press.

Frydman, R. and Goldberg, M.D. (2008) 'Macroeconomic Theory for a World of Imperfect Knowledge', Centre on Capitalism and Society at Columbia University, Working Paper No. 24, May.

Frydman, R. and Goldberg, M.D. (2010) 'Efficient Markets: Fictions and Reality', paper given to the Institute for New Economic Thinking, Cambridge, April.

Goodfriend, M. (2004) 'Monetary Policy in the New Neoclassical Synthesis: A Primer', *Economic Quarterly*, Federal Reserve Bank of Richmond, Summer, pp. 21–45.

Goodfriend, M. (2007) 'How the World Achieved Consensus on Monetary Policy', *Journal of Economic Perspectives*, Vol. 21, No. 4, pp. 47–68.

Goodhart, C. (2010) 'Comments on "Credit Frictions and Optimal Monetary Policy" by Curdia and Woodford': www.bis.org/events/conf080626/goodhart.pdf (accessed 24 January 2013).

Haldane, A.G. (2009) 'Why Banks Failed the Stress Test', speech given at the Marcus-Evans Conference on Stress-Testing, 9–10 February.

Hendry, D.F. and Mizon, G. (2010) 'On the Mathematical Basis of Inter-Temporal Optimization', Working Paper 497, Department of Economics, University of Oxford.

Hicks, J. (1979) 'IS-LM: An Explanation', *Journal of Post Keynesian Economics*, Vol. 3, No. 2, pp. 139–54.

Hume, D. (1888) *Hume's Treatise of Human Nature*, ed. L.A. Selby Bigge, Oxford: Clarendon Press. Originally published 1739–40.

Juselius, K. (2006) *The Cointegrated VAR Model: Econometric Methodology and Empirical Applications*, Oxford: Oxford University Press.

Kahneman, D. and Tversky, A. (1979) 'Prospect Theory: An Analysis of Decision Under Risk', *Econometrica*, Vol. 47, No. 2, pp. 263–91.

Keynes, J.M. (1936) *The General Theory of Employment, Interest and Money*, London: Macmillan.

Keynes, J.M. (1937) 'The General Theory of Employment', *Quarterly Journal of Economics*, Vol. 51, No. 2, pp. 209–23.

Keys, B.J., Mukherjee, T., Seru, A. and Vikrant, V. (2010) 'Did Securitisation Lead to Lax Screening? Evidence from Subprime Loans', *Quarterly Journal of Economics*, Vol. 125, No. 1, pp. 307–62.

Kirchler, M. (2010) 'Partial Knowledge is a Dangerous Thing: On the Value of Asymmetric Fundamental Information in Asset Markets', *Journal of Economic Psychology*, Vol. 31, No. 4, pp. 643–58.

Kirman, A. (1992) 'Whom or What Does the Representative Individual Represent?' *Journal of Economic Perspectives*, Vol. 6, No. 2, pp. 117–36.

Knight, F.H. (1921) *Risk, Uncertainty, and Profit*, Hart, Schaffner and Marx Prize Essays, No. 31, Boston, MA, and New York: Houghton Mifflin.

Krugman, P. (2009) 'How did Economists Get It So Wrong?' *New York Times*, 2 September: www.nytimes.com/2009/09/06/magazine/06Economic-t.html (accessed 24 January 2013).

Leamer, E.E. (2010) 'Tantalus on the Road to Asymptopia', *Journal of Economic Perspectives*, Vol. 24, No. 2, pp. 31–46.

LeRoy, S.F. (1989) 'Efficient Capital Markets', *Journal of Economic Literature*, Vol. 27, No. 4, pp. 1583–621.

Lo, A.W. (2007) 'Efficient Markets Hypothesis', in L. Blume and S. Durlauf (eds), *The New Palgrave: A Dictionary of Economics*, 2nd edn, New York: Palgrave Macmillan.

Lo, A.W. and Repin, D. (2002) 'The Psychophysiology of Real-Time Financial Risk Processing', *Journal of Cognitive Neuroscience*, Vol. 14, No. 8, pp. 323–39.

Lo, A.W., Repin, D.V. and Steenbarger, B.N. (2005) 'Fear and Greed in Financial Markets: A Clinical Study of Day-Traders', *American Economic Review*, Vol. 95, No. 1, pp. 352–9.

Lucas, R.E. (1978) 'Unemployment Policy', *American Economic Review Papers and Proceedings*, Vol. 68, No. 2, pp. 353–7.

Lucas, R.E. (2009) 'In Defence of the Dismal Science', *The Economist*, 6 August: www.princeton.edu/~markus/misc/Economist_Lucas_roundtable/Lucas_article_The_Economist.pdf (accessed 24 January 2013).
McCombie, J.S.L. (2010) 'The Thatcher Monetarist Experiment, 1979–85: An Assessment', in G. Fontana, J.S.L. McCombie and M.C. Sawyer (eds), *Macroeconomics, Finance and Money*, Basingstoke: Macmillan.
McCombie, J.S.L. and Pike, M. (2013) 'The End of the Consensus in Macroeconomic Theory? A Methodological Inquiry', *American Review of Economics and Sociology*, Vol. 72, No. 2, pp. 1–32.
McDonald, I.M. (2009) 'The Global Financial Crisis and Behavioural Economics', *Economics Papers*, Vol. 28, No. 3, pp. 249–54.
Mehrling, P. (2000) 'What is Monetary Economics About?' Barnard College, Columbia University, mimeo.
Meyer, L.H. (2001) 'Does Money Matter?' *Review*, Federal Reserve Bank of St. Louis, September/October, pp. 1–15.
Mian, A.R. and Sufi, A. (2009) 'The Consequences of Mortgage Credit Expansion: Evidence from the U.S. Mortgage Default Crisis', *Quarterly Journal of Economics*, Vol. 124, No. 4, pp. 1449–96.
Mian, A., Sufi, A. and Trebbi, F. (2010) 'The Political Economy of the US Mortgage Default Crisis', *American Economic Review*, Vol. 100, No. 5, pp. 1967–99.
North, D.C. (1999) 'Dealing with a Non-Ergodic World: Institutional Economics, Property Rights, and the Global Environment', *Duke Environmental Law and Policy Forum*, Vol. 10, No. 1, pp. 1–12.
Roubini, N. (2006) Speech to the IMF on the impending financial crisis.
Roubini, N. and Mihm, S. (2010) *Crisis Economics: A Crash Course in the Future of Finance*, London: Allen Lane Press.
Rajan, R.G. (2005) 'Has Financial Development Made the World Riskier?' *Proceedings*, Federal Reserve Bank of Kansas City, August, pp. 313–69.
Rajan, R.G. (2010) *Fault Lines: How Hidden Fractures still Threaten the World Economy*, Princeton, NJ: Princeton University Press.
Samuelson, P.A. (1965) 'Proof that Properly Anticipated Prices Fluctuate Randomly', *Industrial Management Review*, Vol. 6, No. 2, pp. 41–9.
Samuelson, P.A. (1973) 'Proof that Properly Discounted Present Values of Assets Vibrate Randomly', *Bell Journal of Economics*, Vol. 4, No. 2, pp. 369–74.
Samuelson, P.A. (2004) 'Where Ricardo and Mill Rebut and Confirm Arguments of Mainstream Economists Supporting Globalisation', *Journal of Economic Perspectives*, Vol. 18, No. 3, pp. 135–46.
Shefrin, H. (2008) *Ending the Management Illusion*, Columbus, Ohio: McGraw Hill.
Simon, H. (1955) 'A Behavioural Model of Rational Choice', *Quarterly Journal of Economics*, Vol. 69, No. 1, pp. 99–118.
Solow, R.M. (2008) 'Comment: The State of Macroeconomics', *Journal of Economic Perspectives*, Vol. 22, No. 1, pp. 243–9.
Summers, L. (1991) 'The Scientific Illusion in Empirical Macroeconomics', *Scandinavian Journal of Economics*, Vol. 93, No. 1, pp. 129–48.
Taylor, J.B. (1993) 'Discretion Versus Policy Rules in Practice', *Carnegie-Rochester Series on Public Policy*, Vol. 39, pp. 195–214.
Taylor, J.B. (2007) 'Housing and Monetary Policy', NBER Working Paper, No. 13682.
Taylor, J.B. (2009) *Getting Off Track: How Government Actions and Interventions Caused, Prolonged and Worsened the Financial Crisis*, Stanford, CA: Hoover Institution Press.

Tobin, J. (1958) 'Liquidity Preference as Behaviour Towards Risk', *Review of Economic Studies*, Vol. 25, No. 67, pp. 65–86.

Tversky, A. and Wakker, P.P. (1995) 'Risk Attitudes and Decision Weights', *Econometrica*, Vol. 63, No. 6, pp. 1225–80.

Thaler, R.H. (1997) 'Irving Fisher: Modern Behavioural Economist', *Journal of Economic Perspectives*, Vol. 17, No. 4, pp. 191–202.

Thaler, R.H. (2000) 'From Homo Economicus to Homo Sapiens', *Journal of Economic Perspectives*, Vol. 14, No. 1, pp. 133–41.

Wenli, L., White, M.J. and Zhu, N. (2010) 'Did Bankruptcy Cause Mortgage Defaults to Rise?' Federal Reserve Bank of Philadelphia, mimeo.

Yuxiang, K. and Chen, Z. (2010) 'Monetary Policy Credibility and Inflationary Expectation', *Journal of Economic Psychology*, Vol. 31, No. 4, pp. 487–97.

4 The debt trap

Óscar Dejuán

Introduction

A debt trap can be compared with quicksand. Both share the same fate: whatever you do, you become more and more trapped. If people in quicksand stay still, the sand will swallow them up little by little. If, on the contrary, they try to escape by themselves, they will die of exhaustion there and then. If all economic agents are obsessed with cancelling their debts at the same time, aggregate demand, wages, profits and taxes will get stuck while deficit and debt rise. If, on the contrary, they try to move ahead by maintaining or increasing their usual expenditure, they may be punished by an unaffordable risk-premium. A debt trap becomes lethal when agents have to refinance their debt at an ever increasing interest rate.

This chapter analyses how a handful of advanced countries fell into a debt trap and the difficulties of escaping from it. Our analysis is inspired by the post-Keynesian paradigm introduced in the 1930s by Kalecki and Keynes, whose main tenets are the principle of effective demand and the non-neutrality of money and finance (Kalecki, 1971; Keynes, 1936).

Each section of this chapter approaches the credit boom and the debt trap from a different methodological perspective. In the overview offered in the next section, we contrast the sustainable wage-led growth that characterized the golden age of capitalism (1945–1970) and the unsustainable credit-led growth that defines the glittering age of capitalism (1996–2008). At the end of this section we present some empirical evidence about the credit expansion and the debt trap in Spain and other selected countries. The third section deploys the post-Keynesian model behind our arguments. It is useful to analyse the relationship between the four variables that build a debt trap: the rate of growth of demand and output, the prices of assets (real estate bubbles, in particular), the interest rate and the indebtedness ratio. One of the novelties is the introduction of a multiplier whose value depends on the debt burden. The fourth section traces the evolution of debt ratios under different scenarios that replicate what happened in some advanced economies before and after the 2007–2008 crash. The last section of the chapter concludes that economies in a debt trap, like people engulfed in quicksand, need an external saviour whose priority should be the dilution of the debt burden.

A credit-led growth ending in a debt trap

Figure 4.1 illustrates the circuit of income in a given period of production and shows the requirements to close it and grow in a balanced way. Year by year, the incomes generated in the process of production should buy full capacity output. Financial intermediaries are supposed to bridge the gap between surplus and deficit agents. Figure 4.1 may also help to interpret actual paths of growth. *Grosso modo* and with due caveats, the lower part describes the *wage-led growth* that characterizes the *golden age of capitalism* (1945–1970). To describe the *credit-led growth* of the *glittering age of capitalism* (1996–2008) we should add a space for the new financial system (see the shaded area in the upper part of Figure 4.1).

During the golden age, the engines of the economy were the industries producing cars and household electrical appliances. Also new machines, which are the ordinary vehicle of technical progress and allow a rise in real wages, without

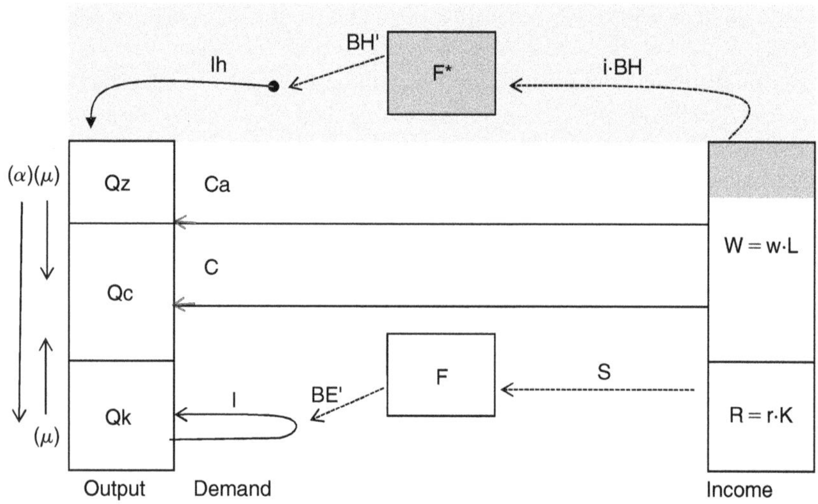

Figure 4.1 The circuit of income and the double role of finance.

Notes

Solid arrows: flows of money in exchange of goods and services; dash-arrows: transfers and property income; dot-arrows: financial flows.

μ: multiplier; α: accelerator.

Factors – L: labour employed; K: stock of capital.

Final Output – Q: production of capital goods (k), consumption goods (c) and goods for autonomous demand (z). In the golden age it is identified with cars. In the glittering age, with luxury goods and houses.

Final demand – Ca: autonomous consumption (of cars and luxuries); C: induced consumption; I: productive investment by firms; Ih: residential investment by households.

Income – W: wages; R: profits; w: real wage; r: rate of profit; i: interest rate.

Finance – S: savings. BE′: net borrowing of firms to finance productive investment; BH′: net borrowing of households (mortgage loans); BH: stock of debt owed by worker-households.

The shaded horizontal area (in the upper part of the figure) illustrates the new role of finance.

damaging the rate of profit. The production of the goods included in the autonomous vector, triggered the demand for and the supply of equipment required for the expansion of capacity (this is the accelerator). Also the consumption goods demanded by workers employed directly or indirectly in the overall process of production (this is the multiplier).

The post-war path of growth was a sustainable one because the incomes generated in the production process were enough to absorb each and every part of final output. By spending their disposable ordinary wages, households purchased the bulk of output which consists in ordinary consumption goods. With the extra wages obtained from the appropriation of productivity gains, they were able to purchase the durable consumption goods included in the autonomous vector. Firms, satisfied with the realized rate of profit, decided to expand capacity in order to match efficiently the expected increases in demand. Financial institutions channelled the savings accruing from profits to new investments.

Previous wage-led growth started to fail in the late 1960s when wages increased above productivity and firms translated the differential into prices, aggravating ongoing international imbalances. The oil crises of 1973 and 1979 speeded inflation up, in the midst of a recession. Apart from fixing these imbalances, the restoration of growth required a new locomotive, since the market for cars and electrical appliances had come of age. Which industry would take up the relay baton? Most economists pointed to ICT (Information and Communication Technologies). They certainly have a huge potential market. Unfortunately, their dragging effects (the ones captured by the multiplier) are very low. After the stock-market crash of ICT firms in 2000–2001, entrepreneurs and bankers tried to exploit the potential of another industry: construction. This is the beginning of our story.

The upper part of Figure 4.1 (shaded area) reflects the effects of the financialization of the economy during the *glittering age of capitalism* (1996–2008) in countries like the USA, the UK, Spain and Ireland, to mention just a few. The economy was dragged by a single industry (construction) funded with cheap credit. Construction has the highest income and employment multipliers but it lacks the advantage of built-in technical progress. Real wages remained constant in an age dominated by financial capital and globalization. The disposable income of workers (after subtracting taxes and mortgage payments from wages) actually fell.

Who would buy the houses driving the new path of growth? They were built on a large scale aimed at a market as big as all the living dwellings needed for workers. But workers could not afford them. Their wages barely met ordinary consumption.[1] Banks filled the gap by granting cheap mortgage loans. These loans inflated the prices of houses so banks were obliged to lend even more. Soon, the indebtedness ratio of households, developers and construction firms surpassed prudent thresholds, whatever your measure of prudence.

Credit conveys debt and debt is bound to have deflationary effects on demand after a point. Households were obliged to set aside an increasing part of their income to pay monthly instalments. These *forced savings* are represented by the shaded area at the top-right of Figure 4.1. They will leak from the circuit of income/demand if banks do not find creditworthy borrowers, as happened from early 2007. Since then, banks were more a "drain" than a "drive". To balance their sheets, banks cut off credit to the few firms and households willing to expand capacity (Graziani, 2003).

Table 4.1 and Figure 4.2 present international empirical evidence about the magnitude of the debt trap and the difficulties of escaping from it. Private debt increased rapidly in the boom period, especially from 2002–2007. The indebtedness ratio remained constant because income was growing at the same pace. The problem emerged in late 2005, when central banks raised the official interest rate to prevent inflation. After the financial crash of 2007 households and firms curtailed their investments and began to focus on debt cancellation with miserable results. The USA and Australia were the only countries where the stock of private debt decreased due to their particular legal systems that allow the cancellation of mortgage obligations in return for the house keys. In the rest of the countries private debt kept roughly constant. All over the world, sovereign debt increased after the expansionary fiscal policies of 2009 and even more after the contractive policies implemented in 2010–2012. In 2009 the central bank set the official interest rate at a historical minimum. Yet, the market interest rate remained high due to the increasing risk premium applied by lenders.

These paradoxes should not surprise post-Keynesian economists. In the next section we shall set up a model to explain them.

A model to explain the interplay between financial stocks and economic flows

In this section we are going to explore the interplay between financial stocks (the burden of debt) and economic flows (income, consumption, investment, etc.). Such interplay is the main tenet of the stock-flow consistent models that here

Table 4.1 Growth of debt

	Change (percentage points)	
	2000–2008 (Q2)	*2008 (Q2)–11*
Australia	77	–14
Canada	39	17
France	89	35
Germany	7	1
Italy	69	12
Japan	37	39
Spain	145	26
UK	177	20
USA	75	–16

Source: National Central Banks and McKinsey Global Institute.

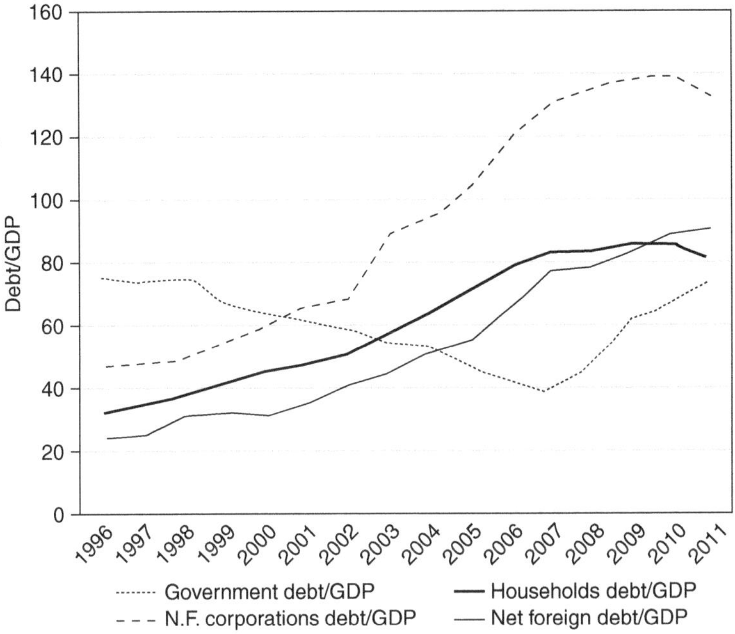

(a)

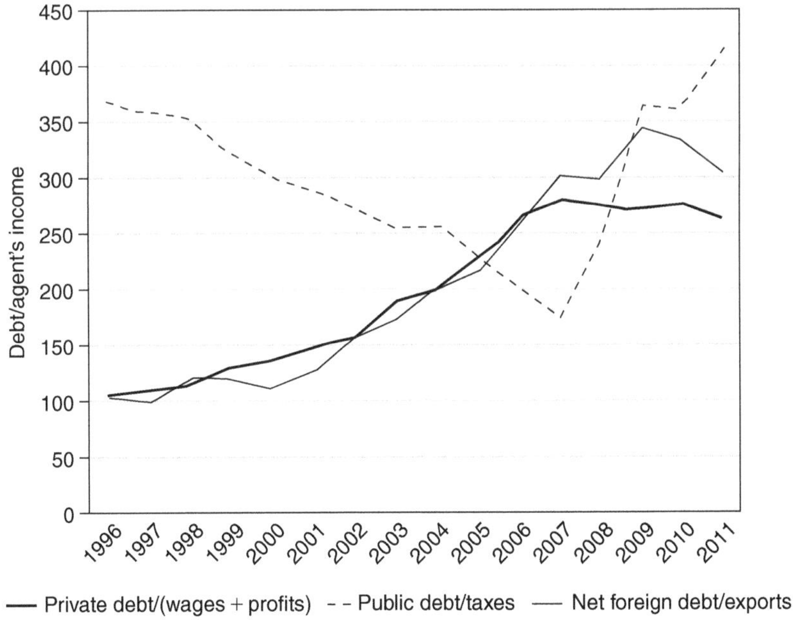

(b)

Figure 4.2 Evolution of debt in Spain (1996–2011) (%) (source of data: Bank of Spain).

will be simplified at the maximum (Godley and Lavoie, 2006). The financial-fragility hypothesis (Minsky, 1975; Minsky and Papadimitriou, 2004) will also play an important part of our story. The quality of debt deteriorates because it represents an increasing part of disposable income and it becomes more speculative.

The supply side: technology, distribution and prices. Real estate bubbles

The economy we are going to analyse produces consumption and capital goods that differ in function but are produced by the same technology. It is represented by the labour coefficient (l, an inverse measure of labour productivity) and the optimal capital coefficient (k) that is supposed to remain constant during the period of our analysis. Firms adapt to changes in demand by speeding up and slowing down the rate of capacity utilization. $u^* = 1$ is the normal rate corresponding to k.

We take as given the real wage (w). It is supposed to increase parallel to labour productivity but, since technical change has been ruled out, we can assume a constant wage. The Sraffian system of equations allows us to determine the *normal prices of production* associated to a given technology and real wage (Sraffa, 1960). Also the normal rate of profit (r^*) corresponding to $k(u^*)$ and w. In our simplified model we can compute relative prices by the following system of equations. Due to the assumption of equal technical coefficients among sectors, all prices equal one.

$$p = w \cdot l + r \cdot p \cdot k = [1,1,\ldots 1] \tag{4.1}$$

Prices of production do not depend on demand. If demand rises, firms will adjust production by increasing the rate of capacity utilization (a short-run adjustment) and by increasing the installed capacity through investment (a long-run adjustment). The inflation theory based on the Phillips curve states that an acceleration of growth may cause tensions in the labour market and raise nominal wages and prices. This did not happen in the glittering age of capitalism. Apparently the globalization of the economy has flattened the Phillips curve.

Houses are the exception to the rule. A quite relevant exception that, surprisingly, does not interest central banks entrusted with the control of the consumption price index (CPI). Demand affects prices of non-produced assets (like land and shares); also house prices that are related to these scarce assets and whose production requires quite a long time.[2] House prices are bound to rise when demand (funded by credit) increases faster than supply. According to the Ricardian theory of rent and asset prices, the natural or fundamental value of a house can be ascertained by capitalizing the yearly rents or, what amounts to the same, the mortgage commitments (Leamer, 2007; Dejuán and Febrero, 2010). This is done in the following expression where f is the annual instalment paid by the borrower, i is the interest rate and n the number of years of the redemption period.[3] Banks that fix these three variables, can be considered the main culprits for the evolution of house prices.

$$P_h = \frac{f}{(1+i)} + \frac{f}{(1+i)^2} + \ldots + \frac{f}{(1+i)^n} = f\left(\frac{(1+i)^n - 1}{i(1+i)^n}\right) \tag{4.2}$$

In our classical Keynesian synthesis, interest is a distributive variable that central banks can control, up to a certain extent, by fixing the official interest rate (i_o). In their medium- and long-term loans to firms and households, banks add the ordinary margin (φ_1) that covers their production costs and the normal rate of profit. When the economy as a whole or a particular borrower is exposed to special risks, banks may charge a second mark-up (φ_2). It is a *risk premium* that rating agencies revise from time to time taking into account all factors affecting the credit-worthiness of borrowers, including their indebtedness ratio. This effect was anticipated by Kalecki in his "principle of increasing risk" (Kalecki, 1971; Dejuán, 2002).

$$i = i_o(1 + \varphi_1 + \varphi_2) \tag{4.3}$$

The risk premium explains why, after the crisis, market interest rates did not fall despite central banks having fixed the official rate at an all time historical minimum.

The demand side: multiplier of consumption and acceleration of investment

According to the Keynesian–Kaleckian principle of effective demand, output and employment are supposed to adjust to the expected aggregate demand (Keynes, 1936; Kalecki, 1971). It includes: autonomous demand (Z'_t), expansionary investment by firms (I_t) and induced consumption by households (C_t).

$$Y_t = D_t = C_t + I_t + Z'_t \tag{4.4}$$

In a more compelling way, output can be considered as a multiple of autonomous demand. This can be defined in a broad sense ($A = I + Z$) or in a strict sense (Z, that subtracts investment from Z'). In the first case we use the ordinary multiplier (μ), in the second, the supermultiplier (μ^*) (see Serrano, 1995; Bortis, 1997; Dejuán, 2005).

$$Y_t = \mu \cdot [(I_t + Z]_t) = \mu^* \cdot Z_t \tag{4.5}$$

The bulk of private consumption is a relatively high and stable fraction of household disposable income. Following the classical tradition we shall consider that workers–households systematically consume all their disposable wages. The consumption out of rents (even if they are received by the same type of households) is autonomous because it does not depend directly on current income.

The disposable income of workers–households can be computed as:

$$YH_t' = W_t \cdot (1 - t - i \cdot \beta_{ht}) \tag{4.6}$$

where t is the tax rate (except when it appears as a sub-index that indicates time); i is the interest rate; $\beta_{ht}=BH_t/W_t$ is the indebtedness ratio of households.

Following Kalecki, the average propensity to consume (c) out of national disposable income (Y') can be replaced by the weighted propensity to consume out of disposable wages and profits. In our model, where all the wages and only wages are systematically consumed, we can write: $c_w=1$; $c_r=0$. The weights are the shares of wages and profits in income. The share of wages, the only one relevant in our case, can be computed as: $\omega=W/Y=w{\cdot}l$. This allows us to compute induced consumption by the following expression:

$$C_t = c \cdot Y_t' = c_w \cdot \omega \cdot (1 - t - i \cdot \beta_{ht}) \tag{4.7}$$

The new term (β_h) should be included in the multiplier that now becomes [4.8] (where m is the import propensity: $m=M/Y$):

$$\mu_t = \frac{1}{1 - c_w(1 - t - i \cdot \beta_{ht}) + m} \tag{4.8}$$

The new multiplier highlights the interrelationship between financial stocks (household debt) and economic flows (private consumption). It depends on the relative *burden of debt* that equals the interest rate times the indebtedness ratio of households ($i{\cdot}\beta ht$). The multiplier is no longer a constant parameter. When the relative burden of debt rises (as happens at the end of a boom and at the beginning of a recession) the multiplier shrinks. Fiscal policy becomes less effective in these situations, contrary to Fazzari (Chapter 11, this volume).

Productive investment, of the expansionary type, refers to the purchase of capital goods by firms in order to match efficiently the expected increases in demand. According to the accelerator principle it is a function of the optimal "capital/output ratio" and the expected rate of growth of demand (g). This rate is the true independent variable of the Keynesian system (Eatwell, 1983). In the long-term perspective that characterized growth models, we'd better relate it to the autonomous trend (g_z) and other objective factors (as supermultiplier theoreticians quoted above suggest). $K{\cdot}g{\cdot}D_t$ is the pure accelerator principle. The flexible accelerator takes into account the excesses/shortages of capacity to get rid of them. If the rate of capacity utilization is above the normal one that we set at unity (if $u'_t=u_t-1>0$), firms will invest more than the level suggested by the pure acceleration principle.[4]

$$I_t = k \cdot g \cdot D_t + a \cdot u_t' \tag{4.9}$$

The excess/shortage of inventories is a second buffer of shocks. Here a positive E_{yt} will be discounted from demand. Output in period $t+1$ will be: $Y_{t+1}=D_{t+1}-E_{yt}$. The shortage of inventories (negative E_{yt}) will be replenished with imports.

The autonomous demand vector draws together expenditure that is not systematically related to current income. It includes the following items:

$$Z_t' = I_{ht} + C_{at} + G_t + X_t' \tag{4.10}$$

where I_h is *residential investment by workers-households.* It is paid entirely with mortgage loans. The initial level of residential investment and its expected rate of growth will be the key independent variables of our model. C_a is *autonomous consumption out of dividends*. Alternatively it can refer to the advertising costs of firms. G is *government expenditures in goods and services*. It is a policy variable. X' is *net exports*, i.e. export (X) minus imports (M). We distinguish: (1) ordinary imports that are related to income via the import propensity: $M'=m\cdot Y$; (2) extraordinary imports that only emerge in boom periods when there are shortages of inventories: $M''=-E_y$; (3) imports that depend on the exchange rate. The last ones are included (with a negative sign) in X. Notice that Z in [4.11] and in the multiplicand of [4.5] does not include imports:

$$Z_t = I_{ht} + C_{at} + G_t + X_t \tag{4.11}$$

The financial side: pumping of debt and its deflationary effect

We are interested in ascertaining the determinants of the indebtedness ratio and its deflationary impact on aggregate demand. The stock of debt of any agent increases with its deficit financed with credit and bonds (B_t' refers to the borrowing needs corresponding to a deficit position). The primary deficit of each agent equals its disposable income minus final consumption, minus investment. The total deficit adds the repayment of debt ($i\cdot B_t$).

To simplify our empirical analysis (later, in the Appendix) we have taken the following assumptions: (a) banks represent all financial institutions – they lend money and purchase bonds; (b) banks are owned by rentiers, so rentiers–households (J) and financial institutions (F) are, somehow interchangeable; (c) loans and bonds are "perpetual", the principal is never returned. The last assumption implies that when we set the borrowing needs at B_t', we mean: "B' units above the repayment level corresponding to year t".

Let us focus on the pilling of debt by workers–households (H) and generalize later. Under the assumption that workers consume their entire disposable income, the primary deficit of workers–households will coincide with the value of residential investment ($Z_h=I_h\cdot P_h$), which is growing at the autonomous trend (g_h). Adding the service of debt ($i\cdot BH$) we obtain the total deficit in year t (BH'_t) and the stock of debt accumulated the last day of year t (BH_t):

$$BH_t = BH_{t-1} + BH_t' = BH_{t-1} + i \cdot BH_{t-1} + Z_{ht} \tag{4.12}$$

Dividing by wages we obtain the *indebtedness ratio* of workers–households (β_h). It increases with the yearly interest payments ($i \cdot \beta_{ht}$) and the primary deficit relative to wages ($z_{ht}=I_h \cdot P_h/W$):

$$\beta_{ht} = \beta_{h(t-1)} + i_t \cdot \beta_{h(t-1)} + z_{ht} \quad (4.13)$$

The same procedure can be followed to determine the indebtedness ratio of rentiers (J, β_j), firms or enterprises (E, β_e), government (G, β_g) and the nation as a whole (N, β).

To analyse the deflationary effect of debt we should remember the dual role of modern finance: "drive" and "drain". The nominal inflow of credit in the circuit of production is the sum of loans granted by the banking system plus the bonds purchased by its owners (rentiers). This is equivalent to the borrowing needs of workers–households, firms and government:

$$INFLOW_t = BH'_t + BE'_t + BG'_t \quad (4.14)$$

The real inflow or banking drive only considers the value (at constant prices) of the resources mobilized by loans and bonds. We are interested in the building of new houses, not in their nominal value that includes the capital gains appropriated by the owners of land. For this reason we should write I_{ht} instead of $BH'_t=I_{ht} \cdot P_{ht}$. Neither are the loans granted for the purchase of real and financial assets a driving force for the economy. Usually they have a speculative purpose and create bubbles:

$$DRIVE_t = REAL\ INFLOW = I_{ht} + BE'_t + BG'_t \quad (4.15)$$

The "banking drain" refers to the outflow of credit from the circuit of income–demand–production committed to the repayment of debt. It is i times the outstanding debt of agents. Notice that this debt grows with their *total* borrowing needs, regardless of their justification. What matters here is $BH'_t=I_{ht} \cdot P_{ht}$ leading to a fast increase in the stock of debt (BH) when house prices are increasing:

$$DRAIN_t = OUTFLOW_t = i \cdot (BH_t + BE_t + BG_t) \quad (4.16)$$

The net drive (ND) is the difference between the real inflow (drive) and the outflow (drain). After dividing by income we obtain the relative net drive (nd):

$$nd_t = ND_t / Y = ((I_{ht} / Y) + (BE'_t / Y) + (BG'_t / Y)) - i \cdot (\beta_{ht} + \beta_{et} + \beta_{gt}) \quad (4.17)$$

At the bottom of Figure 4.4 (below) we also plot the relative net drive in nominal terms which includes total loans. The difference with the previous ratio informs about the inflationary effect of credit (here restricted to the real estate bubble).

Cumulative processes

A debt trap is the result of a series of cumulative processes between the following variables: the rate of growth of output (g) which depends on the autonomous trend (in our model its main element is the rate of growth of residential investment, g_h); the price of houses (P_h); the interest rate (i); and the indebtedness ratio (β). A sustainable path of growth is compatible with different values of these variables. The autonomous trend and the general rate of growth may increase with constant prices, a constant interest rate and a constant indebtedness ratio. Probably a change in distribution will be required to ensure the equilibrium between demand and full capacity supply: a higher rate profit if the new (luxury) goods are produced for rentiers; a higher wage if the new goods (houses) are produced for the mass of workers. Alternatively, the adjustment to a higher rate of growth could be met by a change in consumption and savings propensities of social groups.

The problem with the glittering age of capitalism is that these adjustments never arrived. Banks lent increasing amounts of money to workers–households unable to purchase the new houses built for them. In the left part of Figure 4.3 we see that the acceleration of growth speeded up the indebtedness ratio ($\Delta g \rightarrow \Delta\beta$). The repayment of debt is bound to have a deflationary impact on aggregate demand and growth, although it takes some time to be visualized. The demand for dwellings funded with mortgage loans (always above its supply) raised house prices. In turn, the real estate bubble stimulated residential investment and borrowing. People hurried up to purchase houses before their prices went up. Two cumulative processes superimpose here: (1) $\Delta g \leftrightarrow \Delta P_h$; (2) $\Delta P_h \leftrightarrow \Delta\beta$.

After 2007 the process is reversed. The autonomous trend started to fall for two complementary reasons: the saturation of the dwelling market and the rise in interest rates due to a tightening of monetary policy and credit restrictions.[5] The right panel of Figure 4.3 shows the sources of change: [∇g] and [Δi]. Also the two new cumulative processes that came into play.

The first one occurs in the financial sector and can be summarized in the loop: $\Delta i \leftrightarrow \Delta\beta$. In a heavily indebted economy, a rise in interest rates is bound to

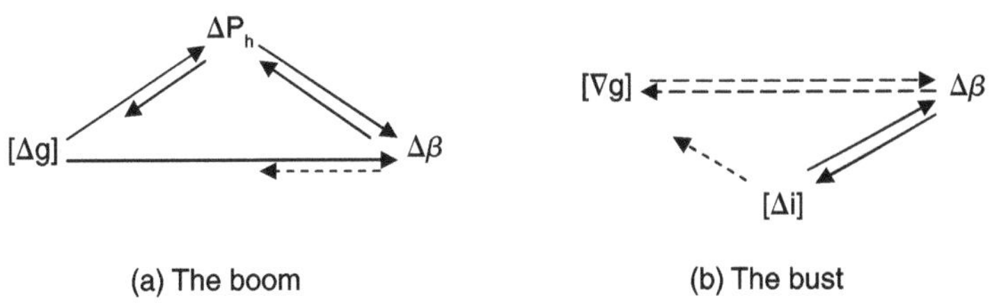

Figure 4.3 Cumulative processes.

Note
Solid arrows: direct relationship. Dash-arrows: inverse relationship ($\Delta \rightarrow \nabla$ or $\nabla \rightarrow \Delta$). The length of the arrow indicates its strength. The square brackets indicate the origin of the change. g: rate of growth; P_h: price of houses; i: interest rate; β: indebtedness ratio.

increase the burden of debt with the consequent deflationary impact on aggregate demand.[6] The corridor $\Delta\beta \rightarrow \Delta i$ is even more dangerous. Beyond a given threshold, an increase in the indebtedness ratio may trigger the risk premium raising the market interest rate to prohibitive levels.

The second cumulative process refers to the interaction between the rate of growth and the indebtedness ratio. Note the reversal of the original arrow's direction. In panel (a) an acceleration of g caused an increase in β. In panel (b) a deceleration of g may increase β giving rise to the following loop: $\nabla g \leftrightarrow \Delta\beta$. To understand this result we have to consider that wages, profits and taxes are in the denominator of the indebtedness ratio. Even if the primary deficit was nil in recessions, the ratio between a constant debt and a falling income is supposed to increase.

These vicious circles make it difficult to escape from the debt trap as we are going to see in the next section.

Simulations to illustrate how difficult it is to escape from a debt trap

Table 4.A.1 (Appendix) simulates the evolution of economic and financial variables under different scenarios for an economy that behaves according to the post-Keynesian model presented in the previous section. Figure 4.4 plots the evolution of the stock of debt of households (*BH*), firms (*BE*), government (*BG*) and the nation as a whole (*BN*) under a given sequence of scenarios. The upper panel represents the weight of these stocks on national income. The medium panel relates them to the primary income of agents. They are the indebtedness ratios (β) introduced in the previous section. The bottom panel examines the net inflow of credit–demand on the circuit of income under the same scenarios as a proportion of national income.

We contemplate six correlative scenarios: (a) equilibrium path of growth; (b) credit-boom; (c) financial constraints; (d) recession; (e) expansive fiscal policy; (f) contractive fiscal policy. They are "correlative" or "sequential" in the sense that each scenario starts off from the values inherited from the previous one. Some changes are provisional; others definitive. The interest rate rises in period 11 and continues at this level until the last period. Growth rates fall in period 16 and continue depressed until the end.

Equilibrium path of growth

The economy we are considering is growing along its warranted path ($g_w = (1 - c - z_t)/k = 0.025$). All the elements of the autonomous demand vector (residential investment, autonomous consumption, real public expenditure and exports) grow at this rate. Productive investment and induced consumption follow suit. The interest rate (uniform for all agents) is $i = 0.025$.

This economy has inherited a high stock of debt. The outstanding debt of firms, government and the nation as a whole represents 0.8 (80 per cent) of

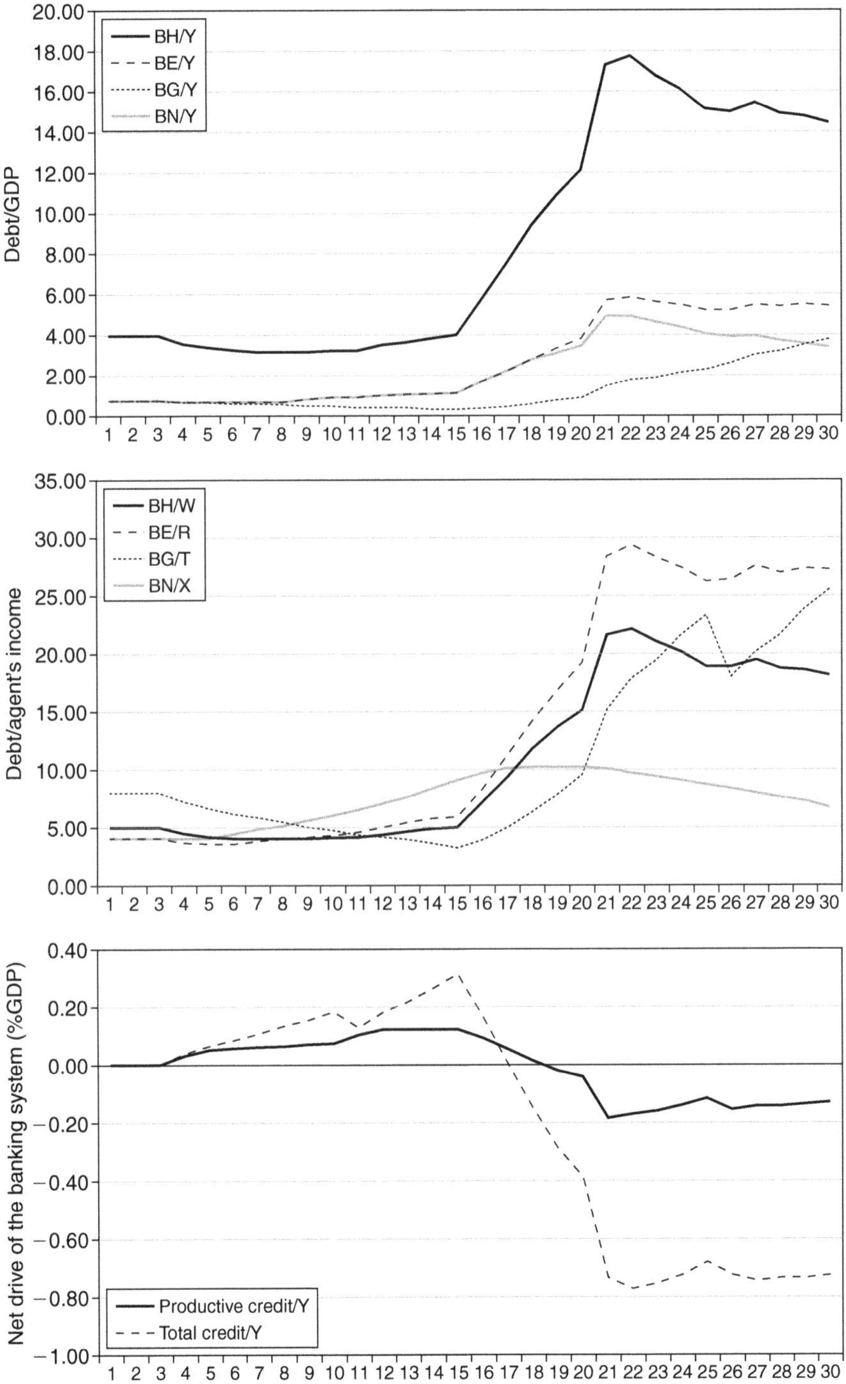

Figure 4.4 Paths of debt.

national income. The percentage of their "primary" incomes is 400 per cent ($\beta_e = \beta_g = \beta_n = 4$). The outstanding debt of households is five times wages ($\beta_h = 5$) and four times national income.

Despite this negative inheritance, the economy is able to grow in a balanced way in the first three quarters. Economic growth keeps the debt ratios constant. The last column of Table 4.A.1 that is plotted in the bottom of Figure 4.4 lets the cat out of the bag: the net drive of credit on aggregate demand is nil. The banking system reallocates savings without impinging on aggregate demand.

These are the implicit conditions to get such satisfactory result: (1) the economy is growing at its warranted rate: all the savings available for expansionary investment are really invested; (2) the interest rate is equal or less than the actual rate of growth; (3) the indebtedness ratios are below the critical threshold that triggers the risk premium; (4) debt grows at the warranted rate or below it (in our case, $B'/B = g_w$)

Credit-boom

In the second scenario (Q4–10), banks propel the construction industry forward by granting cheap mortgage loans to households. The growth of residential investment (g_h) shifts from 0.025 to 0.1. Banks also finance housebuilding but since supply falls behind demand, house prices start rising at 0.1. Autonomous consumption of luxury goods that is somehow affected by wealth effects, speeds up its rate of growth to 0.05. Productive investment increases at 0.04 which is the average rate of the growth in autonomous demand.

A debt-pump starts developing although it is disguised by economic growth. The indebtedness ratios of households and firms will eventually rise but quite slowly. Government debt ratios diminish all the time due to the higher tax revenues accruing from economic prosperity.

Financial constraints

In Q11 the central bank doubles the official interest rate fearing an acceleration of inflation and the ongoing speculative bubbles in the real estate and stock exchanges. The market rate also doubles, shifting from 0.025 to 0.5. Other things stay the same, including the credit boom to finance residential and productive investment. The indebtedness ratios of households, firms and the nation as a whole speed up, but continue to be manageable.

Recession

In period 16 the economy enters into a deep recession due to the collapse of residential investment. From then on mortgage credits decrease at a rate of 25 per cent ($g_h = -0.25$) pushing down house prices ($g_{ph} = -0.1$). Autonomous consumption, fed by dividends and wealth effects, vanishes. Productive investment becomes nil since aggregate demand is not growing. Only government expenditure and exports continue their traditional patterns of expansion.

By checking demand, the recession helps to reduce primary deficits. But secondary deficits continue increasing as a consequence of the application of high interest rates on the enormous stock of debt inherited from the boom period. Since income is falling, the indebtedness coefficients rise very fast. Although the problem was created in the boom, it emerges in the recession.

Expansive fiscal policy

From periods 21 to 25, the government implements an expansive fiscal policy. It raises real public expenditure 10 per cent per year. The economy soon recovers a positive trend but not as fast as Keynesian economists would have expected. Private consumption and productive investment stay stuck, despite the impetus of the government. This failure has to do with the low value of the multiplier after the chronic increase in the burden of debt ($i \cdot \beta_h$). The original multiplier of 1.72, is only worth 0.92 in period 21. Aggregate income is supposed to rise after an increase in public investment financed with bonds, but just by the same amount (or less) of public expenditure. The magic of the Keynesian multiplier vanishes.

The balance sheets of agents are affected in different ways after the expansive fiscal policy. The fall in the indebtedness ratio of households is offset by the increase in the ratio of firms. The true cost of fiscal policy is an increase in the shares in income of the public deficit and sovereign debt.

Contractive fiscal policy

Fearing that the acceleration of public deficit may trigger the sovereign risk premium, the government moves towards a contractive fiscal policy. Public expenditure is frozen and the tax rate rises from 0.1 to 0.15.

By generating a recession, the austerity policy turns into a complete and utter failure. The fall in income checks the ongoing improvements in private balance sheets. The fall in tax receipts also deteriorated public finances. After a transient reduction in the deficit in period 26 (due to the application of a higher tax rate on a given income), the government indebtedness ratio rises as is illustrated in the intermediate panel of Figure 4.4. The "sovereign debt/national income" ratio rises steadily as we appreciate in the upper panel.

Conclusions and policy implications

In the introduction of this chapter we compared a debt trap to quicksand. In the following sections we realized how difficult it is to escape from it: whatever you do, you become more bogged down. Both in quicksand and debt traps, salvation is supposed to come from outside and requires the draining of the land/balance sheets.

The economic saviour has to be a powerful international agency, like the EU and the ECB. An economic draining implies the dilution of debt by shifting its burden to the future. To be efficient and fair, the cost of the operation should be shared by debtors and creditors, especially the banking system which played a major part in the financial mess leading to economic recession.

The dilution of debt requires a specific treatment for each agent. (a) Households unable to repay their mortgage should be allowed to free themselves from debts by handing over their house keys. (b) Indebted firms should be allowed to swap loans and bonds for equity. (c) Banks are supposed to balance loans with deposits and to pay passive interests from the interests earned on loans. Yet, during the crisis, they cannot be obliged to cover the losses resulting from accounting adjustments. Otherwise there would be no credit available for private investment. (d) The ECB should buy sovereign debt in the open market (at the current discount price) to avoid market pressure on interest rates. The new sovereign debt should be repaid over a longer period of time at a reasonable interest rate (let's say, 3 per cent instead of the 6 per cent that some governments are paying nowadays).

So far European policies have moved in a different direction. Instead of helping indebted countries from the outside, the EU urged governments to help banks and urged banks to help governments. Both of them ended up in a financial quagmire. Instead of rearranging debt obligations, the EU approved one bail-out plan after another. The international banking system got a warranty of their credits and bonds at the expense of tax payers. Instead of mobilizing credit towards productive activity, banks were obliged to use all their liquidity to recapitalize themselves. In addition, the EU urged governments to attain fiscal consolidation within a couple of years. The policy has been a resounding failure. In 2012 most economies entered into a second recession, while deficits and debt ratios continue to increase.

Keynesian economists know that austerity, when generalized, is self-defeating. But they should be humble enough to recognize that the expansive fiscal and monetary policies implemented in 2009 failed to stimulate private consumption and investment. As a result, public deficit rose to two digits and the burden of sovereign debt increased so much that the markets penalized some countries with high risk premiums.

The great depression of 1929 led Keynes to conclude that monetary policy ceased to be effective when it was most necessary: in a crisis dominated by a liquidity trap. The great recession of 2008 should lead Keynesians to conclude that expansive fiscal policy may be less effective in a crisis dominated by a debt trap. Our chapter shows that this failure is explained by three factors that depress the value of the multiplier: (a) the interest rate rises in parallel to the risk premium; (b) the disposable income of households falls due to the burden of private debt; (c) the propensity to consume falls when most households are obsessed with cancelling debt. If firms share the same obsession the acceleration mechanism breaks down too.

In our opinion, fiscal policy continues to be necessary but it should be implemented at a higher level (the European Union) and accommodated by the ECB that should act as lender of last resort. In the future, we shall reshape the financial system to avoid the reproduction of a credit/debt bomb. Right now, what matters is to dilute the burden of debt so that the economy can recover sooner and repay it little by little.

Appendix: paths of income and paths of debt

Data

Technology: $l=0.2$: labour coefficient (inverse of labour productivity). $k=4$: capital coefficient

Distribution: $w=4$: real wage; $i=0.25$: interest rate; $t=0.1$: tax rate

Propensities: $c_w=1$, propensity to consume out of disposable wages; $m=0.2$ import propensity.

Scenarios. They differ in the rate of change of autonomous demand and certain prices. (a) Period 1–3: all the elements of the autonomous demand (Z) grow at $g=0.025$; $i=0.025$. (b) From 4 to 15: acceleration of autonomous trends: $g(Ih)=0.1$; $g(Ph)=0.1$; $g(Ca)=0.05$. (c) From 11 to 30: $i=0.05$. (d) From 16 to 30: deceleration of autonomous trends: $g(Ih)=-0.25$; $g(Ph)=-0.1$; $g(Ca)=0$; $I=0$ during recession. (d) Period 21–25: expansive fiscal policy: $g(G)=0.2$. (e) Period 26–30: contractive fiscal policy: $g(G)=0$; $t=0.15$

Economic variables (the initial values appear in row 1)

Ih_t: residential investment; P_{ht}: price of houses; Ca_t: autonomous consumption; G_t: real public expenditure; X_t: exports; $Z_t=(Ih_t{\cdot}Ph_t)+Ca+G_t+X_t$: autonomous demand; $A_t=Z_t+I_t$: autonomous demand in a broad sense.

$I=kgD-a{\cdot}u'$: productive investment computed by a flexible accelerator. u' measures the deviation from normal capacity. The parameter a is obtained econometrically; here it has been fixed at $a=0.5$.

$\mu=1/(1-c_w{\cdot}\omega{\cdot}(1-t){\cdot}(1-i{\cdot}\beta)+m$: multiplier. $c_w=1$: propensity to consume out of wages; $\omega=W/Y$: share of wages in income; t: tax rate; i: interest rate; $\beta=BH/W$: indebtedness ratio of workers–households; m: import propensity.

$D_t=\mu{\cdot}(Z_t+I_t)=Yt$: expected demand to which production adjusts.

$Y_t=D_t-Ey_t$ (Positive excesses of inventories, E_y, should be subtracted from expected demand).

$KR_t=k{\cdot}Y_t$: required capital. $KI_t=KI_{t-1}+I_{t-1}$: installed capacity.

$u'=u_t-1=$deviation from normal capacity normalized at 1. $u_t=Y_t/Y^*_t$ actual rate of capacity utilization. $Y^*=KI_t{\cdot}(1/k)$: full capacity output.

$L_t=Y_t{\cdot}l$: employment. $W_t=w{\cdot}L_t$, wages. $R_t=Y_t-W_t$: profits. $r_t=R_t/KI_t$: current rate of profit. $T_t=t{\cdot}Y_t$: tax rate.

$YH'_t=W_t(1-t-i{\cdot}\beta)=W_t(1-t)-i{\cdot}BH_t$: disposable income of workers–households. BH_t is their accumulated debt.

YJ'_t: disposable income of rentiers–households = dividends + interest payments.

YE'_t: disposable income of firms. We suppose that firms distribute net profits to shareholders (after taxes and interest rates).

$YB'_t = T - i \cdot BG$: disposable income of government.
YN'_t: sum of domestic incomes. If we add net transfer to the rest of the world we get national income.
$C_t = c_w \cdot YH'_t$, private consumption.
$M = M' + M'' = m \cdot Y_t + E_{yt}$ (if there are shortage of inventories, negative E_{yt}).

Financial variables

Note that the absolute value is later divided by the primary income of each agent and by national income.

$BH'_t = YH'_t - C_t - (Ih_t \cdot Ph_t)$: need of borrowing of workers–households. Since $c_w = 1$, it coincides with mortgage credits $= Ih_t \cdot Ph_t$.
$BJ'_t = YH'_t - Ca$: need of borrowing of rentiers–households. Its negative sign implies that rentiers (and the financial sector they represent) are the source of all credits.
$BE'_t = YE'_t - I_t$: need of borrowing of firms. Since they distribute all profits (after taxes), it coincides with productive investment.
$BG'_t = YG'_t - G_t$: need of borrowing of government.
$BN'_t = (-1) \cdot (X_t - M_t - i \cdot BN_t)$: need of borrowing of the nation, it equals the current account deficit.
$BH_t = BH_{t-1} + BH'_{t-1}$: stock of debt of workers–households.
$BJ_t = BJ_{t-1} + BJ'_{t-1}$: stock of debt of rentiers–households. Its negative sign represents the outstanding loans of the banking sector.
$BE_t = BE_{t-1} + BE'_{t-1}$: outstanding debt of firms.
$BG_t = BG_{t-1} + BG'_{t-1}$: outstanding debt of government.
$BN_t = BN_{t-1} + BN'_{t-1}$: outstanding debt of the nation with foreign lenders.
Real inflow: loans to purchase produced goods and services. It is a "drive".
Outflow: interest payments and dividends that reduce disposable income and demand. It is a "drain".
ND: net drive = real inflow–outflow. (A negative value means a "drain" effect.)
nd: ND/Y = relative net drive.

Table 4.A.1a Real side: economic flows

	Ih	*Ph*	*Ca*	*G*	*X*	*Z*	*I*	*A*	*μ*	*D*	*Y*	*g(Y)*	*KR*	*KI*	*u'*
1	10.00	1.00	8.00	10.00	20.00	48.00	10.00	58.00	1.72	100.00	100.00		400.00	400	0.00
2	10.25	1.00	8.20	10.25	20.50	49.20	10.25	59.45	1.72	102.50	102.50	0.025	410.00	410.00	0.00
3	10.51	1.00	8.41	10.51	21.01	50.43	10.51	60.94	1.72	105.06	105.06	0.025	420.25	420.25	0.00
4	11.56	1.10	8.83	10.77	21.54	52.69	17.48	70.17	1.76	120.98	120.98	0.152	483.94	430.76	0.12
5	12.71	1.21	9.27	11.04	22.08	55.09	21.37	76.47	1.77	131.84	131.84	0.090	527.37	448.24	0.18
6	13.98	1.33	9.73	11.31	22.63	57.66	23.87	81.53	1.78	140.57	140.57	0.066	562.28	469.61	0.20
7	15.38	1.46	10.22	11.60	23.19	60.39	25.70	86.09	1.78	148.43	148.43	0.056	593.71	493.49	0.20
8	16.92	1.61	10.73	11.89	23.77	63.31	27.21	90.51	1.79	156.06	156.06	0.051	624.24	519.19	0.20
9	18.61	1.77	11.26	12.18	24.37	66.43	28.60	95.02	1.78	163.83	163.83	0.050	655.33	546.39	0.20
10	20.47	1.95	11.83	12.49	24.98	69.77	29.98	99.75	1.78	171.98	171.98	0.050	687.90	574.99	0.20
11	22.52	2.14	12.42	12.80	25.60	73.34	31.43	104.77	1.55	180.63	182.23	0.060	722.54	604.97	0.20
12	24.77	2.36	13.04	13.12	26.24	77.17	33.14	110.31	1.52	190.19	183.84	0.009	760.77	636.40	0.16
13	27.25	2.59	13.69	13.45	26.90	81.29	34.11	115.40	1.51	198.96	193.78	0.054	795.84	669.53	0.16
14	29.98	2.85	14.38	13.79	27.57	85.71	35.72	121.42	1.49	209.35	202.87	0.047	837.41	703.64	0.15
15	32.97	3.14	15.09	14.13	28.26	90.46	37.51	127.96	1.47	220.62	213.21	0.051	882.50	739.36	0.15
16	24.73	2.82	0.00	14.48	28.97	68.18	39.53	107.71	1.30	185.70	168.18	−0.211	742.82	776.86	−0.13
17	18.55	2.54	0.00	14.85	29.69	63.08	28.83	91.91	1.17	158.47	137.13	−0.185	633.88	816.39	−0.33
18	13.91	2.29	0.00	15.22	30.43	59.56	22.04	81.60	1.05	140.69	114.97	−0.162	562.77	845.22	−0.46
19	10.43	2.06	0.00	15.60	31.19	57.22	18.07	75.30	0.97	129.82	102.07	−0.112	519.29	867.27	−0.53
20	7.82	1.85	0.00	15.99	31.97	55.78	15.89	71.67	0.92	123.57	94.11	−0.078	494.28	885.34	−0.57
21	5.87	1.67	0.00	17.59	32.77	56.23	0.00	56.23	0.74	96.94	66.60	−0.292	387.77	901.23	−0.70
22	4.40	1.50	0.00	19.34	33.59	57.34	0.00	57.34	0.73	98.86	65.55	−0.016	395.43	901.23	−0.71
23	3.30	1.35	0.00	21.28	34.43	59.01	0.00	59.01	0.76	101.74	69.56	0.061	406.97	901.23	−0.69
24	2.48	1.22	0.00	23.41	35.29	61.17	0.00	61.17	0.78	105.47	72.71	0.045	421.89	901.23	−0.68
25	1.86	1.09	0.00	25.75	36.17	63.78	0.00	63.78	0.81	109.96	77.63	0.068	439.85	901.23	−0.66
26	1.39	1.00	0.00	25.75	37.08	64.22	0.00	64.22	0.79	110.72	78.48	0.011	442.88	901.23	−0.65
27	1.04	1.00	0.00	25.75	38.01	64.80	0.00	64.80	0.77	111.72	76.27	−0.028	446.87	901.23	−0.66
28	0.78	1.00	0.00	25.75	38.96	65.49	0.00	65.49	0.79	112.91	79.11	0.037	451.63	901.23	−0.65
29	0.59	1.00	0.00	25.75	39.93	66.26	0.00	66.26	0.79	114.25	79.61	0.006	456.99	901.23	−0.65
30	0.44	1.00	0.00	25.75	40.93	67.12	0.00	67.12	0.80	115.72	81.56	0.024	462.86	901.23	−0.64

	L	*W*	*R*	*r'*	*T*	*YH'*	*YJ'*	*YE'*	*YG'*	*YN'*	*C*	*M'*	*E(y)*	*M''*	
1	20.00	80.00	20.00	0.050	10.00	62.00	12.00	16.00	8.00	98.00	62.00	20.00	0.00	0	1
2	20.50	82.00	20.50	0.050	10.25	63.55	12.30	16.40	8.20	100.45	63.55	20.50	0.00	0	2
3	21.01	84.05	21.01	0.050	10.51	65.14	12.61	16.81	8.41	102.96	65.14	21.01	0.00	0	3
4	24.20	96.79	24.20	0.056	12.10	76.34	12.92	19.62	9.94	118.83	76.34	24.20	−1.33	1.33	4
5	26.37	105.47	26.37	0.059	13.18	83.84	13.27	21.41	11.01	129.53	83.84	26.37	−2.10	2.10	5
6	28.11	112.46	28.11	0.060	14.06	89.74	13.67	22.75	11.88	138.05	89.74	28.11	−2.59	2.59	6
7	29.69	118.74	29.69	0.060	14.84	94.93	14.13	23.89	12.68	145.64	94.93	29.69	−2.91	2.91	7
8	31.21	124.85	31.21	0.060	15.61	99.86	14.66	24.97	13.47	152.97	99.86	31.21	−3.11	3.11	8
9	32.77	131.07	32.77	0.060	16.38	104.78	15.29	26.04	14.29	160.40	104.78	32.77	−3.20	3.20	9
10	34.40	137.58	34.40	0.060	17.20	109.82	16.03	27.16	15.16	168.16	109.82	34.40	−3.19	3.19	10
11	36.45	145.78	36.45	0.060	18.22	101.20	33.83	24.48	14.27	173.79	101.20	36.45	12.71	0	11
12	36.77	147.07	36.77	0.058	18.38	99.94	36.17	23.80	14.51	174.43	99.94	36.77	10.35	0	12
13	38.76	155.03	38.76	0.058	19.38	104.19	39.15	24.48	15.57	183.38	104.19	38.76	12.96	0	13
14	40.57	162.30	40.57	0.058	20.29	107.19	42.63	24.95	16.59	191.35	107.19	40.57	14.83	0	14
15	42.64	170.57	42.64	0.058	21.32	110.36	46.80	25.55	17.76	200.47	110.36	42.64	17.53	0	15
16	33.64	134.54	33.64	0.043	16.82	72.76	51.78	16.09	13.44	154.07	72.76	33.64	21.34	0	16
17	27.43	109.70	27.43	0.034	13.71	46.92	55.56	9.33	10.28	122.09	46.92	27.43	25.73	0	17
18	22.99	91.97	22.99	0.027	11.50	28.60	58.48	4.37	7.84	99.29	28.60	22.99	27.76	0	18
19	20.41	81.65	20.41	0.024	10.21	17.72	60.92	1.16	6.18	85.98	17.72	20.41	29.46	0	19
20	18.82	75.29	18.82	0.021	9.41	10.92	63.04	−1.12	4.91	77.75	10.92	18.82	30.34	0	20
21	13.32	53.28	13.32	0.015	6.66	−9.61	65.01	−6.92	1.61	50.08	−9.61	13.32	33.31	0	21
22	13.11	52.44	13.11	0.015	6.55	−10.86	66.79	−7.45	0.70	49.18	−10.86	13.11	32.18	0	22
23	13.91	55.65	13.91	0.015	6.96	−8.30	68.63	−7.11	0.17	53.40	−8.30	13.91	32.76	0	23
24	14.54	58.17	14.54	0.016	7.27	−6.26	70.48	−6.89	−0.57	56.76	−6.26	14.54	32.33	0	24
25	15.53	62.10	15.53	0.017	7.76	−2.87	72.42	−6.35	−1.28	61.92	−2.87	15.53	32.24	0	25
26	15.70	62.78	15.70	0.017	11.77	−5.49	74.44	−7.30	1.38	63.02	−5.49	15.70	35.45	0	26
27	15.25	61.01	15.25	0.017	11.44	−7.07	76.38	−8.04	−0.17	61.11	−7.07	15.25	33.79	0	27
28	15.82	63.29	15.82	0.018	11.87	−5.18	78.51	−7.96	−1.04	64.33	−5.18	15.82	34.64	0	28
29	15.92	63.69	15.92	0.018	11.94	−4.88	80.71	−8.28	−2.30	65.25	−4.88	15.92	34.16	0	29
30	16.31	65.25	16.31	0.018	12.23	−3.59	83.04	−8.36	−3.41	67.68	−3.59	16.31	34.35	0	30

Table 4.A.1b Financial side: flows and stocks of debt

	BH'	*/W*	*/Y*	*BJ'*	*/Y*	*BE'*	*/R*	*/Y*	*BG'*	*/T*	*/Y*	*BN'*	*/Y*	*BH*	*/W*
														400	5
1	10.00	0.13	0.10	–4.00	–0.04	2.00	0.10	0.02	2.00	0.20	0.02	2.00	0.02	410	5.00
2	10.25	0.13	0.10	–4.10	–0.04	2.05	0.10	0.02	2.05	0.20	0.02	2.05	0.02	420	5.00
3	10.51	0.13	0.10	–4.20	–0.04	2.10	0.10	0.02	2.10	0.20	0.02	2.10	0.02	431	5.00
4	12.71	0.13	0.11	–4.10	–0.03	6.68	0.28	0.06	0.82	0.07	0.01	6.14	0.05	443	4.45
5	15.38	0.15	0.12	–4.01	–0.03	9.23	0.35	0.07	0.03	0.00	0.00	8.70	0.07	459	4.20
6	18.61	0.17	0.13	–3.94	–0.03	10.85	0.39	0.08	–0.57	–0.04	0.00	10.60	0.08	477	4.08
7	22.52	0.19	0.15	–3.91	–0.03	12.02	0.40	0.08	–1.08	–0.07	–0.01	12.19	0.08	500	4.02
8	27.25	0.22	0.17	–3.94	–0.03	12.97	0.42	0.08	–1.59	–0.10	–0.01	13.64	0.09	527	4.00
9	32.97	0.25	0.20	–4.02	–0.02	13.82	0.42	0.08	–2.11	–0.13	–0.01	15.04	0.09	560	4.02
10	39.90	0.29	0.23	–4.20	–0.02	14.64	0.43	0.09	–2.67	–0.16	–0.02	16.42	0.10	600	4.07
11	48.28	0.33	0.26	–21.41	–0.12	19.36	0.53	0.11	–1.47	–0.08	–0.01	19.29	0.11	648	4.12
12	58.41	0.40	0.32	–23.13	–0.13	22.37	0.61	0.12	–1.39	–0.08	–0.01	19.93	0.11	707	4.41
13	70.68	0.46	0.36	–25.46	–0.13	23.32	0.60	0.12	–2.12	–0.11	–0.01	22.26	0.11	777	4.56
14	85.52	0.53	0.42	–28.25	–0.14	25.15	0.62	0.12	–2.80	–0.14	–0.01	24.52	0.12	863	4.79
15	103.48	0.61	0.49	–31.70	–0.15	27.05	0.63	0.13	–3.63	–0.17	–0.02	27.13	0.13	966	5.06
16	69.85	0.52	0.42	–51.78	–0.31	23.44	0.70	0.14	1.04	0.06	0.01	18.77	0.11	1036	7.18
17	47.15	0.43	0.34	–55.56	–0.41	19.50	0.71	0.14	4.56	0.33	0.03	12.77	0.09	1083	9.45
18	31.83	0.35	0.28	–58.48	–0.51	17.68	0.77	0.15	7.38	0.64	0.06	8.24	0.07	1115	11.78
19	21.48	0.26	0.21	–60.92	–0.60	16.91	0.83	0.17	9.42	0.92	0.09	5.31	0.05	1137	13.66
20	14.50	0.19	0.15	–63.04	–0.67	17.00	0.90	0.18	11.07	1.18	0.12	3.20	0.03	1151	15.10
21	9.79	0.18	0.15	–65.01	–0.98	6.92	0.52	0.10	15.98	2.40	0.24	–2.94	–0.04	1161	21.61
22	6.61	0.13	0.10	–66.79	–1.02	7.45	0.57	0.11	18.64	2.84	0.28	–4.11	–0.06	1168	22.14
23	4.46	0.08	0.06	–68.63	–0.99	7.11	0.51	0.10	21.11	3.03	0.30	–4.36	–0.06	1172	20.98
24	3.01	0.05	0.04	–70.48	–0.97	6.89	0.47	0.09	23.97	3.30	0.33	–4.81	–0.07	1175	20.15
25	2.03	0.03	0.03	–72.42	–0.93	6.35	0.41	0.08	27.02	3.48	0.35	–4.94	–0.06	1177	18.92
26	1.39	0.02	0.02	–74.44	–0.95	7.30	0.47	0.09	24.36	2.07	0.31	–5.93	–0.08	1179	18.75
27	1.04	0.02	0.01	–76.38	–1.00	8.04	0.53	0.11	25.91	2.27	0.34	–7.59	–0.10	1180	19.32
28	0.78	0.01	0.01	–78.51	–0.99	7.96	0.50	0.10	26.78	2.26	0.34	–8.35	–0.11	1180	18.64
29	0.59	0.01	0.01	–80.71	–1.01	8.28	0.52	0.10	28.05	2.35	0.35	–9.64	–0.12	1181	18.53
30	0.44	0.01	0.01	–83.04	–1.02	8.36	0.51	0.10	29.16	2.38	0.36	–10.73	–0.13	1181	18.10

	/Y	*BJ*	*/Y*	*BE*	*/R*	*/Y*	*BG*	*/T*	*/Y*	*BN*	*/Y*	*/X*	*ND*	*nd*	
		–480		80			80			80					
1	4.00	–484	–4.80	82	4.00	0.80	82	8.00	0.80	82	0.80	4.00	0.00	0.00	1
2	4.00	–488	–4.72	84	4.00	0.80	84	8.00	0.80	84	0.80	4.00	0.00	0.00	2
3	4.00	–492	–4.65	86	4.00	0.80	86	8.00	0.80	86	0.80	4.00	0.00	0.00	3
4	3.56	–496	–4.07	93	3.56	0.71	87	7.12	0.71	92	0.71	4.00	3.99	0.03	4
5	3.36	–500	–3.77	102	3.52	0.70	87	6.60	0.66	101	0.70	4.18	6.39	0.05	5
6	3.26	–504	–3.56	113	3.63	0.73	86	6.19	0.62	112	0.72	4.46	8.07	0.06	6
7	3.22	–508	–3.40	125	3.80	0.76	85	5.82	0.58	124	0.75	4.81	9.40	0.06	7
8	3.20	–512	–3.26	138	4.00	0.80	84	5.47	0.55	137	0.79	5.21	10.54	0.07	8
9	3.22	–516	–3.13	152	4.21	0.84	82	5.11	0.51	152	0.84	5.64	11.60	0.07	9
10	3.26	–520	–3.00	166	4.41	0.88	79	4.75	0.47	169	0.89	6.10	12.61	0.07	10
11	3.29	–542	–2.86	186	4.56	0.91	78	4.33	0.43	188	0.93	6.60	19.27	0.11	11
12	3.53	–565	–2.95	208	5.05	1.01	76	4.22	0.42	208	1.02	7.17	22.97	0.12	12
13	3.65	–590	–2.92	231	5.37	1.07	74	3.93	0.39	230	1.07	7.74	23.68	0.12	13
14	3.83	–619	–2.91	257	5.70	1.14	71	3.65	0.36	255	1.14	8.36	25.25	0.12	14
15	4.05	–650	–2.90	284	6.02	1.20	68	3.34	0.33	282	1.20	9.02	26.62	0.12	15
16	5.75	–702	–3.87	307	8.43	1.69	69	4.02	0.40	301	1.68	9.74	16.27	0.10	16
17	7.56	–758	–5.12	327	11.20	2.24	73	5.00	0.50	314	2.19	10.13	7.31	0.05	17
18	9.42	–816	–6.59	344	14.20	2.84	81	6.37	0.64	322	2.73	10.30	1.89	0.02	18
19	10.93	–877	–8.00	361	16.86	3.37	90	7.89	0.79	327	3.15	10.32	–1.74	–0.02	19
20	12.08	–940	–9.32	378	19.19	3.84	101	9.56	0.96	330	3.48	10.23	–3.79	–0.04	20
21	17.29	–1005	–14.12	385	28.39	5.68	117	15.17	1.52	327	4.96	10.08	–12.00	–0.18	21
22	17.71	–1072	–15.33	393	29.37	5.87	136	17.85	1.79	323	4.99	9.75	–11.08	–0.17	22
23	16.79	–1141	–15.41	400	28.21	5.64	157	19.50	1.95	319	4.65	9.39	–10.89	–0.16	23
24	16.12	–1211	–15.69	407	27.48	5.50	181	21.56	2.16	314	4.39	9.04	–9.87	–0.14	24
25	15.14	–1284	–15.60	413	26.18	5.24	208	23.28	2.33	309	4.05	8.68	–8.83	–0.11	25
26	15.00	–1358	–16.35	420	26.31	5.26	232	17.65	2.65	303	3.94	8.34	–11.89	–0.15	26
27	15.45	–1434	–17.80	428	27.55	5.51	258	20.29	3.04	296	3.98	7.98	–10.77	–0.14	27
28	14.91	–1513	–18.13	436	27.06	5.41	285	21.75	3.26	287	3.74	7.59	–11.12	–0.14	28
29	14.83	–1594	–19.00	444	27.39	5.48	313	23.85	3.58	278	3.61	7.19	–10.63	–0.13	29
30	14.48	–1677	–19.54	453	27.25	5.45	342	25.57	3.84	267	3.40	6.78	–10.50	–0.13	30

Notes

1 During the glittering age, autonomous consumption (consistent in luxury goods) came from rich households, getting property rents and capital gains.
2 The direction of causality is important. The Ricardian theory of rent concludes that after an increase in the prices of houses (due to an increase in demand), builders will agree to pay more for the land they need. The ultimate winners will be the owners of the strips of previously worthless land. A redistribution of wealth occurs. National accounts will just reflect the increasing transfers from borrowers (worker–households) to lenders (banks and rentiers–households).
3 If the loan is perpetual, expression [4.2] shrinks to: $p_h = f/i$.
4 The reaction of firms to shortages of capacity depends on the parameter *a*. It is supposed to be higher than one, but just enough to get rid of shortages of capacity.
5 Fearing inflation, central banks raised the official interest rates. After realizing their dangerous exposure to the construction business, retail banks raised the gap between the official rate and the market rate of interest.
6 Consider also the negative impact on investment and growth that may result from an increase in interest rates.

References

Bortis, H. (1997). *Institutions, Behaviour and Economic Theory*. Cambridge, UK: Cambridge University Press.

Dejuán, Ó. (2002). El tipo de interés: ese frágil eslabón entre el circuito económico real y financiero. In Oscar Dejuán and Eladio Febrero (eds), *La fragilidad financiera del capitalismo* (pp. 77–96). Cuenca: Universidad de Castilla – La Mancha.

Dejuán, Ó. (2005). Paths of accumulation and growth: towards a Keynesian long-period theory of output. *Review of Political Economy, 17*(2), 231–252.

Dejuán, Ó. and Febrero, E. (2010). The failure of a path of growth driven by household indebtedness (Spain, 1997–2009). *Économie Apliquée, LXIII*(1), 63–78.

Eatwell, J. (1983). The long period theory of employment. *Cambridge Journal of Economics, 7*, 269–285.

Godley, W. and Lavoie, M. (2006). *Monetary Economics: An Integrated Approach to Credit, Money, Income, Production and Wealth*. New York: Palgrave.

Graziani, A. (2003). *The Monetary Theory of Production*. New York: Cambridge University Press.

Hein, E. (2012). *The Macroeconomics of Finance-Dominated Capitalism: And its Critics*. Cheltenham, UK: Edward Elgar.

Kalecki, M. (1971). *Selected Essays in the Dynamics of the Capitalist Economy (1933–1970)*. Cambridge, UK: Cambridge University Press.

Keynes, J. M. (1936). *The General Theory of Employment, Interest and Money*. London and New York: Harcourt Brace Jovanovich.

Leamer, E. (2007). Housing is the business cycle. *NBER Working Papers* (13428).

Minsky, H. P. (1975). *John Maynard Keynes*. New York: Columbia University Press.

Minsky, H. P. and Papadimitriou, D. (2004). *Induced Investment and Business Cycles*. Cheltenham, UK: Edward Elgar.

Serrano, F. (1995). Long period effective demand and the Sraffian supermultiplier. *Contributions to Political Economy, 14*, 67–90.

Sraffa, P. (1960). *Production of Commodities by Means of Commodities: Prelude to a Critique of Economic Theory*. Cambridge, UK: Cambridge University Press.

Part II

The balance of payments constraint

Trade deficits as a source of risky debt

5 Controversial and novel features of the Eurozone crisis as a balance of payment crisis[1]

Sergio Cesaratto

Europe and the 'this time is different' syndrome

The European crisis appears as the nth 'this time is different' episode of the financial liberalisation sequence cum fixed exchange rates, capital flows from the centre to the periphery, housing bubble, current account (CA) deficit and indebtedness, default. Although I find Reinhart and Rogoff (2009) to be a poorly organised account of the history and nature of defaults, their title really conveys the sense of a recurring pattern of unfortunate events (a better summary is Reinhart 2011). The title of a seminal paper 'Good-bye financial repression, hello financial crash?' (Diaz-Alejandro 1985) also sums up the essence of those events.

In this chapter I examine some explanations that have been given for the nature of the balance of payments (BoP) disequilibrium of the Eurozone (EZ) members in relation also to the presumed German mercantilism (second, third and fourth sections). I then discuss two interpretations of the causes of the rise in the sovereign spread of periphery countries (fifth section) that pay insufficient attention to the EZ BoP crisis. Finally, I shall focus on the novel and controversial features of the EZ BoP crisis compared to previous experiences and particularly on the role of the European Central Bank in refinancing banks in peripheral countries (final two sections).

The neoclassical view

According to conventional theory, international trade and factors' mobility are substitutes (Mundell 1957). An advanced country, for instance, might export goods and services produced with relative high capital/labour intensive techniques, and import labour-intensive commodities or, alternatively, export capital and import labour. In both cases, factors' marginal products would level off globally and per-capita incomes would converge. Accordingly, conventional economists were convinced that capital flows from industrialised to catching up countries, from countries where capital is relatively abundant and their 'marginal product' relatively low to countries where capital is scarce, were proving their theory (cf. e.g. Holinski *et al.* 2012: 3). Blanchard and Giavazzi (2002: 148; see also 154–5; B&G hereafter), for instance, championed this view in a paper in which they examined the Portuguese and Greek cases. Impressively cool and prescient was the comment to B&G by Pierre-Oliver Gourinchas (2002: 204) who promptly recognised in the Portuguese and Greek experience a reminiscence of the still fresh standard Latin-American events (particularly Argentina's default in the same year).

In this regard, two aspects will be outlined here. In the first place, in the case of open economies, no less than in closed economies, the idea that core countries' savings find an automatic debouche in investment in periphery countries depends on the neoclassical saving–investment relationship and it is therefore subject to the Keynesian and capital theory critiques (Garegnani 1983). In other words, in the non-orthodox context there is no automatic mechanism that translates a larger (potential) saving supply into domestic or foreign investment since a fall in the rate of interest does not affect investment either in the domestic economy or in that of other countries. So in an open economy, no less than in a closed one, it is investment that – both in the short and long run – determines saving (both domestic and foreign). The world economy is, after all, a closed economy (Dalziel and Harcourt 1997: 628).

Second, a trade deficit is not necessarily generated by an investment boom financed by foreign financial capital inflows: these flows may well, and more likely will, finance consumption booms (Prasad *et al.* 2007). The fact that a CA deficit corresponds to the excess of domestic investment over national saving may mistakenly lead people to believe that foreign saving is financing an investment boom. It is not necessarily so, as an example in Note 1 promptly shows.[2]

The conventional approach to international capital flows, according to which surplus countries – those which present an excess of domestic saving over domestic investment – lend this excess to borrowing countries (those who invest more than the domestic saving supply) should be so re-expressed. In the absence of controls over capital inflows and assured by commitments to pegged exchange rates, the international and domestic private financial institutions are able to create credit facilities in periphery countries that typically finance housing bubbles rather than investment in the tradable sector. The increasing demand of imports from core countries generates, for a given domestic autonomous demand, the 'twin surpluses' in these countries – an excess of savings over public and/or private consumption and a current account surplus – and the corresponding 'twin deficits' in the periphery countries.

The German view

A variation of the neoclassical story has been proposed by the influential German economist Werner Sinn (e.g. 2012; CESifo 2011). Summing up, he maintains that the capital outflows from Germany impoverished the investment capacity of his country and this (and not the repression of domestic consumption) would explain Germany's low growth in the European Monetary Union (EMU) pre-crisis decade. After the crisis, capital outflows ended. The ensuing recovery of investment reinforced by wage moderation, so the argument goes, led to the German recovery in spite of the periphery troubles.

It may, in the first place, be asked why the EMU favoured credit demand in the periphery and not in Germany. One may dare to think that, on the one hand, countries such as Spain and Ireland were already in a process of catching up, while suffering from financial repression – for instance, mortgages were available only at high interest rates and for a short duration, the opposite happened after the EMU. This attracted foreign financial flows. On the other hand the German market was unpromising as far as investment was concerned: wage moderation, the traditional German household aversion for debt and the low propensity towards home-ownership. So credit went where the economic climate was more favourable to autonomous (credit financed) spending decisions. In no sense, moreover, could financial flows to the periphery have constrained credit availability in Germany. Sinn clearly argues as if a *given* amount of German saving was available for alternative purposes, either in the core or in the periphery. But, as has already been said, German savings are the end result of a financial circuit which starts from the creation of purchasing power by peripheral or subsidiaries of core banks in favour of autonomous spending in the periphery. German (foreign) savings are thus the outcome of (actually by definition identical to) the German foreign trade surplus – more precisely of its current account surplus.

In the second place, the general opinion is that the German recovery in mid-2010 has been led by exports (who would say otherwise?) to extra-EZ markets and certainly not by investment driven by the 'capital reversal' that followed the crisis. Export growth was the result both of the good performance of the emerging economies and of the euro depreciation against the US $ and, in particular, against the yen – that helped German exports in China. According to Professor Makoto (2012) the 'Euro's exchange rate against a dollar has fallen from around 1.6 dollars in 2008 to 1.31 dollars, about 20 per cent, and against yen from 160 yen to 100 yen, about 38 per cent'.

A big fuss was also raised by Professor Sinn in late spring 2011 when he accused the ECB of providing unlimited financial support to the periphery countries with persisting current account deficits and capital flights. The story has to do with a complicated mechanism through which the ECB manages in an ordered way the payments flow within the EZ, called TARGET 2 (T2), that involves the Eurosystem central banks (CBs) along with the ECB itself (Garber 2010). As explained, e.g. by Febrero *et al.* (2012; see also Cesaratto 2013), credit that finances net imports in the EZ periphery is created by local banks. This spending eventually becomes foreign saving (net exports) in core countries and, normally, financial lending by core EZ banks to periphery banks. To simplify, whenever a Greek citizen borrowed money from a Greek bank in order to buy a German commodity, the German exporter would eventually lend to the Greek bank, through its German bank, the revenues received as payment for its exports. Ordinarily, the ECB is involved in this circuit only as an intermediary, as a clearing house. Since 2008 onwards, however, Germans began to distrust the solvency of the peripheral European countries and stopped the recycling of their export revenues. These earnings began, therefore, to remain deposited in the very German banks that re-deposited them, via the Bundesbank, in the ECB. Once the interbank market fails, it was the selfsame ECB that, as part of its normal duty as a Central Bank in a currency union, began to replenish the reserves of the peripheral banks. Sinn does not seem mistaken in calling our attention to the role of the ECB in making European imbalances financially sustainable – although he typically overstretches his case to maximise the German role as a victim. What Sinn fails to see, indeed, is that the ECB, by constantly refinancing German exports towards the periphery, is actually preventing the circuit from collapsing.[3] In addition, as the crisis unfolded, in order to keep the financial system stable, the ECB's refinancing operations also make good the capital flights from the peripheral to the core European banks by replenishing, in practice, the peripheral banks' reserves. This is mirrored by a T2 liability of the peripheral CBs at the ECB. Symmetrically, in this case, the capital outflows from the periphery that reach, say, German banks are re-deposited, via Buba, in the ECB. This is mirrored by a T2 net claim of the Bundesbank. (I shall return to T2 in the sixth section of the chapter.)

The Kaleckian view

Championed by Martin Wolf (2012), the interpretation of the European crisis as a BoP crisis is becoming dominant. Accordingly, the cause of the crisis must be found in the easier access for a number of peripheral EMU countries to the European financial markets at low nominal interest rates. Financial liberalisation and the removal of the exchange rate risk encouraged massive capital flows from core to periphery countries in the 'periphery' (see: Merler and Pisani-Ferry 2012; Bagnai this volume; Tilford and Whyte 2011: 4; Jaumotte and Sodsriwiboon, 2010: 8–9; European Commission 2009, 2010). Credit-financed autonomous consumption determined a growth both of domestic demand and of nominal wages higher than in core EZ. Higher inflation rates in the periphery determined low real interest rates, a further support to domestic demand. The growth of domestic demand was associated to a housing bubble in Spain and Ireland, and to the growth of public spending in Greece. This sequel of events, and its consequences, foreign indebtedness and 'sudden capital stops' are basically not so different from those that typically took place in developing countries and ended in sovereign defaults (Diaz-Alejandro 1985; Frenkel and Rapetti 2009: 688–9; Reinhart 2011: 27–9).

These events took place in a context in which monetary policy was tailored to core Europe. Nechio (2011) shows how much the ECB monetary policy followed a mechanical application of the Taylor's Rule applied to core Europe. Of course, I do not subscribe to the Taylor's Rule and the idea that monetary policy should have, as a consequence, been more restrictive, quite the opposite: rather fiscal and wage policies in the core should have been much slacker. Had monetary policy been more restrictive, given the German austerity stance, the

EZ would have avoided its foreign imbalances but at the price of a generalised stagnation. The ECB policy stance is also indicative of the (self-interested) 'benign neglect' under which light the effects of financial liberalisation and the mounting European imbalances had been looked at up to the crisis.

Growth based on the construction sector is ephemeral, i.e. it usually does not generate significant productivity and export growth (this seems particularly true for Spain and Greece; Ireland has a strong export sector based on FDI). Moreover, the above-average *nominal* wage dynamic (although not the *real* dynamic), led periphery countries to a progressive loss of international competitiveness. The combination of bubbly imports and inadequate exports led them to persistent current account deficits and to the deterioration of their net international investment position (NIIP). *Core* Europe's exports benefited from these events because they compensated for their languid domestic demand. Parallel to the deficit countries, in Germany domestic demand stagnated due to wage moderation, an outcome of the labour market reforms carried out by Schroeder's government, restrictive fiscal policies and relatively high real interest rates (in opposition to the low real interest rates of the inflation-prone periphery).[4]

In this respect, Cesaratto and Stirati (2011) see continuity with what an important German economic historian has defined as 'Monetary Mercantilism' (Holtfrerich 2008: 34; see also Holtfrerich 1999: 242–3 *et passim*), a strategy inaugurated in the early 1950s under the auspices of Erhard. Taking advantage of fixed exchange rates, as during the Bretton Woods epoch, the German strategy was to maintain the inflation rate a little below that of competitors to sustain exports while enjoying a strong currency. The three institutional pillars of 'monetary mercantilism' are: neo-corporativism, mercantilist micro and macro institutions and policies, and the Bundesbank.

The former implied a direct involvement of the labour movement both at the micro and the macro level in the maintenance of a competitive system, particularly in the export sector (Carlin and Soskice 2009). At the micro level Germany has an excellent training, educational and R&D system while the reliance on export-led growth creates an ideological climate that induces cooperation and discipline (Crouch 2008). At the macro level the system keeps wage growth below or in line with productivity growth. Paternalism is a traditional attitude of the German government, while its domestic and foreign policies prioritise German exports. The sense of the national community, traditions and nature are the main components of the 'German ideology'. This model suits the mercantilist tradition perfectly, particularly the German version of it (Cameralism, Historical School, cf. Riha 1985: chs 4 and 5). But, of course, as Voltaire said (and the late Vianello liked to repeat): 'Incantations will destroy a flock of sheep if administered with a certain quantity of arsenic'. The watchdog role of the model was thus assumed by the Bundesbank in a unique wage bargaining process directly involving the CB and the leading trade union IG-Metall (Franzese and Hall 2000: 182–3). This role of the Bundesbank as the watchdog of the German mercantilist model is very important to understand German opposition to the reform of the ECB from its present 'monetarist' constitution. The German export-oriented policy was widely criticised by its Keynesian-oriented Western partners during the 1950s and later, up until the criticism of German passivity vis-à-vis growing world unemployment in the second half of the 1970s (when international Keynesianism lived out its final swansong with the locomotive theory). With the European Monetary System and later with the EMU, Italy, France and the other European peripheral partners wanted to imitate Germany and 'German discipline'.[5]

In the light of Kaleckian theory, 'Monetary Mercantilism' is a perfect strategy for capitalists: low domestic wages (relative to productivity) imply a high surplus (i.e. capitalists' profits) that can be successfully sold in the uncompetitive periphery. The financial capital flows provide the periphery with the purchasing power required to absorb the core capitalists' surplus. More specifically, mercantilism regarded the trade surplus as the only net wealth source for the nation. This is a nebulous idea, but it makes sense in a Kaleckian/Rosa Luxemburg context. The surplus (S) in a Classical–Marxian–Sraffian approach is that part of the social product (P) left to the capitalists as profits, once the 'necessities' (N) to the workers have been paid: $P-N=S$ (Garegnani 1984). Exports are a way to realise (in a Marxian sense) the surplus. Assuming that the social product is composed by the necessities N and net exports $E-M$, then: $P=N+(E-M)$. It follows that: $S=E-M$, net exports are equal to capitalists' profits. According to Kalecki the central countries must 'export' financial capital first in order to export physical goods later[6] (what happened in the EMU and also with a number of Eastern-Europe and Baltic states). Of course, the limit is that deficit countries may not be able, in the long run, to redeem their debt (but, paraphrasing Kalecki, capitalists do many things as a class, yet they do not plan the international trade as a class).

The controversial rise of sovereign spreads

From the blast of the global crisis in 2008 until spring 2011 Italy had somehow managed to escape unnoticed by the financial markets by not adopting any anti-cyclical budget policy although at the price of the largest fall in GDP in 2009 among OECD countries. After all, the high Italian public debt (PD) had existed for three decades without a major financial crisis. The spreads between Italian ten-year Treasury bonds and the analogous German Bunds reached unsustainable levels within a few months when competing with the Spanish ones.

After the rise of Spanish and Italian sovereign spreads, many economists begun to puzzle over why Japan, with a much higher PD/GDP ratio was paying much lower interest rates (e.g. Krugman 2011). We can envisage two positions with regard to this. On the one hand, there are those (e.g. Gros 2011) who maintain that the puzzle is mainly to do with the proportion of PD held by foreigners, relatively high in the case of European periphery countries. On the other hand, there are those (e.g. Nersisyan and Wray 2010 and their Modern Monetary Theory (MMT) disciples) who maintain that the key explanation of the relative height of sovereign spreads is in the backing or not of a sovereign CB (SCB), national or, in a currency union, super-national. Both these are only partially true.

Public debt sustainability in a closed economy with a sovereign currency

Let us begin by discussing the sustainability of PD in a closed economy with an SCB – so none of the causes of the relative higher spreads, a relatively high foreign ownership of the PD or the absence of a SCB are present.[7] The main thesis in favour of PD sustainability in a closed economy with a sovereign currency[8] is that in economies in which the private sector is unable to generate sufficient demand to lead to the full utilisation of output capacity, public deficits generate income and savings so that the private sector would voluntarily and happily absorb the newly emitted government bonds. Hence,

> a superior limit to the ratio debt/income would entail, ceteris paribus, envisaging a limit to the accumulation of wealth and to the income levels the private sector may achieve, that evidently renders the imposition of such limits as unacceptable without any adequate justification.
>
> (Ciccone 2002: 128–9, my translation)

While Ciccone's implicit emphasis is on the (real) Keynesian multiplier process whereby government deficit generates the savings that eventually finance it, the MMT leitmotiv is rather on the monetary mechanisms whereby the government spends first by crediting private bank accounts or by drawing a cheque on its CB account, without having to tax or issue any bonds in advance (cf. Lavoie 2011: 12–19 for a clarification of the mechanisms behind these statements).[9] In both perspectives no obvious limit can be envisaged with regard to the PD/GDP ratio as far as, for instance, a public deficit is necessary to keep capacity at full utilisation or reach full employment.

Actually, any expenditure financed out of purchasing power creation, either by public or private subjects, generates, within the limits of existing capacity, additional financial wealth for the remaining subjects. Wray distinguishes between 'inside' and 'outside' debt. The former is held, for instance, by a household relative to another household (that holds 'inside wealth'), while 'if the domestic private sector taken as a whole spends more than its income, it must issue "outside debt" held as "outside wealth" by at least one of the other two sectors (domestic government sector and foreign sector)' (Wray 2011b). So the specific difference between public and private debt is that the former sector, *so long as it controls a sovereign bank*, can issue at will the monetary equivalent of its debt, 'monetise' it for short. As a result, it cannot by definition default and PDs appear less fragile than private debts (e.g. Wray 2006: 4).

A monetisation of PD would take place if the private sector (we are assuming a closed economy), for some reason preoccupied with the solvency of the State, refused to subscribe new or rolled-over treasury bonds (these might have been issued, of course, at higher interest rates that, however, just amplify that anxiety). Preoccupation in the private sector can be seen as a rightward shift in the liquidity preference curve – that is, for a given interest rate financial investors prefer to hold relatively more liquidity in their portfolio. What the CB would do is to satisfy this desire, and since the additional liquidity is hoarded, monetisation does not have inflationary effects (see for instance Kalecki 1943: 347–8). An inflationary process might ensue if the private sector tries to convert money into real assets, such as equities, real estate investment etc. (Ciccone 2002: 133–5). The transmission of inflation to prices of general commodities is, however, uncertain, and depends on the nature of the direct and indirect input utilisation of some of those real assets (say office buildings).[10] According to Ciccone (ibid: 136) only an irrational preoccupation of the private sector about the sustainability of the PD – sustainability that ultimately depends on the self-fulfilling confidence of the same private sector – may lead to the necessity of monetisation, which appears to be an unlikely event in a closed economy.

The presence of an SCB plays the essential role of seconding the liquidity preference of the public to prevent panic. An extreme case might be one of a liquidity trap in which herd behaviour pushes the interest rates on sovereign bonds up to very high and perhaps increasing levels in a self-fulfilling confidence crisis that the monetary authority is unable to stop. Even in this extreme case, Wray seems to sustain the unlimited solvency of a sovereign State with a sovereign currency (Nersisyan and Wray 2010: 15). Of course, in extreme situations the confidence in the currency might be undermined by current and expected inflation which is a way to extol from the private sector any amount of resources the state wishes, and is a de facto default with respect to existing treasury bonds. Certainly such an extreme situation seems to describe a political default if not a technical one. We may think that a panic would develop after witnessing some 'real' signs, like a PD/GDP ratio that is currently rising rapidly or expected to do so. Reinhart and Rogoff (2009: 132) state that 'overt domestic default tends to occur only in times of severe macroeconomic distress'. At this point we should distinguish between the *real triggers* (I deliberately refrain from saying *causes*) of a financial crisis, like an escalating PD/GDP ratio, and *financial panic*. In the case of PD a 'fundamental' is the PD/GDP ratio that evokes a relation between debt and its tax base. How likely a sovereign default is in a closed economy is difficult to say since this scenario is very abstract and not really separable from the events that concern the foreign sector (ibid: 123).

Unsustainability depends on the proportion of PD held by foreigners

In a widely quoted post Gros (2011) indicated a significant positive correlation between sovereign spreads relative to German Bunds and current account imbalances. The explanation he provided is that as long as sovereign debt is held by nationals then, in the case of difficulties financing it, the State would be able to tax national bond holders, something which is precluded in the case of foreign holders.[11]

The easiest way to execute a wealth tax that hits domestic bondholders directly is precisely a downright default. So, it is not clear in what sense a domestically held sovereign debt would be 'safer' (although not precisely from the bond-holders' point of view) from the point of view of (domestic) investors. With free capital movements, worries about a domestic default, a wealth tax, monetisation or 'financial repression', could generate capital flights. If a country feels no necessity and, perhaps more importantly, lacks the will to turn to international financial markets, one may say that a PD is 'safer' if it is 'frozen' within the domestic boundaries in the context of 'financial repression', i.e. by forcing domestic savings to be invested in government bonds at a relatively low interest rate through controls on the domestic financial sector and on capital flows. In this case the government can also resort to an open domestic default, masked by a wealth tax on domestic bondholders, through monetization.

So, while domestic ownership of the PD is not per se a no-default insurance, the prevalence of foreign ownership of the PD might be a warning sign for another problem (so a domestically owned PD might be safer, but for different reasons from those adduced by Gros and others). These deeper problems have to do with a country's negative foreign balances (CA and NIIP) that are associated with negative domestic private and/or public balances (as noted above, the perceived credit risk of the public sector also reflects that of the private sector which the former might be called on to bail out). Persistent negative trade imbalances, with consequently increasing foreign stock imbalances (NIIP) and negative net income flows that worsen the CA, would signal that the level of domestic aggregate demand (AD) – which is the consequence of the spending decisions of the two domestic sectors – is inconsistent with the foreign equilibrium, given the marginal propensity to import and the level of exports. This means that the private or the public sectors (or both) do not generate, in these circumstances, enough domestic saving and/or tax revenues and will persistently need foreign savings. This entails increasing foreign held public and/or private debt, which is the domestic manifestation of the worsening NIIP of the country. It is in this respect that we view a relative large foreign ownership of the PD as a signal, *ceteris paribus*, of difficulty.

It is again useful to separate the change in the 'fundamentals', basically a worsening of the CA and NIIP of a country associated to a current or expected worsening of the PD/GDP ratio, from the ensuing financial anxiety that leads to a 'sudden stop' of capital flows and to the difficulty of re-financing the PD. These events, by increasing the sovereign spread, aggravates the negative pattern of the 'fundamentals'.

In principle, a country's current account deficit just creates financial wealth for the foreign sector, so why should the 'irrational' behaviour of foreign investors pave the way to a default by a 'capital flow reversal' (as Ciccone wondered in the case of a domestically held PD)? The main reason is that in a foreign unbalanced country there is a devaluation risk that is absent in a closed economy, and although a country might try to reassure foreign investors by letting sovereign rates reflect this very risk, the fact that this worsens the imbalances just augments the expectation of a devaluation. A devaluation is not only a masked default – both external, given the promises of redeeming sovereign debt at a given exchange rate, and internal, given the probability of ensuing inflation – but also a way to re-address the loss of competitiveness that is likely to be one of the causes of foreign and domestic imbalances, a temptation for any government. Moreover, a government might find it easier to default with foreign rather than with domestic bondholders. The share of foreign held sovereign debt is therefore only a warning signal of a deeper BoP crisis.

Unsustainability depends on the absence of a sovereign central bank

The absence of a truly European central bank to guarantee the liquidity of European sovereign debts aggravated (although it did not cause) the crisis by letting sovereign spreads spiral upwards. As consequence of the ECB's deficient running, according to De Grauwe (2011: 8–10) the periphery's public debts (PD) moved from a low risk to a high risk equilibrium, in his view from a liquidity to a solvency crisis. This is not totally correct since the original troubles with the European periphery seem to be related to solvency, not just to liquidity, and indeed they emerged when liquidity was abundant and sovereign spreads were low. According to Wray and his MMT disciples this abundance just delayed the *redde rationem* of the deficient monetary organisation of the EZ, so that they attribute an almost exclusive relevance to the renunciation of a national SCB as the explanation for the European financial crisis.

In short, Wray argues that as long as a country retains a sovereign currency, it retains the privilege of making payments by issuing its own currency and makes no promises to redeem its debt at any fixed exchange rate or even worse in a foreign currency, then it cannot default and the nationality of the debt holders is irrelevant (Nersisyan and Wray 2010: 12–14).

It is certainly right that if a fixed exchange rate leads to a CA deficit, a country is exposed to 'sudden stops' in capital flows, while the higher interest rates needed to avoid capital flights and to keeping parity will worsen the external and domestic imbalances. Wray seems, however, to hold a different view. Given full monetary sovereignty, the MMT scholars apply the same argument envisaged for a closed economy to an open economy: a public deficit corresponds to net private wealth desired either by the domestic private sector or by the foreign sector, so there are no limits to the foreign holdings of Government bonds 'so long as the rest of the world wants to accumulate its IOUs':

> a country can run a current account deficit so long as the rest of the world wants to accumulate its IOUs. The country's capital account surplus 'balances' its current account deficit.... We can even view the current account deficit as resulting from a rest of world desire to accumulate net savings in the form of claims on the country.
>
> (Wray 2011a)

The devil is, notoriously, in the details, and the proviso 'so long as the rest of the world wants to accumulate its IOUs' seriously circumscribes Wray's view that countries with a fully sovereign currency and no promise of convertibility at a given exchange rate can have faith in unlimited foreign credit. But for most countries, the non-convertibility at a given exchange rate is precisely the case in which they will not get (cheap) foreign credit. *Indeed, it is by promising at-pair convertibility that periphery countries can finance in a cheap way their CA deficits.* Of course, this will often create future problems, while certainly a floating exchange rate would discourage cheap foreign lending. One may also say that a competitive (real) exchange rate policy is what periphery countries need, a position largely shared by development economists nowadays, not least because it is not conducive to fictitious foreign-borrowing-led growth.

Wray (2011c) elsewhere admits that the proposition that any State 'can run budget deficits that help to fuel current account deficits without worry about government or national insolvency' applies indeed only to the US:

> precisely because the rest of the world wants Dollars. But surely that cannot be true of any other nation. Today, the US Dollar is the international reserve currency – making the US special.... The two main reasons why the US can run persistent current account deficits are: a) virtually all its foreign-held debt is in Dollars; and b) external demand for Dollar-denominated assets is high – for a variety of reasons.

The main reason seems that the US issues the main reserve currency, an internationally fully accepted liability even without a commitment to convert it in something else (i.e. fiat money). So, when Wray says that PD and CA debts, with a sovereign currency, are not a problem, this only applies to the US.

With fixed exchange rates, it is not so much the promise to redeem the debt at a fixed exchange rate or in a foreign currency that creates problems. It would not be a problem in CA surplus countries, for instance. The problem is that fixed exchange rates lead periphery countries to a CA deficit, to the fear of devaluation, unsustainable interest rates, 'sudden capital stops' etc. Remember that the European imbalances initially grew when the ECB was pursuing very low interest rates that with financial liberalisation and the end of a devaluation risk led to the bubbles in the periphery and eventually to the imbalances. This is not to say that the role of an SCB is not relevant: quite the opposite. Lately, the ECB should and could have operated to avoid the increase in sovereign spreads, but it could not have avoided the preceding sequence of events.

It may be added that with the right institutional setting, the EZ could be a perfect US-MMT style country. With the full backing of the ECB the infra-European financial imbalances would be manageable for a region with external balanced accounts that, what's more, issues an international currency. The institutional change required for the EZ to resemble the US includes the transfer of the conspicuous part of existing PDs along with many government budget functions to a federal government (to avoid moral hazards),[12] while national States would work like American local States. Monetary policy should cooperate with fiscal policy to pursue full employment and, subordinated to this, price stability. Federal transfers from dynamic to troubled areas should dramatically increase while a minimum standard of welfare rights should be universally recognised for all European citizens. Labour mobility and infra-EZ direct investment should be incentivised. Actually, fiscal pacts were already included in the Maastricht (1992) and Amsterdam (1997) treaties, in which the European periphery exchanged budgetary discipline with German inflation 'credibility' and low interest rates. As experience has shown, the troubles have not derived from fiscal indiscipline, although part of the problems certainly derived from a deregulated financial sector. At the European and national level, financial resources should therefore be re-regulated to sustain public, social and environmental investment rather than construction or consumption bubbles. Public or semi-public investment banks should be used at both levels for this purpose. Unfortunately, this project appears too challenging for the EZ, a club of independent States. Short of this full institutional unification, pro-active monetary and budget policies at the European level, particularly in the surplus countries, would of course also help towards a solution.

But can EZ countries really default? Target 2 and LTRO

In December 2011 the ECB adopted a special-term refinancing operation extending LTRO (longer-term refinancing operation) – an existing refinancing facility usually limited to three months at a variable interest rate, but already extended to one year in 2009 by a earliest special-term refinancing operation – to three years at a fixed 1 per cent interest rate allocating one trillion euros to the operation (at the same time mandatory bank reserves were reduced from 2 per cent to 1 per cent of all deposits). The scope was to ring fence banks with weak capitalisation and mark-to-market devalued assets; to avoid a credit crunch; to stimulate local banks to support their respective domestic sovereign bonds. On the one hand, the last objective has had limited success, but the reduction of sovereign spreads on the Spanish and Italian bonds has been limited since, at the same time, the austerity measures were squashing growth. On the other hand, this intervention has avoided the capital outflows from the periphery rapidly leading the periphery to a default stage – since foreign investor clearly did not wish to roll-over previously acquired peripheral private and government debts. According to Credit Suisse (2012),

> about 20 per cent of the peak cumulative portfolio and other investment made since 2002 [till January 2012] has been withdrawn recently … these capital outflows could become much larger, if domestic investors were to join foreign investors in pulling money out.

This is a phoney situation: the ECB is financing CA deficits at the same time as capital outflows, i.e. it is *ex-post* financing previous CA deficits that foreign investors do not want to roll-over.

As a result, the ownership of PD is becoming pretty domestic, although this is backed not by domestic savings (this is impossible given the enduring CA deficit) but by the ECB. A prompt intervention of the ECB as a lender of last resort of peripheral states would have possibly avoided the capital outflow reducing the sovereign spread. This would not have solved, of course, CA imbalances and the recourse to T2 that, however, might also have been lower in a more confident climate. The solution for CA imbalances would have required, as suggested above, reversing past patterns of domestic aggregate demand in the EZ with strong and moderate expansion in core and in peripheral Europe, respectively.

Epilogue: the hybrid nature of the EMU and its destiny

A traditional objection to the interpretation of the EZ crisis as a typical 'this time is different' crisis is that there cannot be a BoP crisis in a currency union. The question is that the EZ is a hybrid between a full currency union (which also implies a fiscal union) and a traditional fixed exchange agreement. One main difference with the latter is that in a currency union capital flights are automatically compensated by the CB, in the EZ by T2 and refinancing operations (Mayer *et al.* 2012; Cesaratto 2013). As everybody knows, assuming zero variation of foreign currency reserves, the BoP sheet would read: $CA+KA=0$, where KA is the capital account. Normally, in a two countries world, if country A has (all magnitudes are balances) a negative CA_A-, country B symmetrically shows CA_B+, then KA_A+ and KA_B- (country B is lending to country A). Suppose country B does not lend to country A (so the CA flow imbalance is not financed), and even worse that there are capital outflows from country A (so the stock of debt acquired by B in the past is not rolled-over as it expires). Then both CA_A- and KA_A-. What happens in a currency union is that through T2: $CA_A+KA_A+T=0$, where $T>0$ means that country A is overdrawing from its CB account. It is as if the ECB were creating *foreign currency reserves* in a fixed exchange rate system (Leppanen 2012); or as if the deficit countries were creating the international reserves, like the US in Bretton Woods (I or II) (Kohler 2012); or better still, it is as if the EMU worked in an ultra-Keynesian fashion as an *International Clearing Union* (ICU), with even less prudence than Keynes envisaged.[13] With T2, the EZ country A has indeed an infinite overdraft possibility (Milbrandt 2012; CESifo 2012). What has happened in the periphery from 2007/8 is that CA_A- and KA_A-, $T+$ and symmetrically in the core: $CA+$, $KA+$, $T-$ (core banks receiving hot money from the periphery and reducing their overdraft at their NCB).

Not so paradoxically, given the hybrid nature of the EMU: 'If, in the framework of a political union, the euro central banks were integrated as dependent branches of the ECB, the consolidation of the branches would dissolve the Target balances in thin air' (Neumann 2012; also Ulbrich and Lipponer 2012; CESifo 2012). This makes clear that through T2 the ECB is acting as a regular CB: normally banks rely on the interbank market to finance their imbalances (when they fall short of reserves); if, in exceptional circumstances, this does not work the ECB just fills the gap. So, in this respect EMU is not like, say, the European Monetary System (EMS). If the ECB interrupts T2 and the refinancing operations (i.e. it stops acting as a CB with the peripheral banks) this is the end of the EMU. Of course, T2 is not the cause of the problems, but it prevents the EMU from exploding as the EMS did in 1992.

In this regard one might think that if the EZ was a real Federal State, the financial crisis would be a 'normal' domestic crisis: if some local banks and some local governments (deprived of monetary sovereignty) are not solvent, nobody would talk of a BoP crisis. Even considering the grand scale of the EZ crisis, a 'normal' state would intervene by socialising part of the local government and banks' debt, imposing austerity and balanced budgets on them; saved banks would be nationalised, restructured or shut down. The CB would cooperate by sustaining the sovereign/federal debt. At the same time the Federal administration would use fiscal transfers to attenuate the crisis. Fine, but this is not Europe! If it were, it would manage to solve the situation without too much hardship.[14]

The question is that the EZ is a hybrid, in between a fixed exchange rate system among independent countries and a fully integrated economy, sharing the possibility of a BoP crisis with the former and national banking principles with the latter. In this spurious set up the ECB has acted somewhat similarly to the US Federal Reserve: through T2 and LTRO it is injecting liquidity and absorbing toxic assets as collateral, letting insolvent local banks and governments survive. A fiscal pact has been imposed, but there is no Federal government assisted by an SCB on hand to heal the local states and banks.[15] To sum up, the EZ crisis is not a classical fixed exchange rate crisis; it is not a domestic financial crisis; it is what it is: a BoP crisis in an imperfect currency union. If the union were perfected, the crisis could be solved in the same way as a traditional domestic crisis. If it is not perfected, it is an unedited BoP crisis with a still unwritten final (Cesaratto 2013).

Notes

1 I wish to thank the participants of a workshop held at the Centro Sraffa at the University of Rome, 3 May 2012. A longer, working paper version of this chapter has been published as Cesaratto (2012).

2 Take a peripheral economy with the following data (standard notation): $c=0.5$, propensity to import $m=0.2$, $I=250$ and $E=100$. Income is 500 and the trade balance in equilibrium: $S-I=E-M=0$. Now suppose that core countries' banks finance autonomous spending $Ca=100$. The new income level will be 643 (approx.), $M=129$, $S=Y-C-Ca=221$, $S-I=E-M=29$. This looks like the Portuguese and Greek result illustrated by B&G: a lower saving rate (or average propensity to save), due to the expansion of Ca, accompanied by an unaltered I.

3 The way the "credit circuit" works (see Note 2) in the T2 context proves that it is financial lending in support of spending in the periphery that generates – via higher German net export, production and income – higher German (foreign) savings. So it is not correct to say that German savings financed Greece's (presumed) profligacy, since it is actually Greek "profligacy", financed out of credit created by the financial system, that has generated German savings. This is not surprising for those who have fully understood Keynes. Without that spending, *nicht* saving.

4 The EU Commission points out that the periphery's troubles came from increasing imports rather than by a poor performance of exports (European Commission 2009: 26–7; European Commission 2010: 8). This suggests that had core Europe been more expansive, the imbalances would not have occurred, at least to the extent they have done. Holinski *et al.* (2012: 12) also note the role of the fall in the EU net transfer to the EZ periphery as a consequence of the enlargement of the Union in the mid-1990s as a further cause of CA imbalances. Of course, interest payments on a mounting foreign debt were a further cause of CA imbalances (ibid: 10).

5 It is relevant to note that official think tanks *do not* attribute German competitive gains to above average productivity gains (e.g. European Commission 2009: 25).

6 Political reasons – German unification – have been adduced as a main reason why France pushed for the currency union. More practically, Vianello (2005: 12) points out that France was paying too high an interest rate to keep parity in the EMS.

7 Kalecki (1934 [1971]) associates the realisation of the social surplus in foreign markets to the 'domestic exports' constituted by government deficit spending. In his marvellous paper on Tugan-Baranowsky and Rosa Luxemburg (1967 [1971]) both markets were subsumed to the label of 'external markets', i.e. markets outwith the conventional 'income-spending circuit'.

8 In his critical review of the issue, Ciccone (2002: 114ff.) pertinently refers to two notions of sustainability, one based on the belief that the public sector meets an inter-temporal balanced budget constraint; a second that refers to the ratio between PD and GDP. The second indicator vaguely compares the size of the debt to the levy capacity of the State. I shall refer to the second.

9 A sovereign currency means that a country promises to honour any sovereign debt written in this currency by issuing its own notes, without feeling committed to exchanging it for any foreign currency at a prefixed exchange rate.

10 The idea that taxation and savings are a result and not a pre-requisite of government spending is, of course, very clear in Keynes and expressed with even more clarity by Kalecki (1943: 347–8).

11 This inflation process would of course reduce the real value of monetised debt, and also of the part that the private sector still holds in bonds as long as the nominal interest rate does not fully incorporate expected inflation.

12

> [A]s long as Eurozone members retain full taxing powers, they can always service their domestic debts, even without access to the printing press. This is why, I believe, it is foreign debt that constitutes the underlying problem for the solvency of a sovereign, even in the Eurozone.
>
> (Gros 2011)

13 As Nersisyan and Wray (2010: 16) argue:

> With a sovereign currency, the need to balance the budget over some time period determined by the movements of celestial objects or over the course of a business cycle is a myth, an old-fashioned religion. When a country operates on a fiat monetary regime, debt and deficit limits and even bond issues for that matter are self-imposed, i.e., there are no financial constraints inherent in the fiat system that exist under a gold standard or fixed exchange rate regime. But that superstition is seen as necessary because if everyone realizes that government is not actually constrained by the necessity of balanced budgets, then it might spend 'out of control,' taking too large a percent of the nation's resources.

14 Indeed Keynes regarded the International Clearing Union as an extension of the principles that govern a national banking system, the same principle that informs T2. In 1941 he even called it 'Currency Union':

> The idea underlying my proposals for a Currency Union is simple, namely to generalise the essential principle of banking, as it is exhibited within any closed system … This principle is the necessary equality of credits and debits, of assets and liabilities. If no credits can be removed outside the banking system but only transferred within it, the Bank *itself* can never be in difficulties. It can with safety make what advances it wishes to any of its customers with the assurance that the proceeds can only be transferred to the bank account of another customer. Its problem is solely to see to it that its customers behave themselves and that the advances made to each of them are prudent and advisable from the point of view of its customers as a whole.
>
> (Keynes 1980 [1941]: 44, emphasis in original)

15 According to Sinn (2012) and his disciples (Kohler 2012) the situation is bound by the limits the Bundsbank meets in sterilising the liquidity flooding to Germany once the BuBa has sold all its assets (including gold, foreign currencies etc.), with dubious inflationary consequences. Others, including ECB economists (Bindseil *et al.* 2012), say that this money can remain deposited at the ECB. Perhaps the question is that at some point German savers might become unhappy with the returns on hoarded liquidity and start to spend it.

References

Bindseil, U., Cour-Thimann, P. and König, P. (2012) 'Target2 and Cross-border Interbank Payments during the Financial Crisis', *Forum*, 13 (Special Issue January): 83–101.

Blanchard, O. and Giavazzi, F. (2002) 'Current Account Deficits in the Euro Area: The End of the Feldstein-Horioka Puzzle?' *Brookings Papers on Economic Activity*, 147–86.

Carlin, W. and Soskice, D. (2009) 'German Economic Performance: Disentangling the Role of Supply-Side Reforms, Macroeconomic Policy and Coordinated Economy Institutions', *Socio-economic Review*, 7 (1): 67–99.

Cesaratto, S. (2012) 'Controversial and novel features of the Eurozone crisis as a balance of payment crisis', *Quaderni del Dipartimento di Economia Politica e Statistica*, www.econ-pol.unisi.it/dipartimento/it/node/1649.

Cesaratto, S. (2013) 'The Endless Eurozone Crisis, Where Do We Stand? A Classical-Kaleckian Overview', *Quaderni del Dipartimento di Economia Politica e Statistica*, www.econ-pol.unisi.it/dipartimento/it/node/1813.

Cesaratto, S. and Stirati, A. (2011) 'Germany in the European and Global Crises', *International Journal of Political Economy*, 39 (4): 56–87. Working paper version: www.econ-pol.unisi.it/dipartimento/it/node/1267.

CESifo (2011) *Bogenberg Declaration: Sixteen Theses on the Situation of the European Monetary Union*: www.cesifo-group.de/cesifo/newsletter/Bogenberg_Declaration.htm.

CESifo (2012) *Forum*, 13 (Special Issue January).

Ciccone, R. (2002) *Debito pubblico, domanda aggregata e accumulazione*, Aracne, Roma.

Credit Suisse (2012) *TARGET2: I'm a Euro, Get Me Out of Here!* Economics Research.

Crouch, C. (2008) 'What will follow the Demise of Privatised Keynesianism', *Political Quarterly*, 79 (4): 476–87.

Dalziel, P.C. and Harcourt, G.C. (1997) 'A Note on "Mr Meade's Relation" and International Capital Movements', *Cambridge Journal of Economics*, 21 (5): 621–31.

De Grauwe, P. (2011) 'Managing a fragile Eurozone', *CESifo Forum*, 2.

Diaz-Alejandro, C. (1985) 'Good-bye Financial Repression, Hello Financial Crash', *Journal of Development Economics*, 19 (1–2): 1–24.

European Commission (2009) 'Competitiveness Developments within the Euro Area', *Quarterly Report on the Euro Area*, 8 (1).

European Commission (2010) 'The Impact of the Global Crisis on Competitiveness and Current Accounts Divergences in the Euro Area', *Quarterly Report on the Euro Area*, 9 (1).

Febrero, E., Uxó, J. and Bermejo, F. (2012) 'El funcionamiento del sistema TARGET2 desde la Gran Recesión: Una aproximación desde la óptica del circuito monetario', *Jornadas de Economía Crítica*, XIII (February) Sevilla.

Franzese, R.J. and Hall, P.A. (2000) 'Institutional Dimensions of Coordinating Wage-Bargaining and Monetary Policy', in Iversen, T., Pontusson, J. and Soskice, D. (eds), *Unions, Employers, and Central Banks: Macroeconomic Coordination and Institutional Change in Social Market Economies*, Cambridge University Press, Cambridge.

Frenkel, R. and Rapetti, M. (2009) 'A Developing Country View of the Current Global Crisis: What should not be Forgotten and What should be Done', *Cambridge Journal of Economics*, 33 (4): 685–702.

Garber, P. (2010) 'The Mechanics of Intra Euro Capital Flight', *Deutsche Bank*: http://fincake.ru/stock/reviews/56090/download/54478.

Garegnani, P. (1983) 'Notes on Consumption, Investment and Effective Demand', in Eatwell, J. and Milgate, M. (eds), *Keynes's Economics and the Theory of Value and Distribution*, Duckworth, London.

Garegnani, P. (1984) 'Value and Distribution in the Classical Economists and Marx', *Oxford Economic Papers*, 36 (2): 291–325.

Gourinchas, P.O. (2002) 'Comments and Discussions', *Brookings Papers on Economic Activity*, 2002 (2): 187–209.

Gros, D. (2011) 'External versus Domestic Debt in the Euro Crisis', *VOX*, 24 May.

Holtfrerich, C.L. (1999) 'Monetary Policy under Fixed Exchange Rates (1948–70)', in Baltensperger, E. (ed.), *Fifty Years of the Deutsche Mark: Central Bank and the Currency in Germany since 1948*, Oxford University Press, New York.

Holtfrerich, C.L. (2008) 'Monetary Policy in Germany since 1948: National Tradition, International Best Practice or Ideology', in Touffut, J.P. (ed.), *Central Banks as Economic Institutions*, Edward Elgar, Cheltenham.

Holinski, N., Kool, C. and Muysken, J. (2012) 'Persistent Macroeconomic Imbalances in the Euro Area: Causes and Consequences', *Federal Reserve Bank of St. Louis Review*, January/February 1: 1–21.

Jaumotte, F. and Sodsriwiboon, P. (2010) 'Current Account Imbalances in the Southern Euro Area', *IMF Working Paper*, 10/139.

Kalecki, M. (1934) 'On Foreign Trade and "Domestic Exports"', in Kalecki, M. (1971) *Selected Essays on the Dynamics of the Capitalist Economy 1933–1970*, Cambridge University Press, Cambridge.

Kalecki, M. (1943) 'Political Aspects of Full Employment', *Political Quarterly*, 14 (4): 322–31.

Kalecki, M. (1967) 'The Problem of Effective Demand with Tugan-Baranowski and Rosa Luxemburg', in Kalecki, M. (1971) *Selected Essays on the Dynamics of the Capitalist Economy 1933–1970*, Cambridge University Press, Cambridge.

Kalecki, M. (1971) *Selected Essays on the Dynamics of the Capitalist Economy 1933–1970*. Cambridge University Press, Cambridge.

Keynes, J.M. (1980 [1941]) *The Collected Writings of John Maynard Keynes*, vol. XXV, Activities: 1940–1944, Shaping the Post-War World: the Clearing Union, (eds Robinson, A., Johnson, E. and Moggridge, D.), Macmillan, for the Royal Economic Society, London: St. Martin's Press, for the Royal Economic Society, New York.

Kohler, K. (2012) 'The Eurosystem in Times of Crises: Greece in the Role of a Reserve Currency Country?' *Forum*, 13 (Special Issue January): 14–22.

Krugman, P. (2011) *Italy Versus Japan*: http://krugman.blogs.nytimes.com/2011/07/16/italy-versus-japan/.

Lavoie, M. (2011) *The Monetary and Fiscal Nexus of Neo-chartalism: A Friendly Critical Look*, Department of Economics, University of Ottawa, mimeo.

Leppänen, O. (2012) *Eurosystem TARGET Balance Deviations call for Cautious Changing of the EU Banking Landscape*: www.voxeu.org/index.php?q=node/7884.

Makoto, I. (2012) *From the Subprime to the Sovereign Crisis: Why Keynesianism does not Work?* paper presented at the Congreso de economistas heterodoxos, Buenos Aires, March.

Mayer, T., Möbert, J. and Weistroffer, C. (2012) 'Macroeconomic Imbalances in EMU and the Eurosystem', *Forum*, 13 (Special Issue January): 35–42.

Merler, S. and Pisani-Ferry, J. (2012) *Sudden Stops in the Euro Area*, Bruegel Policy Contribution, March.

Milbradt, G. (2012) 'The Derailed Policies of the ECB', *Forum*, 13 (Special Issue January): 43–9.

Mundell, R.A. (1957) 'International Trade and Factor Mobility', *American Economic Review*, 47 (3): 321–35.

Nechio, F. (2011) 'Monetary Policy When One Size Does Not Fit All', *Federal Reserve Bank of San Francisco Economic Letter*, 2011–18.

Nersisyan, Y. and Wray, R.L. (2010) 'Does Excessive Sovereign Debt really Hurt Growth? A Critique of this Time is Different, by Reinhart and Rogoff', *Working Paper*, No. 603, Levy Institute, June 2010: www.levyinstitute.org/pubs/wp_603.pdf.

Neumann, M.J.M. (2012) 'The Refinancing of Banks Drives Target Debt', *Forum*, 13 (Special Issue January): 29–32.

Prasad, E.S., Rajan, R.G. and Subramanian, A. (2007) 'Foreign Capital and Economic Growth', *National Bureau of Economic Research, Working Paper 13619*.

Reinhart, C.M. and Rogoff, K.S. (2009) *This Time is Different: Eight Centuries of Financial Folly*, Princeton University Press, Princeton, NJ.

Reinhart, C.M. (2011) 'A Series of Unfortunate Events: Common Sequencing Patterns in Financial Crises', *Rivista di Politica Economica*, 100: 11–36.

Riha, T. (1985) *German Political Economy: The History of an Alternative Economics*, MCB University Press, Bradford.

Sinn, H.W. (2012) 'The European Balance of Payments Crisis: An Introduction', *Forum*, 13 (Special Issue January).

Tilford, S. and Whyte, P. (2011) *Why Stricter Rules Threaten the Eurozone*, Centre for European Reform: www.cer.org.uk/sites/default/files/publications/attachments/pdf/2011/essay_eurozone_9nov11–4084.pdf.

Ulbrich, J. and Lipponer, A. (2012) 'Balances in the Target2 Payments System: A Problem?' *Forum*, 13 (Special Issue January): 73–6.

Vianello, F. (2005) *La moneta unica europea*, Università di Roma La Sapienza, mimeo.

Wolf, M. (2012) 'Why the Bundesbank is Wrong', *Financial Times*, 10 April.

Wray, L.R. (2006) 'Extending Minsky's Classifications of Fragility to Government and the Open Economy', *Working Paper No. 450*, Levy Economics Institute.

Wray, L.R. (2011a) *Sovereign Currency and Government Policy in the Open Economy:* http://neweconomicperspectives.org/2011/11/mmp-blog-26-sovereign-currency-and.html.

Wray, L.R. (2011b) *MMT, Sectoral Balances and Behaviour*: http://neweconomicperspectives.org/2011/06/mmt-sectoral-balances-and-behavior.html.

Wray, L.R. (2011c) *Currency Solvency and the Special Case of the US Dollar*: http://neweconomicperspectives.org/2011/11/mmp-blog-25-currency-solvency-and.html.

6 Unhappy families are all alike

Minskyan cycles, Kaldorian growth, and the Eurozone peripheral crises

Alberto Bagnai[1]

Introduction

Four years after the onset of the Eurozone peripheral crisis, neither the scientific nor the public debate seem to have reached a consensus view about its causes. While in academia the opinion slowly prevails that regional external imbalances were at the root of the crisis, as they led to the massive accumulation of net external liabilities from the private sector (Eichengreen, 2010; De Grauwe, 2010), in the Eurozone media the current (May 2012) fashionable interpretation puts the blame on fiscal profligacy from the peripheral governments, leading to the accumulation of an unsustainable government debt. This shift in attitude between the two debates depends on many things, including the different political and distributional implications of the two explanations, and the difficulty in explaining to the general public what external debt is, as compared to public debt.

Be it as it may, these debates seem to have reached an agreement on at least one point, namely, that every Eurozone peripheral country was hit by the crisis in its own way: Greece would have been destroyed by its government's "creative finance" and corruption, leading eventually to a solvency crisis, while the Italian government would be "illiquid but not insolvent", Spain and Ireland would have experienced a real estate bubble (possibly fuelled by government neglect or profligacy) and so on. This is what I call the "Anna Karenina" paradigm, from the well-known Tolstoj novel which begins: "Happy families are all alike; every unhappy family is unhappy in its own way". The "Anna Karenina" paradigm is a particular case of the "this time is different" attitude, criticised by Reinhart and Rogoff (2008), i.e. of the idea that each financial crisis would be the consequence of a series of unfortunate and mostly idiosyncratic events, that would make each crisis unpredictable and a case in its own, with no particular relation with other crisis episodes. This view is disproved by economic history, which instead tells us that some common features were present in most previous episodes of financial crisis. European economists however push the "this time is different" argument even further, by claiming that "this time *and in this place* it is different".

Analysing differences between different situations is no doubt a useful task. However, Occam's razor warns us against multiplying unnecessary explanations.

Moreover, in this particular case I think that insisting on the synchronic and diachronic differences of the Eurozone peripheral crises leads to biased and perhaps unintended outcomes. On the one hand, by insisting on "differences" one runs the risk of dispersing the attention on anecdotal evidence: the leaves conceal the tree. On the other hand, insisting on the "novelty" of the present Eurozone predicament, amounts to denying the usefulness of any historical analysis.

However, this is certainly not the first, and probably not the last time, that a country or a group of countries are crushed under the weight of too heavy a currency. Many cases have already been analysed, more or less in depth, in the economic literature, and it would be questionable, if not suspect, to suggest (even implicitly) that there is nothing to be learned from these experiences. Just to mention a few cases, consider Churchill's decision to re-enter the gold standard in 1925 at the pre-First World War gold parity (Keynes, 1931), which promoted a similar decision by Mussolini to reach the so-called "quota 90" (90 Italian liras for one pound), or, coming to more recent experiences, the dramatic experience of the so-called "credible EMS" between 1987 and 1992 (Frankel and Phillips, 1992). All these experiences occurred, at different points in time, in Europe, and they all ended up in the same way: the "strong currency policy", whatever its intended motivations, and whatever the global economic and political context, failed, and had to be abandoned.

Developing countries provide many more examples of what happens when a country decides (or is advised to decide) to adopt too strong a standard of value, in particular by pegging to the US dollar, be it through a "soft peg", such as the one implemented by some Asian countries before the 1997 financial crisis (Calvo and Reinhart, 2002), or through straight "dollarization", as was the case in the "currency boards" adopted in Latin America (Berg *et al.*, 2002). A particularly telling case for the Italian public is that of Argentina, which is well known in Italy both for the very close cultural ties between the two countries,[2] and for the consequences of its 2001 default, which hurt a number of Italian small creditors. For this reason, in the last decade Argentina has been omnipresent in the Italian debate: initially as an example of the dangers that the euro would ward off (which is rather paradoxical in my view, if one considers the close analogy between tying the peso to the dollar, on the one hand, and the lira to the Deutsche Mark, on the other); nowadays, as an example of how leaving the euro would rescue (or destroy) Italy, as well as other Eurozone peripheral economies.

In this chapter I try to reverse the "Anna Karenina approach" to the Eurozone peripheral crises. What I would like to show is that, contrary to current conventional wisdom, these crises "are all alike": they reproduce, in their essence, the main features of Minsky's (1982) "boom and bust" cycle in developing countries, as described by Taylor (1998) and more recently by Frenkel and Rapetti (2009). In my opinion, this reversal of perspective, besides being supported by empirical evidence, provides many further useful insights. First, it allows us to identify the common roots of the apparently different crises and possibly to define common management or exit strategies, looking at the previous historical experiences; second, the adoption of a common framework allows us to gauge the effective relevance of country idiosyncratic features in the explanation of what is going on in the Eurozone.

In this respect, our analysis shows that as far as the two major peripheral countries are concerned, i.e. Italy and Spain, the "market-driven destabilization" mechanism described by Taylor (1998) has interacted with another well-known tenet of post-Keynesian development economics, the Verdoorn (1949)–Kaldor (1957) model of cumulative growth, as set out by Thirlwall (2002) or León-Ledesma (2002). The basic intuition of Taylor (1998) is that in developing countries the Minskyan cycle is set off by an exogenous change of macroeconomic policy, which invariably comprises the adoption of a "credible" (i.e. fixed) nominal exchange rate. The post-Keynesian cumulative growth model implies that, besides its effects on the financial market, the shock determined by this nominal rigidity feeds back, through exports and output growth, on productivity, thereby inducing a further divergence in price competitiveness between the peripheral and core countries. This mechanism compounds its cumulative effects with the Minskyan cycle, leading to a particularly perverse situation where a country may see its net external liabilities grow, even if its real growth rate is not booming (as envisaged in the standard explanation by Frenkel and Rapetti, 2009).

The remainder of the chapter is as follows. The next section briefly describes the two models taken as a starting point for our interpretation of the Eurozone peripheral crises. Then, we discuss some features of these crises that are apparently at odds with the reference framework. The next step is to analyse the sectorial financial balances of selected Eurozone core and peripheral countries in order to investigate the responsibility of the private and public sectors in the evolution of the countries' net foreign assets. After this is done, the chapter presents in a standardized way the patterns of the macroeconomic fundamentals in Greece, Italy, Portugal and Spain, assessing their consistency with the Minskyan reference frameworks, and the last section draws some conclusions and indicates directions for future research.

The reference frameworks: Minskyan cycles and Kaldorian growth

In this section we briefly set out the theoretical reference framework used in this chapter to reconcile the apparently disparate evidence on the Eurozone peripheral crises (the "unhappy families"). This framework integrates two well-known models: the Minskyan boom-and-bust cycle, and the Verdoorn–Kaldor model of cumulative growth. We do not make any attempt to integrate these models at a formal level: we just single out their main implications in terms of observable variables and use them to interpret the main stylized facts of the Eurozone crisis.

Minskyan cycles in peripheral countries

Since the outbreak of the crisis, references to Minsky's analysis of financial instability have become usual in the economic literature (see Seccareccia, 2010). The standard explanation of the Minskyan mechanisms emphasizes the endogenous nature of the instability (for a survey and an analytical explanation see Charles, 2008), determined by the agents' changing risk perception in different stages of the economic cycle, coupled with the destabilizing role of financial innovation. Moreover, most of these explanations refer to closed economies, or, at least, do not assign a distinct role to foreign capital flows. For several reasons, these features are somehow unsatisfactory when it comes to the analysis of the developing countries' financial crises of the last three decades. Consider for instance that in developing countries repressed financial markets and backward financial institutions do not provide a particularly favourable environment to (destabilizing) financial innovation; moreover, the huge literature on "current account reversals" (Bagnai and Manzocchi, 1999) or "sudden stops" (Calvo, 1998) stresses that financial crises in developing countries are always anticipated by massive inflows of foreign capital: therefore, the destabilizing role of *foreign* finance is an important stylized fact that must be taken into account.

This is done among others by Taylor (1998) and Frenkel and Rapetti (2009), who revise the standard model in two ways: first, they consider the trigger of the boom phase to be not an "endogenous" change in domestic agents' risk perception, but rather an exogenous macroeconomic policy change (usually required by foreign multilateral institutions); second, they explicitly take into account the role of international capital flows in the build-up of the crisis. Following Frenkel and Rapetti (2009), a typical "peripheral" country's crisis occurs through the following seven steps:[3]

1 Multilateral agencies "suggest" that the peripheral country considers a "structural reforms" package typically including:

   a domestic financial market liberalization;
   b international capital movement liberalization;
   c adoption of a "credible" or fixed nominal exchange rate with respect to the "core" or "anchor" country.

2 By reducing the exchange rate risk and raising domestic interest rates this policy change brings about favourable arbitrage opportunities between domestic and foreign financial assets. Domestic players issue foreign debt (bought by foreign creditors) to take advantage of these opportunities.

3 Capital inflows determine an increase in domestic liquidity, hence in domestic credit to the private sector, which in turn brings about:

   a a fall in domestic interest rates (as well as in interest rate spreads);
   b an increase in output and employment;
   c an increase in prices.

4 The ensuing real exchange rate appreciation sets off a cumulative process through two channels:

   a a financial one: capital inflows are fostered by the expectations of capital gains on domestic assets;

   b a real one: a worsening of the trade balance leads to a current account deficit, hence to further capital inflows.

5 At a given point in time, some players realize that the fixed exchange rate is not credible anymore, and begin to undo their position in domestic assets, in order not to bear the risk of devaluation. This determines a "sudden stop" or even a "reversal" in foreign capital inflows.
6 The domestic central bank "defends" the exchange rate parity by raising interest rates, in order to attract foreign capital. This, however, usually worsens the financial position of the public sector, sending even more negative signals to the markets. Further rises in domestic interest rates are required, but the rise in interest spreads makes the markets increasingly nervous.
7 A "run" on the domestic central bank reserves follows, which usually forces the country very quickly out of its "credible" exchange rate rule. This leads to nominal devaluation and a "twin" (financial and balance-of-payments) crisis.

Some features of this cycle are worth noting.

First, in the early stage of the Minskyan cycle the peripheral economy does generally experience a real growth boom, fuelled by massive foreign capital inflows.

Second, the financial crisis does not originate in the public sector. On the contrary, real growth expansion in the early stages of the cycles generally ensures that the government budget balance and the public debt-to-GDP ratio improve. As a rule, the financial fragility in the peripheral economy is determined by an increasing financial exposure of the private sector.

Third, the cycle is initially fostered by nominal divergence among the core and peripheral economies. In the early stages, it is the spread between domestic and "core" interest rates that sets off the mechanism by attracting foreign capitals to the periphery. The cumulative causation sets in through divergence between the peripheral and core inflation rates, which feeds back into the current account deficits (following a real exchange rate appreciation in the peripheral country), which in turn determines further capital inflows.

Fourth, it is worth mentioning that the claim that the subprime crisis can be interpreted as a "Minsky moment" has been questioned by some post-Keynesians authors (e.g. Davidson, 2008). The subprime mortgage crisis has no doubt been the trigger of the Eurozone peripheral crises, contributing in particular to step 5 of the mechanism set out above. As such, a reflection on its true origin is obviously relevant. However, in this chapter I concentrate on a different issue. Rather than investigating whether the "classical" Minsky model explains what happened in the US in 2007 (which is the point raised by Davidson), I will focus on whether the "core-periphery" Minsky model developed by Taylor (1998) and Frenkel and Rapetti (2009) contributes to the explanation of what happened afterwards in the Eurozone.

Verdoorn–Kaldor cumulative growth model

In *The nature of economic growth* Tony Thirlwall (2002), building on his seminal work (Thirlwall, 1979), sets out a model of cumulative causation that explicitly recognizes the role of aggregate demand in determining a self-sustained increase in the rate of real growth. At the heart of the model lies the so-called Verdoorn law (from Verdoorn, 1949), also known as "Kaldor's second law of growth" (from Kaldor, 1966), stating that the rate of growth of productivity depends on the rate of growth of output (plus an autonomous productivity growth component). This empirical regularity has been subject to extensive empirical testing, and was generally found to be robust across countries and sectors. Its rationale lies in the presence of increasing returns and dynamic returns of scale. In Thirlwall's (2002) words, Verdoorn's law "opens up the possibility of a virtuous circle of export-led growth". This cumulative and circular causation develops along the following lines:

1 any shock that induces a faster export growth determines a faster output growth, through Hicks' (1950) open-economy supermultiplier (or any other export-led growth mechanism);
2 the increase in output growth brings about an acceleration in labour productivity, through Verdoorn's law;
3 the acceleration in productivity determines a fall in unit labour costs, hence an improvement of the country's price competitiveness;
4 this increase in price competitiveness feeds back on export growth, thus giving rise to a self-sustained increase in real growth.

This process however can also go the other way round: any shock that depresses the rate of growth of real exports can bring about a sustained decrease in the rate of growth of average labour productivity.

What are the bearings of this model to the Minskyan cycle described above? There are at least two points where the interactions between these two models are relevant to our analysis.

First, Verdoorn's law implies that any nominal shock that depresses the exports growth rate can exert a lasting effect on the growth rate of average labour productivity. Thus, a nominal revaluation, or, in a dynamic context, the adoption of a more rigid or even fixed exchange rate (which prevents the peripheral country from accommodating an adverse inflation differential) may exacerbate stages (3) and (4) of the Minskyan mechanism through its effects on labour productivity, and hence on price competitiveness. A previous attempt to integrate the two models in this respect has been done by Frenkel and Taylor (2006).

Second, central to Thirlwall's (1979, 2002) analysis is the concept of balance-of-payments constrained long-run growth rate, i.e. the rate of growth above which an economy incurs in a structural current account deficit. The BoP-constrained rate could also be defined as the (maximum) financially sustainable growth rate, namely the rate of growth that cannot be overcome without resorting to a net inflow of foreign financial resources. Thirlwall shows that under fairly general conditions a sustained real appreciation lowers this financially sustainable rate. Such a sustained real appreciation may be determined by a fall in the rate of growth of labour productivity, initiated by the adoption of a "credible" or "fixed" exchange rate. This implies that after an exogenous policy change such as the one considered at stage (1) of the Minskyan cycle, a country may start to accumulate net external liabilities even if its real growth rate is not booming by historical standards, simply because the shock determined by the policy change has lowered the country's financially sustainable growth rate in the first place.

These remarks will be useful when looking at the differences between the Eurozone peripheral crises.

An example: Italy in the "new EMS"

Developing countries provide uncountable examples of the Minskyan mechanism: an exhaustive list is presented by Frenkel and Rapetti (2009), who also examine five of them in detail (Chile 1982, Mexico 1988–1995, Thailand 1997, Korea 1997, Argentina 2001). It has gone unnoticed, as far as I know, how closely this mechanism explains some industrial countries crises, such as the 1992 EMS crisis in Italy. Table 6.1, following the same scheme as the tables in Frenkel and Rapetti (2009), illustrates this point.

The exogenous policy shock that set off the cycle was the inception of the so-called "new EMS". This new regime was informally adopted after the DM-area revaluation occurred on 1 January 1987 and was characterized by two typical features: a move towards financial liberalization (of international capital flows in particular), and the decision to proceed to exchange rate realignment only under exceptional circumstances (Giavazzi and Spaventa, 1990; Frankel and Phillips, 1992). Moreover, since 5 January 1991, Italy entered the narrow band of oscillation around its central parity (±2.5 per cent instead of the previous ±6 per cent), thereby introducing a further nominal rigidity. This was part of a strategy inspired by Giavazzi and Pagano's (1986, 1988) analysis, according to which governments in peripheral countries would have benefited from large credibility gains by "tying their hands" with a stronger commitment towards the nominal anchor of the EMS (Germany), and this would have helped them in pursuing nominal convergence (i.e. deflationary policies).

As shown in Table 6.1, things went differently: the developments following this policy change adhered closely to the Minskyan scheme described above, rather than to the masochistic "advantages of tying one's hands" tale.

First, the adoption of a "credible" exchange rate rule determined a raise in foreign capital inflows, which increased steadily from 0.3 GDP points in 1986 to 3.8 GDP points in 1990 (stage (2) of the Minskyan cycle). Domestic liquidity increased, and domestic credit to the private sector rose steadily from 50 to 60 GDP points between 1987 and 1992. As a consequence, the interest rate spread corrected for the nominal devaluation first rose to 2.9 in 1988, then declined reaching 0.7 in 1991 (the year before the crisis). In the early stages of the cycle real growth was positively affected by the increase in domestic liquidity, topping 4.2 per cent in 1988 (also because of a buoyant world demand). Prices kept rising at a faster pace than in the "anchor" country: in other words, Italy got no clear advantage in terms of deflationary policies from having tied its hands to

Table 6.1 Italy: selected macroeconomic variables, 1986–1993

	1986	*1987*	*1988*	*1989*	*1990*	*1991*	***1992***	*1993*
Real growth	2.9	3.2	4.2	3.4	2.1	1.5	**0.8**	–0.9
Trade balance (% GDP)	0.8	0.0	–0.1	–0.2	–0.1	–0.2	**0.0**	2.8
Current account balance (% GDP)	0.4	–0.3	–0.8	–1.4	–1.5	–2.0	**–2.3**	0.8
Financial account balance (% GDP)	0.3	1.1	1.9	2.8	3.8	2.0	**0.9**	0.5
Change in official reserves (USD millions)	2348	5470	8417	11358	11623	–6718	**–23992**	–3135
Domestic credit to private sector	49.5	50.1	52.3	52.5	54.9	57.4	**60.4**	60.6
Government bond yield (Italy)	11.5	10.6	10.9	12.8	13.5	13.3	**13.3**	11.2
Lending rate (Germany)	8.8	8.4	8.3	9.9	11.6	12.5	**13.6**	12.9
ITL/DEM exchange rate (% change)	1.7	6.2	–0.3	2.1	0.5	0.1	**20.6**	7.9
Interest rate spread	1.0	–4.0	2.9	0.8	1.4	0.7	**–20.9**	–9.5
Productivity growth spread (% points)	0.3	0.5	0.4	0.0	–2.4	–3.6	**–1.2**	0.5
Inflation differential	–5.9	–4.5	–3.8	–3.5	–3.7	–2.7	**0.0**	0.0
% change of the reer	4.2	2.1	–1.2	4.3	4.5	1.5	**–2.1**	–14.6
External debt (GDP points)	–7.2	–6.4	–6.4	–8.8	–11.0	–12.1	**–10.8**	–10.6
Government budget balance (% GDP)	–11.2	–10.9	–11.0	–11.4	–11.4	–11.4	**–10.4**	–10.0

Data sources: the main data source is IMF (2010). Real growth, inflation rates and government budget balance come from IMF (2012b). Domestic credit to the private sector comes from World Bank (2012). Average labour productivity comes from OECD (2012). External debt data come from Lane and Milesi-Ferretti (2007).

Germany (Acocella, 1998): on the contrary, the inflation, after a first decrease, rose slightly in 1990, despite a sharp fall in the real growth rate (stage (3) of the Minskyan cycle). After a moderate depreciation in 1988, the real exchange rate appreciated steadily. The trade balance turned to a moderate deficit. The much larger worsening of the current account was driven by a fall in net foreign income from abroad, because of interest payments on foreign capitals (stage (4)). The bell tolled in 1991. Until 1990 the capital inflows had more than compensated the current account deficit, resulting in an accumulation of official reserves. In 1991, when Italy entered the "narrow band", the trend of capital inflows was reversed (from 3.8 to 2.0 GDP points) and Italy experienced the first tensions in the currency market, as witnessed by a decrease in official reserves (stage (5)). The final stage took place in 1992, when the Italian lira, after a record of six growing current account deficits, underwent a massive speculative attack that pushed it out of the EMS. A massive run on Italy's official reserves ended up with a 20 per cent nominal devaluation. Interestingly enough, the nominal devaluation not only reversed the trade balance, bringing it to 2.8 GDP points in 1993 after five years of moderate deficits, but it also reversed the sign of the productivity growth spread: in 1993 average labour productivity growth in Italy was 0.5 points above the value it took in Germany, after a minimum of –3.6 points reached in 1991 (the year in which Italy entered the "narrow band"). This pattern is fully consistent with the Kaldor–Verdoorn mechanism.

The only feature that distinguishes this case from those studied by Frenkel and Rapetti is the pattern of the government budget balance. In Italy the government balance was negative and almost constant around –11 GDP points. Real growth was not fast enough to determine any noticeable improvement. This was partly determined by the fact that since 1979 the EMS partnership had forced Italy to raise its interest rates in order to "defend" the central parity of the lira. This change in monetary policy was further strengthened by the so-called "divorce" of Italy's central bank from the Ministry of Treasury, i.e. by the decision of the central bank not to intervene anymore in the primary market for public debt securities. As a result, the average real government bond yield jumped by ten points, from about –6 per cent in 1980 to about 4 per cent in 1982, and was on average equal to 6 per cent afterwards, setting the public debt-to-GDP ratio on a dynamically unstable path and overburdening the Italian government budget with huge interest expenses.

Two optical "Euroillusions"

Although the Minskyan framework seems to explain well what went on in Italy in 1992, does it provide any clue about what is going on 20 years later in the Eurozone peripheral countries?

If we believe the conventional interpretation of the current crisis, the answer must be negative. As a matter of fact, in the Minskyan framework the financial crisis originates in the private sector, in a context of buoyant real growth, and it is fuelled by nominal divergences (in interest and inflation rates) between the core and the peripheral economies. These three features are at odds with today's fashionable tale of the Eurozone crisis, according to which the villain is the "sovereign" debt, the crisis developed in a context of stagnant growth (supposedly by lack of mostly unspecified "structural" reforms) and it was determined by the peripheral governments' inability to take advantage of the beneficial nominal convergence brought about by the euro, which had reduced the burden of the debt.

The view that the Minskyan framework is inappropriate in the current crisis is consistent with the "this time is different" principle (Reinhart and Rogoff, 2008), and after all, the idea that something may have changed in Europe since 1992 sounds plausible. But of course another possibility is still open: the conventional explanation of the crisis could be false. In this section I explore this hypothesis, by analysing two statements that are often repeated in the public debate, namely that European peripheral countries would have benefited:

1 from low and converging inflation rates;
2 from low and converging (nominal) interest rates.

These statements, if true, would obviously contradict two important transmission mechanisms of the Minskyan cycle: convergence of the interest rates would imply the absence of any incentive for the "core" countries to lend to the "peripheral" ones (why lend to less trustworthy countries if the returns are the same?); convergence of the inflation rates would imply the absence of any real exchange rate appreciation in the peripheral countries, thus any further accumulation of net external liabilities (or, looking at the current account of the balance of payments, any persistent imbalance in trade flows).

I call these two sentences the "optical euroillusions", because while they may seem self-evident if one takes a glance at the (inappropriate) data, a more thorough analysis quickly unveils that their conventional wisdom is nothing but retrospective wishful thinking. In other words, a closer look at the data reveals that, unsurprisingly enough, nominal divergences of the kind stressed by Frenkel and Rapetti were at work in the peripheral countries before the present crisis, and were part of its mechanism.

Interest rates convergence

Figure 6.1 presents the government bond yields spreads between the peripheral countries and Germany. The figure is almost unreadable, but in economic terms this is so to speak an advantage rather than a disadvantage: the clutter in the middle of the graph depends on the fact that from Greece entry in the euro (2001) to the eve of the Lehman Brothers crack (early 2008) the sovereign spreads of Eurozone members collapsed to nearly zero, becoming undistinguishable from each other. This is exactly what politicians and newspapers keep repeating, when they mention the so-called "euro dividend", i.e. the reduction in the burden of sovereign debt, determined by the convergence of peripheral country interest rates to the German ones.

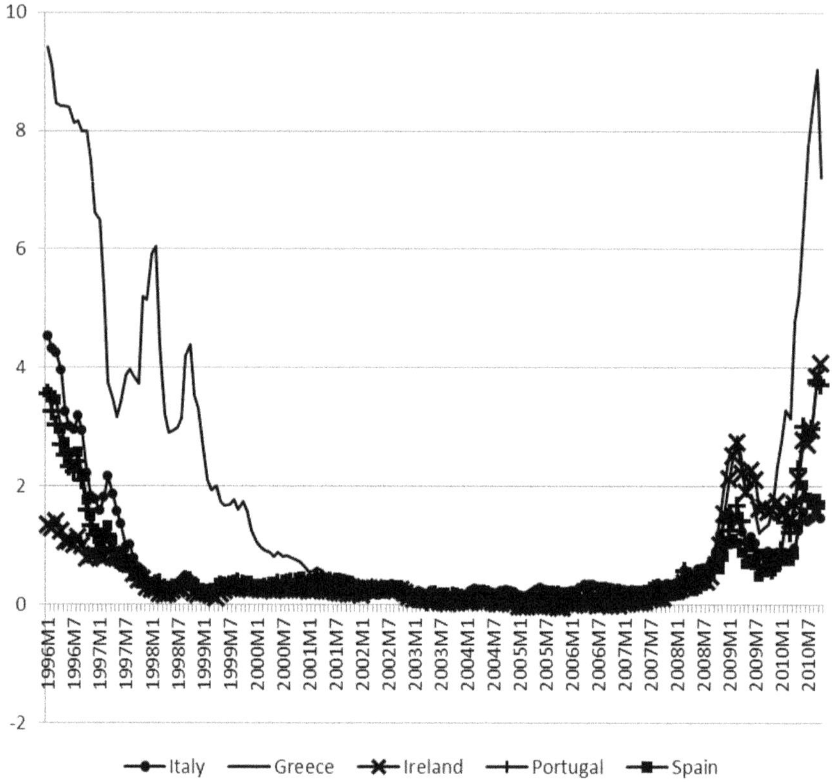

Figure 6.1 Government bond yield spread (source: IMF, 2010).

The conventional argument runs as follows: why were sovereign spreads higher before the onset of the euro? Because profligate peripheral governments lacked the "discipline" and "credibility" of the euro. So why did the spreads become higher after, when the euro was "disciplining" these governments? Because unfortunately profligate governments were profligate governments: they spoilt the benefit determined by the euro dividend, by postponing the structural reforms, and markets lost confidence in them. It has already been noticed in the literature that this explanation is a bit tautological and self-contradictory (Acocella, 1998): in fact, if the euro had effectively enforced "discipline", by definition profligate governments could no longer have kept their "vicious" habits. The very fact that they did, demonstrates that there is no such thing as an externally enforced "discipline", and the Italian experience in the "new EMS" offered some lessons in this respect.

But apart from the above, this explanation focuses on the wrong variables. If the crisis is presented as a sovereign debt crisis, sovereign interest rates spreads seem the right variables to look at, and there is no incentive to look any further.

But let us have a look at the spreads on private debts: if we do this, we immediately get a completely different picture from the conventional one, a picture which is more consistent with both the Minskyan framework and the stylized facts of the crisis. Figures 6.2 to 6.6 report the interest rate spreads between the peripheral Eurozone countries and Germany, on the government bond yield as

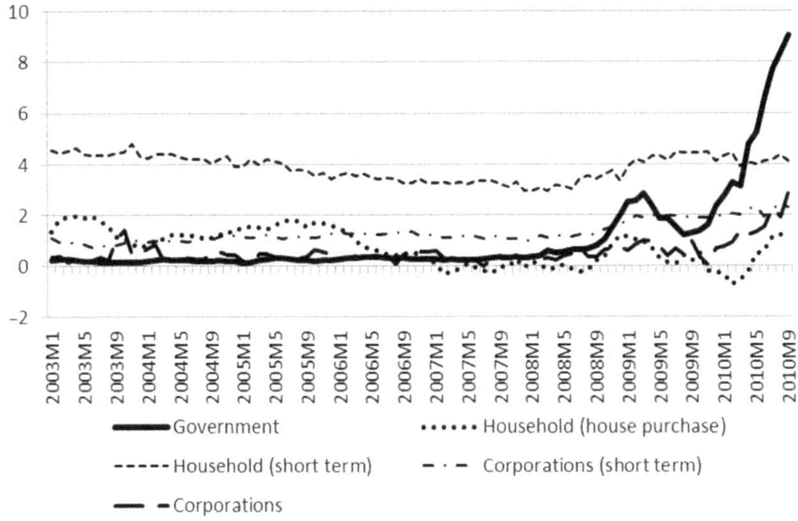

Figure 6.2 Spreads on public and private debts: Greece (source: IMF, 2010).

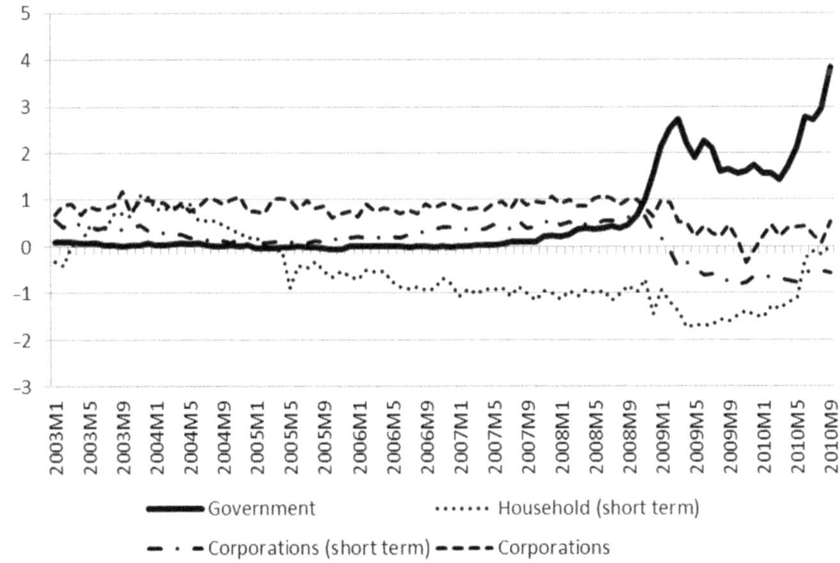

Figure 6.3 Spreads on public and private debts: Ireland (source: IMF, 2010).

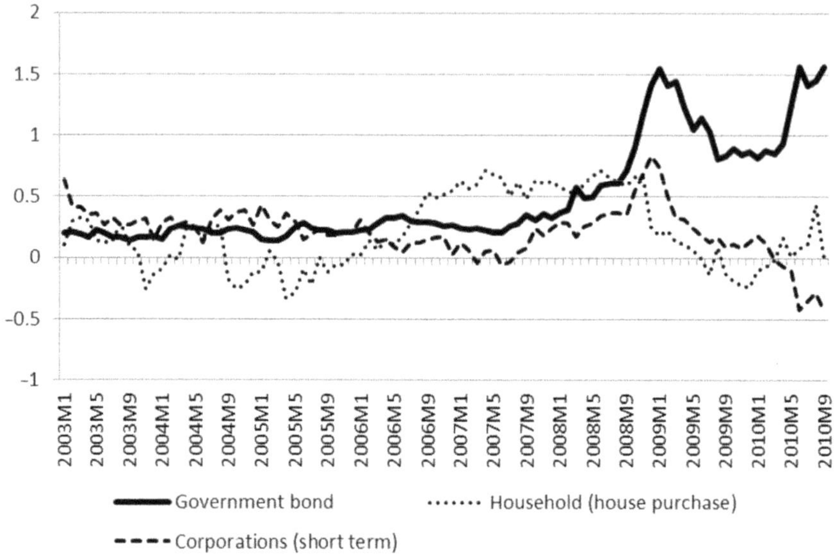

Figure 6.4 Spreads on public and private debts: Italy (source: IMF, 2010).

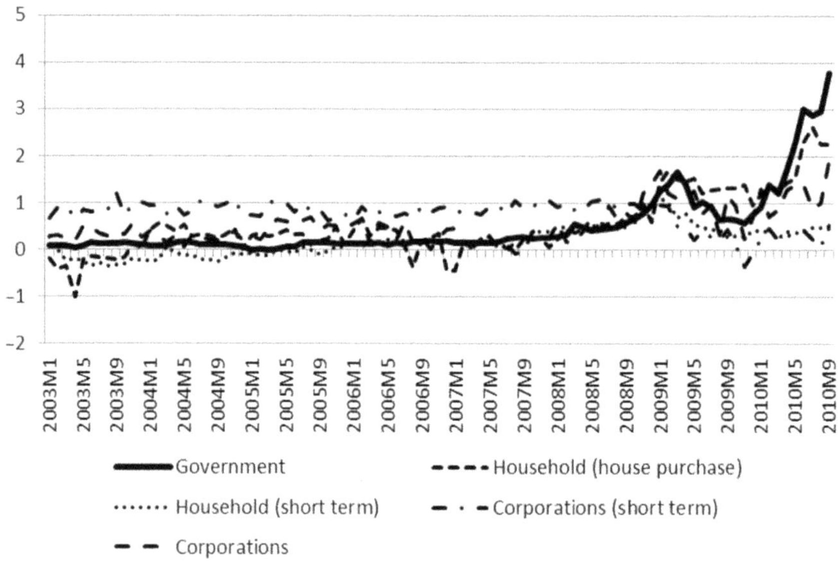

Figure 6.5 Spreads on public and private debts: Portugal (source: IMF, 2010).

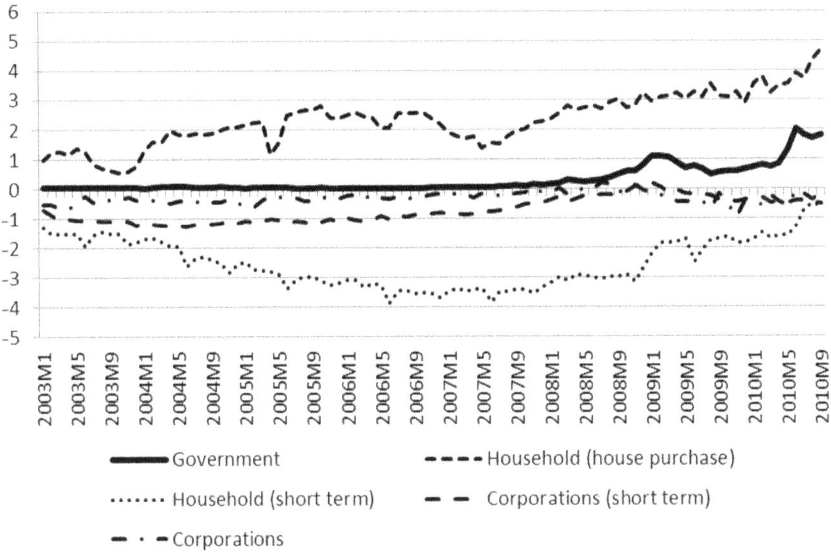

Figure 6.6 Spreads on public and private debts: Spain (source: IMF, 2010).

Table 6.2 Interest rate spreads between peripheral countries and Germany on public and private debts (average, 2003:1–2007:12)

	Government bond yield	*Household (house purchase)*	*Household (short term)*	*Corporations (short term)*	*Corporations*
Greece	0.25	0.98	3.85	1.10	0.38
Ireland	0.03	–0.22	0.29	0.86	–
Italy	0.23	0.19	–0.99	0.22	–0.28
Portugal	0.13	0.15	–0.01	0.86	0.33
Spain	0.05	1.85	–2.73	–0.99	–0.33

Data sources: see Note 3 in the text.

well as on four other categories of private debts: short-term (up to one year) loans to households, house purchase loans to households, short-term loans to firms, loans to firms over one million euro. The data run from January 2003 to September 2010 and came from the IMF (2010). Table 6.2 summarizes the same information by taking the sample averages from 2003:1 to 2007:12. All in all, these data show that while the spread on government debt narrowed to almost zero, four years after the inception of the euro loans to the private sector provided still a lot of interesting arbitrage opportunities for the "core" countries' creditors. This is evident in Greece, where all the "private" interest rates spread were above the "public" one. In the other countries the picture is mixed. For instance, in Portugal and Ireland the spread on corporation debt was positive, while in Spain it was the spread on house purchase loans to household. In other words, despite what Figure 6.1 suggests, there was enough nominal divergence in private sector interest rates to ignite stage (2) of the Minskyan cycle as described before.

Once you look at the right data, the virtuous convergence towards the German rates reveals itself to be an optical euroillusion.

Inflation rates convergence

The same applies to inflation convergence, another supposed benefit of euro membership. Figure 6.7 reports the inflation rates in the Eurozone from 1980 to 2010. The time series patterns of the data display a remarkable convergence since the early 1990s. This evidence supports the often repeated claim that the inception of the euro would have offered to the member countries a period of beneficial stability, by bringing their inflation rates closer to that of the "virtuous" countries of the core. Figure 6.7, however, conceals more than it discloses. In fact, after the inception of the euro the inflation rates, while becoming lower, continued to be very persistent. Inflation differentials with respect to the nominal

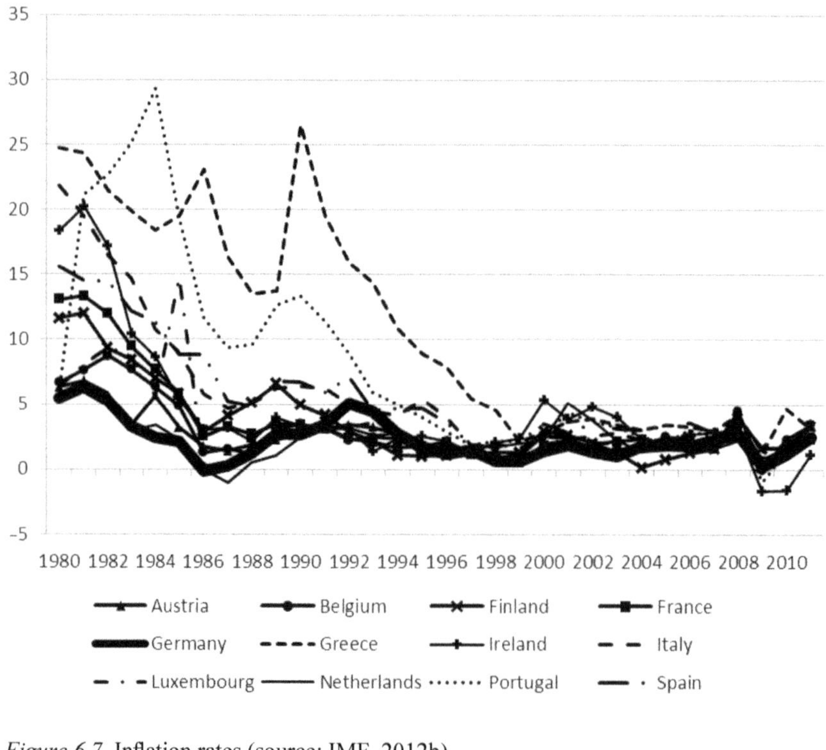

Figure 6.7 Inflation rates (source: IMF, 2012b).

Table 6.3 Inflation differentials with Germany, sample averages

	1980–2010	*1980–1992*	*1993–1998*	*1999–2007*	*2008–2010*
Austria	0.29	0.55	–0.15	0.18	0.39
Belgium	0.72	1.36	–0.32	0.42	0.89
Finland	1.40	3.43	–0.72	–0.01	1.03
France	1.36	3.24	–0.45	0.22	0.29
Greece	8.95	16.67	6.62	1.64	2.05
Ireland	2.38	4.78	–0.07	1.82	–1.42
Italy	3.53	7.04	1.61	0.74	0.59
Luxembourg	1.14	2.13	–0.13	0.73	0.64
Netherlands	–0.07	–0.73	–0.02	0.84	–0.01
Portugal	5.85	12.33	1.61	1.37	–0.33
Spain	3.45	6.32	1.49	1.55	0.60

Data source: IMF (2012a).

anchor of the system were consistently positive. As Table 6.3 shows, from 1999 to 2007 in all the Eurozone countries inflation was higher than in Germany (with the possible exception of Finland). In fact, over the larger sample from 1980 to 2010 we see that every (prospective) Eurozone member had had higher inflation than Germany (with the possible exception of Netherlands). This empirical regularity weakens in each post-crisis period. From 1993 to 1998 some core countries (in particular, Finland and France) were able to offset a (small) share of their cumulated inflation differential with Germany. After 2008 this happened in only two peripheral countries, Ireland and Portugal.

The persistence of such a wedge between the member countries' inflation rates means that these rates were not converging. The study by Busetti *et al.* (2006) shows that after a remarkable convergence effort in the 1990s, with the inception of the euro the Eurozone was split into three "inflation convergence" clubs: the virtuous countries of the former Deutsch Mark (DEM) area, Italy and the other peripheral countries, each evolving along separate paths. It is worth noting that this is exactly what the Minskyan framework presented before predicts, namely, that the exogenous policy change determined by the adoption of a "credible" exchange rate will foster nominal divergence (or at least impede nominal convergence). While Busetti *et al.* (2006) use sophisticated econometric methodologies, a rough picture of what is going on in Europe before the crisis can be obtained by looking at how often the inflation differentials between each member country and Germany changed sign. From 1999 to 2007 there were only 14 changes of sign (corresponding to 14 per cent of the sample), all occurring within the "virtuous" club, except one (Italy managed to have a lower inflation than Germany in 2007). As Cesaratto and Stirati (2010–11) illustrate, this behaviour of inflation rates finds its historical roots in the explicit decision of the German elites to adopt an export-oriented growth model, by practising a real competitive devaluation against the European partners. Summing up, as for nominal interest rates, inflation convergence too qualifies itself as an optical euroillusion.

This has important consequences and raises many questions. As a matter of fact, while economic theory does not provide definite theoretical or empirical support to the idea that the optimal inflation rate is close to zero, as implicitly assumed in the current political debate (see, e.g. Acocella *et al.*, 2010; Khan and Senhadji, 2000), it is trivially true that the persistence of inflation differentials within a monetary union *must* lead to disruptions in trade flows, through a progressive deterioration of price competitiveness in the high-inflation countries which necessarily leads to the accumulation of net foreign liabilities in these countries (Fleming, 1971).

Why did this phenomenon go unnoticed for so many years? Why did inflation disappear from the political debate, despite the persistence of non-negligible inflation differentials, and despite the obvious threats that these differentials posed to the Eurozone stability? Since persistent inflation differentials necessarily lead to external imbalances, these questions are akin to another question: why did the Maastricht treaty and the Stability and Growth Pact neglect the monitoring of external imbalances? Why did they not set any quantitative reference parameter for them?

It is difficult to find a rational answer to these questions, especially if one considers that Article 3A of the Treaty on the European Union explicitly quotes a "sustainable balance of payments" among the "guiding principles" of the Member States, and Article 109j recalls that "the situation and development of the balances of payments on current account" (i.e. net foreign indebtedness) shall be taken into account in the reports of the Commission and of the European Monetary Institute during the process towards the euro. The Treaty therefore expresses a clear awareness of the dangers determined by unsustainable external imbalances among member states.

The only rational motivation for ignoring them is as old as the world itself: these imbalances (and, before them, the underlying nominal divergences that fuelled them) were ignored for the very reason that (and as long as) they benefited the stronger partners of the Union, as Cesaratto and Stirati (2010–2011) explain. This is best understood if we look at the sectorial financial balances of the member countries. We turn to this task in the next section.

Which debt?

In the previous section we showed that despite the boasted advantages of nominal "convergence", after the inception of the euro there were still enough nominal divergences between the core and peripheral economies of the Eurozone to ignite and sustain a Minskyan cycle through disrupting external imbalances and the associated international capital flows. In other words, this evidence is consistent with the view, nowadays shared by a large part of the economic profession, that the Eurozone crisis is in its essence a balance of payments crisis, or, in other words, an external debt sustainability crisis. Media and politicians across Europe keep repeating instead that the Eurozone crisis is a sovereign debt crisis. In principle, these two statements do not contradict each other: if a government borrows an "excessive" amount of money from foreign creditors, ending up in a default, the ensuing debt crisis will be *both* a sovereign debt crisis (because the debtor is the government) *and* an external debt crisis (to the extent that the creditors are non-resident entities). However, for this to happen, the country must have obeyed to the so-called "twin deficits" mechanism, namely, capital inflows (the current account deficit) must have been determined mostly by the government budget deficit. This is what happens in the Mundell–Fleming model with perfect capital mobility and fixed exchange rates: an expansionary fiscal policy (i.e. an increase in government deficit) raises the domestic interest rates, thus attracting capital from abroad, thereby determining an increase in the current account deficit. Unlike our reference framework, in the Mundell–Fleming model the nominal divergences that open to arbitrage possibilities, hence to the inflows of foreign capital, are caused by the behaviour of the public sector: it is the peripheral government, rather than the families and households, which start borrowing from the core creditors.

We will now move a little step further in our analysis of how closely the Minskyan paradigm adapts to the Eurozone crisis by addressing this question: which debt determined the crisis? Or, in other words, which sector was mainly responsible (if any) for the massive accumulation of net foreign liabilities? Was it the public one, or the private one? Before delving into the data, it is worth noting that at this point we have at least two indirect evidences that support the Minskyan hypothesis of a private debt-driven crisis.

First, the data on the interest rate spreads set out show that the government bond yield spread collapsed to zero in the years before the crisis, whereas the spreads on different kinds of private debt were positive: in principle, this suggests that foreign capitals were not attracted by expansionary fiscal policies (which would have raised the government bond yield); at the same time, the persistence of positive spreads in some segments of the financial market indicates that creditors from the core countries had obvious incentives to lend money to private (rather than sovereign) debtors in the peripheral countries. Second, evidence on the "twin deficit" mechanism suggests that the relation between government and external deficit is rather tenuous. Panel studies such as Chinn and Prasad (2003) or Bartolini and Lahiri (2006) find very low coefficients (between 0.1 and 0.3), indicating that each euro of government deficit causes only 10 to 30 cents of current account deficit. Country specific studies like Bagnai (2006) show that in Italy, Spain and Portugal there is no long-run relation between the two deficits, while in Greece and Ireland a relation exists but weakens over time. In particular, contrary to what could be expected given the usual accounts of the Greek crisis, the government deficit loses its significance as an explanatory variable of the Greek current account at the end of the 1980s (on a sample ranging from 1960 to 2004). As we shall see in the next section, the data patterns are consistent with the stylized facts stressed by the empirical literature, rather than with the conventional wisdom about "government profligacy".

Sectorial balances in the Eurozone: unhappy families are all alike

In this section we present the evolution of the sectorial balances in selected Eurozone countries from 1993 to 2007, i.e. from the last but one crisis to the eve of the present one, expressed as shares of GDP. The arithmetic of sectorial balances is expounded in the Appendix. It is worth remembering here that the sectorial balances are a mere accounting device, which provides a descriptive account of the data patterns. It would be wrong to infer from these patterns, which simply reflect the fact that *ex post* the national accounts identities *must* be satisfied, any "causal" explanation about the mechanism that triggered the crisis. Moreover, since the data are measured in GDP points, they obviously do not say anything about GDP growth, nor are intended to do so. As a matter of fact, this is not a limit of the analysis, because the sustainability of an agent financial position (hence, of its financial balance) depends on its ratio to the sector's revenues. For this reason, sustainability testing is mostly based on debt-to-GDP ratios (Chalk and Hemming, 2000). Summing up these remarks, in this section we are only interested in assessing whether the accumulation of net foreign liabilities by peripheral countries has coexisted with growing public or private indebtedness.

We begin with Figure 6.8 that describes by means of simulated data the pattern of sectorial balances in a hypothetical country, "Twinsland", where the sectorial balances strictly obeys a "twin deficits" mechanism. The figure shows

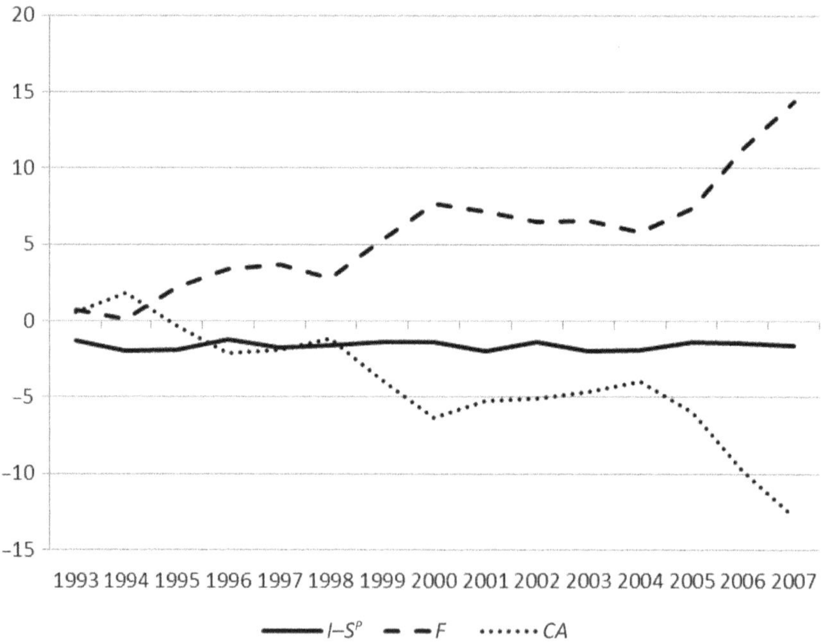

Figure 6.8 Typical sectorial balance patterns in a "twin deficits" country (source: author's simulations).

that in the presence of a moderate and stable private surplus ($I-S^P$, the solid line), the increasing borrowing requirements of the government (F, the dashed line) are satisfied by borrowing money from abroad, i.e. through a current account deficit (i.e. a foreign sector surplus, CA, the dotted line). It should be considered that owing to the way the balances are defined, the "twin" behaviour displays graphically as "mirror" behaviour. This pattern where a rising government deficit mirrors a falling current account balance is exactly what we would expect to find in the data if the conventional story on the Eurozone crisis was true: profligate governments increase their indebtedness by borrowing on foreign markets.

As a matter of fact, such a long-run pattern is never observed in any Eurozone country. Before going into the details, it is perhaps worth getting a general picture by looking at Table 6.4, which reports some summary statistics on the sectorial balances: the sample correlations between the current account balance on the one hand, and either the private or the public deficit on the other hand, and the variations of the balances over the whole sample considered (1993–2007).[4] The table is split into three panels: simulated economy, "unhappy families" and "happy families". In the simulated economy of Twinsland there is a perfect negative correlation between the government deficit and the current account balance (Figure 6.8), and the increase in government deficit over the whole sample, equal to 13.63 GDP points, is almost perfectly mirrored by a worsening in the current account balance.

Figure 6.9 Greece (source: IMF, 2012b).

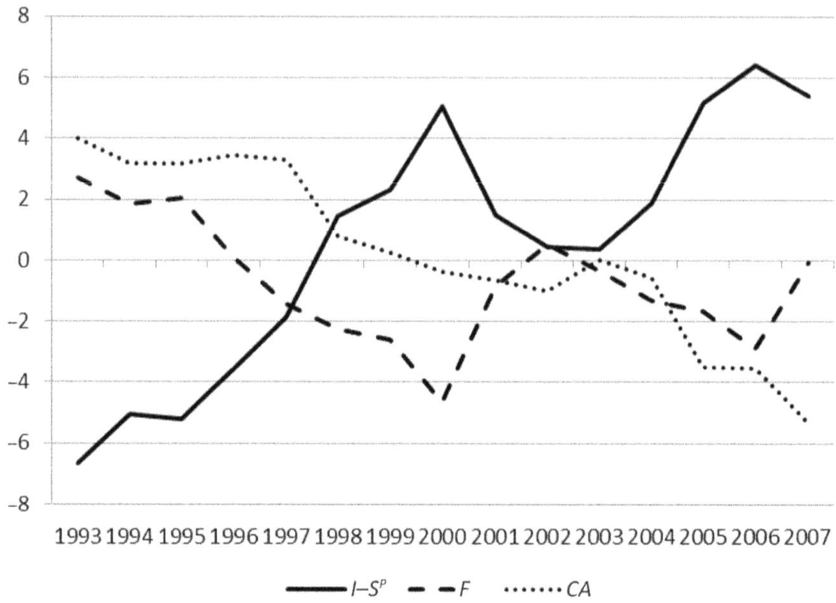

Figure 6.10 Ireland (source: IMF, 2012b).

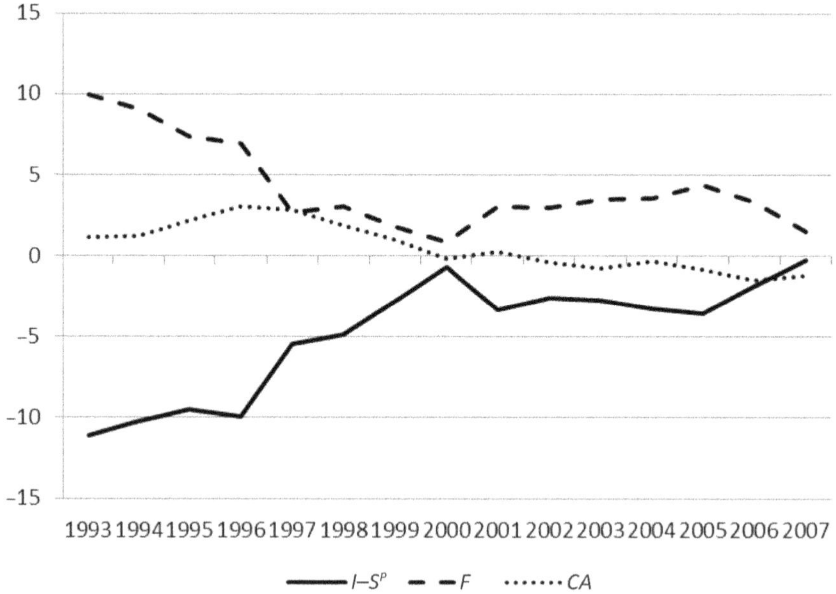

Figure 6.11 Italy (source: IMF, 2012b).

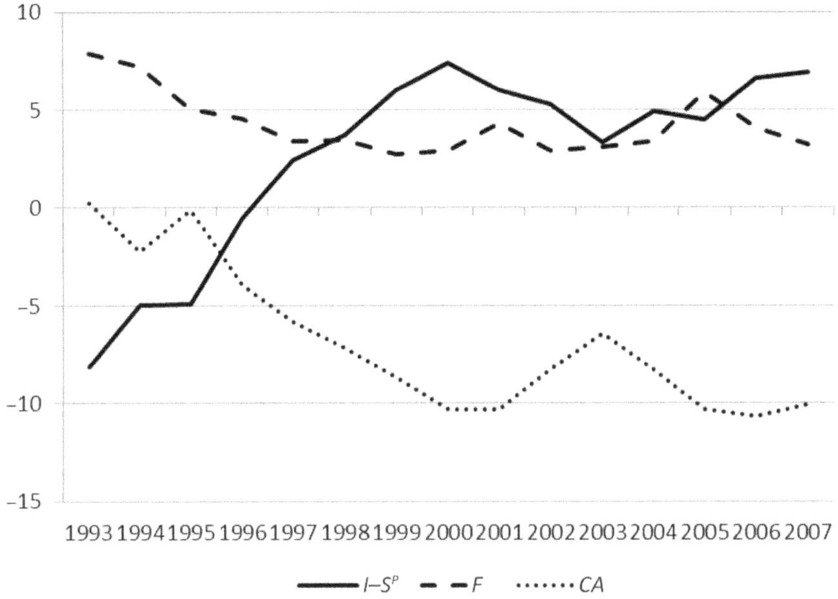

Figure 6.12 Portugal (source: IMF, 2012b).

Figure 6.13 Spain (source: IMF, 2012b).

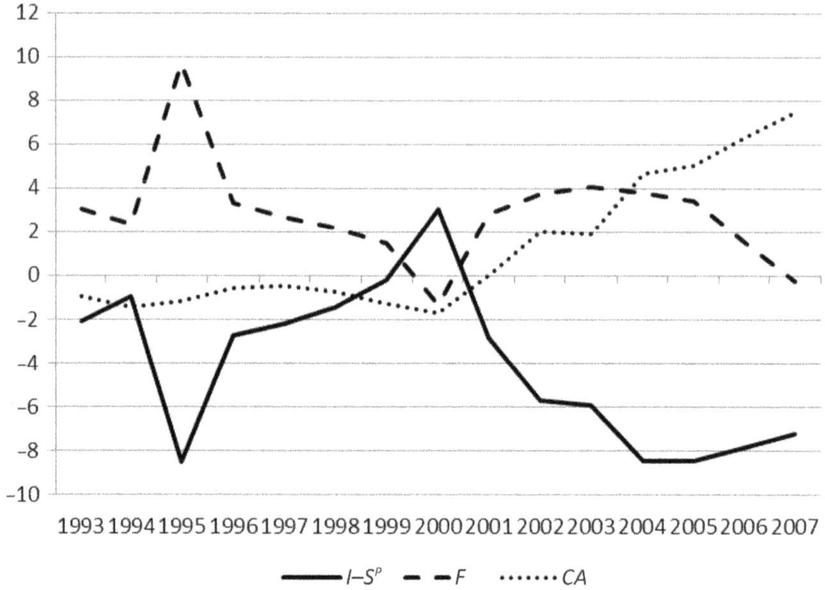

Figure 6.14 Germany (source: IMF, 2012b).

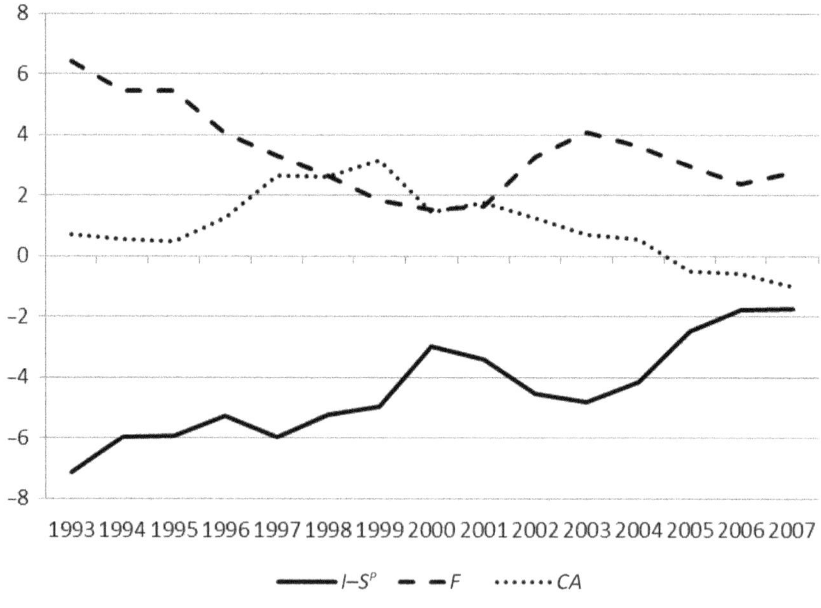

Figure 6.15 France (source: IMF, 2012b).

Table 6.4 A descriptive analysis of financial balances in selected European countries

	Sample correlations (1993–2007)		*Variation (2007 over 1993)*		
	*CA, I-S^P^*	*CA, F*	*I-S^P^*	*F*	*CA*
Simulated economy					
Twinsland	–0.22	–1.00	–0.27	13.63	–13.36
Unhappy families					
Belgium	–0.71	0.35	10.43	–6.98	–3.45
Greece	–0.91	0.40	19.36	–5.73	–13.63
Iceland	–0.99	0.93	26.29	–9.85	–16.44
Italy	–0.73	0.43	10.90	–8.50	–2.40
Ireland	–0.91	0.47	12.06	–2.75	–9.30
Portugal	–0.97	0.64	15.01	–4.66	–10.35
Spain	–0.97	0.88	17.39	–8.46	–8.92
Happy families					
France	–0.51	–0.26	5.38	–3.67	–1.71
Germany	–0.75	–0.16	–5.12	–3.28	8.40

Data source: IMF (2012a).

This happens in any of the "unhappy families" considered, which include, along with the peripheral Eurozone countries, also Belgium (a former DEM-area country that ran into troubles during the crisis because of its fragile banking sector) and Iceland (a non-Eurozone country whose crisis anticipated that of many peripheral Eurozone countries). Let us look first at the sample correlation between the balances, reported in the leftmost part of Table 6.4. In all these countries it is *private* rather than *public* deficit that displays a strong *negative* correlation with the current account balance (above 0.9 in absolute value in Greece, Iceland, Ireland, Portugal and Spain). This behaviour is also evident in Belgium and Italy, where the correlation is still large (above 0.7 in absolute value) and negative. On the other hand, in all these countries the government deficit displays a moderate to strong *positive* correlation with the current account balance, instead of a perfect negative correlation (as we would expect in the "twin deficits" case). This correlation is particularly strong in Iceland (0.93) and Spain (0.88), two countries that were experiencing a significant fiscal consolidation just before the outbreak of the crisis.

All in all, there is strong evidence that the growing external indebtedness is correlated with the excess of private sector expenditure over its revenues, while the correlation of the current account balance with government deficit is much weaker and positive. In the countries considered the steady increase in external indebtedness has gone hand in hand with an increase in the private sector borrowing requirement (or, more precisely, with a reduction of its net saving), in the presence of a falling public sector borrowing requirement. This hypothesis is supported by the variations of the balances, reported in the rightmost part of Table 6.4. In all the countries considered the current account balance worsened, from a minimum of –2.4 GDP points in Italy to a maximum of –16.44 GDP points in Iceland. At the same time, in all these countries the government deficit fell (instead of increasing), from a maximum of 9.85 GDP points in Iceland to a minimum of 2.4 GDP points in Italy. The simple, but inexorable, arithmetic of the balances implies therefore that the worsening of the current account balance reflects a reduction in the private sector net savings (an increase in the private sector deficit). In fact, $I\text{–}S^P$ has increased in all the unhappy families, with increases ranging from a maximum of 26.29 GDP points in Iceland to a minimum of 10.90 in Italy. The cross-country correlation between the increase in the private deficit and the current account balance is –0.90. Moreover, it is worth noting that in all the "unhappy families" the reduction in private net savings was larger (in absolute value) than the worsening in the current account balance: the increase in the financing needs of the private sector was not completely reflected in an increase of foreign capital inflows because it was partly offset by an increase in government net saving (a reduction in government deficit). This evidence is completely at odds with the claim that the public sector has been the engine of the financial crisis: on the contrary, fiscal consolidation in *all* the "unhappy families" seems to have contributed to reining in the adverse trend of external indebtedness.

Going now into some detail, the pattern described is particularly evident in Spain (Figure 6.13), where the steady worsening of the current account, starting in 1997, was accompanied by a constant improvement of the government balance (that eventually went into surplus in 2005), more than offset by a steady increase in the private sector deficit. In this case it is quite apparent that the "twins" are the external and the private deficits, rather than the external and the public ones. Portugal (Figure 6.12) displays a similar pattern, although the development is more abrupt, with the increase in private deficit (and the reduction in public deficit) occurring in the first half of the sample, followed by a stabilization of the balances.

The picture in Greece is substantially similar in the long run, with some distinct episodes. Unlike Spain (and like Ireland and Italy), Greece slightly loosened up its fiscal discipline after its entry in the Eurozone. However, during that period (approximately from 2000 to 2004) the current account balance *improved* (hence, once more we do *not* find twin deficits), because the private deficit, which had improved by 15 GDP points from 1993 to 2000, fell by more than public deficit rose. On the contrary, the sharp worsening in external indebtedness in the three years before the onset of the crisis clearly depended on the sharp increase of private deficit. A similar pattern, much more pronounced, is observed in Ireland, where the government balance had reached in 2000 a 4.6 GDP points surplus (shown in Figure 6.10 as a negative deficit, dashed line). This was partly reversed leading in two years to a "close to balance" position, followed by a new episode of fiscal consolidation up to the onset of the crisis. As in the previous cases, during the two fiscal consolidations (1993 to 2000 and 2002 to 2006) the current account balance kept worsening: once more, external indebtedness was mirrored by an increase in the private sector deficit.

In the case of Italy the picture is more complex (although the summary statistics in Table 6.4 show that in its essence the mechanisms at work were similar). After the 1992 devaluation an improvement in the current account balance was mirrored by a fall in the government deficit, with an almost stable private sector deficit: this typical "twin deficits" pattern lasted until 1996. By the end of 1996 Italy re-entered the EMS narrow band: the current account balance worsened, along with an improvement of the government deficit. From 1996 to 2000 it is the fall in private savings, rather than in government savings, that explained the fall in the current account balance. In the change-over year the government deficit improved sharply. This increase was partly mirrored by a decrease in the private deficit: as a result, the current account balance kept worsening (at a slow but steady rate). Starting in 2006, another structural change: the government tightened its fiscal stance, but at the same time the private sector net savings went to zero: as a result, the current account balance kept falling, even in the presence of a fiscal consolidation (which we found to be the typical pattern in all the "unhappy families"). All in all, Italy alternates episodes where the current account dynamics seems to be driven by the government deficit, with episodes in which the private deficit takes the lead. The general picture, however, as summarized in Table 6.4, does not differ in the medium run from that of the other "unhappy families".

More on balances in the Eurozone: happy families are happy in their own way

What about the happy families, i.e. about the so-called French–German axis? A look at the bottom panel of Table 6.4, and at Figures 6.14 and 6.15, shows that they are happy (if ever) each in its own way.

Unlike the "unhappy families", France and Germany display a *negative* correlation between the current account balance and government deficit. This correlation in principle would signal a "twin deficits" behaviour: however, it is very weak (which is to be expected, given the existing evidence on the "twin deficits" behaviour recalled above), and almost inexistent in the case of Germany. In both cases, the pattern of the external balances is more correlated with the private deficit.

If we look at the variation of the balances over the sample considered, we realize that despite many claims, there is no such thing in the economic fundamentals as a "French–German" axis. True, the government deficit has improved in both countries by about the same amount (around 3.5 GDP points), but (i) the correlations show that the government deficit is not an important determinant of the external balance, and (ii) the behaviours of the current account balances, hence of the private deficits, differ widely between the "happy" countries. While from 1993 to 2007 the current account balance of Germany has improved by 8.4 GDP points, the current account balance of France worsened by –1.71. This figure actually conceals the real dimension of the phenomenon, because, as it is easily checked in Figure 6.15, the current account balance of France had reached a maximum of 3.15 GDP points in 1999, falling steadily thereafter by more than 4 GDP points. This steady fall can be divided into several episodes: in the first year after the inception of the euro (from 1999 to 2000) the current account worsens following a drop in private savings (an increase in the private deficit). From 2000 to 2003 the worsening is related to an increase in public deficit, matched only in part by an increase in private net savings (we have therefore a four year window of "twin deficits" behaviour). From 2004 until the eve of the crisis the situation is reversed again: the current account balance keeps falling, owing to the presence of fiscal austerity (a drop in *F*), we assist a sharp reduction in private net saving. If we enlarge the zoom, we see that the private balance has kept worsening along a relatively steady path, starting from a surplus position of about 7 GDP points ($I-S^P=-7$), and shrinking by more than five points (Table 6.4). This pattern is very similar to the one followed by the private sector balance in Italy, and also, *toute proportion gardée*, in Spain and Greece. The situation in Germany is completely different. A glance at Figure 6.14 shows that the take-off of the German current account balance occurs together with a strong increase in its private sector surplus (a drop in $I-S^P$) by more than 10 GDP points from 2000 to 2004, in the presence of rising government deficit (an increase in *F*). Unlike in France, in Germany the public and current account deficits become "twins" starting in 2004, in the presence of a stable and sizeable surplus (negative deficit) of the private sector.

Flows and stocks

Summing up the discussion so far, we have seen that all the "unhappy" families have witnessed a huge increase in the private sector deficit (a reduction in the private sector net savings), in the presence of a falling government deficit, and of a worsening current account balance. This suggests that the financial distress in these countries has been caused by the accumulation of private, rather than public, external liabilities against foreign creditors. In other words, this evidence disproves the argument that the Eurozone peripheral crisis is an external debt crisis caused by fiscal profligacy.

As is to be expected, the behaviour of the stocks obeys that of the underlying flows. As Figure 6.16 shows, the four countries most hit by the crisis (Greece, Ireland, Portugal and Spain) experienced a dramatic worsening of their net international investment position from 1999 to 2007, ranging from –48 GDP points in Spain to –70 GDP points in Greece. In two out of these four countries the public debt was falling. In fact, the only sizeable increase in general government gross debt took place in Portugal, where the debt increased by 19 GDP points, reaching a still reasonable level of 68 GDP points in 2007. A worsening of the net external position, coupled with a reduction of public debt, features also in two other countries affected by the crisis: Italy and Belgium (where the crisis hit the banking sector, leading to the nationalisation of Dexia). As usual, Germany features a completely different pattern: instead of a reduction in public debt and a worsening in the net international investment position (hereafter, NIIP), Germany displays a small increase in public debt and a sizeable improvement in the NIIP.

The same data are reported in Table 6.5 along with the change in domestic credit to the private sector. The change in the NIIP is almost uncorrelated with the change in public debt (the cross-country sample correlation is 0.03), while it is strongly correlated with the change in private debt (domestic credit to the

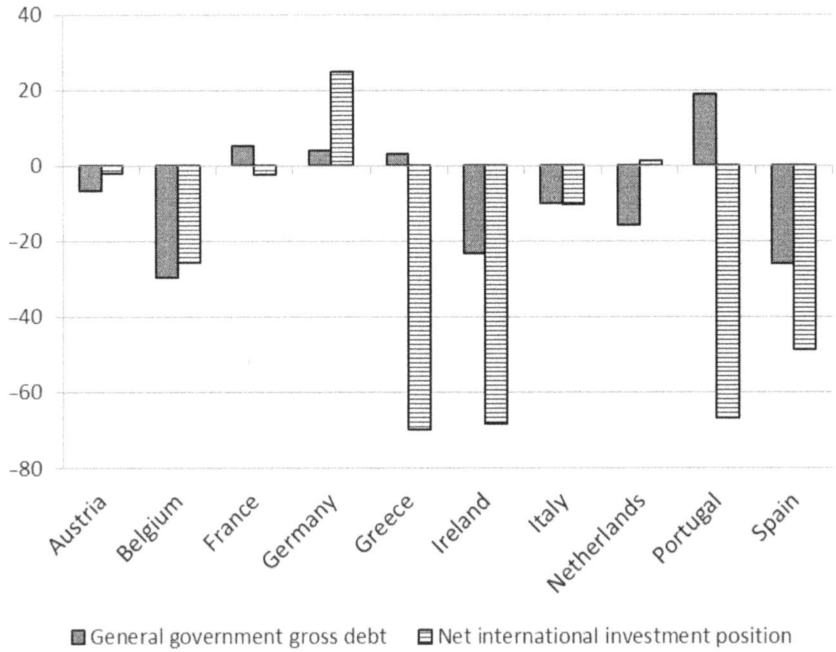

Figure 6.16 Change in public and external debt to GDP ratio (1997–2007) (source: general government gross debt comes IMF (2012b); net international investment from IMF (2010)).

private sector), with a negative coefficient equal to –0.70. While the correlation does not per se indicate causation, we stress that this stylized fact is perfectly consistent with the Minskyan framework (accumulation of net external liabilities by the private sector), while it does not match the "sovereign debt" explanation of the peripheral crises.

The patterns of macroeconomic fundamentals in the "unhappy families"

Summing up, the evidence presented so far shows that after the exogenous policy change determined by the adoption of the euro, the peripheral countries of the Eurozone experienced both a significant nominal divergence (in the private debt spreads, as well as in the inflation rates) and a private-sector-driven accumulation of net foreign liabilities. These two features, while contrasting the usual narrative of the crisis, are perfectly consistent with the Minskyan framework presented before. In this section we further explore the analogy between the Minskyan cycle and the Eurozone crisis by looking at the patterns of the macroeconomic fundamentals in the period preceding the crisis, and checking whether they follow the steps described above. This is done in Tables 6.6 to 6.9, which are built following Frenkel and Rapetti (2009).

Table 6.5 The change in private, public and external debt from 1999 to 2007 (GDP ratios)

	Austria	*Belgium*	*France*	*Germany*	*Greece*	*Ireland*	*Italy*	*Netherlands*	*Portugal*	*Spain*
Domestic credit to private sector	16.1	10.4	23.9	–11.1	52.4	98.0	30.5	62.7	53.1	98.2
General government gross debt	–6.6	–29.5	5.3	3.9	2.9	–23.2	–9.9	–15.8	18.8	–26.1
Net international investment position	–2.1	–25.8	–2.4	24.8	–69.8	–68.4	–10.4	1.3	–66.9	–48.7

Data source: domestic credit comes from World Bank (2012); general government gross debt from IMF (2012a); net international investment position from IMF (2010).

Table 6.6 Spain: selected macroeconomic variables, 1996–2009

	1996	*1997*	*1998*	*1999*	*2000*	*2001*	*2002*	*2003*	*2004*	*2005*	*2006*	*2007*	*2008*	*2009*
Real growth	2.4	3.9	4.5	4.7	5.1	3.6	2.7	3.1	3.3	3.6	4.1	3.5	0.9	–3.7
Trade balance (GDP points)	–2.6	–2.5	–3.6	–5.1	–6.4	–5.7	–5.0	–5.1	–6.4	–7.5	–8.5	–8.7	–8.0	–4.3
Current account balance (GDP points)	–0.4	–0.1	–1.2	–2.9	–4.0	–3.9	–3.2	–3.5	–5.2	–7.4	–9.0	–10.0	–9.8	–5.5
Financial account balance (GDP points)	3.5	1.6	–2.2	–1.7	2.6	3.0	2.6	0.5	3.5	6.5	8.7	9.6	9.5	5.9
Change in official reserves (USD millions)	24280	11755	–14354	–22795	–2880	–1341	3690	–15490	–6412	–1920	578	215	688	5970
Domestic credit to private sector	73.2	78.3	85.2	89.6	97.7	101.1	105.7	113.2	124.9	145.7	167.2	187.8	202.8	210.9
Long-term interest rate	8.7	6.4	4.8	4.7	5.5	5.1	5.0	4.1	4.1	3.4	3.8	4.3	4.4	4.0
Long-term interest rate (Germany)	6.2	5.7	4.6	4.5	5.3	4.8	4.8	4.1	4.0	3.4	3.8	4.2	4.0	3.2
% change of the ESP/ECU exchange rate (+=devaluation)	1.7	4.3	1.3	0.0	0.0	0.0	0.0	0.0	0.0	0.0	0.0	0.0	0.0	0.0
Interest rate spread (corrected for the devaluation)	0.8	–3.5	–1.0	0.2	0.3	0.3	0.2	0.1	0.1	0.0	0.0	0.1	0.4	0.8
Productivity growth spread (% points)	–1.1	–2.1	–1.2	–0.8	–2.7	–2.4	–0.9	–0.2	–0.3	–0.6	–2.8	–0.2	0.9	5.3
Wage inflation differential	0.7	2.3	0.7	–0.2	–0.5	0.9	1.4	3.3	2.1	2.1	3.0	2.6	1.7	2.4
% change of the reer (+=appreciation)	2.6	–1.7	–0.2	–2.7	–0.9	1.1	2.5	6.2	4.1	3.5	2.9	4.8	5.1	3.1
External debt (GDP points)	–17.1	–15.4	–19.6	–23.5	–24.3	–27.9	–36.8	–43.3	–48.0	–46.0	–71.6	–85.1	–75.1	–96.1
Government budget balance (GDP points)	–4.9	–3.4	–3.2	–1.4	–1.0	–0.7	–0.5	–0.2	–0.3	1.0	2.0	1.9	–4.2	–11.2

Data sources: the main data source is IMF (2010). Real growth, inflation rates and government budget balance come from IMF (2012b). Domestic credit to the private sector comes from World Bank (2012). Long-term interest rates as well as average labour productivity come from OECD (2012). External debt data before 1999 come from Lane and Milesi-Ferretti (2007).

Table 6.7 Italy: selected macroeconomic variables, 1996–2009

	1996	*1997*	*1998*	*1999*	*2000*	*2001*	*2002*	*2003*	*2004*	*2005*	*2006*	*2007*	*2008*	*2009*
Real growth	1.1	1.9	1.4	1.5	3.7	1.9	0.5	0.0	1.7	0.9	2.2	1.7	–1.2	–5.5
Trade balance (GDP points)	4.3	3.3	2.9	1.9	0.9	1.4	1.1	0.8	0.6	0.0	–0.7	0.2	0.0	0.2
Current account balance (GDP points)	3.2	2.7	1.6	0.7	–0.5	–0.1	–0.8	–1.3	–0.9	–1.7	–2.6	–2.4	–3.4	–3.1
Financial account balance (GDP points)	–0.6	–0.6	–1.5	–1.4	0.7	–0.3	0.9	1.3	0.5	1.4	1.7	1.8	3.5	1.4
Change in official reserves (USD millions)	11907	13150	–21472	–8051	3247	–588	3169	1115	–2844	–1030	–566	1893	8204	9003
Domestic credit to private sector	54.6	55.3	57.9	70.6	76.0	77.9	80.0	83.6	85.2	89.4	95.0	101.1	105.2	111.0
Long-term interest rate	9.4	6.9	4.9	4.7	5.6	5.2	5.0	4.3	4.3	3.6	4.0	4.5	4.7	4.3
Long-term interest rate (Germany)	6.2	5.7	4.6	4.5	5.3	4.8	4.8	4.1	4.0	3.4	3.8	4.2	4.0	3.2
% change of the ITL/ECU exchange rate (+=devaluation)	–8.1	–1.5	0.7	–0.4	0.0	0.0	0.0	0.0	0.0	0.0	0.0	0.0	0.0	0.0
Interest rate spread (corrected for the devaluation)	11.3	2.7	–0.4	0.6	0.3	0.4	0.3	0.2	0.2	0.2	0.3	0.3	0.7	1.1
Productivity growth spread (% points)	–2.4	–0.2	–1.5	–0.4	–0.2	–1.7	–2.0	–2.1	0.2	–0.7	–3.3	–1.6	–0.6	0.5
Wage inflation differential	–1.5	1.8	0.7	–0.4	–0.9	–1.6	–0.4	1.3	1.4	1.7	1.9	1.2	–0.7	–0.1
% change of the reer (+=appreciation)	13.9	3.6	0.3	0.1	–5.4	1.4	4.6	11.3	5.4	2.5	1.3	3.6	6.9	5.9
External debt (GDP points)	–5.6	–6.4	–11.2	–12.6	–13.2	–9.7	–15.2	–16.8	–17.8	–14.8	–21.5	–22.9	–20.2	–20.5
Government budget balance (GDP points)	–6.9	–2.7	–3.1	–1.8	–0.9	–3.1	–3.0	–3.5	–3.5	–4.4	–3.3	–1.5	–2.7	–5.4

Data sources: the main data source is IMF (2010). Real growth, inflation rates and government budget balance come from IMF (2012b). Domestic credit to the private sector comes from World Bank (2012). Long-term interest rates as well as average labour productivity come from OECD (2012). External debt data before 1999 come from Lane and Milesi-Ferretti (2007).

Table 6.8 Portugal: selected macroeconomic variables, 1996–2009

	1996	*1997*	*1998*	*1999*	*2000*	*2001*	*2002*	*2003*	*2004*	*2005*	*2006*	*2007*	*2008*	*2009*
Real growth	3.6	4.4	5.1	4.1	3.9	2.0	0.8	–0.9	1.6	0.8	1.4	2.4	0.0	–2.9
Trade balance (GDP points)	–8.1	–9.1	–10.5	–11.4	–12.9	–12.4	–10.5	–9.4	–11.0	–11.8	–11.4	–11.4	–13.3	–10.4
Current account balance (GDP points)	–4.0	–5.7	–6.8	–8.1	–10.4	–10.3	–8.2	–6.5	–8.3	–10.3	–10.7	–10.1	–12.6	–10.2
Financial account balance (GDP points)	3.7	4.9	4.6	7.1	9.8	9.9	7.4	0.4	5.7	8.2	8.3	8.2	11.1	9.6
Change in official reserves (USD millions)	723	1245	508	216	371	853	1017	–6455	–1863	–1741	–2357	–962	115	1095
Domestic credit to private sector	70.3	78.1	89.5	109.4	126.6	133.7	136.3	135.8	136.4	141.2	152.5	162.5	173.7	186.7
Long-term interest rate	8.6	6.4	4.9	4.8	5.6	5.2	5.0	4.2	4.1	3.4	3.9	4.4	4.5	4.2
Long-term interest rate (Germany)	6.2	5.7	4.6	4.5	5.3	4.8	4.8	4.1	4.0	3.4	3.8	4.2	4.0	3.2
% change of the ITL/ECU exchange rate (+=devaluation)	–0.5	2.5	2.0	–0.7	0.0	0.0	0.0	0.0	0.0	0.0	0.0	0.0	0.0	0.0
Interest rate spread (corrected for the devaluation)	2.8	–1.8	–1.7	1.0	0.3	0.4	0.2	0.1	0.1	0.1	0.2	0.2	0.5	1.0
Productivity growth spread (% points)	2.6	1.5	1.8	1.0	1.8	–2.6	–1.1	0.2	–0.4	0.5	–3.0	2.5	–1.3	4.1
Inflation differential	1.7	0.4	1.6	1.5	1.4	2.5	2.3	2.2	0.7	0.2	1.3	0.1	–0.1	–1.1
% change of the reer (+=appreciation)	–2.1	–1.9	2.9	1.7	–2.2	0.0	2.1	2.5	2.5	2.4	1.8	–2.1	1.3	–1.9
External debt (GDP points)	–11.3	–16.4	–27.1	–28.5	–38.3	–44.8	–60.2	–65.0	–69.1	–63.8	–82.7	–95.4	–90.8	–112.7
Government budget balance (GDP points)	–4.5	–3.4	–3.5	–2.7	–2.9	–4.3	–2.9	–3.1	–3.4	–5.9	–4.1	–3.2	–3.7	–10.2

Data sources: the main data source is IMF (2010). Real growth, inflation rates and government budget balance come from IMF (2012b). Domestic credit to the private sector comes from World Bank (2012). Long-term interest rates as well as average labour productivity come from OECD (2012). External debt data before 1999 come from Lane and Milesi-Ferretti (2007).

Table 6.9 Greece: selected macroeconomic variables, 1996–2009

	1996	*1997*	*1998*	*1999*	*2000*	*2001*	*2002*	*2003*	*2004*	*2005*	*2006*	*2007*	*2008*	*2009*
Real growth	2.4	3.6	3.4	3.4	4.5	4.2	3.4	5.9	4.4	2.3	4.6	3.0	–0.1	–3.3
Trade balance (GDP points)	–11.4	–11.5	n.a.	–13.0	–15.9	–14.6	–14.5	–13.1	–13.7	–14.1	–16.7	–18.3	–18.7	–13.1
Current account balance (GDP points)	–3.3	–3.7	n.a.	–5.3	–7.7	–7.2	–6.5	–6.6	–5.9	–7.5	–11.1	–14.3	–14.7	–11.0
Financial account balance (GDP points)	6.4	0.1	n.a.	5.4	8.5	0.4	7.8	3.3	3.0	6.4	9.7	12.2	12.7	10.7
Change in official reserves (USD millions)	4215	–4515	n.a.	2435	2573	–5699	1863	–4723	–3277	–104	279	457	39	1213
Domestic credit to private sector	31.3	32.4	34.4	41.7	47.4	57.4	61.0	64.8	70.8	79.6	85.1	94.1	97.5	94.1
Long-term interest rate	–	9.8	8.5	6.3	6.1	5.3	5.1	4.3	4.3	3.6	4.1	4.5	4.8	5.2
Long-term interest rate (Germany)	6.2	5.7	4.6	4.5	5.3	4.8	4.8	4.1	4.0	3.4	3.8	4.2	4.0	3.2
% change of the ITL/ECU exchange rate (+=devaluation)	0.6	2.3	7.5	–1.7	3.3	1.2	0.0	0.0	0.0	0.0	0.0	0.0	0.0	0.0
Interest rate spread (corrected for the devaluation)	–	1.8	–3.6	3.5	–2.5	–0.7	0.3	0.2	0.2	0.2	0.3	0.3	0.8	2.0
Productivity growth spread (% points)	1.9	3.6	–1.7	0.3	1.2	1.6	0.3	4.1	2.1	0.1	1.5	1.0	–1.3	2.2
Wage inflation differential	6.7	3.9	3.9	1.5	0.3	–1.9	1.3	16.2	3.2	0.3	0.8	1.8	–0.4	2.1
% change of the reer (+=appreciation)	3.6	7.5	–4.2	–3.3	–5.3	–0.8	19.8	2.3	0.0	–4.0	3.6	2.0	–5.9	5.8
External debt (GDP points)	–6.7	–16.6	–20.7	–31.6	–38.8	–45.8	–58.8	–65.8	–73.4	–72.5	–88.4	–101.4	–71.5	–88.2
Government budget balance (GDP points)	–6.8	–6.0	–3.9	–3.1	–3.7	–4.4	–4.8	–5.7	–7.4	–5.6	–6.0	–6.7	–9.7	–15.6

Data sources: the main data source is IMF (2010). Real growth, inflation rates and government budget balance come from IMF (2012b). Domestic credit to the private sector comes from World Bank (2012). Long-term interest rates as well as average labour productivity come from OECD (2012). External debt data before 1999 come from Lane and Milesi-Ferretti (2007).

Step 1

We recall that in step 1 the Minskyan cycle is set off by an exogenous shock, determined by the adoption of an exogenous macroeconomic policy package including financial liberalization (both domestic and external) and a "credible" exchange rate policy. Some remarks are needed. First, in the Eurozone financial liberalization had largely occurred before the adoption of the single currency: in other words, a component of the exogenous shock (liberalization) had been "diluted" over the previous two decades. Second, the timing of the adoption of the "credible exchange rate" differs from one country to the next, because Greece entered the Eurozone two years later than the other peripheral countries (in 2001 instead of 1999), and also because the nominal exchange rate before the onset of the euro was managed differently in the different countries: just to give an example, Italy experienced a nominal revaluation by 8 per cent in 1996, and afterwards pegged its exchange rate to the ECU, while Portugal and Spain in 1997 engineered a moderate devaluation.

Step 2

Taking these differences into account, it is fair to say that the institutional shock had the effects envisaged by the Minskyan framework (step 2 above): the *ex post* interest rate spreads (adjusted for the exchange rate variation) increased everywhere by about one point (see Tables 6.6 to 6.9). For the reasons explained above (financial liberalization had already occurred), in the peripheral Eurozone countries this effect was determined mostly by the elimination of the exchange rate risk. Consider also that, due to data availability, the tables consider the sovereign spread (spread on long-term government bonds), but the detailed analysis shows that the spreads on the other segments of the credit market were in most cases higher.

Step 3

Be that as it may, this behaviour of the spreads seems to have prompted the effects described in step 3 of the Minskyan framework: first of all, capital inflows and an increase in domestic liquidity, as witnessed by the increase of domestic credit to the private sector. This pattern is evident in Figure 6.17: the domestic credit-to-GDP ratio had been stable to declining in Italy and Spain, and moderately increasing in Portugal: in each case, there is a visible change of pace around 1999 (more apparent in Italy and Portugal). This increase in liquidity produced the effects envisaged by the Minskyan framework:

i the interest rates fell and the spreads reduced;
ii output increased;
iii prices increased.

As for the interest rates, in 2005 the *ex post* sovereign spread reached a minimum everywhere. This minimum was equal to zero in Spain, in coincidence with a

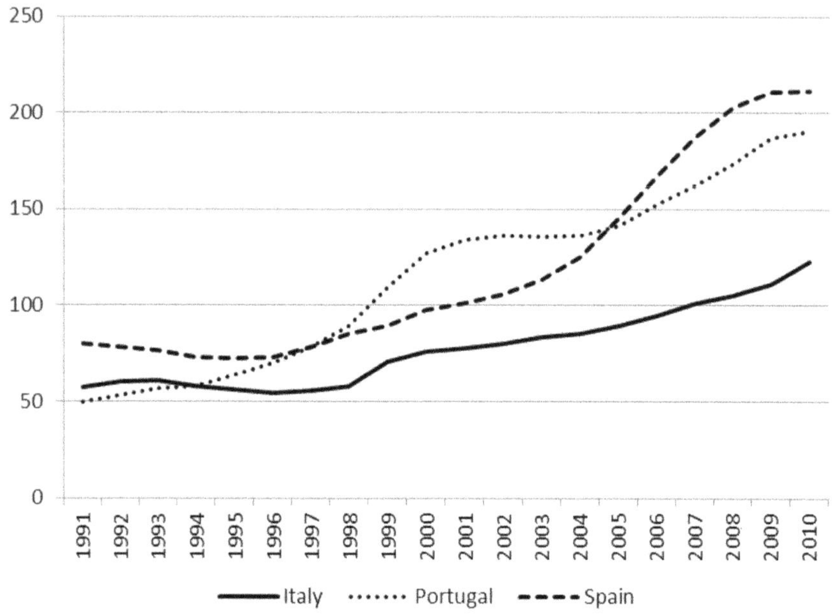

Figure 6.17 Domestic credit to the private sector (% GDP) (source: World Bank, 2012).

positive government balance; the other sovereign spreads did not vanish (owing to the large debt stock in Greece and Italy, and to an insufficient fiscal consolidation in Portugal). A similar pattern applies also to some – but not all – segments of the private credit market, see Figures 6.2 to 6.6.

As for output growth, its increase is especially evident in Italy (where growth jumped from 1.5 to 3.7 per cent, in correspondence with a five point increase in the domestic credit-to-GDP ratio) and Spain (where growth reached 5.1 per cent in 2000). Contrary to Portugal (that was badly hit by the recession in 2003), and to most core countries (like Belgium, Finland and Netherlands), and despite the global recession determined by the burst of the dotcom bubble in the US (which had occurred in 2000), the Mediterranean countries experienced on average an increase in real growth in the 2000–2007 period, as compared to the 1993–1999 post-crisis and pre-euro period.

The dynamic of prices presents some interesting differences from one country to the next. Tables 6.6 to 6.9 report for each country the wage inflation and the productivity growth differential with respect to Germany (in the case of Portugal we report the consumer price inflation differential, owing to the lack of data). It is interesting to look at these data together with the dynamics of the nominal and real exchange rate. Table 6.10 displays the average productivity growth spreads between the peripheral countries and Germany. The productivity spreads are defined as the difference between the peripheral and the core rates of growth in the average productivity of labour. In the two major peripheral countries, as well as in Portugal, the productivity spread behaves exactly as predicted by the Kaldor–Verdoorn model: an adverse shock (revaluation) in the nominal exchange rate reduces the productivity growth rate through its effect on exports and output growth. It is worth noting that the only notable exception in this respect is Greece, where productivity growth increases with respect to Germany after the inception in the Eurozone (the result does not change significantly if one takes 1999 or, more correctly, 2001 as the inception date). The data therefore tells a completely different story from the one that is currently told in the media, according to which Greek people are paying for their laziness (and for the profligacy of their governments). As far as Italy is concerned, the fall in productivity is sizeable, but it becomes even larger if we split the sample not after 1999, but after 1995, i.e. when Italy did actually change its currency policy, by revaluating the lira against the ECU. With the only exception of Greece, the Kaldor–Verdoorn effect therefore seems to explain the dynamics of productivity in the three largest peripheral countries.

The behaviour of prices and of real exchange rate however differs from one country to the next. Italy displayed a reasonable degree of wage moderation. Its wage differential with Germany was on average negative up to 2002, averaging –0.9 per cent in the first three years of the euro era. As a consequence, despite the drop in productivity, its average real appreciation was close to zero in the same period (Table 6.7).[5] In Spain there was less wage moderation relative to Germany (the average wage differential was positive at 0.6 per cent); therefore, the real appreciation rate was higher (0.9 per cent instead of 0.2 per cent). By the way, this pattern is consistent with the fact that real growth in Spain was on average twice the real growth in Italy. Even in Portugal we observe the same dynamics: the productivity spread went from 1 per cent in 2000 to –1.1 per cent in 2002, the consumer price inflation differential from 1.5 to 2.3 per cent, and the real appreciation rate from 1.7 to 2.1 per cent. An interesting common feature to Italy and Spain (the two major peripheral countries) is that their wage inflation differential increases sharply in 2003 (going from –0.4 to 1.3 per cent in

Table 6.10 Average productivity growth spread

	Greece	*Italy*	*Portugal*	*Spain*
1993–1999	–0.3	–0.3	0.3	–0.4
2000–2007	1.5	–1.4	–0.3	–1.3
change	1.8	–1.1	–0.6	–0.9
1993–2001	–0.1	–	–	–
2002–2007	1.5	–	–	–
change	1.7	–	–	–
1993–1995	–	0.9	–	–
1996–2007	–	–1.3	–	–
change	–	–2.2	–	–

Data source: OECD (2012).

Italy, and from 1.4 to 3.3 per cent in Spain), with immediate effects on the real appreciation rate (which jumps from 4.6 to 11.3 per cent in Italy and from 2.5 to 6.2 per cent in Spain). A glance at the data shows that this jump in relative wage inflation was determined by a drop in the rate of growth of German nominal wages. Wage inflation, which had been close to 3 per cent in Germany in the first four years of the euro era, dropped sharply to an average of 1.4 per cent from 2003 to 2007, as a result of wage moderation introduced by the so-called Hartz reforms of the labour market (ILO, 2012). As the International Labour Organisation puts it, at the European level this reforms package

> has created conditions for a prolonged economic slump as other member countries increasingly see only even harsher wage deflation policies as a solution to their lack of competitiveness. This is all the more discomforting as it is unclear to what extent these wage deflation policies in Germany have contributed to higher employment levels, which in 2006 were barely higher than in 1991.
>
> (ILO, 2012, box 4)

This aggressive mercantilist policy from the core country is a distinct feature of the Minskyan cycle in the Eurozone. It is worth stressing that it is precisely the feature one should legitimately expect not to find in a region that has decided to call itself an economic "union".

Step 4

Whatever the reasons, the accelerating real appreciation in the periphery brings us to step 4 of the crisis. The financial effects are especially evident in Spain, where capital inflows, which had been on average equal to 1.2 GDP points from 1996 to 2003, jump to an average of 7.1 from 2004 to 2007. The same applies to Italy, which up to 2001 had had a negative financial account balance (indicating that it was repaying the external debt accumulated during the "credible EMS" period). After 2003 the financial account balance jumps to an average of 1.3 GDP points, whereas it had been on average negative at –0.4 GDP points from 1996 to 2003. And the same applies also to the two minor peripheral countries, although with some minor differences in the time profile of the balances.

As widely acknowledged (Berger and Nitsch, 2010; De Grauwe, 2012), these capital inflows were largely devoted to the financing of the growing trade deficits towards the Eurozone countries. This effect is more apparent in the smaller economies, as is to be expected, since smaller economies are necessarily more open and more dependent on foreign trade than larger ones. Therefore, after 2003 the trade balance worsens both in Portugal (where it had already reached a minimum of –13 GDP points in 2000) and in Greece (where a minimum had also been reached in 2000 at –16 GDP points). In both countries however the current account balance, while being negative, is smaller in absolute value than the trade balance. This indicates that the balance on services and incomes is positive. In Italy instead the trade balance is positive (with the only exception of 2006), but it converges rather quickly to zero after 1999; at the same time, the current account balance decreases steadily, changing from positive to negative in 2000. This indicates a negative services and incomes balance. The situation of Spain is somewhat different: both the trade and the current account balances are negative, but up to 2005 the latter is smaller in absolute value than the former.

The crisis

Even keeping these differences into account, the situation described so far matches closely the framework outlined before. The next step is the beginning of the crisis, announced by a rise in the interest rate spreads (from 2008), as well as by a reduction in capital inflows (measured by the financial account balance). Yet, owing to the existence of the single currency, the final stage of the Eurozone crisis, which is still not over, differs from the standard one: rather than a run on the peripheral country's central bank foreign exchange reserves, carried out by selling the peripheral country's currency on the foreign exchange market, in order to "force" it out of the peg, what we see today in the Eurozone looks rather like a run on the peripheral country's political sovereignty, welfare systems and real assets, carried out by selling the peripheral country's government bonds, thus forcing up the spreads and inducing a huge turmoil in the peripheral stock markets. This pushes down the market value of both the government bonds and the equities of the periphery, and allows "technical" bodies like the ECB to intervene in a more and more pervasive way in the political process of the peripheral countries on behalf of the core countries, in order to impose meaningless fiscal austerity policies such as the so-called "fiscal compact" (EU, 2012).

If one looks at the last few years, fiscal austerity may seem the right answer. In fact, government debt has increased almost everywhere, as a result of automatic and discretional fiscal policies in response to the global recession. As it happens, the increase in public debt has been larger in the countries that were most severely hit by the crisis. However, public debt is an effect, rather than a cause, of the crisis: as a matter of fact, its increase is strongly correlated with the increase in private debt before the crisis (Figure 6.18). The cross-country sample correlation between the increase in domestic credit to private sector from 1999 to 2007 (reported in Table 6.5) and the increase in general government gross debt from 2007 to 2011 (reported in Table 6.11) is equal to 0.74.[6] As an example, Ireland had the largest decrease in public debt among the crisis-hit countries (–23 GDP points, Table 6.5), together with the largest increase in private debt (98 GDP points, as in Spain, Table 6.5), and after the crisis it underwent the largest increase in public debt (80 GDP points), following the private banks' "rescue plan" (Department of Finance, 2010).

In all evidence, public debt reduction strategies are aiming at the wrong target. By compressing the revenues of domestic households and companies, restrictive fiscal policies reduce their ability to reimburse their debts with the

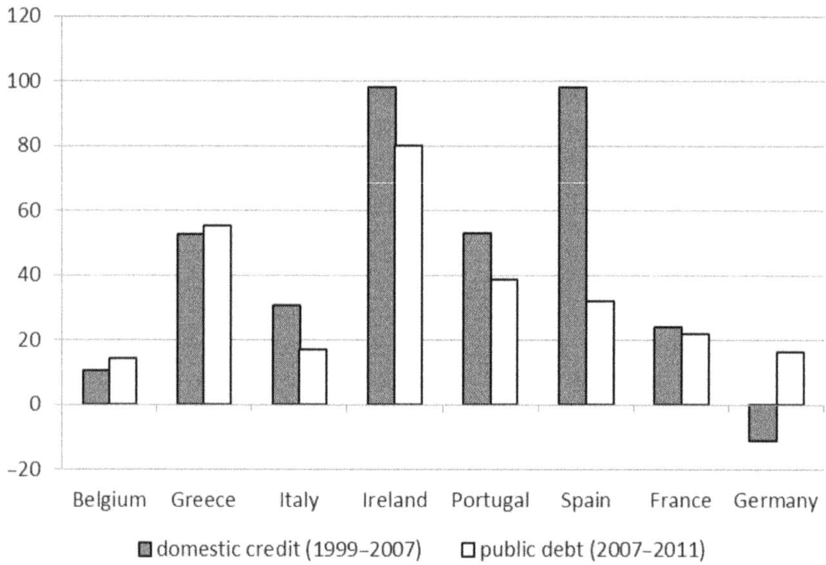

Figure 6.18 Change in domestic credit before and public debt after the crisis (% GDP) (source: domestic credit comes from World Bank (2012), public debt from IFS (2012a)).

Table 6.11 Flows and stocks in the Eurozone crisis

	Cumulated balances (2007–2011)			*Variation in stocks (2011 over 2007)*		
	I-Sp	*F*	*CA*	*Domestic credit*	*Public debt*	*NIIP*
Belgium	–15.5	15.8	–0.4	3.9	14.4	45.8
Greece	7.9	51.8	–59.7	21.9	55.4	28.3
Italy	–5.0	18.0	–13.0	21.4	17.0	5.6
Ireland	–49.3	62.6	–13.3	10.7	80.1	–74.5
Portugal	19.1	30.9	–50.1	28.3	38.5	–13.7
Spain	–16.6	11.2	5.4	23.8	32.2	–2.1
France	–17.9	26.1	–8.2	8.9	22.1	–9.1
Germany	–39.8	8.4	31.4	2.5	16.3	4.8

Data sources: the sectorial balances come from IMF (2012a); domestic credit from World Bank (2012); public debt from IMF (2012a); net international investment position (NIIP) from IMF (2010).

banking system. This increases the fragility of the banking system and prompts for further public or multilateral intervention to rescue it (at the time of writing – May 2012 – such a plan was being discussed in Spain). The "conditionality" clauses included in the multilateral intervention agreements make plain that not only the multilateral bodies (EC, IMF, ECB, the so-called "troika") are aiming at the wrong target, but they are deliberately doing so for ideological reasons. Take for instance the IMF memorandum on Greece (IMF, 2012b). The idea herein expressed by Prime Minister Papademos that "productivity-enhancing structural reforms" should "fundamentally reduce the footprint of government in the economy through bold structural fiscal reforms and by privatizing public assets" is completely at odds with the data summarized in Tables 6.5 and 6.9 as well as in Figure 6.9. The "footprint of government" has little to do with the increase by 52 GDP points of domestic credit to the private sector, in the presence of a stable public debt-to-GDP ratio (Table 6.5), while the euro, for the reasons set out in this section, has a lot to do with the fact that the liabilities to non-residents of the Greek banking system have increased by 31 GDP points from 2001 to 2009, bringing the share of liabilities to non-residents from 16 to 56 per cent of the total liabilities of the banking system.[7]

No matter how counterproductive they will be, austerity plans of this kind are now being proposed to all the crisis-hit countries, as they satisfy three needs of the core countries' financial capitalism: in the short run, the need to socialize the losses by charging the taxpayers of the periphery with the burden of the peripheral banking systems' external liabilities; in the medium run, the need to acquire real assets (in particular, public utilities and other strategic infrastructure) of the peripheral economies, which may constitute an interesting investment opportunity for the huge financial surpluses acquired by core countries in the first decade of the euro (this is what "privatization" is aimed at); in the long run, the need to repress the role of the government as a financial intermediary, in order to channel to the private financial market the flow of savings which are now being intermediated by the State, both through its public debt and through the welfare systems. In other words, the solutions that are now being proposed aim at accelerating the transformation of the Eurozone into a "coupon-pool capitalist system" as described by Froud *et al.* (2001) in their interesting and somehow overlooked paper, where the stock market is given a dominant role, bringing higher dynamic instability and rising income inequality.

Conclusions

It is now time to draw some lessons, define some policy options and indicate some avenues for future research.

The long collection of stylized facts presented in this chapter confirms the usefulness of the developing countries' version of the Minskyan boom-and-bust cycle as a tool for interpreting the Eurozone peripheral crises. This prompts a question: why does a theoretical framework elaborated with reference to developing countries fit so well the stylized facts of the Eurozone peripheral crises?

The answer is relatively simple: this evidence confirms De Grauwe's (2011) statement that Eurozone membership has transformed member countries into "developing" countries from a financial point of view. By entering the Eurozone, the countries lose control over the currency in which their debt is issued. As a consequence, the markets can force their governments to default. As Frenkel and

Rapetti (2009) put it, the key difference between a developed and a developing country is that in the latter "the set of risky assets includes public bonds and domestic corporate debt, which are all subject to country risk". But this is precisely what is happening in the Eurozone peripheral countries now, and with precisely the same consequences as outlined by Frenkel and Rapetti: the occurrence of a crisis triggers capital outflows, as a result of domestic and foreign investors' "flight to quality". As shown by De Grauwe (2011), nominal exchange rate flexibility would provide a useful stabilizing mechanism: besides its obvious medium-run effects on price competitiveness, a large enough nominal depreciation has the immediate financial effect of inducing foreign investors to buy the currency of the crisis-hit country, which would therefore not experience a massive capital outflow and liquidity crisis. As a consequence, this country keeps control over its interest rate and can finance easily expansionary fiscal policies.

It is worth stressing that the working of an equilibrium mechanism is impeded in the Eurozone by *two* facts: a technical one, and a political or ideological one. The technical fact is of course the adoption of a single currency, which by definition rules out the possibility of a nominal devaluation. But this would not be enough without the political fact: the decision to treat external imbalances in an asymmetric way, with surpluses being praised as a sign of virtue, and deficits being despised as a sign of vice. This moralistic attitude implies that the burden of the adjustment is put on the deficit countries, where the rise in interest rates makes it increasingly difficult to re-equilibrate the government and the current account balance. At the same time the surplus countries, that can finance their public debt at a negative real interest rate (as a consequence of the "flight to quality"), refrain from practising expansionary policies (that would help the rebalancing of the whole area, by inducing a real appreciation in surplus countries), claiming that it is the peripheral countries' responsibility to become more "competitive", i.e. to implement an "internal" real devaluation through structural reforms. This approach misses a very simple point: since the largest share of the Eurozone trade occurs between member countries, the deficit of the periphery *are*, to a large extent, the surpluses of the core. In fact, our descriptive analysis shows how these deficits were engineered by European institutions dominated by core countries' governments, through a well-known mechanism (well-tested in developing countries), whose aim is to provide favourable arbitrage opportunities to the core financial institutions, and an outlet to the core industrial production.

At an even more general level, nobody seems to notice how this approach contradicts the rhetoric of the European "Union". A glance at periphery newspapers shows that most people trace the origin of the periphery problems back to insufficient price competitiveness towards Germany, and they seem to believe that these countries should accept Germany's suggestions on how to successfully compete against Germany itself. These people are missing the point that it would be extremely irrational of the German government to give suggestions of this kind to its partner countries (possibly through the institutions it largely controls, like the ECB)! As argued above, the unconfessed goal of the structural reform packages seems to be rather that of socializing the losses of the private banks from the core, and of paving the way to a massive acquisition of periphery real assets from the core countries' capitalists. But setting aside these obvious considerations, nobody seems to grasp that the rationale of a Union should be cooperation through coordination of policies, not fratricidal competition among members. Union through competition has another name: annexation (*Anschluss* in German). The cessions of sovereignty that have been asked in the last year (including the "fiscal compact") give worrying signals in this respect.

Be that as it may, this experience has useful lessons at the theoretical and political level.

First and foremost, our descriptive analysis confirms that there is no such thing as an "endogenous" currency area. The idea that an exogenous institutional change, such as the adoption of a single currency, may induce the condition for its sustainability, either by synchronizing the member countries' business cycle through the promotion of trade, as advocated by Rose (2000, 2001), or by facilitating nominal convergence through the credibility gains, as claimed by Giavazzi and Pagano (1986), proved false. The effects of the exogenous institutional change, rather than stabilizing, as in the "endogenous OCA" theories, were clearly destabilizing, as anticipated by the Minskyan model and described in this chapter. The decision of the European policy makers to dictate the agenda of European integration by ignoring the warnings issued by many qualified economists (for a survey see Jonung and Drea, 2010), even if taken in good faith, was disastrous. An inescapable, even though painful, consequence of this fact is that undoing the single currency in some way will necessarily be part of the solution of the Eurozone crisis, the only alternative being that of waiting for a disorderly break-up.

Second, the crisis demonstrates that "market fundamentalism", as expressed in many European treaties, as well as in the "rescue" packages that are now being proposed, has failed (and keeps failing, as the case of Greece demonstrates). The financial distress we are now facing disproves the optimistic views expressed by Blanchard and Giavazzi (2002), according to which external imbalances in the Eurozone were the result of a catching-up process favoured by financial market integration. What seems here at stake is the neoclassical idea that international factor movements are intrinsically stabilizing, because they obey the law of diminishing returns. The recent wave of financial crises, first outside, then within the Eurozone, seems much more consistent with the Minskyan framework, and with the Keynesian intuition that markets ruled by the "liquidity" principle will necessarily fail to allocate saving in an efficient way, as they will inevitably and legitimately look at short-term capital gains, rather than at the long-term returns of investments. This massive market failure is clearly inscribed in the data. The countries that ran into difficulties are those that experienced the largest foreign capital inflows, and where private (not public) debt experienced the largest increases. What attracted foreign capital in the peripheral economies was the "Ponzi game" logic of the financial bubble capitalism, rather than a prudent appreciation of the long-term returns possibly provided by the relatively undercapitalized economies of the periphery. It is unjust and even racist to put the blame of this massive diversion of financial resources on the peripheral countries' microeconomic units (households, firms). Why should a family that lives in a thriving economy refuse to borrow money at a convenient interest rate in order to, say, live in a better house? In a capitalist economy, the banking system has the task of assessing the merit and monitoring the development of investment projects. The banking system of the Eurozone failed in accomplishing this task and it needs to be reformed in such a way as to avoid in the future the moral hazard problems underlying its failure. A part of this reform will certainly be the (re)nationalization of a part of the banking system, the split of the banks that are "too big to fail", and the introduction in Europe of the separation between commercial and investment banks (as envisaged by the Glass–Steagall Act in the United States).

But even before that, the Eurozone political institutions failed to recognize a simple truth: too much is too much. If on the one hand debt sustainability remains a controversial field (see Chalk and Hemming, 2000), on the other hand empirical studies such as Manasse and Roubini (2005) provide clear indications about what variables to monitor in order to prevent a sovereign debt crisis. Interestingly enough, the most important variable in their analysis turns out to be the total (i.e. public *and* private) net external debt-to-GDP ratio: a result fully consistent with the Minskyan framework. On the other hand, the two variables considered by the Maastricht Treaty seem to have little or no empirical relevance for the forecast of a sovereign default: the public debt-to-GDP ratio ranks 48th for predictive power, and the general government balance-to-GDP ratio has no clear predictive power. The "financial indicators dashboard" inscribed in the Maastricht Treaty has been very poorly designed (as clearly anticipated by Buiter *et al.*, 1993). Interestingly enough, looking at the right variables would have given the right signals. Manasse and Roubini show that the total external debt-to-GDP ratio reaches 54.7 per cent in the year before the outbreak of a crisis. In the Eurozone this attention level was overcome by Greece and Portugal in 2002 and by Spain in 2004. Something could have been done. But the European policy makers were blinded by their dull ideological hatred for the "government footprint" in the economy (to borrow IMF's words). This explains their decision to put an upper limit to government, but not to external debt: in fact, putting a limit on government debt amounts to repressing the role of the State, while putting a limit on external debt would mean repressing the role of international financial markets. Even though the empirical evidence shows that too much private finance can harm an economy (Arcand *et al.*, 2011), while public debt is less harmful to growth than usually believed (Panizza and Presbitero, 2012), European policy makers have fought the battle they were asked to fight by the markets: a battle against the State, which eventually turned out to be a battle against prosperity and peace in the European continent.

Several issues raised in this chapter deserve further investigation. To mention a few: it would be interesting to formalize the Minskyan framework proposed above and to integrate it with the export-led post-Keynesian model; the causality relationship between private and external deficits, implied by the Minskyan framework and suggested by the data, should be investigated formally through causality tests; but over and above that, the most urgent question is to design viable and feasible scenarios of an orderly dismantling of the euro area. Only by escaping the "golden cage" of the euro will the peripheral economies recover their full sovereignty and their status of advanced economies. It would be a gross mistake to label this aspiration as short-sighted and dangerous nationalism. The experience of the Eurozone has shown instead that a political "vision" which does not reckon with the facts is an avenue to unmitigated economic and political turmoil. And the facts tell us that the Eurozone is not a optimal currency area.

Appendix: the arithmetic of sectorial balances

The sectorial balance analysis starts from the GNP identity:

$$Y^N = C + G + I + X - M + NFI \tag{6.1}$$

where Y^N is GNP, *NFI* are the net foreign incomes from abroad and the other variables have their usual meaning. By defining the current account balance as:

$$CA = X - M + NFI \tag{6.2}$$

and national savings as:

$$S^N = Y^N - C - G \tag{6.3}$$

and substituting these definitions in Eq. (6.1) we get the well-known relation:

$$CA = S^N - I \tag{6.4}$$

Equation (6.4) shows that the current account balance corresponds to the excess of national savings over domestic investment: if a country's savings exceeds its investment, *ex post* this difference will be lent abroad, while if a country's savings fall short of investment, the country will need to borrow from abroad. By adding and subtracting net direct taxes from Eq. (6.3) we get:

$$S^N = Y^N - T - C + T - G = S^P + S^G \tag{6.5}$$

where S^P is private saving (national income less taxes less private consumption) and S^G is government saving (government revenues less government expenditure).

Finally, by substituting Eq. (6.5) into Eq. (6.4) and rearranging terms we get:

$$I - S^N + F + CA = 0 \tag{6.6}$$

where $F = -S^G$ is the government *deficit*. Eq. (6.6) expresses the three sectorial balances as deficits (excess of expenditure over revenues): $I - S^N$ is the private sector deficit, F the government deficit, CA the foreign sector deficit.[8] A positive value indicates the borrowing requirement of the corresponding sector, while a negative value indicates its lending capability (surplus). Eq. (6.6) shows that the three sectors cannot be all in deficit: if a sector is in deficit (positive value), at least another *must* be in surplus (negative value). It is worth noting that Eq. (6.6) expounds a mere accounting fact that *must* be verified *ex post* and as such it does not endorse a particular causal explanation of any kind. It is instead a descriptive tool, which is in principle compatible with any possible causal mechanisms.

Notes

1 I am grateful to Eladio Febrero Paños and to Roberto Frenkel for their useful comments. Usual disclaimers apply.
2 Argentina hosted more than 26 million Italian migrants between 1876 and 1976, and Italy, in turn, was chosen by many Argentinians as a refuge in the years of the military dictatorship.
3 This numbering of the different stages of the crisis is proposed here only to simplify future reference and does not feature in Frenkel and Rapetti's paper.
4 Since most balances are trending over the period considered, we find the change to be more informative than, say, sample averages.
5 It should be stressed that the unit labour cost based measure of the real exchange rate takes into account all the trade partners, not only the Eurozone core ones. Therefore, its behaviour is influenced not only by the inflation differentials within the Eurozone, but also by the behaviour of the nominal exchange rates and wages in the other trade partners. By and large, trade with the Eurozone accounts for slightly more than a half of total trade in each peripheral country, while the United States is in general the second largest partner after the Eurozone, with a market share typically between 5 and 10 per cent.
6 The correlation is calculated among the eight countries considered in Table 6.11.
7 The data come from the consolidated depository corporation balance sheets reported by IMF (2010).
8 It should be noted that $CA > 0$ implies that the reporting country's exports exceeds its imports (i.e. the reporting country has an external surplus), which of course implies that the rest-of-the-world exports fall short of its imports (i.e. the rest of the world runs an external deficit).

References

Acocella, N. (1998) *The foundations of economic policy: values and techniques*, Cambridge: Cambridge University Press.

Acocella, N., Di Bartolomeo, G., Tirelli, P. (2010) "The optimal inflation rate revisited", *MEMOTEF Working Papers*, No. 76, University of Rome "La Sapienza" (November).

Arcand, J.-L., Berkes, E., Panizza, U. (2011) "Too much finance?" mimeo, http://upanizza.blogspot.it/2011/03/too-much-finance.html.

Bagnai, A. (2006) "Structural breaks and the twin deficits hypothesis", *International Economics and Economic Policy*, 3, 137–155.

Bagnai, A., Manzocchi, S. (1999) "Current account reversals in developing countries: the role of fundamentals", *Open Economies Review*, 10, 143–163.

Bartolini, L., Lahiri, A. (2006) "Twin deficits, twenty years later", *Current Issues in Economics and Finance*, 12, 1–7.

Berg, A., Borensztein, E., Mauro, P. (2002) "An evaluation of monetary regime options for Latin America", *North American Journal of Economics and Finance*, 13, 213–235.

Berger, H., Nitsch, V. (2010) "The euro's effect on trade imbalances", *IMF Working Paper*, No. 226 (October).

Blanchard, O., Giavazzi, F. (2002) "Current account deficits in the Euro area: the end of the Feldstein-Horioka puzzle?" *Brookings Papers on Economic Activity*, 33, 147–210.

Buiter, W.H., Corsetti, G., Roubini, N. (1993) "Excessive deficits: sense and nonsense in the Treaty of Maastricht", *Economic Policy*, 8, 57–100.

Busetti, F., Forni, L., Harvey, A., Venditti, F. (2006) "Inflation convergence and divergence within the European Union", *ECB Working Paper Series*, No. 574 (January).

Calvo, G.A. (1998) "Capital flows and capital-market crises: the simple economics of sudden stops", *Journal of Applied Economics, Universidad del CEMA*, 0, 5–54.

Calvo, G.A., Reinhart, C.M. (2002) "Fear of floating", *Quarterly Journal of Economics*, 117, 379–408.

Cesaratto, S., Stirati, A. (2010–11) "Germany and the European and global crises", *International Journal of Political Economy*, 39, 56–86.

Chalk, N., Hemming, R. (2000) "Assessing fiscal sustainability in theory and in practice", *IMF Working Papers*, No. 81 (April).

Charles, S. (2008) "Teaching Minsky's financial instability hypothesis: a manageable suggestion", *Journal of Post Keynesian Economics*, 31, 125–138.

Chinn, M.D., Prasad, E.S. (2003) "Medium-term determinants of current accounts in industrial and developing countries: an empirical exploration", *Journal of International Economics*, 59, 47–76.

Davidson, P. (2008) "Is the current financial distress caused by the subprime mortgage crisis a Minsky moment? Or is it the result of attempting to securitize illiquid noncommercial mortgage loans?" *Journal of Post Keynesian Economics*, 30, 669–676.

De Grauwe, P. (2010) "The financial crisis and the future of the Eurozone", *Bruges European Economics Policy Briefings*, No. 21.

De Grauwe, P. (2011) "The governance of a fragile Eurozone", *CEPS Working Document*, No. 346 (May).

De Grauwe, P. (2012) "In search of symmetry in the Eurozone", *CEPS Policy Brief*, No. 268 (May).

Department of Finance (2010) *National Recovery Plan 2011–2014*, Dublin: Department of Finance – Department of Public Expenditure and Reform, www.budget.gov.ie/The%20National%20Recovery%20Plan%202011–2014.pdf.

Eichengreen, B. (2010) "Imbalances in the euro area", University of California at Berkeley, mimeo (November), http://elsa.berkeley.edu/~eichengr/Imbalances_ Euro_ Area _5-23-11.pdf.

EU (2012) *Treaty on stability, coordination, and governance in the Economic and Monetary Union*, http://european-council.europa.eu/home-page/highlights/treaty-on-stability,-coordination-and-governance-signed?lang=en.

Fleming, J.M. (1971) "On exchange rate unification", *Economic Journal*, 81, 467–488.

Frankel, J., Phillips, S. (1992) "The European Monetary System: credible at last?" *Oxford Economic Papers*, 44, 791–816.

Frenkel, R., Rapetti, M. (2009) "A developing country view of the current global crisis: what should not be forgotten and what should be done", *Cambridge Journal of Economics*, 33, 685–702.

Frenkel, R., Taylor, L. (2006) "Real exchange rate, monetary policy and employment: economic development in a garden of forking paths", *Alternative to Inflation Targeting: Central Bank Policy for Employment Creation, Poverty Reduction and Sustainable Growth*, Amherst (MA): Political Economy Research Institute.

Froud, J., Johal, S., Haslam, C., Williams, K. (2001) "Accumulation under conditions of inequality", *Review of International Political Economy*, 8, 66–95.

Giavazzi, F., Pagano, M. (1986) "The advantages of tying one's hands: EMS discipline and central bank credibility", *CEPR Discussion Papers*, No. 135 (October).

Giavazzi, F., Pagano, M. (1988) "The advantage of tying one's hands: EMS discipline and central bank credibility", *European Economic Review*, 32, 1055–1075.

Giavazzi, F., Spaventa, L. (1990) "The 'new' EMS", *CEPR Discussion Papers*, No. 369 (January).

Hicks, J. (1950) *The trade cycle*, Oxford: Clarendon Press.

Hodrick, R.J., Prescott, E.C. (1997) "Postwar U.S. business cycles: an empirical investigation", *Journal of Money, Credit, and Banking*, 29, 1–16.

ILO (2012) *Global employment trends 2012: preventing a deeper job crisis*, Geneva: International Labour Organisation.

IMF (2010) *International financial statistics*, 2010#12 CD-Rom edition.

IMF (2012a) *World economic outlook database*, Washington: International Monetary Fund, www.imf.org/external/pubs/ft/weo/2012/01/weodata/index.aspx.

IMF (2012b) *Greece: letter of intent, memorandum of economic and financial policies, and technical memorandum of understanding*, International Monetary Fund, (9 March), www.imf.org/external/np/loi/2012/grc/030912.pdf.

Jonung, L., Drea, E. (2010) "It can't happen, it's a bad idea, it won't last: US economists on the EMU and the Euro, 1989–2002", *Economic Journal Watch*, 7, 4–52.

Kaldor, N. (1957) "A model of economic growth", *Economic Journal*, 67, 591–624.

Kaldor, N. (1966) *Causes of the slow rate of economic growth in the United Kingdom*, Cambridge: Cambridge University Press.

Kaldor, N. (1970) "The case for regional policies", *Scottish Journal of Political Economy*, 17, 337–348.

Keynes, J.M. (1931) *Essays in persuasion*, London: Macmillan.

Khan, M., Senhadji, A. (2000) "Threshold effects in the relationship between inflation and growth", *IMF Working Paper*, 110, Washington: IMF.

Lane, P.R., Milesi-Ferretti, G.M. (2007) "The external wealth of nations mark II", *Journal of International Economics*, 73, 223–250.

León-Ledesma, M. (2002) "Accumulation, innovation and catching-up: an extended cumulative growth model", *Cambridge Journal of Economics*, 26, 201–216.

Manasse, P., Roubini, N. (2005) " 'Rules of thumb' for sovereign debt crises", *IMF Working Paper*, No. 42.

Minsky, H.P (1982) *Can it happen again?* Armony (NY): ME Sharpe.

OECD (2012) *OECD statistics extracts*, http://stats.oecd.org/Index.aspx.

Panizza, U., Presbitero, A.F. (2012) "Public debt and economic growth: is there a causal effect?" *MoFiR Working Paper*, No. 65.

Reinhart, C.M., Rogoff, K.S. (2008) "This time is different: a panoramic view of eight centuries of financial crises", *NBER Working Paper*, No. 13882.

Rose, A.K. (2000) "One money, one market: the effect of common currencies on trade", *Economic Policy*, 30, 9–45.

Rose, A.K. (2001) "Currency unions and trade: the effect is large", *Economic Policy*, 33, 449–461.

Seccareccia, M. (2010) "Keynes, Minsky, and analyses of the financial crisis", *International Journal of Political Economy*, 39, 3–4.

Taylor, L. (1998) "Capital market crises: liberalisation, fixed exchange rates and market-driven destabilization", *Cambridge Journal of Economics*, 22, 663–676.

Thirlwall, A.P. (1979) "The balance of payments constraint as an explanation of international growth rate differences", *Banca Nazionale del Lavoro Quarterly Review*, 128, 45–53.

Thirlwall, A.P. (2002) *The Nature of Economic Growth*, Cheltenham (UK), Northampton (USA): Edward Elgar.

Verdoorn, P.J. (1949) "Fattori che regolano lo sviluppo della produttività del lavoro", *L'Industria*, 1, translated in Pasinetti, L. (ed.) *Italian Economic Papers*, vol. II, Oxford: Oxford University Press, 1993.

World Bank (2012) *World development indicators*, http://data.worldbank.org/data-catalog/world-development-indicators/.

7 The adjustment of current account imbalances within the European Monetary Union since the beginning of the Great Recession

Some strengths and many weaknesses

Jesús Paúl and Jorge Uxó

Introduction

High and persistent current account imbalances in its Member States have been a feature of the European Monetary Union (EMU)[1] from its onset. Although the euro area as a whole has remained relatively close to external balance with the rest of the world,[2] this balance has been the result of a highly differentiated behavior between countries (Figure 7.1). On the one hand, Greece, Portugal and Spain[3] have experienced significant current account deficits and, on the other hand, Germany and other small countries such as the Netherlands and Finland have registered large surpluses.

In the early years of the EMU, policymakers (and many academic economists) didn't see current account imbalances as a danger for the stability of the countries registering them, let alone for the stability of the whole monetary union. On the contrary, they considered significant external imbalances as an indicator of a correct functioning of the EMU, because they made possible the transfer of financial resources from higher-income countries towards lower-income countries, boosting real convergence between Member States. Likewise, to the extent that external imbalances arose as a result of optimizing behavior of private economic agents in their saving and investment decisions and not as a manifestation of high fiscal deficits, they were not viewed as a destabilizing factor.

However, countries that ran large current account deficits experienced a sharp deterioration in their net international investment positions, as a consequence of the build-up of external liabilities derived mainly from the jump in private-sector debt. Furthermore, in some Member States, particularly Spain and Ireland, this was associated with booms in property investment. When the international financial crisis broke in 2007, the size and dispersion of intra-EMU current account imbalances had reached its peak. Debtor international investment positions of deficit Member States were between 80 and 100 percent of GDP, and indebtedness of nonfinancial private sectors exceeded 200 percent of GDP.

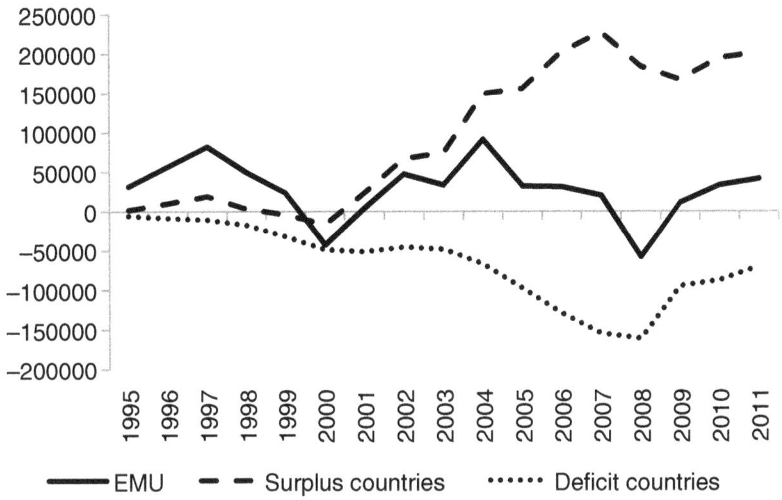

Figure 7.1 Current account positions in EMU (millions of euros) (source: AMECO).

Note
Surplus countries: Germany, the Netherlands, Finland; deficit countries: Greece, Portugal, Spain.

From the onset of the international financial crisis, current account imbalances within the euro area and the way policymakers are facing them have been affected in two dimensions.

First, the European authorities have begun (slowly) to show increasing concern about intra-EMU current account imbalances. The existence of countries with high external deficits and countries with large surpluses has come to be considered a major source of macroeconomic instability and a threat to the viability of the single currency project. As a consequence, a new specific Macroeconomic Imbalances Procedure (MIP) has been implemented as a part of the EU economic governance framework which includes current account balances and international investment positions in the Scoreboard of Indicators designed to detect and prevent these imbalances.[4]

In our opinion, this is a step forward. The correction of global imbalances is considered a key factor in achieving the restoration of a balanced growth of the world economy (e.g. Blanchard and Milesi-Ferretti, 2009; Horn *et al.*, 2009). In the same way, the reduction of the external imbalances of EMU Member States is a necessary condition to achieve a solid economic growth capable of generating employment. In turn, restoring a robust and sustained growth path is essential to give credibility back to the EMU project (Semieniuk *et al.*, 2012).

However, the official view about the causes of the external imbalances and their relationship with the roots of the crisis is inadequate. Current account imbalances are considered almost exclusively a problem of a lack of competitiveness of the deficit countries, closely related to their economic policy mistakes and "bad behavior". Consequently, the proposals to address them focus on strengthening policies of wage restraint and fiscal tightening and the implementation of structural adjustment reforms, which would theoretically introduce more flexibility in goods, services and labor markets, boosting productivity growth and raising the competitiveness of deficit countries. Nevertheless, these proposals will lead to extremely low economic growth prospects, threatening the viability of the Monetary Union itself.

Specifically, it must be emphasized that the primary concern about fiscal discipline shown by European governments is not justified. Indeed, the differential behavior during the current crisis of EMU countries with large external deficits ratifies the fact that macroeconomic stability is not only associated to the reduction of public deficits. The four countries that in 2007 recorded higher current account deficits have required financial assistance – Greece, Portugal and Ireland – or have been involved in sovereign debt crises, such as Spain.[5] However, until the beginning of the crisis, Ireland and Spain had never exceeded the budgetary thresholds established in the Stability and Growth Pact, and their vulnerability came exclusively from private sector borrowing.

Second, the financial and economic crisis has led to a reversal in the divergent trend in current accounts within the EMU (see Figure 7.1) as a result of its effect on variables such as unit labor costs, real exchange rates or domestic demand.

This chapter aims to assess whether the change in the relevance that European economic authorities assigned to external imbalances within the EMU and the reduction they have recently experienced, suggest its gradual correction and, with it, the restoration of higher and more balanced economic growth.

The rest of the chapter is structured as follows. First, we analyze the adjustment of the current account imbalances within the euro area since the beginning of the crisis and the factors that have influenced its evolution. Then we present the new Macroeconomic Imbalances Procedure and the policies proposed to deal with them, and the main reasons that make them inadequate. The last section sets out our main conclusions and summarizes some basic guidelines to facilitate sustainable external adjustment and balanced growth within the EMU.

The impact of the global financial crisis on current account balances within the euro area

The narrowing of current account differences in the euro area and the role of the adjustment of trade balances

The Great Recession has not significantly altered the current account balance of the whole euro area, which remains very close to equilibrium. However, it has had a significant impact on the external imbalances of Member States. In fact, between 2007 and 2011 there has been a reduction in current account imbalances in almost all the euro area countries, with the only exception of Italy, France and the Netherlands (Figure 7.2). The dispersion of current accounts, which had increased steadily since the late 1990s until 2007, has been reduced to a slightly higher level than that of the early years of the euro (Figure 7.3).

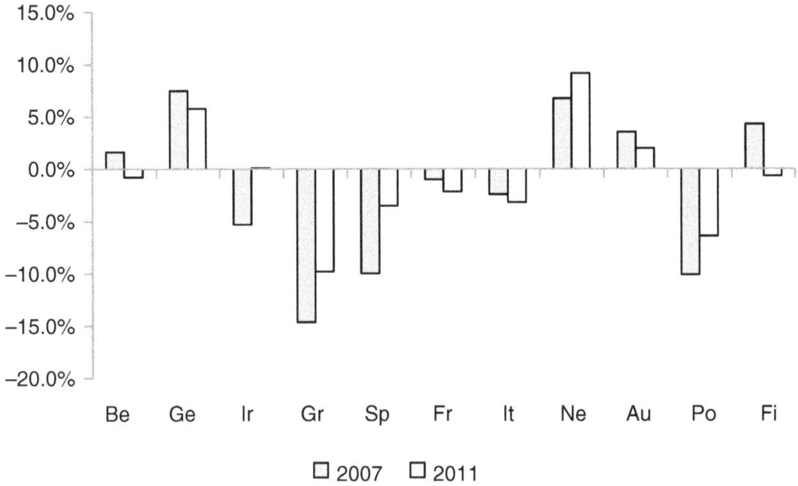

Figure 7.2 Current account balances (% of GDP) (source: AMECO).

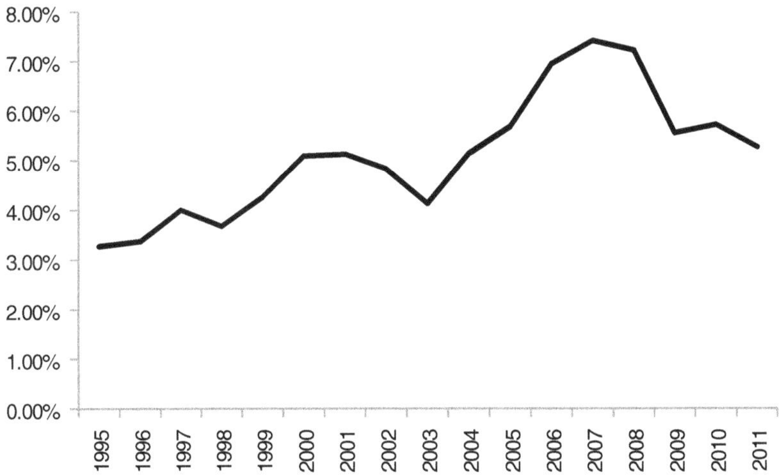

Figure 7.3 Dispersion of current account balances of EMU Member States (standard deviation – % of GDP) (source: AMECO).

These external adjustments have taken place both in Member States which entered the Great Recession with large current account deficits and those showing large current account surpluses, but they have been higher in the deficit countries. Greece, Portugal and Spain recorded an average deficit of over 11 percent of GDP in 2007, which fell to about 4.8 percent in 2011. On the other hand, the average current account surplus of Germany, the Netherlands and

Finland dropped from 7.1 percent of GDP in 2007 to 6.0 percent in 2011.[6] It is this difference in the intensity of the adjustment between deficit countries and surplus countries, together with the maintenance of external balance of the whole euro area, which explains the increase in France and Italy's current account deficits.

The external adjustment that the global financial crisis has led to, not only shows some differential behavior between deficit and surplus countries, but also within each of these two groups, as is reflected in Table 7.1.

Spain has managed to substantially reduce its current account deficit, from the 10 percent recorded in 2007 to 3.5 percent in 2011. To a large extent, this is the result of an improvement in its trade balance. Greece has also experienced a substantial reduction in its current account deficit but it still remains at an exceptionally high rate (–9.8 percent) and this is causing a rapid deterioration in its already high debtor international investment position. Finally, Portugal has improved its trade balance but it still amounts to –6.4 percent GDP, despite the significant drop in domestic demand.

Concerning Member States which entered the crisis with high current account surpluses, in 2011 the Netherlands registered even a higher current account surplus than in 2007, around 9.2 percent of GDP, the largest of the whole EMU. Germany had slightly adjusted its current account surplus as a result of a small decline in its trade surplus, but it still maintains a positive balance close to 6 percent of GDP. Finally, Finland shows a significant adjustment in its surplus, reaching a small deficit in 2011.

What has driven the adjustment of external imbalances within the EMU?

The reduction of current account imbalances within the EMU Member States must be framed in a crisis whose intensity and duration are unknown in recent economic history. The Great Recession has affected all the variables that determine the behavior of the external sector.

First, the narrowing of current account differences is closely related to the contraction in domestic demand, which has been much higher in deficit countries than in surplus countries (Figure 7.4).

A second important factor is the evolution of unit labor cost (ULC). As shown in Table 7.2, they had remained virtually stagnant in Germany between 1999 and 2007, which resulted in a significant improvement in its competitiveness, in contrast to Portugal, Spain and Greece where ULC grew above the average. However, nominal unit labor costs recorded a slower growth in Spain and Portugal than in the three surplus countries between 2007 and 2011. In Greece, meanwhile, this adjustment has not taken place, despite the sharp contraction in wages in 2010 and 2011.

It is important to separate the influence of nominal wages and productivity on unit labor cost, and to distinguish what happened at the beginning of the crisis and in the years 2010 and 2011, when austerity policies have been fully implemented.

Table 7.1 Current account balances (% of GDP)

	Greece			*Portugal*			*Spain*			*Average*		
	2007	*2011*	*Change*	*2007*	*2011*	*Change*	*2007*	*2011*	*Change*	*2007*	*2011*	*Change*
Trade balance	–18.6	–12.7	5.9	–11.3	–7.7	3.6	–8.7	–3.7	5.0	–10.5	–5.5	5.0
Services balance	7.4	6.8	–0.6	3.9	4.5	0.6	2.2	3.2	1.0	3.2	3.9	0.7
Income balance	–4.2	–4.2	0.0	–4.2	–5.0	–0.8	–2.9	–2.4	0.5	–3.2	–3.0	0.2
Current transfers	0.7	0.3	–0.4	1.5	1.8	0.3	–0.7	–0.6	0.1	–0.2	–0.2	0.0
Current account	–14.6	–9.8	4.8	–10.1	–6.4	3.7	–10.1	–3.5	6.6	–10.7	–4.8	5.9

	Germany			*Netherlands*			*Finland*			*Average*		
	2007	*2011*	*Change*	*2007*	*2011*	*Change*	*2007*	*2011*	*Change*	*2007*	*2011*	*Change*
Trade balance	8.2	6.0	–2.2	7.3	7.0	–0.3	5.1	–0.6	–5.7	7.9	5.8	–2.1
Services balance	–1.2	–0.8	0.4	1.6	1.6	0.0	0.3	0.5	0.2	–0.6	–0.3	0.3
Income balance	1.8	1.9	0.1	–0.1	2.2	2.3	–0.3	0.3	0.6	1.3	1.8	0.5
Current transfers	–1.3	–1.3	0.0	–2.1	–1.6	0.5	–0.8	–0.9	–0.1	–1.4	–1.3	0.1
Current account	7.4	5.7	–1.7	6.7	9.2	2.5	4.3	–0.7	–5.0	7.1	6.0	–1.1

Source: Eurostat.

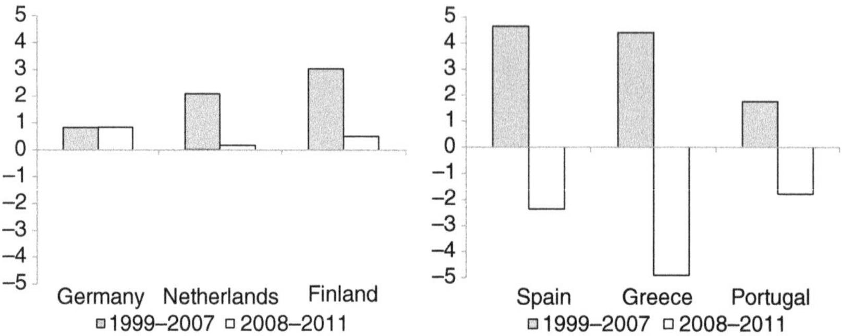

Figure 7.4 Domestic demand (annual average rate of growth) (source: AMECO).

Table 7.2 Nominal unit labor costs

	Euros			*EMU12 = 100*		
	1999	*2007*	*2011*	*1999*	*2007*	*2011*
Germany	0.57	0.56	0.61	108.8	95.8	95.7
Netherlands	0.49	0.58	0.63	92.6	98.7	98.8
Finland	0.51	0.56	0.64	97.3	95.0	101.6
Spain	0.46	0.59	0.60	88.3	101.4	95.3
Greece	0.46	0.57	0.62	88.3	96.4	97.6
Portugal	0.49	0.61	0.63	93.1	103.5	99.5
EMU12	0.53	0.59	0.63	100.0	100.0	100.0

Source: AMECO.

In Spain the lower growth in unit labor cost has been due mainly to the increase in "apparent" labor productivity,[7] and to the sharp reduction in wage growth in 2010 (0 percent) and 2011 (0.8 percent), while in Portugal this is the result of wage moderation. On the other hand, Greece registered a significant wage restraint (in 2010 and 2011 wages have fallen a total of more than 3 percent)[8] but this has not led to a lower ULC growth due to the sharp drop in apparent labor productivity (Figure 7.5).

The behavior of nominal unit labor costs in Germany is also noteworthy. It has experienced an average annual growth of 2 per cent since the start of the crisis, compared to its stagnation from 1999 to 2007. However, this increase is mainly due to the fall in apparent labor productivity as a result of a lower job destruction than in other countries. Although the rate of growth in nominal wages has increased recently (2.5 percent in 2010–2011, slightly higher than the increase in labor productivity), during the period 2008–2011 it still registered an average growth lagging behind the euro zone average, and the German authorities' public declarations don't show any change in their policy of wage restraint.

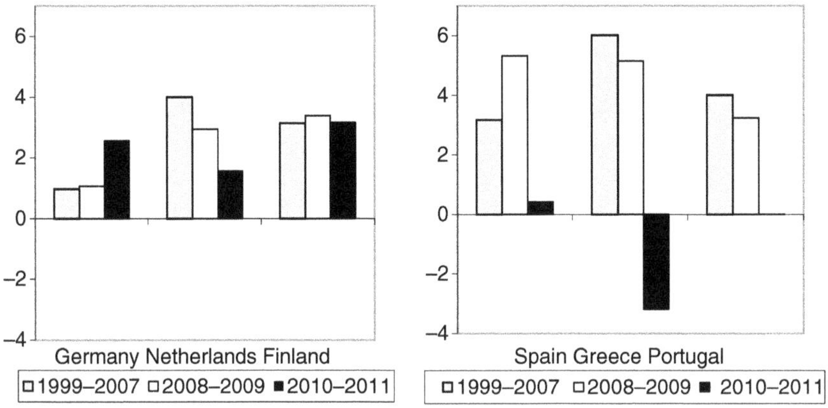

Figure 7.5a Nominal compensation per employee, total economy (annual average rate of growth (source: AMECO).

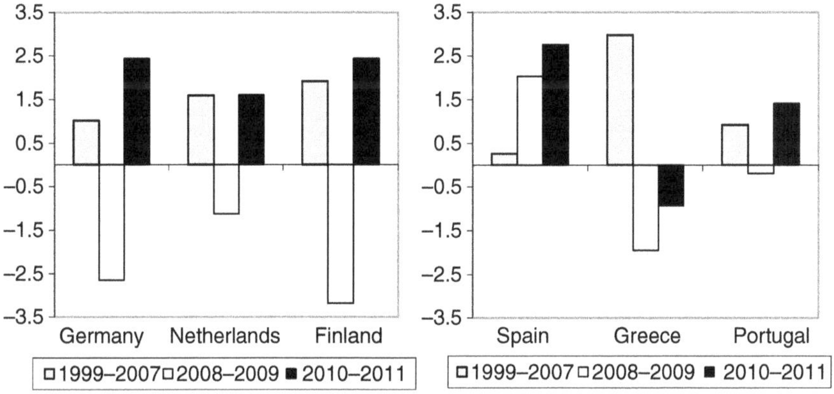

Figure 7.5b GDP per person employed, at 2005 market prices (annual average rate of growth) (source: AMECO).

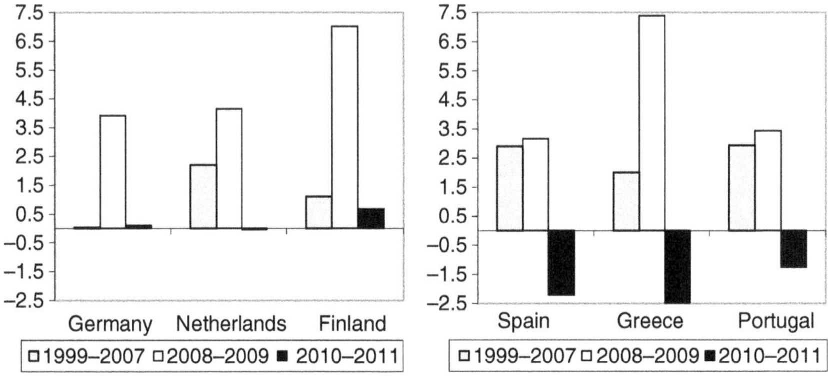

Figure 7.5c Nominal unit labor cost, total economy (annual average rate of growth) (source: AMECO).

This is probably one of the most important changes needed in the current European scenario to solve the crisis.

These different behaviors in unit labor costs have had their effect on competitiveness, measured by the real effective exchange rates (Figure 7.6). Spain and Portugal have corrected, but only partially, the cumulative loss of competitiveness in the decade preceding the global economic crisis, while Greece continued to lose competitiveness in 2008 and 2009, and its real effective exchange rate is still higher than in 2007. Meanwhile, Germany has experienced a very small real appreciation since 2008 (compared to the rest of the euro zone) but it had benefited from a sharp depreciation in the previous years.

The adjustment of external imbalances is still pending

It could be said that, despite some advances, the correction of current account imbalances within the euro area that has taken place so far is still insufficient:

- On the side of surplus countries, Germany has reduced its imbalance very moderately and the Netherlands has even increased it between 2009 and 2011. In turn, Greece and Portugal keep on experiencing very large deficits, which are leading to a rapid deterioration in their international investment positions.
- The recent adjustment is not due to profound changes in the economic policies of Member States, but it derives principally from the negative effects of the economic crisis on income and employment, the falls in domestic demand and the increases in apparent labor productivity registered in deficit countries. On the contrary, the unbalanced growth model, which is the ultimate source of external deficits and surpluses, remains unchallenged.[9] The factors that fueled current account surpluses in some countries in the past (weak growth in domestic demand and improvements in competitiveness

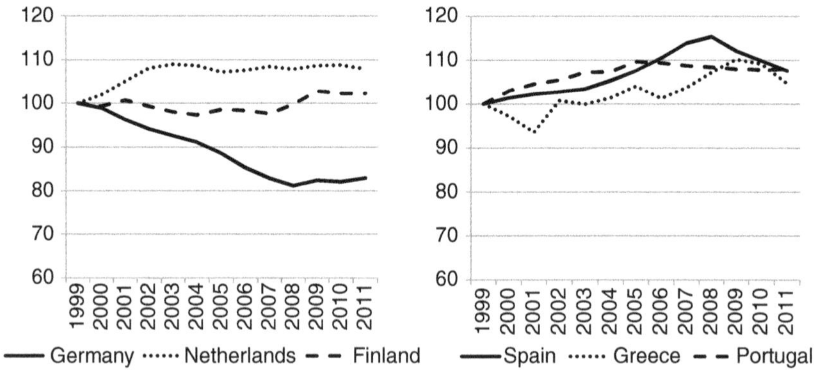

Figure 7.6 Real effective exchange rate, based on labor unit costs (performance relative to the rest of EU17) (cumulative change) (source: AMECO).

achieved through wage moderation) remain, with no real desire from these countries to change their export-led growth strategies.
- A coordinated strategy does not exist with a clear commitment to reducing external imbalances, both in deficit and surplus countries, but rather an asymmetric adjustment which will have high costs in terms of lower growth and rising unemployment.

In this sense, if surplus countries, particularly Germany, keep giving priority to the achievement of balanced public accounts, another widening in their current account surpluses will take place,[10] unless the nonfinancial private sector reduces its net lending. But this seems rather unlikely, especially if we consider the behavior of German nonfinancial corporations and households before and during the crisis, when they continuously increased their net lending.

Meanwhile, in the current institutional framework of the EMU, deficit countries face the need to reduce simultaneously their budget and current account deficits. And although these goals are not theoretically incompatible, their achievement will most likely lead to a very deep economic recession, to the extent that fiscal contraction will be accompanied by the deleveraging of the nonfinancial private sector. This challenge appears particularly difficult for Greece and Portugal, where large current account deficits remained in 2011, despite the huge weakness in their domestic demand, and where the level of external openness is very low.[11]

As Semieniuk *et al.* (2012) have highlighted, the stability programs presented by euro area Member States in April 2011 confirmed the absence of a coordinated and symmetrical strategy for reducing external deficits. In fact, when the forecasts of Member States' current accounts are taken as a whole, it is found that an external surplus of the euro area as a whole should exist, which is actually not the case.

How can some headway be made in the correction of external imbalances? The weaknesses of the macroeconomic imbalance procedure and of current economic policies

One of the most prominent features of the economic policy framework in the euro area is the excessive attention paid, sometimes almost exclusively, to the balancing of public budgets. However, the crisis has shown that macroeconomic stability requires not only the sustainability of public finances, but also the avoidance of persistent current account imbalances.[12] To put it more bluntly: the high and persistent external imbalances recorded since the introduction of the euro are one of the root causes of the crisis within the monetary union, more so than fiscal imbalances. The sovereign debt crisis is a consequence of the crisis, not its cause.

Recent European governance reforms continue to emphasize, without any justification, fiscal discipline over and above any other objective.[13] But European authorities have finally understood that it is also necessary to establish additional mechanisms for the prevention and correction of other macroeconomic imbalances and losses in competitiveness. This is reflected in the Macroeconomic Imbalances Procedure (MIP) launched in February 2012.

This procedure begins with an Alert Mechanism Report by the European Commission in which a scoreboard of ten main indicators is used to identify possible imbalances in some Member States. In the second stage, a more in-depth analysis is developed to determine the driving forces behind these observed imbalances and, if appropriate, the Commission proposes policy recommendations, and a phase of political pressure (and eventually economic sanctions) is started to force the country to adopt corrective measures (European Commission 2012b).

In Table 7.3 we outline the ten indicators included in the MIP scoreboard and the indicative thresholds established. They give us a clear idea of the prevailing view among European authorities regarding the origin of the current account imbalances and the economic policy measures that are required to correct them, as well as their limitations. We should underline three main aspects of this approach:

1 Asymmetry in the responsibility of the imbalances. Surveillance is established in principle both for deficit and for surplus countries, but in fact is much stricter for the former. For example, while the limit for current account deficits is 4 percent of GDP, the surplus limit can be extended up to 6 percent of GDP. Also, the European Commission itself recognizes that

Table 7.3 Scoreboard and indicative thresholds for the surveillance of macroeconomic imbalances

External imbalances and competitiveness

- Three-year backward moving average of the *current account balance* in % of GDP, with a threshold of +6% and –4%.
- *Net international investment position* in % of GDP, with a threshold of –35%.
- Five-year percentage change of *export market shares* measured in values, with a threshold of –6%.
- Three-year percentage change in *nominal unit labor cost*, with thresholds of +9% for euro-area countries and +12% for non-euro-area countries, respectively.
- Three-year percentage change of the *real effective exchange rates* based on HICP/CPI deflators, relative to 35 other industrial countries, with thresholds of –/+5% for euro-area countries and –/+11% for non-euro-area countries, respectively.

Internal imbalances

- *Private sector debt* in % of GDP with a threshold of 160%.
- *Private sector credit flow* in % of GDP with a threshold of 15%.
- Year-on-year *changes in the house price index* relative to a Eurostat consumption deflator, with a threshold of 6%.
- *General government sector debt* in % of GDP with a threshold of 60%.
- Three-year backward moving average of the *unemployment rate*, with a threshold of 10%.

Source: European Commission (2012b).

although all Member States must comply with these thresholds, this is more urgent in the case of deficit countries, to the extent that it can affect their ability to cope with their external debt and, ultimately, prevent the proper functioning of the EMU itself.

2 The origin of the imbalances is attributed to the lack of competitiveness, linked mainly to an excessive growth of unit labor costs in the peripheral countries. An upper limit for nominal unit labor costs is set (9 percent in the last three years), but the application in a country of a deliberate strategy of wage compression to improve its competitiveness at the expense of its neighbors is not penalized to the same extent (indeed, it is promoted).

3 The lack of domestic demand in some countries is not considered in any sense as a leading factor that could explain external imbalances. It is more than obvious that if a big country, such as Germany, develops a strong wage restraint policy and strict fiscal austerity and this weakens its domestic demand and drives it to a current account surplus, there will be symmetrical current account deficits in other countries. However, it is not clear that the Procedure will put any pressure on a country whose domestic demand is too low to change its economic policy.

In short, although the correction of external imbalances is formally seen as a task for both the deficit and surplus countries, in practice the causes of external imbalances in the euro area are attributed almost exclusively to the debtors: economic policy mistakes and the "bad behavior" of the peripheral countries, excessive spending, lack of competitiveness and export capacity, inefficient allocation of funds raised in international markets and excessive wage growth.[14] On the contrary, surplus countries are seen as a demonstration of efficiency and "virtue": austere fiscal policies, wage moderation and high productivity.

Consequently, the proposed economic policies to correct the external imbalances, like the Euro Plus Pact,[15] focus on strict adjustment programs to restore competitiveness in the deficit countries, mainly through wage cuts, fiscal austerity and structural reforms to improve their ability to compete in international markets, while specific measures to reinforce domestic demand in surplus countries are not called for.

In our opinion, this way of approaching the causes of current account imbalances within the EMU and its relation with the origin of the crisis is inappropriate, and these economic policy proposals are going in the wrong direction.

The correction of external imbalances and the restoration of sustainable growth in the EMU requires a greater coordination of the economic policies of the Member States. However, current proposals actually seek to promote a global convergence toward what we might call the "German model", and we think that this will have very negative consequences for the whole monetary union, and especially for the peripheral countries.

This growth pattern is based on the central role of exports and is characterized by the following three basic pillars:

- Improvements in competitiveness should constitute the main strategy of the economic authorities and this requires a strict policy of wage restraint and deep structural reforms.
- Exports are better than imports and countries should pursue external surpluses. Or, in terms of savings and investment, countries should live "within – below, we would say – their means".
- Fiscal austerity should be a fundamental element of public policies, to the extent of raising the budget balance to the category of law.

According to the economic authorities and, in general, mainstream economists, the goodness of this model is indisputable, as has been seen by the improvement in the behavior of the German economy since the beginning of the Great Recession, especially when it is compared to the peripheral economies in Europe. So the German economy becomes the best example of economic virtue, with households and companies spending within their means and the external surplus reflecting the ability of its industries to compete in international markets. Therefore, all the other economies should aspire to be like Germany, especially the "spendthrift" and "uncompetitive" Southern economies.

However, the "Germanization" of the EMU will actually weaken domestic demand in the whole euro area. Germany's large current account surplus is not an unambiguous indicator of competitiveness, but also the result of its lack of domestic demand, which has been offset thanks to the strong spending of the peripheral countries. But this growth model could only be generalized to the whole euro area if the monetary union registered a larger surplus vis-à-vis the rest of the world, which in turn would aggravate the problem of global imbalances. As Boyer (2012: 300) states,

> this repeats the pre-Keynesian fallacy that ignores that the surpluses of some countries are the strict counterparts of the deficits of others. Clearly, the German strategy has been sustainable only because the European Union and the rest of the world had dynamic domestic demands that created space for German exports.

Since an export-led growth is highly unlikely in the whole euro area, what can be expected for the future is the continuance of the imbalances within the EMU together with weak global demand and economic stagnation. This will continue to cast doubts on the viability of the European project (Wolf, 2010).

In short: the attempt to turn the euro zone into an expanded version of the economic policies applied in Germany will have adverse effects on the German economy itself, the rest of EMU and the global economy (Whyte, 2010).

Palley (2011) highlights, in relation to the world economy, that the benefits of the export-led growth model have been overrated, when, in fact, its extension is only leading to stagnation and confrontation among countries. Specifically, from a Keynesian perspective[16] we can make two major critiques of the export-led growth model:

- The first was identified by Joan Robinson (1947) to refer to competitive devaluation strategies applied by some countries in the 1930s and which led her to speak of "macroeconomic mercantilism". When countries try to compensate a demand shortage through increased exports and apply policies of "beggar-thy-neighbor", they are harming, albeit indirectly, their trading partners, by adversely affecting demand and employment.
- The second is labeled the "structural Keynesian critique" (Palley, 2004). The argument is that export-led growth leads to low-quality growth and that the strategy of gaining competitiveness by any means is a "race to the bottom" that harms the welfare and prosperity of its citizens.

The German experience since the introduction of the euro is a clear example of these two critiques. Germany has undergone a "macroeconomic mercantilism" to sustain its growth. The gains in competitiveness that have occurred since the introduction of the euro have not been achieved by high growth in productivity and improving living standards for workers. On the contrary, it was a strict wage moderation policy which paved the way to the decline in unit labor costs and with them the reduction of the real effective exchange rate.[17]

This model has resulted in increased inequality and deteriorating living standards for the German population. In fact, Germany has been one of the EMU countries that has registered a lower per capita income growth rate since the introduction of the euro. It is true that the German labor market has weathered the crisis better than other countries and that its unemployment rate remains very low now, but at the expense of stagnating living standards of its population and the generation of imbalances in other EMU countries. Germany's chronic weakness in aggregate demand was partially offset by the expansion in demand in the peripheral countries, financed by increased borrowing, which has proved to be unsustainable.

But if the alleged positive effects of export-led growth are already questionable for the German economy itself, even more so is the desire of a wholesale "Germanization" of the EMU. Germany, at the beginning of the last decade, began a process of strong wage restraint, labor market liberalization and deregulation, enabling it to achieve improvements in its relative competitiveness. In turn, German exports benefited from the strong growth in the domestic demand of the peripheral countries, driven by the sharp reduction in interest rates. However, if the idea is to apply this strategy across the board, the end result can only be increased inequality and reduced global aggregate demand leading to lower economic growth, accompanied by deflationary pressures. Ultimately, this will further hinder the private and public deleveraging which deficit countries necessarily face.

Conclusions and proposals

The adjustments in current account imbalances that have taken place since the beginning of the crisis are limited. Neither surplus countries, like Germany and the Netherlands, nor deficit countries, such as Greece and Portugal, have significantly advanced in the correction of external imbalances. Moreover, cuts have largely responded to factors associated to the crisis (increases in apparent labor productivity resulting from rising unemployment and declines in the growth of domestic demand) with strong recessionary effects. Meanwhile, the underlying problems that led to current account imbalances are still present and threaten not only the continuity of the process of narrowing external imbalances, but the achievement of a sustainable economic growth path in the medium term, capable of generating sufficient quality employment.

The current account deficits of some countries in the EMU and the surpluses of others are two sides of the same coin: the existence of an unbalanced growth model. Some countries with exceptionally low wage growth and weak domestic demand have offset their negative effects on economic growth and employment through a strategy of export-led growth. Meanwhile, other countries have based their growth on the expansion of domestic demand fuelled by increasing borrowing. In short, there have been two interdependent strategies: the growth of the core countries was sustained by the demand of the periphery and, at the same time, these countries needed the surplus countries to finance their current account deficits.

This unbalanced growth model is characterized by a global demand shortage, driven largely by the deterioration in income distribution, which has been temporally corrected by the accumulation of debt in some countries. However, what the global financial crisis has highlighted is that this model is unsustainable because it fuels growing imbalances, in particular the accumulation of private and external debt.

With the inclusion of current account balances in the new surveillance procedure for the prevention and correction of macroeconomic imbalances (MIP), European policymakers have begun to show concern for one of the negative symptoms of this growth model. However, their proposals for reform-wage competition, labor reforms, fiscal consolidation – will not solve the origin of the problem and will lead to a permanent weakness of aggregate demand, with grave social costs. This can seriously put at risk the viability of the single currency project, or at the very least provoke the exit of some countries outside the euro zone.

In our view, to overcome current account imbalances within the euro area and, in turn, restore robust growth, sustainable both from a macroeconomic and social point of view, the following principles should be observed:

- *Economic policy coordination.* Coordination does not mean convergence toward the policies of fiscal austerity and strong wage restraints that countries that have followed a model based on exports, and especially Germany, have carried out. It is true that some countries, such as Greece and Portugal and to a lesser extent Spain, still require significant improvements in competitiveness, but this is a relative concept and, therefore, their achievements will depend on the policies pursued in the euro area as a whole. Moreover, high public deficits cannot be maintained over the medium term, but the cost in terms of income and employment resulting from their reduction is conditioned by the behavior of domestic demand in other countries, particularly in the European core. In this sense, the economic policies of the peripheral countries to reduce external and public deficits should be accompanied by a strengthening of domestic demand in those countries like Germany that have sufficient leeway to adopt more expansionary fiscal and wage policies.

- *Symmetrical adjustment*. The correction of current account imbalances within the EMU cannot only rest in countries with high deficits, but it is also necessary that the authorities of surplus countries set a target for reducing balances. The newly created MIP should be more explicit in the role to be played by surplus countries than it has been. Moreover, as suggested by some authors when they analyze global imbalances (for example, Skidelsky, 2010; Davidson 2011) it is desirable to recover the basic principles of Keynes's proposals in the Bretton Woods Conference, and particularly the existence of some automatic mechanism to "recycle" the current account surplus in effective demand increases. This would result in an expansive adjustment of current account imbalances in the euro, instead of the tightening bias that results from the economic policies currently proposed.
- *The waiver of "beggar-thy-neighbor" policies*. Continuing the "competitive race" among EMU countries is doomed to failure. The individual search for improved competitiveness through wage cuts, the dismantling of labor standards and, in general, the welfare state, only serve to worsen the quality of the European model of development, to increase social inequalities and to further depress global aggregate demand. Of course, the waiver of such policies can only be achieved if there is an agreement between countries regarding the establishment of common standards on labor, environmental taxes and wages. In this sense, Stockhammer's (2011) proposal is particularly interesting. He suggests the establishment of a standard wage growth in the whole of the EMU based on productivity growth in each country, the overall inflation target and – temporarily – the purpose of correcting the real exchange rate that is considered necessary to address existing imbalances. This rule should not be exceeded, but neither should lower wage growth be allowed.
- *The guarantee of sufficient growth in global demand*. The unbalanced growth model cannot be replaced by the extension to the whole of the EMU of the export-led growth model. This strategy, hitherto used in countries like Germany, has increased inequality and has been a source of imbalances. Moreover, its extension to all of the countries in the Monetary Union is not feasible. Incidentally, what countries are we going to export to? Instead of this strategy, it is necessary to implement measures to boost domestic demand. Increasing certain public investments, improving the provision of some public goods, such as education and health care, the establishment of certain "social standards" to reduce "precautionary savings" or a tax reform to increase taxes on higher income groups to the benefit of lower income

groups, are some measures that would increase demand (for a more extensive treatment of these and other measures as well as their justification, see Hein and Truger, 2009).

To be honest, it is unlikely that the policies of the Monetary Union countries will be governed by the above principles in the near future. On the contrary, the recent reforms of the economic governance of the EMU are clearly focused on imposing the convergence toward a growth model based on wage restraint and social cuts as a way of improving competitiveness and enhancing exports. That is, a competitive strategy (a national solution) instead of the cooperative model (a European solution to European problems) that we have advocated in this chapter. The difficulties faced by this shift have a lot to do with the conflict between different national interests within the monetary union, but also between different class interests within each country, as reflected in the worsening income distribution that lies at the root of the crisis and, paradoxically, the policies supposedly designed to solve this. At the end of the day, this competition between countries ends up being a competition between workers in these countries through the deterioration of their wages and working conditions. Likewise, as noted by Arestis and Sawyer (2010), to adopt an alternative approach faces the predominance of the neoliberal agenda in the institutional design of the whole monetary union. However, as they also point out, "without basic and fundamental change, many (perhaps all) Euro area countries face a bleak economic future".

Notes

1 In this chapter, when we refer to EMU we only consider EMU12, except Luxembourg, which because of its distinctive features, has a current account surplus of around 10 percent of GDP.
2 From 1999 until 2011 the euro area as a whole had an average current account surplus of 0.3 percent of GDP.
3 Ireland had a significant current account deficit in 2007 (5.3 percent of GDP). However, this has not been its normal behavior since the launch of the euro. This is the reason why we do not include Ireland amongst large current account countries in this chapter.
4 In the following section, we critically explain the content of this new surveillance procedure of economic policies for European countries. See European Commission (2012a) for a detailed analysis of the indicators used for the surveillance macroeconomic imbalances and European Commission (2012b) for the first monitoring report of these indicators with data referring to 2010.
5 Italy has also been strongly affected by the sovereign debt crisis, and although it did not have a large current account deficit when the crisis began, in recent years it has suffered a significant deterioration in its external balance, unlike the other countries of the EMU.
6 Averages weighted by GDP.
7 This increase in productivity is not the result of technical progress, but it is related to the reduction in the number of jobs, especially in those sectors characterized by lower levels of skills.
8 As a result, real wages have fallen in 2010 and 2011 by 13 percent in Greece and 4.5 percent in Spain and Portugal (European Commission 2012c).

9 See Uxó *et al.* (2011) for a detailed explanation of the origin of current account imbalances in the euro area and their relationship with the unbalanced growth model in which some countries follow an export-led growth strategy, whereas others base their growth on the expansion of domestic demand financed by debt.

10 The current account balance, considered as net lending or borrowing of the nation, coincides with the sum of net lending/borrowing of the private sector and net lending/borrowing of the public sector.

11 For a discussion of the difficulties that Portugal and Greece have to face to return to a situation of external sustainability see Gross (2010).

12 On the other hand, the joint sustainability of public finances and the external sector necessarily involves paying greater attention to the private sector financial balance.

13 For a critical review of the major reforms recently introduced in the framework of economic governance in the EU, see Uxó and Paul (2011).

14 A clear example of this point of view is the former Bundesbank President Axel A. Weber (2011), who states that the actual problem of the monetary union

> is that a number of countries have obviously failed to meet the obligations and requirements of a currency union.... The financial crisis has revealed unsustainable developments in some countries – developments which were already in existence before the crisis: too much public spending, unproductive use of capital inflows, losses of competitiveness.

15 European Council (2011).

16 Keynes (1936: 382) pointed out that in a context of insufficient aggregate demand some countries may try to avoid unemployment through international trade. However, if this strategy succeeds it simply shifts the problem of lack of demand to other countries:

> If nations can learn to provide themselves with full employment by their domestic policy ... there need be no important economic forces calculated to set the interest of one country against that of its neighbours.... There would no longer be a pressing motive why one country need force its wares on another or repulse the offerings of its neighbour ... with the express object of upsetting the equilibrium of payments so as to develop a balance of trade in its own favour. International trade would cease to be what it is, namely, a desperate expedient to maintain employment at home by forcing sales on foreign markets and restricting purchases, which, if successful, will merely shift the problem of unemployment to the neighbours which is worsted in the struggle.

17 Cesaratto (2010) also believes that Germany is a good example of a "mercantilist" economy with its emphasis on the trade surplus, productivity, wage moderation and restraint for domestic consumption, and notes the difference between "benign" and "aggressive or malevolent" mercantilism. Aggressive mercantilism would be the one that has characterized economic policy in recent years. In the same vein, Hein and Truger (2009) define the strategy of German economic policy as "dysfunctional mercantilism" and stress that has had a restrictive effect on Germany and the whole European economy.

References

Arestis, P. and Sawyer, M. (2010) "The problems of the Economic and Monetary Union: is there any escape?" *Journal of Economic Issues*, 1 (1): 1–14.

Blanchard, O. and Milesi-Ferreti, G.M. (2009) "Global imbalances: in midstream?" *IMF Staff Position Note*, December.

Boyer, R. (2012) "The four fallacies of contemporary austerity policies: the lost Keynesian legacy", *Cambridge Journal of Economics*, 36 (1): 283–312.

Cesaratto, S. (2010) “Europe, German mercantilism and the current crisis”, *Quaderni del Dipartimento di Economia Politica, Università degli Studi di Siena*, no. 595.
Davidson, P. (2011) “The Keynes solution for preventing global imbalances”, Paper presented at the conference “From crisis to growth? The challenge of imbalances, debt and limited resources”, Berlin, Germany, Research Network Macroeconomics and Macroeconomic Policies.
European Commission (2012a) “Scoreboard for the surveillance of macroeconomic imbalances”, *European Economy Occasional Papers 92*, February.
European Commission (2012b) *Alert Mechanism Report*, COM (2012) 68 final, 14 February.
European Commission (2012c) “European economic forecast, spring 2012”, *European Economy*, 1/2012.
European Council (2011) *Conclusions of the Presidency*, 24–25 March. www.consilium.europa.eu/uedocs/cms_data/docs/pressdata/en/ec/120296.pdf (accessed 17 March 2012).
Gross, D. (2010) “Adjustment difficulties in the GIPSY Club”, *CEPS Working Document No. 326*, March.
Hein, E. and Truger, A. (2009) “How to fight (or not to fight) a slowdown”, *Challenge*, 52 (3): 52–75.
Horn, G., Joebges, H. and Zwiener, R. (2009) “From the financial crisis to the world economic crisis (II). Global imbalances: cause of the crisis and solution strategies for Germany”, *IMK Report*, 40, December.
Keynes, J.M. (1936) *The General Theory of Employment, Interest and Money*, Cambridge University Press, Cambridge.
Palley, T.I. (2004) “The economic case for international labor standards”, *Cambridge Journal of Economics*, 28 (1): 21–36.
Palley, T.I. (2011) “The contradictions of export-led growth”, *Public Policy Brief*, Levy Economics Institute of Bard College, No.119.
Robinson, J. (1947) *Essays in the Theory of Emplo*yment, 2nd edn, Basil Blackwell, Oxford.
Semieniuk, G., van Treeck, T. and Truger, A. (2012) “Nothing learned from the crisis? Some remarks on the Stability Programmes 2011–2014 of the Euro area governments”, in Jespersen, J. and Madsen, M.O. (eds.), *Keynes's General Theory for Today*, Edward Elgar, Cheltenham, 186–206.
Skidelsky, R. (2010) “Keynes, global imbalances and international monetary reform, today”, in *Rebalancing the Global Economy: A Primer for Policymaking*, edited by Claessens, S., Evenett, S. and Hoeckman, B., CEPR, London, 173–180.
Stockhammer, E. (2011) “Peripheral Europe's debt and German wages: the role of wage policy in the euro area”, *International Journal of Public Policy*, 7 (1/2/3): 83–96.
Uxó, J. and Paúl, J. (2011) “The reform of the economic governance of the eurozone: macroeconomic supervision and coordination”, *International Journal of Public Policy*, 7 (4/5/6): 205–225.
Uxó, J., Paúl, J. and Febrero, E. (2011) “Current account imbalances in the Monetary Union and the Great Recession: causes and policies”, *Panoeconomicus*, LVIII/5: 571–592.
Weber, A. (2011) “Challenges for monetary policy in EMU”, *Federal Reserve Bank of St. Louis Review*, July/August, 93 (4): 235–242.
Whyte, P. (2010) “Why Germany is not a model for the eurozone”, *Centre for European Reform, Essays*, October.
Wolf, M. (2010) “Why Germany cannot be a model for the eurozone”, *Financial Times*, 30 March.

8 The effects of the great recession of 2008 on the neo-Keynesian development experiences

The cases of Argentina and Brazil

Fabián Amico and Alejandro Fiorito[1]

Introduction

This chapter aims to analyze the effects of the great recession of 2008 on a group of developing countries, such as Argentina and Brazil, in the context of a new pattern of growth adopted in 2000. As a general framework of analysis, we will summarize the main features of the new pattern of international growth, beginning with the emergence of China. In this context, we will discuss the main strategies undertaken by developing countries. Of these three strategies, this analysis will focus on one of them. Following Medeiros (2010), we will refer provisionally to this strategy as "neo-Keynesian", which in Latin America is represented by the cases of Brazil and Argentina. In this analytical framework, the term "neo-Keynesian" means a strategy that results in increased economic growth by an expanding domestic market, reducing poverty and increasing real wages. But at the same time, these improvements are achieved without substantive policies aimed at changing patterns of trade specialization as well as inducing a structural change.

Thus, the aim of this chapter is to present and discuss the main features of the new "engine" of global growth in 2000. At this point we follow closely the early vision of Lewis (1980), particularly with regard to China's rise as a major trading power. It will also be described how several developing countries have redefined their strategies for growth in this new context. Then the emergence of a new pattern of growth will be analyzed, which we have called "neo-Keynesian", and outline its main features and the results produced within the framework of the specific cases of Argentina and Brazil between early new millennium until the crisis of 2008.

Having established the main features of the new pattern of growth, we will analyze the specific mechanisms of transmission of the great recession of 2008 on these growth experiences. We will show that the crisis did not change the main structural features that characterize the new world "engine of growth" for less industrialized countries. The next step will analyze the novel factors of these cycles of growth which allowed them to tackle the crisis with more and better instruments, reducing its internal impact, and which finally allowed them to recover a path of growth quickly. Some important differences between the cases under review will also be highlighted, and we will describe some important features of economic interaction between Argentina and Brazil. At this point some policy implications and some potential dilemmas for the future growth of these countries will be discussed briefly. Finally, the chapter ends with some brief concluding remarks.

The new engine of global growth in 2000

In the context of the change in the growth pattern from 2000s (and especially from 2003), the Less Developed Countries (LDC) showed three strategies of development. The first, a "passive" and "integrationist" strategy followed by Mexico and South East European countries.[2] This began in the 1990s and it is continuing today despite its weak results. The second is the so-called "new-developmental" strategy taken by China and other Asian countries (like Taiwan and Singapore) focusing on the upgrade of their industrial structures. In this case, the macroeconomic policies are subordinate to industrial change aimed to reduce the technological gap.

Since the beginning of the millennium the world's economy has changed quite a lot due to the very important irruption of China into the world market after it became a member of WTO (World Trade Organization) in 2001. At this stage the growth of developing countries was decoupled from the developed world, even in the case of Latin America, which from 2003–2007 experienced strong growth (6 percent in average) due to high export commodity prices and good conditions of financing.

This change is to a great extent related to new China dynamics. China's economy seems to constitute an autonomous pole of growth day by day, a possibility that Lewis had anticipated in his speech upon receiving the Nobel Prize in 1979. Lewis's idea was simple: "instead of trade determining the rate of growth of less-developed countries (LDC), it will be growth of LDC production that determines LDC trade, and internal forces that will determine the rate of growth of production" (Lewis, 1980: 562). The necessary condition was that a leader country would have autonomous growth and high demand from other developing exporters. Thus, these countries could base their growth on internal markets by relaxing their restrictions on the balance of payments.

This is one possible interpretation for some stylized facts of global growth in 2000. In this decade there was a considerable acceleration of economic growth in developing countries. While in the 1980s and 1990s, the cycles in advanced countries and developing countries were highly correlated (and the average growth rates of both groups were similar), in the 2000s the cyclical correlation between the two groups of countries persisted, but during this period, for the first time in more than three decades, developing countries (including Latin America and the Caribbean economies) grew at consistently higher rates than the advanced economies (Damill and Frenkel, 2011; Medeiros, 2011).

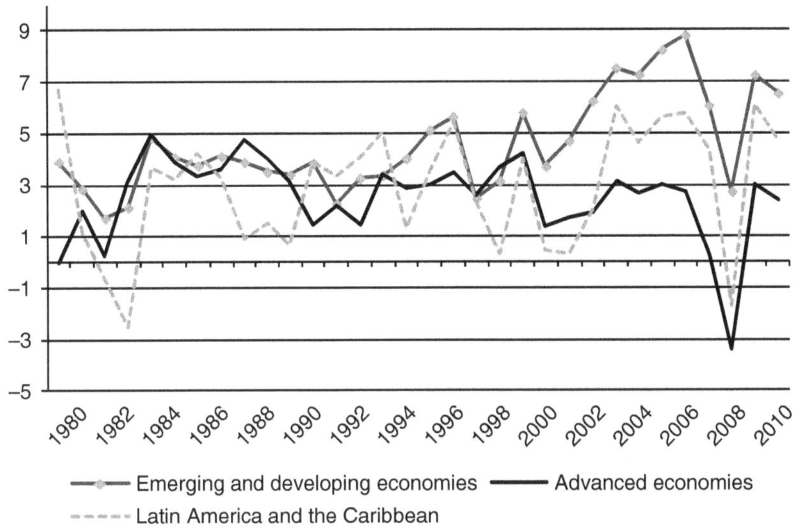

Figure 8.1 GDP growth rates: advanced, emerging and Latin American economies (source: IMF, World Economic Outlook Database, 2011, www.imf.org/external/pubs/ft/weo/2012/01/pdf/text.pdf).

The emergence of China, with its huge economies of scale and relatively low wages (in international terms), generates a clear trend toward lower industrial costs compared to production costs of raw materials. It is also China's currency policy, which has managed to avoid the appreciation of the yuan against the dollar, boosting the competitiveness of Chinese production and eliminating a possible mechanism that could counterbalance the trend of deteriorating terms of trade of industrial products. In fact, since China has become the leading exporter in broad industrial sectors, its internal costs determine international prices. And the terms of trade of these products are not immune to the exchange rate policy of the country.

Along with these factors, and as a result of increasing industrialization and improved consumption patterns, China has increased its demand for raw materials and food traditionally produced in the periphery of the global economy. Under current conditions (in which Asia cannot supply all the requirements of raw materials and food), the growing Asian demand has contributed to this remarkable tendency of commodity prices rising in recent years.[3]

Current trends differ from the one imagined by traditional structuralist literature, since the terms of trade have been reversed in favor of the periphery and this trend looks sustainable. However, Lewis (1980) anticipated this possibility. Lewis argued that the principles governing the terms of trade were dependent on the characteristics of the exporting countries or regions rather than the type of product involved. Thus, according to Lewis's approach, the products from backward agricultural regions, which have structural surplus labor and low wages, should be cheap in relation to those produced in countries with modern agriculture, high wages and lower proportions of surplus population. Following this logic, Lewis predicted that the continuity of Asian industrialization would lead to a reversal of the terms of trade, which would benefit countries producing raw materials.

These circumstances, as discussed below, have profound implications because they do not create favorable incentives for industrialization strategy, as in the times of Prebisch. On the contrary, given the new international situation, industrialization is seen as more expensive and more difficult than in the past. In contrast, the traditional strategy of international integration based on the export of agricultural commodities and opposite to the promotion of industrialization, today may be viewed as a more convenient option

In short, in Lewis's theory the main difference in terms of trade between North and South was not really between industrial and primary exports (as in the Prebisch–Singer thesis) but between the country level of productivity and wages in production of food and on the surplus labor. Thus, for example, the low wages paid in China kept down the prices of the commodities produced (directly or affected indirectly by them), *irrespective* of its material composition.

However, the strong fall in labor share in China and India have in turn strong effects on world economy. On the one side, in the case of the US, the global commodities chains and the declining power of unions and workers put a stop to the growth of industrial wages. On the other side, they have a strong impact on the primary production and contribute to the high level of commodities prices. Serrano (2008) points out this unusual feature of the price cycle and especially its low influence on world inflation. Basically, the decline of union and labor power in developed countries is the principal reason for this change contributing

Table 8.1 Industrialized and developing countries: contribution to global GDP growth, 2008–2011 (percentage points)

Countries and groupings	*2008*	*2009*	*2010*	*2011*
Industrialized countries	0.1	–1.8	1.6	1.2
United States	0.0	–0.5	0.6	0.5
European Union	0.2	–0.9	0.4	0.4
Japan	–0.1	–0.4	0.2	0.1
Others	0.0	0.0	0.4	0.3
Developing countries	2.7	1.3	3.5	3.2
Sub-Saharan Africa	0.1	0.1	0.1	0.1
Latin America and the Caribbean	0.4	–0.2	0.5	0.4
Developing Asia	1.6	1.7	2.3	2.1
China	1.1	1.2	1.4	1.4
Middle East and North Africa	0.3	0.1	0.2	0.2
Central and Eastern Europe	0.1	–0.1	0.2	0.1
World	2.9	–0.5	5.0	4.4

Source: ECLAC on the basis of data from IMF.

for the perseverance of the high commodities prices (and TOT favorable to primary production).

Thus, the South–South trade grew very fast. Furthermore, the interaction between the economies of Argentina and Brazil (with the particular strategy followed by Brazil in the region) co-determined the final results in terms of growth and policy options. In general terms, this view of the role of China in the world growth pattern differs to the so-called "global imbalances" postulated for mainstream economics (Serrano, 2003; Dooley *et al.*, 2003). In our approach, in some ways US is a "cyclical center" for China, but then China is a "cyclical center" for the countries producing primary commodities and raw materials like Argentina and Brazil. In this way, China's growth determines the "engine of growth" of the peripheral primary exports countries during 2003–2008, and after the great recession this tendency still continues.

In this context, various countries began constructing new development strategies situated *between* neo-developmental strategy and a "passive and integrationist" strategy. This third way, which we call "neo-Keynesian", tries to keep distance, on one hand, from the previous strategy of national development and, on the other, from the pro finance and liberal macroeconomic policy. This road was taken by several natural resources export countries (like Argentina and Venezuela) or countries with a more diversified but "unbalanced" industrial sector (like Brazil or Russia). In reality, these four countries, despite the different levels of industrial development achieved, have an "unbalanced productive structure" and are strong exporters of primary products.[4] Beyond their ideological, political and structural differences, these countries have been following more pragmatic economic policies. Thus, a higher economic growth led by the domestic market, social progress and higher real wages was achieved *without* significant policy focused on changing their patterns of trade specialization.

However, in this third way the State has less power to induce structural change. The economic and social cohesion needed to accomplish this task has disappeared (if it ever existed, for example, in Argentina). In fact, in the main Latin American countries, those large private economic groups, which in the past were the main beneficiaries of industrial policy, did not survive the process of radical liberalization (Argentina) or have moved to the exploitation of natural resources and its support activities, such as services and construction (Brazil).

Anyway, in both countries these industrial interests are now more diffuse and less powerful to exercise leadership in economic policy and to build political support for a comprehensive industrial policy. The boom in commodity prices, in turn, makes the effort to strengthen the industrial policy more difficult and sets a higher "opportunity cost" to the diversification of production and also the attempts of structural change.

This new "engine of growth" influences the growth dynamics of economies like Argentina and Brazil in two ways. On one hand, it pushes up the growth rates in South American countries due to *demand effect* caused for exports to China. Moreover, even if these economies are growing due to the expansion of domestic markets, it is possibly thanks to the positive effect of exports to China

Table 8.2 Balance on current account (percentages of GDP)

	Argentina	*Brazil*	*Total region**
2003	6.3	0.8	0.5
2004	2.1	1.8	1
2005	2.9	1.6	1.4
2006	3.6	1.3	1.6
2007	2.8	0.1	0.4
2008	2.1	−1.7	−0.7
2009	3.6	−1.5	−0.5
2010	1	−2.3	−1.1

Source: Statistical Yearbook (2011), ECLAC.

Note
* Latin America and Caribbean.

on the external constraint on growth (*the balance of payments effect*). As we shall see, the *balance of payments effect* is the main transmission channel in both countries. The persistent process of the domestic growth of China at high rates has allowed many developing countries of the region to keep a positive current account. Indeed, since 2002 to 2006 both Brazil and Argentina have maintained a positive growth in their external gap. However, since 2006 gradually the external current account showed a deficit trend, becoming negative in the case of Brazil since 2008.

The amount of benefits due to an improvement in export prices were bigger in the countries that produce minerals and energy (Andean countries and also Brazil), than in others (Argentina) that produce agricultural crops.

Indeed, as shown in the Table 8.3, the terms of trade improved in both countries, but while in Argentina the increase amounted to 18 percent between 2003 and 2010, in Brazil the increase was nearly 100 percent over the same period.

Table 8.3 Terms of trade (2005 = 100)

	Argentina	*Brazil*
2003	100	74
2004	102	89
2005	100	100
2006	106	131
2007	110	136
2008	125	118
2009	119	119
2010	118	146

Source: Statistical Yearbook (2011), ECLAC.

Growth's "neo-Keynesians" experiences: Brazil and Argentina

Brazil's economy had grown at very low rates until 2003 and it is only since the mid-2000s that GDP growth and employment has begun to accelerate. At first, in the context of the strong expansion of international trade, the growth was led by exports. However, due to its structural characteristics, the Brazilian economy cannot grow significantly when growth is driven by external demand. For that reason, only since 2006 the internal market began to expand at a faster pace through a series of changes in macroeconomic policy and on the international level. Thus, the average GDP growth rate in 2004–2010 period was 4.4 percent, more than double the 1.9 percent average for the 1999–2003 period (Serrano and Summa, 2011).

Other authors have similarly characterized the long phase from the mid-1990s to the first decade of the 2000s. The period from 1996 to 2001/2002 is known as a *stop–go cycle*, while in 2002 a "*long cycle*" began and has continued up to the present (Carneiro, 2010). It thus verifies discrepancies between the contribution of external and domestic demand, which were even more intense in the 1990s. These two periods of growth have in common a high rate of growth of domestic demand, a weaker contribution from net exports and a significant appreciation of the domestic currency.

In turn, the pattern of growth in Brazil in 2000 was marked by two central features of macroeconomic policy: a system of inflation targets (whose main manifestation is a high level of interest rates) and a fiscal policy based on obtaining large primary surpluses.[5] The inflation-targeting framework is based on the supposition that inflation is caused by demand factors. Then, when inflation accelerates, this will lead to higher interest rates in order to reduce demand pressures. But several authors have shown that in Brazil an empirical relationship between demand (i.e. output gap) and inflation acceleration does not exist (Serrano, 2010; Summa, 2010).

Thus, the system works in a different way from the postulate for the conventional theory. A rise in domestic interest rates generates positive interest differentials and produces a revaluation of domestic currency. In turn this revaluation transforms the *negative* supply shocks (i.e. increasing commodities prices in the world market) into a *positive* supply shock in terms of domestic inflation. Given the obvious need to increase public investment, the official argument is that it was necessary to reduce government spending on consumption and social transfers in order to free up resources for public investment. In turn, high interest rates reduce credit growth and hence GDP.

In short, the need to promote stronger growth is a direct contradiction to the inflation targeting system in a period characterized by high commodity prices (and thus, by a high incidence of external factors on inflation in Brazil). But the high rates, and their *unjustified* connection with fiscal surpluses, lead to tightened domestic credit and limit the possibilities of public investment expansion. Finally, the resulting low growth is interpreted (and justified) as a "cautious" policy aimed at maintaining effective GDP growth around its potential level, and so contain inflation. It is a truly self-fulfilling prophecy.

Obviously another possible outcome of this interest rate policy would be less demand (by its effects on net exports), slower output growth and higher unemployment. Possibly these effects would result in a low growth of nominal wages. But some economists argued that this seems not to occur in Brazil since the distributive effect of the appreciated exchange rate has been seen to increase in real wages and consumption by much more than the reduction in net exports, "so much that aggregate demand increases when the real exchange rate appreciates" (Serrano and Summa, 2011).

This kind of low-growth trap imposed by high interest rates and large fiscal surplus was avoided thanks to the improvement of certain international conditions. The new global conditions prevailing since 2003 came at the hands of lower interest rates in the US and a significant reduction in spreads for emerging countries. Thus, the Brazilian central bank could keep large interest rate differentials positive even with *declining* domestic interest rates since 2006.

Additional steps were also taken to increase the availability and access to credit (Barbosa, 2010). In turn, despite large primary surpluses, fiscal policy was not very expansionary, but had a positive impact (albeit small) on aggregate demand (Rodrigues and Pinkusfeld, 2009). Since 2006, however, there was faster growth in government spending and social transfers. A key factor in this context was the rapid growth of real minimum wage, which had a strong effect on public wages, pensions and the salaries of some informal workers.

These changes in macroeconomic policy (albeit small), in combination with an improvement in external conditions, explain why the growth rate of the Brazilian economy finally began to rise in mid-2000. The government

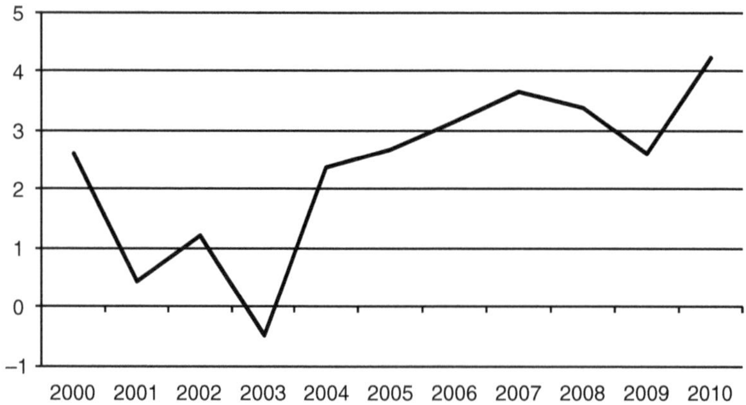

Figure 8.2 Brazil: households' final consumption (contribution to GDP growth, percentage points) (source: Ipeadata, www.iadb.org/intal/intalcdi/PE/2012/09632.pdf).

introduced some changes and economic policy was slightly expansionary, especially from 2006. This led to rapid growth in domestic demand in general and private consumption, in particular, that after a time induced a boom in private investment.

In a way, the path of growth of Argentina's economy in 2000 is not so different in important respects from those discussed in the Brazilian case. Under the convertibility regime, Argentina experienced two periods of sustained capital inflow that spurred growth. The first occurred between 1991 and the contagion of the Mexican crisis in 1995. The second was shorter; it began after the "tequila effect" and stopped in mid-1998. Then the economy remained in a strong depression that led to the dramatic collapse of the regime in 2001–2002, and concluded with the abandonment of the currency board, a big devaluation and default on the external public debt.

The recovery of economic activity since 2002 has been associated with pragmatic macroeconomic policies that offset the external imbalance, while providing incentives for tradable activities. It was also noted that exchange rate policy aimed at maintaining a competitive real exchange rate would have been a decisive factor. However, this approach exaggerates the role of exchange rate policy and completely underestimates the impact of fiscal policy.

In fact, between 2002 and 2007 the primary surplus increases at first and then decreases slightly to stabilize at around 3 percent until at least 2007. This change in the fiscal stance might suggest that the government is making a contractionary policy. But as is known from the pioneering work of Haavelmo, fiscal policy can be expansionary still maintaining a balanced budget.[6] Also, in the case of Argentina, there is an additional point related to the role of export taxes, which have the property of not being contractionary for the level of activity, as they are actually paid by the rest of the world (by consumers of Argentine exports). Therefore, there is an increase in tax revenues without reducing disposable income.

This characteristic of export taxes has some interesting implications in the Argentine case. For example, between 2002 and 2009 the average annual fiscal surplus was exactly equal to the average of export taxes (2.2 percent of GDP). Also, the interest paid on debt during the same period was equivalent on average to little more than that: 2.7 percent of GDP. So, from the fiscal point of view, Argentina paid the interest on foreign debt virtually without contractionary effect (quite the contrary, thanks to the action of other components of fiscal policy), simply transferring part of the rents of commodities exports to the public debt holders.

This way, it was possible for the government to have an expansionary fiscal policy and also exhibit a significant fiscal surplus. This expansionary fiscal policy record since 2003 is due to a direct increase in social transfers (pensions), the increase in the salaries of state employees, the largest public consumption and particularly the recovery of public investment (which had reached ridiculous levels in 2002 due to fiscal adjustment policies of the previous period). In turn, this higher public expenditure had a positive impact in autonomous consumption (pensions, social programs, and wages).

For example, social security spending (which in 2002 represented 20 percent of primary expenditure) had suffered a decline in nominal terms (–4 percent in 2001 and –2 percent in 2002) and went on to grow at a rate of 14 percent annually since 2003 to accelerate further in 2006. Although these numbers are nominal values, they are still very significant. The most striking change was the evolution of capital spending, which had suffered heavy nominal reductions in previous years (32 percent in 2000, –13 percent in 2001, and –22 percent in 2002) and began to grow at impressive rates (87 percent in 2003, 118 percent in 2004) to finally stabilize around a rate increase of 25 percent per annum by 2009.

Following this strategy Argentina experienced one of the most successful growth episodes in its economic history. From mid-2002 to mid-2008, the economy grew at 8.5 percent average annual rate. The favorable external conditions were important, but they only explain a part of the economic performance. In fact, since 2003 the economy grew steadily led by domestic demand (consumption and investment).

As a source of demand, exports combined with the other components of aggregate demand; they determine the level and the rate of growth of actual output. As a source of finance for imports, exports set the limit (and other sources of international finance) beyond which actual output cannot expand.

Besides, in the period 2000–2010 private consumption growth accounted for more than 50 percent of the increase in aggregate demand, while investment contributed nearly 30 percent to the expansion of demand. On the other hand,

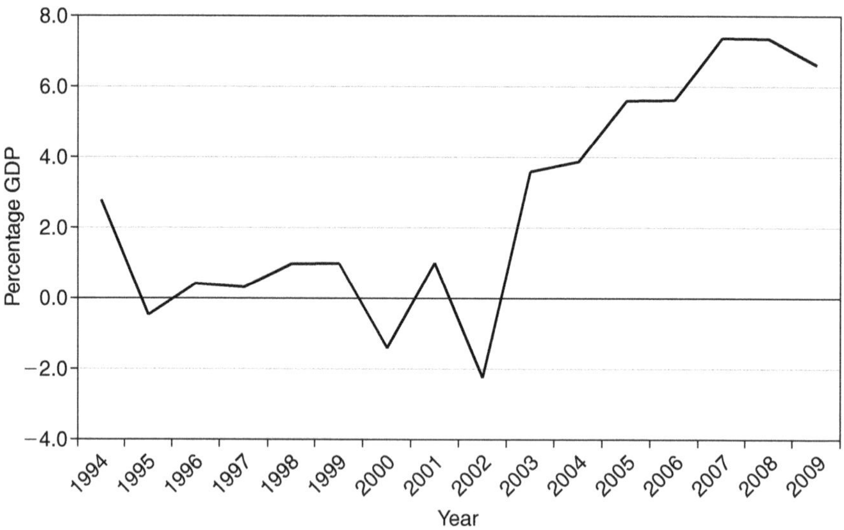

Figure 8.3 Argentina: impact of fiscal policy, 1994–2009 (percentage points on growth of aggregate demand) (source: Ministerio de Economía y Finanzas de la República Argentina).

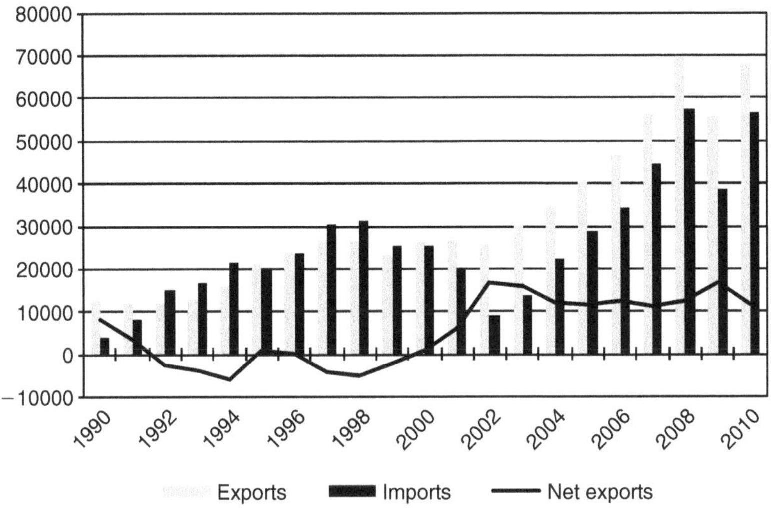

Figure 8.4 Argentina: net exports (millions of US$) (source: Ministerio de Economía y Finanzas de Argentina).

the contribution of net exports to growth in demand was declining and it became negative by 2008. However, although the contribution of net exports was decreasing, and in recent years turned negative (either at constant prices or current prices in domestic currency), when looking at net exports *in dollars*, things look very different.

It emerges very clearly that the foreign exchange contribution of net exports (estimated by the dollar value of imports and exports) has been essential to maintaining a positive trade balance and thus preventing the external constraint on growth. Besides, together with the maintenance of a competitive real exchange rate, it has allowed a significant accumulation of international reserves resulting from the trade balance.

Impact of the great recession on Brazil and Argentina

In both Argentina and Brazil there are two main channels of transmission of the international crisis: the financial channel and the channel of foreign trade. Then, indirectly, these impacts have effects on other variables such as the level of activity, investment and employment. The financial transmission channel in Argentina took place through an intense capital flight. The main cause of this was the "flight to quality" produced by the international financial uncertainty.

Since mid-2007 until the first quarter of 2009 the accumulation of foreign assets of non-financial private sector reached 33.535 million dollars, equivalent to half the export foreign exchange earnings in 2008 (Damill and Frenkel, 2009).

However, the disruptive effects of capital flight were much more limited than they had been in the past. By the late 1970s and in the last years of the model of convertibility, Argentina's economy had a greater external vulnerability due to the existence of large and growing current account deficits, in a context of strong and persistent appreciation of the domestic currency. In addition, the financial system showed a rapid expansion and was affected by exchange rate risk.

These factors were not present when the crisis started in 2007–2008, first because Argentina's economy showed robust current account surpluses from 2003 onwards. Thus, from mid-2007 to early 2009, the trade balance surplus was 31120 million, equivalent to 93 percent of the accumulation of foreign assets by the private sector in the same period. Unlike past experiences, currency accumulated by the private sector was counterbalanced by the foreign trade surplus, and the level of international reserves of the central bank had minor variations.

In Argentina, the main channel of transmission of the crisis was the fall in exports (–20.5 percent in 2009).[7] As exports account for about 20 percent of global demand, the *direct* impact of its reduction is equivalent to a contraction of about 4 percent of GDP. Besides, there was a strong reduction in the investment.

Some economist argued that this strong reduction was due to the expectations of a stronger appreciation of domestic currency initiated in 2008.[8] These economists argue that investment has been growing at a decreasing rate since 2002 due to the continuing real appreciation of domestic currency following the large devaluation of early 2002. However, this investment behavior is fully consistent with the *accelerator principle*, under which investments adjust production capacity following the trend of output and effective demand (Serrano, 1996; Dejuán, 2010).

Thus, the investment growth rate will tend to follow the rate of increase in aggregate demand and GDP. If the GDP growth rate is constant, the rate of increase in investment will tend to converge at that rate. As shown in Figure 8.5, this is what happened in Argentina in the stage that began in 2002. Obviously, when there are changes in the rate of GDP growth, investment will tend to overreact (to "accelerate"), as occurred with the downturn of 2009 and the upswing in 2010. This "overreaction" of the investment is necessary to adjust the size of production capacity to the expected expansion of demand.

In short, the *overall* impact of the decline in exports is amplified by the multiplier and accelerator effects. First, the decline in exports leads to a reduced level of activity and employment in export industries. Then, this initial contractionary effect of reduced employment adds a further contractionary effect, associated with lower consumption wage (or induced), as the decline in employment levels leads to a reduction in the size of the multiplier. Finally, due to the accelerating effect, this decline in exports led to a fall in investment of 10 percent in 2009.[9]

As explained in the preceding section, Brazil has been growing vigorously since the mid-2000s. The components of domestic demand have been leading the growth, while investment grows at higher rates, because of the operation of the accelerator principle. It means the productive capacity tends to adjust following the trend of aggregate demand.

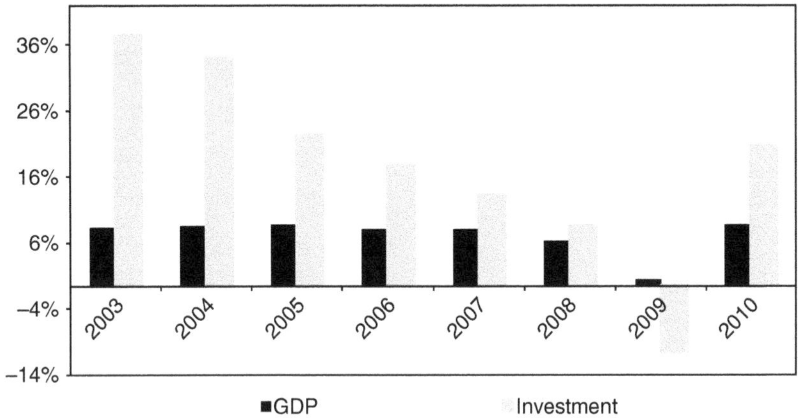

Figure 8.5 Argentina: GDP and investment (growth rates) (source: Ministerio de Economía y Finanzas de Argentina).

On the real side, it should be considered that until 2008/2009 the worst decline in world trade since World War II (in annual terms) had occurred in the 1982 recession, with a reduction in world exports from 6.3 percent. In fact, the decline in world exports in 2009 was about 22 percent, i.e. three times the previous value (Pinkusfeld, 2010). Also in the Brazilian case, the drop in exports (–22.7 percent in 2009) would add the multiplier effect of consumption induced and the effects of the fall in autonomous consumption (due to credit crunch). Then, the accelerating effect would produce a fall in investment.

On the financial side, the fourth quarter of 2008 saw a major reversal of capital flows. Thus, the combination of current account deficits with a net loss of financial resources led to devaluation. There was also a decline in the account of profits and dividends transferred by TNC affiliates abroad, resulting from the process of denationalization of the Brazilian economy in the 1990s. The new orientation of economic policy implemented in Brazil since the mid-2000s opened a space for a strong countercyclical response to the global crisis of late 2008. The official reaction allowed the Brazilian economy to shrink less in 2009 and recover faster than other countries.

How did this dramatic recovery of the Brazilian growth occur (from –0.6 percent in 2009 to 7.5 percent in 2010)? These structural measures taken before the crisis by the government (Barbosa, 2010) point out the expansion in the mechanisms of social protection, the increase of the minimum wage, the expansion in public investment and the tax cuts associated with new industrial policy, among many others. Note that, similar to Argentina, a comfortable level of international reserves gives the government more policy alternatives to fight the impacts of international crises.

Also important were the existence of social protection mechanisms, which helped countercyclical policies and the traditional instruments of "developmental

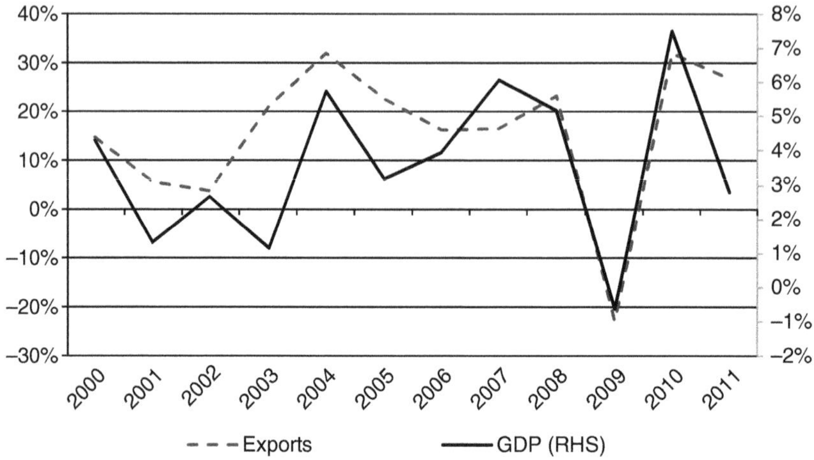

Figure 8.6 Brazil: GDP and exports (growth rates) (source: Ipeadata).

state" facilitate the government's actions.[10] Besides, a "heavy" prudential regulation was also useful not only to prevent crises, but also to fight their effects. The low leverage and the high reserve requirements demanded from the Brazilian banks by the central bank proved to be extremely useful during the credit crunch. Finally, the pragmatism of the government was very important in order to adopt countercyclical measures, because the authorities did not lose too much time in debating the ideological implications of each policy initiative.

As noted by Serrano (2010) and Summa (2010), the central bank of Brazil did not stop the expansion. However, by some change in its policy approach, and by the fall in international interest rates and reduced spreads, the Central Bank achieved its inflation targets, using lower interest rates (both nominal and real). Also during the crisis in late 2008, the countercyclical policy was only possible due to the sharp devaluation of the exchange rate (necessary to stop capital outflows) and was counterbalanced in terms of domestic inflation by the simultaneous fall of commodities in dollar prices. Then, the devaluation was quickly reversed when emerging market spreads returned to levels similar to those existing before the crisis. In a way, strong countercyclical policy in Brazil in the midst of the crisis was not due to a new orientation in economic policy, but rather was a result of the same policy in different cyclical conditions (basically the lower world interest rates and also lower the international prices of commodities).

New performance and policy dilemmas

Compared with previous decades, there are significant positive changes in the behavior of developing economies in general, and in Brazil and Argentina in

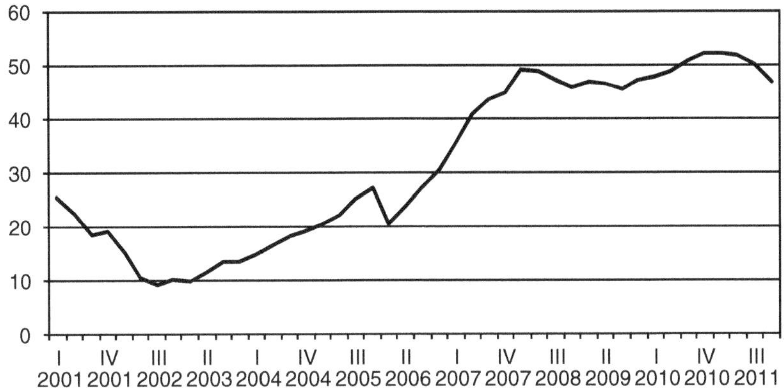

Figure 8.7 Argentina: international reserves (billion US$) (source: CEI, BCRA and Indec).

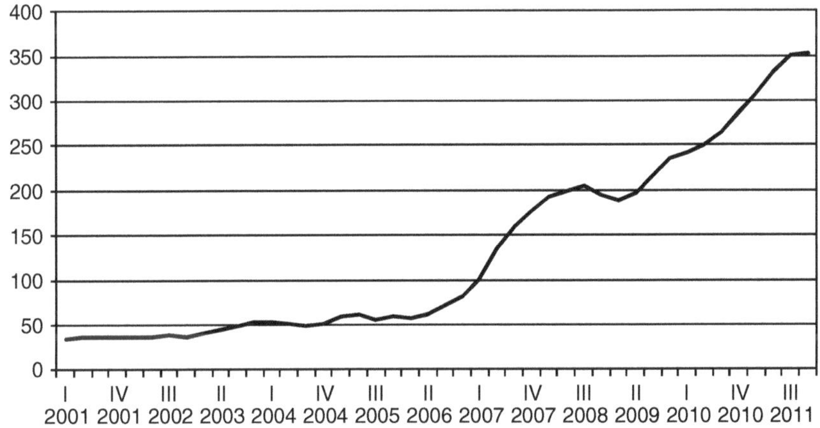

Figure 8.8 Brazil: international reserves (billion US$) (source: CEI, Banco Central do Brazil, IBG and IMF).

particular. These changes are primarily associated with changes in patterns of integration in the international system and macroeconomic policy regimes. In turn, the changes in the modalities of integration led to a reduced financial vulnerability.

Furthermore the new macroeconomic policy orientations, including the adoption of managed floating exchange rate regimes, and an exchange rate policy aimed at either preserving competitive real exchange rates or avoiding large appreciations, and voluminous accumulation of international reserves, were a prominent factor.[11] Besides, the reversal of the results of the current account resulted in an effect of reversing the direction of net capital flows.

External vulnerability and fiscal policy

At this point fiscal deficits on the external deficit should be clearly distinguished. A country with a degree of monetary sovereignty cannot have a debt default in its own currency. However (except for the nation issuing the international reserve currency), all countries need to earn foreign exchange through exports.[12] Thus, in a context of low financial vulnerability, i.e. when a country (even a developing country) has a positive current account and a large stock of international reserves, there is no economic need to maintain a balanced budget.

Obviously, the continued reduction of unemployment (i.e. resulting from an expansionary fiscal policy) can lead to exacerbation of the distributional conflict between wages and profits, and this can lead to accelerating inflation. But the causal mechanism of this type of inflation is quite different from that which can be found in the literature on fiscal policy. In addition, Haavelmo (1945) proved that fiscal policy can be expansionary even with a balanced budget. Indeed, the budget balance says little about whether fiscal policy is expansionary or contractionary.

In fact, during the 2009 crisis, when the budget deficit was increasing, the Argentine government implemented the so-called "Universal child allowance" (*Asignación universal por hijo*), a social program consisting of a subsidy for all children who belong to households of informal workers. The budget deficit initially increased, but months later when the economy returned to a path of growth, the fiscal deficit turned into a slight surplus due to the significant increase in tax receipts associated with a higher level of activity and employment. Brazil did something similar with the implementation of the plan *Bolsa familia* (to financially aid poor families). Although it had been implemented before, it was extended

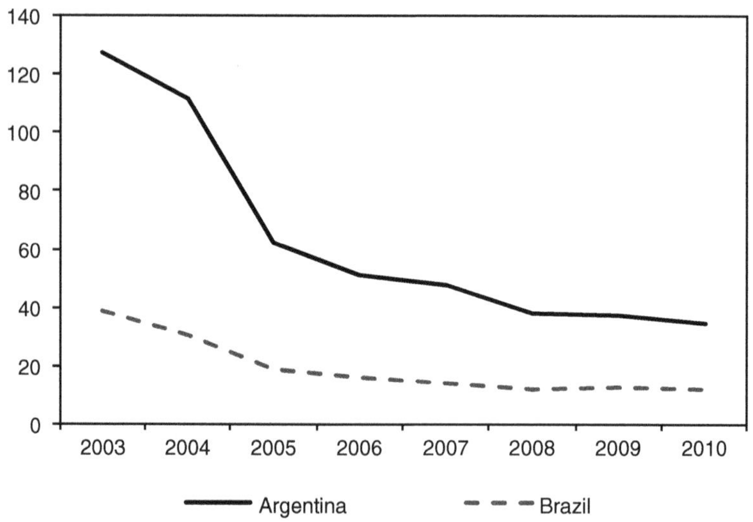

Figure 8.9 Argentina and Brazil: external debt (percentage points of GDP) (source: ECLAC).

during the 2009 crisis, alleviating the effects of the recession on poverty and adding an expansionary effect to the economy. Also, thanks to the new macroeconomic regime, the economies of the region could avoid the "financial traps" of the past,[13] and the reduction of the foreign debt burden is an indicator of a reduced financial vulnerability.

Exchange rate policy and structural imbalance

But, in general terms, there are important differences between the cases analyzed. While Argentina bases its reserve accumulation on a current account surplus and especially its positive commercial result, Brazil accumulated reserves through capital inflows. Also it has a deficit in current transactions. Moreover, while Argentina holds a competitive exchange rate combined with low interest rates, Brazil has very high real interest rates, resulting in a persistent appreciation of the exchange rate. In response to external shocks, in 1999 Brazil adopted a floating exchange rate regime and an inflation targeting system. Argentina continued with the RER appreciated until the 2001 crisis, when it adopted a floating exchange rate regime. Thus, the RER tended to depreciate since the late 1990s: since 1999 in Brazil and since 2002 in Argentina. The real exchange rates (both Argentina and Brazil) reached their peaks in 2002–2003 and then experienced a sustained trend toward appreciation.[14]

Also, in both countries the real exchange rate average for the period 2002–2008, was significantly more depreciated than it was in the 1990s, despite

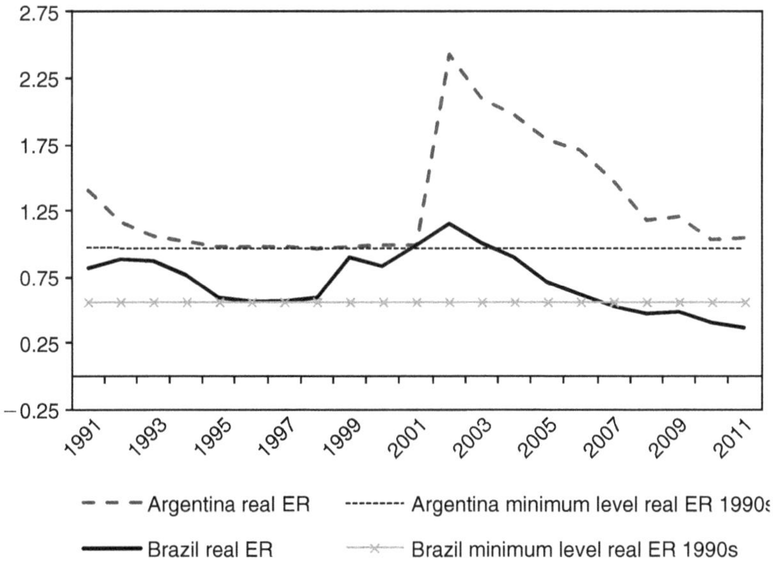

Figure 8.10 Argentina and Brazil: RER (2001 = 1) (source: Ipeadata, www.ipeadata.gov.br/, BCRA, CEI, Indec and Cenda).

the continuing trend toward appreciation. Finally, currency devaluations during the crisis period (2008–2009) represented only a brief interruption of the appreciation trend. Thus, by 2011 the real exchange rates were at levels similar to those minimum levels in the 1990s. However, while in the case of Argentina by 2011 the real exchange rate was still slightly higher than the minimum of the 1990s, Brazil had passed that level by 2007.

The level of real exchange rate is important in connection with the concept of "unbalanced productive structure" (UPS). According to this view, both Argentina and Brazil exhibit a structural imbalance between the productivity of the primary export sector and industrial productivity (Diamand, 1986). The exchange rate level is based on the costs of the more productive (primary) sector. Thus, when the prices of industrial goods are expressed in dollars (calculated on the basis of the exchange rate for the primary sector), they are higher than the international ones. Therefore, unless the industry receives special incentives or a higher real exchange rate, the industrial sector only produces for the domestic market. Marcelo Diamand called these agreements an unbalanced productive structure (see Amico, 2011).

In this arrangement, without special intervention from the state, the exchange rate will eventually adjust to the level of competitiveness of primary production. This level of real exchange rate, as is said, is insufficient to allow the industry to export. A higher real exchange rate (i.e. a more depreciated currency) would be a solution for industrial production. But a higher exchange rate means lower real wages, which the unions are reluctant to accept. At this point there is a significant difference between Brazil and Argentina. A characteristic of the Brazilian economy in the 2000s was the almost complete absence of "wage resistance" to the point that there was a strong inverse relationship between the level of *nominal* exchange rate and average real wages. In Argentina, given the higher wage resistance, there is obviously an inverse relationship between *real* exchange rate and real wages, while the association of wages with the nominal exchange rate is not as straightforward as it is in the case of Brazil.

Thus, high prices (and high demand) for commodities produces a continuing trend toward exchange rate appreciation that strengthens the structural imbalance. The key point is the evolution of the relative profitability of industrial manufacturing. There is empirical evidence that unit labor costs in foreign currency increased steadily since the minimum values reached in the early 2000s. But, while in 2010 in Argentina the unit labor cost in dollars was still 7 percent lower than in 2001, in the case of Brazil it was already over 12 percent for the same period (Frenkel and Rapetti, 2011).

The evolution of the relative profitability is reflected in the structure of exports. Thus, while Argentina increased the proportion of industrial exports (from 60.6 percent of total exports in 2002–2003 to 68.4 percent in 2010), Brazil reduced the incidence of industrial exports (from 69.4 to 53.4 percent over the same period) (Frenkel and Rapetti, 2011; see also Carneiro, 2010).

Long-run growth and regional integration

During the long period associated with the state-led development strategy (from the late 1940s to 1980) Brazil grew at an average of 7.4 percent per year. With the debt crisis and the so-called lost decade, and later with the neoliberal era, the long period from 1980 to 2002 shows average annual growth rates of GDP only slightly above 2 percent.

Starting in the late 1980s, a significant process of liberalization in the context of the Washington Consensus doctrines has been implemented in Brazil (Vernengo, 2011). This policy approach did not change substantially in 2000.[15] However, despite all, Brazil has in recent years had an increase of its average growth rates. In the period 1999–2010, the average annual growth rate of GDP was 3.4 percent. But if the period considered is 2002–2010, this rate increased to 4 percent, which represents twice the average of 1980–2002.

How was this possible in the framework of a macroeconomic model of bias orthodox and almost exclusively focused on inflation? Certainly, the change in international economic conditions allows, through small changes in domestic policy, implied that the greatest growth took place. But this, in turn, is due to broader conditions. In fact, evidence seems to suggest that Brazilian governments institutionalized a *hybrid* policy regime that articulates the priorities of the current macroeconomic consensus, based on orthodox principles (fiscal and price stability and economic openness) with more interventionist policies associated with neo-developmentalist thinking (Ban, 2011). Thus, while defending the goal of macroeconomic stability and neglecting the Keynesian policies of full employment, Brazilian governments also reduced reliance on foreign

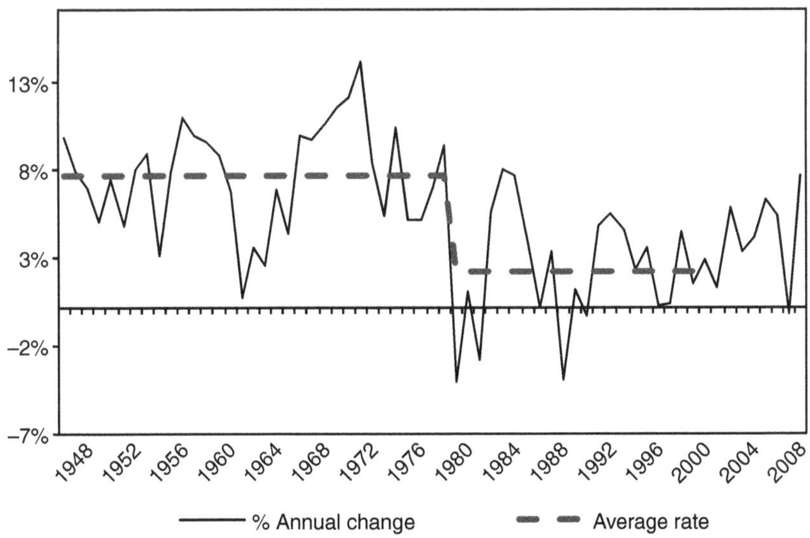

Figure 8.11 Brazil: GDP growth rate (source: Ipeadata, www.ipeadata.gov.br/).

savings and employed a largely *off-the-books* stimulus package during the crisis.

Brazil experienced significant reforms of liberalization and deregulation. But at the same time (in a very different way from Argentina), the Brazilian state held (and even strengthened in some areas) its role as the owner and investor in industry, banking and infrastructure, despite using a policy of open industrial economy (especially due to the appreciation of national currency). Somehow, Brazilian governments did not replace the orthodox scheme with a neo-developmentalist scheme, but, rather, *superimposed* interventionist policies and social welfare programs on the same neo-liberal regimen which were established in the country in the previous decades.

But the articulation of these essentially different things is not an easy task and the current economic regime seems to face structural problems. The main problem is that the exchange rate is the only anti-inflationary tool. Their systematic use (via persistent appreciation) affects the country's external accounts and damages the competitiveness of industry. Several studies show a significant increase of import content in the Brazilian manufacturing industry (Serrano and Summa, 2011; Carneiro, 2010; Pinkusfeld, 2010), and the import penetration is more intense in the most technologically advanced industries.

The Brazilian economy could (at least partially) compensate for this loss of competitiveness by increasing industrial exports to the Southern Common Market (Mercosur, for its acronym in Spanish), and also by the extractive industry exports to the rest of world. But, although the country has had a large volume of international reserves in recent times, these reserves have increased almost exclusively by the entry of short-term capital. To a great extent, Brazil's trade surplus is due to the positive outcome of non-industrial products and low technology that is unrelated to the appreciation of the domestic currency. The increases of the technological content of foreign trade will raise the participation of transnational corporations and the balance trade becomes negative, because of new imports. We can say then that the combination of appreciation of the exchange rate, denationalization and the strategy of transnational corporations is causing negative pressure on Brazil's external accounts.

In a long-term view, in turn Argentina shows much lower GDP growth rates than Brazil. While in the stage of the so-called import substitution industrialization (1950–1976), the country grew at an average annual rate of 3.5 percent in the period of rule of the Washington Consensus, the average was just 0.93 percent per year. With this background, the average growth rates of GDP for the period 2003–2010 (7.6 percent) is an exceptional event.

But if the Argentine government does not apply aggressive industrial policies to diversify exports, substitute imports and produce a structural change, the fate of Argentina's growth in the future will depend on *exogenous* factors, which could alleviate the traditional balance of payments constraint and allow maintained high growth rates of output and employment. These exogenous factors are basically the ability of the economies of Brazil and China (in that order) to pull their imports from Argentina.

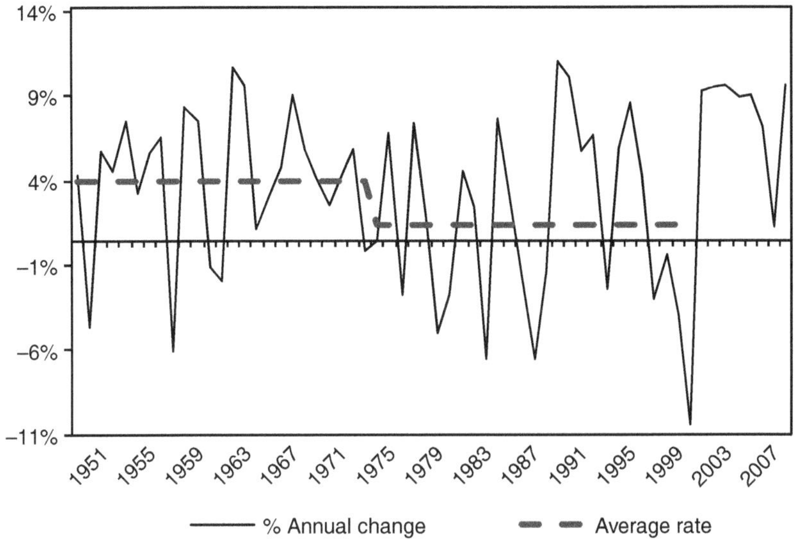

Figure 8.12 Argentina: GDP growth rate (sources: Ferreres, 2005; Cepal e Indec).

From 2000, the level of primary exports from Argentina is similar to the 1990s, and imported from Brazil a large number of vehicles, capital goods and intermediates, that led to a growing trade deficit in Argentina in relation to Brazil.

This result is an obstacle to the regional integration process. Certainly the most lasting benefits of regional integration should come from the increase in scale of production and technological learning process industries, which in turn come from the diversification of the domestic market. In this sense, the Mercosur presents strong ambiguities and limitations, and still failed to give the integration process a broader perspective than the simple customs union. Thus, the integration process ends up being led by the markets, and their beneficiaries end up being the major companies operating in sectors with economies of scale. This integration model ends up, in fact, *expanding* the existing asymmetries (Medeiros, 2008; Prebisch, 1959).

To the extent that it constitutes an expansive integration process, the Mercosur requires the economic leadership of Brazil, who should regain its industrial export growth to fulfill this role. In this hypothetical scheme, called "regional Keynesianism" (Medeiros, 2008), with greater dynamism of industrial exports, Brazil could increase its imports from the regional bloc, which would allow the reduction of asymmetries. Also, the smaller countries of the common market may increase their imports from Brazil, raising the level of economic integration and the size of national markets and overall productivity. The regional common market would then be a way to alleviate the external constraints of the member

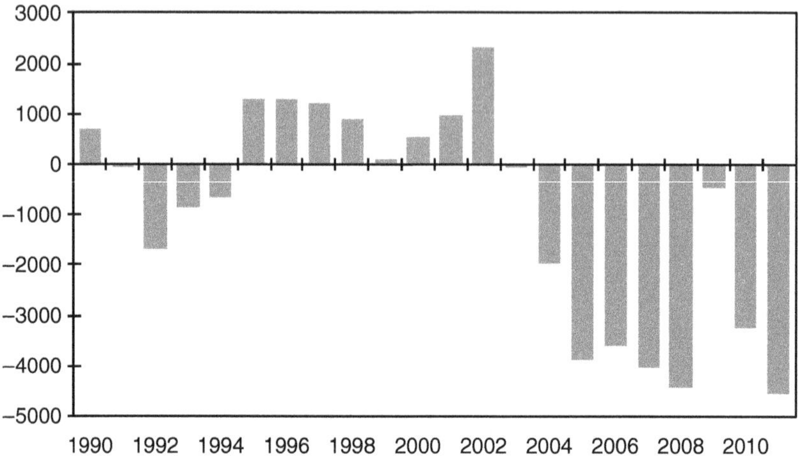

Figure 8.13 Argentina–Brazil: trade balance (million US$) (source: Indec).

countries, allowing higher and sustainable growth rates, in logic similar to that described by Prebisch more than four decades ago.

However, if the regional common market remains within the logic of free trade, the potential for future growth in the region will be weakened. In the case of Argentina, a possibility of expansion within the existing scheme is that the country achieves greater integration of national parties in the production of automobiles, which today constitutes the main export to Brazil. Also, the substitution of some imports of intermediate goods and capital would allow the country more foreign exchange savings and greater domestic market integration, which would extend the current growth cycle. The need for Argentina to implement strong industrial policies is imperative, given that since 2004 it has had a growing trade deficit with Brazil and since 2008 it has also had a trade deficit with China.

For its part, Brazil could mitigate the problems of competitiveness through large exchange rate devaluation. The first problem of this measure is the impact it could have on income distribution. While in Argentina a strong devaluation of the exchange rate generates, sooner or later, a rise in nominal wages to compensate for the decline in real wages generated by the exchange rate adjustment. In Brazil (due to the absence of "real wage resistance") a nominal devaluation will produce a *permanent* fall in real wages. This fall in real wages has a negative effect on consumption and effective demand and may thus have a contractionary effect on aggregate spending, despite the expansionary effect of the improvement in exports and reducing imports.

However, the prevailing economic opinion in Brazil not only postulates a large devaluation without concern for their distributional impacts, it also stresses the need for significant fiscal *contraction* in order to reduce persistently domestic interest rates, which is necessary to "liberate" the nominal exchange rate of its task of controlling inflation.[16]

Technically, it is possible to adjust the exchange rate, reduce its impact on income distribution and keep inflation under control. One way is by setting export taxes (to prevent the export price increases induced by the exchange rate that are passed to domestic inflation) and subsidizing imports. It is also suggested that further control over excessive profit margins in the prices of some services be introduced. The alternative would be complemented by a strong increase of public investment in infrastructure, in order to reduce export costs and other industrial policy measures.

However, the concept and practice of fiscal policy in line with the old tradition of "sound finance" is one of the main obstacles to sustained growth in the future both in Argentina and Brazil. Marx (1852: ch. 1) stated that "the tradition of all dead generations weighs like a nightmare on the brains of the living" and over 80 years later, Keynes (1936: ch. 24, V) said, in a similar vein, that "Practical men, who believe themselves to be quite exempt from any intellectual influence, are usually the slaves of some defunct economist".

Final remarks

At the beginning of the new millennium, China's rise as a major trading power was at the center of the global economic changes and this circumstance has brought better economic opportunities for many peripheral countries. Brazil and Argentina benefited from the strong demand for (and high prices of) commodities. This allowed an unprecedented combination of high economic growth, positive current account and significant reduction in debt levels. The financial crisis of 2008 that led to a major recession in most developed countries did not change some of these new and structural circumstances for less industrialized countries.

In this context, Argentina and Brazil have been following a pragmatic economic policy, which leads to a higher economic growth and social progress led by internal markets. These results have been achieved in these countries without strong efforts to change their pattern of trade specialization. These improvements were achieved through horizontal Keynesian policies without direct State intervention to promote industrial change.

Of course there are some important differences in these experiences. Two of these differences explain the relatively better performance of Argentina. On the one hand, economic policy did not use contractionary fiscal adjustment as an anti-inflationary mechanism. Furthermore, in Latin America, Argentina is the only country that after the strong exchange rate devaluation of 2002 kept a competitive rate of exchange until the end of the present decade.

Indeed, in addition to the beneficial terms of trade with China, the exchange rate appreciated in Brazil (the main trade partner of Argentina) favored the maintenance of competitive exchange rates in Argentina. Thus, the same historical dilemma (the structural imbalance) is in place. However, the same factor that allowed this cycle of growth in Argentina and Brazil (even with their differences) is a challenge for the future. In fact, since the middle of the decade, in a context of the gradual appreciation of their currencies, Brazil and Argentina began to notice the increasing penetration of Chinese imports.

Today, both countries have trade deficits with China, and these deficits are compensated for with difficulty by trade surpluses obtained with other smaller Latin American countries. On the one hand, Brazil is balancing its deficit with China by obtaining surplus with Argentina. Furthermore, Argentina is balancing its trade deficits with Brazil and China by obtaining surpluses with the smaller countries in Latin America. But gradually the structural imbalance is reflected in a persistent deficit trend of the external current account in the two countries.

An alternative development strategy is possible, which would require a strong recovery of the ability and willingness of the state to invest (Pérez Caldentey and Vernengo, 2008). Public investment would provide a basis for policy (industrial, trade and exchange) aimed at stimulating export diversification and selective substitution of imports. This would open up greater space for macroeconomic policies to promote the expansion of domestic markets.

Unfortunately, in regard to public investment and development financing, the rejection of the Washington Consensus in these countries has been more rhetorical than real. In fact, national States have lost the capacity to regulate the economy, or have been captured by social groups with strong interests in the continuation of a development model which emphasizes primary and financial integration. Thus, while Brazil instituted a hybrid political system that we can tentatively call "neo-liberal development" with a "big government", Argentina encouraged a more heterodox Keynesian regime but with the weakness of a "small government".

Finally, the same mechanisms that create favorable conditions for trade in some peripheral countries also impose difficulties on the resumption of their industrialization. The increasing centrality of China's economy and its growing impact on terms of trade, and on the parameters of international competitiveness, change the basic conditions in which they should consider the development strategies of these countries. In this context, these "neo-Keynesian" experiences such as in Argentina and Brazil, based on the expansion of their domestic markets, will find increasing difficulties in the future to continue without changing the predominant pattern of economic growth.

Notes

1 Universidad Nacional de Luján and CIGED-UNSAM (Universidad Nacional de General San Martín), Buenos Aires, Argentina.
2 One common response to the new challenges was the pursuit of an "integrationist" strategy (Amsden, 2001), or as put by Lall (2000) "a passive strategy dependent on foreign direct investment (FDI)".
3 Basically, the main mechanism is that the growing demand makes profitable areas of production of raw materials, which previously were not profitable due to their higher production costs.
4 The definition and implications of the so-called "unbalanced productive structure" will be discussed in the section entitled "New performance and policy dilemmas".

5 It is argued that rapid growth in the long term required a sharp increase in the primary fiscal surplus. This higher fiscal surplus would significantly reduce the public debt–GDP, which in turn allows more permanent reductions in real interest rates in the "long term", resulting in a greater increase in private investment (see Serrano and Summa, 2011).

6 The theorem balanced budget multiplier shows that the variation in the product induced by an increase in public expenditure accompanied, in turn, a variation of the tax is equal to unity (the multiplier is 1).

7 The production of auto parts, automobile industry and agriculture were the most affected branches.

8 Damill and Frenkel, 2009: 40.

9 For a deeper analysis about this *supermultiplier* effect in Argentina see Amico*et al.* (2011) and Fiorito (2011).

10 On one side, a comprehensive system of personal income transfers is very useful for quickly assisting poor and low income families during periods of crisis. On the other side, the existence of public banks, state companies, industrial policy and government investment programs may also facilitate and expedite the action of the State in stabilizing the economy.

11 Even Brazil, which used the persistent appreciation of domestic currency as anti-inflationary instrument, had a very "dirty" floating exchange rate. This flexibility allowed the government to adjust its exchange rate in times of crisis, facilitating the adjustment of the economy.

12 For a discussion about the conditions in which growth can be financed by external debt or foreign direct investment and its implications, see Kregel (1996).

13 On the so-called "financial traps" of low growth and high financial vulnerability see Frenkel (2003).

14 A more general view on Latin America can be seen in Damill and Frenkel (2011).

15 As pointed out by Serrano and Summa (2011) "in terms of its essential features the overall macroeconomic policy framework adopted in Brazil is basically the same since 1999".

16 As noted by Serrano and Summa (2011),

> fiscal contraction will certainly slow down the growth of aggregate demand, but precisely because it does not by itself tend to make the currency appreciate; it has, we must repeat, no direct and systematic impact on the trend of inflation.

References

Amico, F. (2011) "Import substitution, growth and productivity: Looking inward for the source of competitiveness outward", *ESHET Conference*, Unam, Meico City, 9–12 November.

Amico, F., Fiorito, A. and Hang, G. (2010) *Producto Potencial y Demanda en el Largo Plazo: Hechos Estilizados y Reflexiones sobre el caso Argentino Reciente*. Cefid-Ar.35 (available at: http://grupolujan-circus.blogspot.com/2011/04/producto-potencial-y-demanda-en-el.html).

Amsden, A. (2001) *The Rise of the Rest Challenges to the West from Late-industrializing Economies*. New York: Oxford University Press.

Ban, C. (2011) "Brazil's Liberal Neo-Developmentalism: New Paradigm or Edited Orthodoxy?" Forthcoming in *Review of International Political Economy*.

Banco Central del Brasil, www.bcb.gov.br/pt-br/paginas/default.aspx.

Barbosa, N. (2010) "Latin America: Counter-Cyclical Policy in Brazil: 2008–09", *Journal of Globalization and Development*, 1 (1), Art. 13.

BCRA, Banco Central de la República Argentina.

Carneiro, R. (2010) "Desenvolvimento brasileiro pós-crise financeira: oportunidades e riscos", Text prepared for 7th Economic Forum of FGV-SP (available at: www.iececon.net/foco.htm).

CEI, Centro de Economía Internacional, www.cei.gov.ar/.

CEPAL, Comisión Económica para América Latina y el Caribe, www.eclac.org/.

Damill, M. and Frenkel, R. (2009) "Las políticas macroeconómicas en la evolución reciente de la economía argentina", CEDES, Buenos Aires.

Damill, M. and Frenkel, R. (2011) "Macroeconomic policies and performances in Latin America 1990–2010", CEDES, Buenos Aires, December.

Dejuán, O. (2010) "The Accelerator: A Stable and Stabilizing Mechanism", Sraffa International Conference, Rome, 2 and 4 December.

Diamand, M. (1986) "Overcoming Argentina's Stop and Go Economic Cycles", in J. Hartlyn and S. Morley (eds) *Latin American Political Economy: Financial Crisis and Political Change*. Boulder, CO: Westview Press.

Dooley, M., Folkerts-Landau, D. and Garber, P. (2003) "An Essay on the Revived Bretton Woods System", *NBER Working Paper Series*, WP9971.

Ferreres, O. (2005) *2 siglos de economía argentina, 1810–2004*, Buenos Aires: El Ateneo.

Fiorito, A. (2011) "Desacople Financiero sin 'desacople' de la Ortodoxia", Congreso Internacional: Crisis de la Teoría Económica y Políticas Alternativas ante la Crisis Global, Mexico.

Fiorito, A. and Amico, F. (2010) "Exchange Rate Policy, Distributive Conflict and Structural Heterogeneity. The Argentinean and Brazilian cases", International Conference Sraffa's Production of Commodities by Means of Commodities 1960–2010, Rome (available at: http://host.uniroma3.it/eventi/sraffaconference2010/html/papers_submission_01.html).

Frenkel, R. (2003) "From the Boom in Capital Inflows to Financial Traps", Cedes, Buenos Aires.

Frenkel, R. and Rapetti, M. (2011) "Fragilidad externa o desindustrialización: ¿Cuál es la principal amenaza para América Latina en la próxima década?", Cepal, División de Desarrollo Económico, Santiago, November.

Haavelmo, T. (1945) "Multiplier Effects of a Balanced Budget", *Econometrica*, 13 (4): 311–318.

IBGE, Instituto Brasileiro de Geografia e Estatística, www.ibge.gov.br/home/.

IMF, International Monetary Fund, www.imf.org/external/index.htm.

INDEC, Instituto de Estadísticas y Censos de la Rep. Argentina, www.indec.gov.ar/.

Keynes, J.M. (1936) *The General Theory of Employment, Interest and Money*. London: Macmillan.

Kregel, J. (1996) "Riscos e implicações da globalização financeira para a autonomia de políticas nacionais", *Economia e Sociedade*, Campinas, 7: 29–49.

Lall, S. (2000) "The Technological Structure and Performance of Developing Country Manufactured Exports, 1985–98", *Oxford Development Studies*, 28: 337–369.

Lewis, A. (1980) "The Slowing Down of the Engine of Growth", *American Economic Review*, 70 (4): 555–564.

Marx, K. (1852) "The Eighteenth Brumaire of Louis Bonaparte", New York.

Medeiros, C. (2008) "Os dilemas da integração sul-americana", *Cadernos do Desenvolvimento*, 3 (5), Centro Internacional Celso Furtado de Políticas para o Desenvolvimento.

Medeiros, C. (2010) The Decoupling of Economic Growth in World Economy in the Last Decade and Development Strategies (available at: http://cemacro.fgv.br/sites/cemacro.

fgv.br/files/Carlos%20Medeiros%20-%20The%20Decoupling%20of%20Economic%20Growth%20in%20World%20Economy%20in%20the%20Last_0.pdf).

Medeiros, C. (2011) "The Political Economy of the Rise and Decline of Developmental States", *Panoeconomicus*, 58 (1): 43–56.

Pérez Caldentey, E. and Vernengo, M. (2008) "Back to the Future: Latin America's Current Development Strategy", Paper no. 07/2008, IDEAS Working Paper Series.

Pinkusfeld, C. (2010) "Setor Externo da Economia Brasileira: da crise de 2008 à valorização cambial do Banco Central 2009/2010", UFRJ, mimeo.

Prebisch, R. (1959) "El mercado común latinoamericano", *Comercio Exterior*, Tomo XI, no. 5, mayo.

Rodrigues, R. and Pinkusfeld, C. (2010) "Análise Recente das Finanças Públicas e Política Fiscal no Brasil", Third Encounter of the Brazilian Keynesian Association (III Encontro da Associação Keynesiana Brasileira).

Serrano, F. (2003) "From 'Static' Gold to the Floating Dollar", *Contributions to Political Economy*, 22 (1): 87–102.

Serrano, F. (2008) "A Economia Americana, o padrão dólar flexível e a expansão mundial nos anos 2000", in C. Medeiros, F. Serrano and J.L. Fiori (eds) *O Mito do Colapso Americano*. Rio de Janeiro; São Paulo: Record.

Serrano, F. (2010) "Juros, câmbio e o sistema de metas de inflação no Brasil", *Revista de Economia Política*, 30: 63–72.

Serrano, F. and Summa, R. (2011) "Macroeconomic Policy, Growth and Income Distribution in the Brazilian Economy in the 2000s", Center for Economic and Policy Research, Washington (available at: www.cepr.net/documents/publications/brazil-2011-06.pdf).

Summa, R. (2010) "Uma avaliação crítica das estimativas da curva de Phillips no Brasil", UFRRJ/ITR. Dinheiro, Finanças internacionais e Crescimento Sub-área: 5.1. Economia Monetária e Financeira Sessões ordinárias.

Vernengo, M. (2011) "The Brazilian Economy after Lula: What to Expect", *Focus*, CESifo Forum 1/2011.

Part III

The real side of the economy

The problem of effective demand and the failure of austerity policies

9 Net private savings in relation to the government's financial balance

Some basic principles of macroeconomics disregarded by the European Union's economic policy makers

Kazimierz Laski and Leon Podkaminer

The private sector's desire to run a financial surplus cannot be realised without the government's willingness to run a deficit

Looking at a national economy from both the income and expenditure sides, one gets the following identity:

$$YD + T + M = CP + IP + G + X \tag{9.1}$$

where *YD* denotes the disposable income of the private sector, *T* is the disposable income of the government (all taxes net of all monetary transfers to the private sector) and *M* is the income of the rest of the world (RoW) from imports of the national economy in question (the left-hand side of (9.1)). On the right-hand side of (9.1) we have private sector expenditures on consumption (*CP*) and that sector's gross investment (*IP*), government expenditure on goods and services (*G*) and RoW expenditure on the national economy's exports (*X*). By simple rearrangement, we get

$$[(YD - CP) - IP)] = (G - T) + (X - M)$$

This is equivalent to:

$$(SP - IP) = (G - T) + (X - M)$$

or, finally:

$$NPS = D + E \tag{9.2}$$

Private savings ($SP = YD - CP$) comprise household savings and profits retained by firms. In (9.2) we denote by $NPS = (SP - IP)$ the *net* private savings, by

$D=(G-T)$ the budget deficit and by $E=(X-M)$ the RoW deficit (or the current account of the country concerned).

Ex post, the formula (9.2) always holds because it is an identity. However, even as an identity it points up interesting relationships between sectors, especially when statistical data covering longer periods are available. For the world as a whole, we obviously have $NPS=D$. This is an identity which links the financial balances of the private and government sectors aggregated globally. Budget surpluses ($D<0$) and even balanced budgets ($D=0$) do occur, albeit rarely; thus, for monetary economies worldwide, budget deficits ($D>0$) seem to be the rule rather than an exception. This applies not only to times of war and disasters, but – at least for the industrial countries disposing of longer statistical records – also to periods of peace as well.[1]

The world public debt/GDP ratio increased over the last 120 years from about 40 per cent to about 70 per cent and for advanced countries from about 50 per cent to about 100 per cent (IMF 2011). Although there were also periods of decline of this ratio its increasing trend implies not only the increase of the debt but also its increase ahead of GDP growth. It implies also – taking into account the fact that the rate of interest (for public debt) was for long periods below the growth rate of GDP – that the budget deficit in most countries must have been positive.

Given that for the world as a whole $E=0$ by definition and $D>0$ (as shown by long-term statistical records) we have, according to (9.2), $NPS>0$. The private sector of the entire global economy displays a sustained tendency to save more than it invests. The same observation can be made with respect to the European Union (EU). The EU is a group of countries with negligible E. Almost all EU countries have consistently run budget deficits (very much in violation of the Maastricht Treaty). Thus, for the EU as a whole we also have $D>0$. In actual fact, the consolidated budget deficits for the entire euro area have been positive since at least 1995.[2] It follows that the NPS for the EU as a whole is also positive. Last but not least, we observe that for $NPS=0$ – which can be understood as a minimum requirement to the effect that the private sector should not become indebted in the long run – all countries with a passive current account ($E<0$) must record budget deficits $D>0$. Of course, all these observations are to be understood as referring to a trend and average values for longer periods – and not as a rule for each country and every year. We also observe that those countries, which happen to report budget surpluses ($D<0$), very often (although not always) record high E. This must be the case if $E>NPS>0$ (e.g. the case of Norway since becoming a major oil exporting country).

Within the private sector we have two subsectors: private households and firms. It is normally assumed that for most of the time, firms invest more than they save (in the form of profits retained), hence incurring a flow of debt, the volume of which increases over time. This debt makes it possible to increase the firms' productive capacities beyond the levels funded from their own savings (i.e. profits retained). One also assumes that private households are net savers, whose financial assets increase over time. The assumption $NPS>0$ is thus normally interpreted as a situation in which private households save in excess of the new debts which firms are ready to incur.

The fact that as a rule (or mostly so) NPS is positive can be interpreted as reflecting the *desired* level of private savings (SP) being higher than actual private investments. Positive $(D+E)$ helps to narrow the gap between private savings and investments. Alternatively it can be said that the positive NPS must be reflected in the sum $(D+E)$ being positive as well. However, NPS equal to $(D+E)$ is an identity; as such, it does not say anything about the direction of causality. In any event, positive NPS must be *counterbalanced* by the sum of the government and foreign deficits. The private sector's desire to run a financial surplus ($NPS>0$) cannot be realised without the willingness of government and foreign sectors (taken together) to run a deficit. Similarly, the government and foreign sectors (once again taken together) cannot run financial surpluses ($D+E<0$) without the private sector's net dis-saving (NPS falling below 0) without private sector savings falling short of private sector investment.

At present, the understandable trend throughout much of the industrialised world is for the private sector to increase net savings ($\Delta NPS>0$). 'Deleveraging' should strengthen private sector balance sheets. Both households and firms (including in the financial intermediation sector) feel they have incurred excessive debt. The deleveraging trend, however, actually clashes with the present overall orientation of fiscal policies. Those policies prescribe fiscal austerity – reducing budgetary deficits. Should austerity prevail, one would have $\Delta D<0$. Should the private sector succeed to deleverage, $\Delta NPS>0$ would be the outcome. Clearly, the identity $\Delta NPS=\Delta D$ would necessarily be violated. However, by their very nature, the identities hold under any circumstances. In reality, the identity $\Delta NPS=\Delta D$ *will* hold no matter what policy is pursued and irrespective of private sector preferences. What kind of outcome will emerge out of the two conflicting tendencies or which of them will ultimately prevail is very much an open issue. In any case, that conflict is likely to incur some 'collateral damage' in the form of weaker growth and higher unemployment.

Why do net private savings tend to be positive?

One consequence of (9.2) is that in a 'textbook economy' (consisting solely of a private sector – devoid of government and the 'outside world'), NPS would have to be zero. Indeed, in such an economy $D=E=0$, hence $NPS=0$. In such a 'textbook economy', investment is equal to savings (both are private) so that $SP-IP=0$. It must be understood that in such an economy, the private sector as a whole would be unable to accumulate *net* (outside) financial wealth – simply because there would be no party beyond the private sector to supply the financial debt that would constitute the private sector's financial wealth. Surely, economies that rule out accumulation of private sector net financial wealth are conceivable. In all probability, the early 'natural' economies would have fitted that description. However, it is hard to imagine (unless one adheres to 'mainstream ideas') a modern monetary economy without private sector accumulation of net (outside) financial wealth. In a modern economy the private sector accumulates net financial wealth – if not in the form of government bonds, then at least in the form of hoards of cash/fiat money issued by the government's own central bank. To gain access to the money hoarded, the private sector would have willingly supplied the government with goods and services that it had produced on its own. (Thereby the government would have had to acquire such goods and services, without paying for them fully with the proceeds of proper taxation levied on the private sector.) Of course, the private sector's net (outside) wealth would have to be matched by the debt issued by the government[3] (plus, eventually, the debt issued by foreign parties that the private sector had acquired).

Why does the private sector tend to accumulate outside debt (in particular, that of its own government)? The simplest answer is that the private sector greatly values such debt. For the private sector, public debt *must be* wealth – no matter what the proponents of '*Ricardian equivalence*' claim. Otherwise, the private sector would not waste 'good money' on acquiring it. (Or, the private sector would not trade goods and services it produces for the government's 'paper'.)

What kinds of benefits follow from the ownership of public debt? The opportunity to earn interest income on that debt may certainly be one motive. That motive alone, however, does not seem to be decisive. In many countries the rate of interest on public debt is purely symbolic. Japan with its soaring public debt has no difficulty in floating its massively expanding public deficits at interest rates of less than 1 per cent. Interest rates on Switzerland's public debt gravitate towards zero. Essentially, public debt is in such great demand in the private sector for liquidity reasons (as, of course, stressed by Keynes) or as the trusted store of value or as the necessary capital reserves that facilitate firms' access to capital markets (and thus private investment, as in Kalecki). In Laski and Podkaminer (2012) our hypothesis was that private sector demand for public debt is even likely to strengthen secularly. This will be accompanied by private sector savings in general rising more rapidly than private investment. Changes observed in the structure of private sector income (with rising inequality in disposable incomes and the emergence of a super-rich class whose members derive their incomes from trade/speculation in various assets and financial instruments rather than from capital investment in productive capacities) is one of the factors contributing to the yawning gap between private sector savings and investment.[4] The emergence of the super-rich is, of course, intimately linked to the ever-progressing financialisation/privatisation of services traditionally provided by the public sector (*inter alia*, health, education and old-age pensions). Financialisation/privatisation also induces a higher propensity to save for precautionary reasons – without the requisite rise in the propensity to invest productively. The flip side of financialisation of the services formerly provided by the public sector is the rise in private funds, such as the pension funds.[5] These funds may tend to acquire – especially in turbulent times – growing chunks of public debt. Ageing in a time of ever-increasing financialisation of the pension system may add strength to the private propensity to save. Moreover, technological change may be another factor. The productivity of fixed assets is likely to improve secularly owing to advances in technology – the investment of smaller amounts of real assets is capable of producing more output. This trend may be temporarily interrupted by major inventions (such as 'electricity' which called for high initial investment in the construction of power stations, transmission grids, etc.). In the long term, as the supply of goods produced by the private business sector can perhaps be expected to outstrip demand for the same, the desire to save could systematically outstrip the desire to invest.

Destructive fiscal consolidation

The EU policy stance has always stressed the need to limit public-sector deficits. Actually, the Stability and Growth Pact 'lays down the obligation for Member States to adhere to the medium-term objective for their budgetary positions of close to balance or in surplus'.[6] The Fiscal Compact agreed upon by majority of EU leaders is designed to strengthen 'fiscal discipline' across the euro area (and beyond). Moreover, the Fiscal Compact imposes the obligation to *reduce* public debt/GDP ratios. In so doing, it actually imposes, on most euro-area countries, the obligation to run – on a long-term basis – the budgetary surpluses. Taxation of the private sector (net of transfers to the same) should be persistently higher than income earned by the private sector on sales on goods and services to the government. The private sector in most euro-area countries will 'bleed' for many years to come – for the sake of 'healthy public finances'. The latter are deemed indispensable to the long-term robustness of the private sector itself. (An analogy to the medieval 'medical science' and the practice of bloodletting inevitably comes to mind.) The economic and social costs of this austerity hysteria will no doubt be immense.

Supposing D is negative (as required by the Fiscal Compact), NPS would have to be negative as well. Or (remembering that $NPS=SP-IP$) private sector savings would have to be consistently lower than private sector investment. The private sector's financial wealth would then have to drop: for example, via the government redeeming its debt to the private sector (with the proceeds then serving to finance private investment). It is at least debatable whether the private sector would be eager to engage in investment under such conditions. The falling financial wealth and contracting domestic consumer demand might more likely induce falling investment and rising savings, thereby initiating spiralling recessionary adjustment.

The question worth asking is whether it will be possible at all – and under what conditions – to run a euro-area-wide policy, which in fact requires that the net private savings of the member states are persistently negative. Of course, the current account E for some euro-area countries may, on occasion, be positive and high enough to render $D+E$ still positive. A small country (such as Luxembourg) can combine large budgetary surpluses with current account surpluses over extended periods of time – without this having a perceptible impact on its trading partners. A large country (such as Germany) is unlikely to persist indefinitely with high budgetary surpluses combined with massive current account surpluses, the reason being that German current account surpluses are the current account deficits of its partners, such as Italy. The latter country's NPS would then have to be unambiguously negative – on account of both E and D

being negative. Thus, any attempts to run budgetary surpluses in one (or more) euro-area countries can only be successful (via expansion of current account surpluses), if those attempts fail in some other euro-area countries.[7] Incidentally, under the present circumstances it is an illusion to expect that the EU as a whole could become a major net exporter to the rest of the world. Germany and some other EU member countries can continue – at least for some time – to run mercantilist (and deflationary) policies which negatively affect other countries (also outside the EU). But there are limits to the beggar-thy-neighbour policies. Such policies will sooner or later provoke retaliatory reactions. The rest of the world (and the USA in particular) is unlikely to remain passive should the whole EU start recording gigantic trade surpluses (for example matching China's). Otherwise, the successful beggar-thy-neighbour policy is self-defeating because it implies accumulation of foreign debt of the persistent trade deficit countries. Once that debt is acknowledged to be unsustainable, growth in the persistent trade surplus countries would have to flag as well. Moreover, the creditor countries would have to write off the chunks of their 'bad assets'.

The idea of fiscal consolidation as a way out of the present difficulties is related to the diagnosis of the present crisis. In the world as a whole – and especially in advanced countries – over the last decades the debt/GDP ratio increased but private debt increased faster than the government debt. The crisis started when the private household sector could not serve any more its debt, which reached about 100 per cent of GDP in the US (financial institution debt another 125 per cent, and total debt ratio 500 per cent of GDP). The necessary fiscal interventions of the governments in the US and Europe caused significant growth of public debt in relation to GDP; thus the increase of government debt was the consequence of the crisis not its cause. Hence to interpret the present crisis as a sovereign debt problem is totally misleading. It is rather a sudden break of a speculative financial bubble which dark side is increasing debt and inequality.[8] Also the expression "balance sheet recession" introduced by Koo (2003) pinpoints to the notion that the real cause of the present crisis is over indebtedness of private households and firms requiring the repair of their balance through lower expenditure and higher savings, the real factors limiting their demand.

However, the diagnosis prevailing in Europe politics is quite different. The reason of the crisis is too high public debt and excessive government spending, hence the necessary solution is to increase the fiscal discipline. Wolfgang Schaüble, Finance Minister of Germany put its this way: 'The main reason for the lack of demand is the lack of confidence; the main reason for the lack of confidence is the deficits and public debts which are seen as unsustainable' and in another place: 'We won't come to grips with economies deleveraging by having governments and central banks throwing – literally – even more money at the problem. You simply cannot fight fire with fire'.[9]

First, it happens that fire may be – and is being – used very effectively in fighting fire when e.g. we burn parts of the forest in order to prevent its further uncontrollable spread. Second, much more important: what is the intellectual basis of the 'doctrine of expansionary austerity' or what Krugman (2012) calls the 'confidence fairy tale' (the idea that the confidence fairy would come in and reward policy makers for their fiscal virtue)? Confidence of business depends first of all upon profits. Let us therefore have a look at the consequences of fiscal consolidation upon profits.

From (9.2) taking into account that $SP=PR+SH$ we get

$$PR=IP+D+E-SH$$

and by adding to both sides distributed profits *PD* equal per definition to the sum consumption out of distributed profit *CPD* plus savings out of distributed profits *SPD* we get

$$PR+PD=IP+CPD+SPD+D+E-SH$$

$$P=IP+CPD+D+E-SH' \qquad (9.3)$$

P (gross) profits equal to $PR+PD$ and SH' savings of private households minus SPD

Assuming $D=E=0$ i.e. a closed economy without a government we get

$$P=IP+CPD-SH' \qquad (9.3')$$

a formula corresponding to the famous Kalecki's profit equation: profits are determined by private investment and capitalist consumption (here: consumption out of distributed profits without the *time lag*) expenditures minus workers' savings (here: private households' savings outside savings out of profits). Equation (9.3) says that profits of firms are equal to private investments *plus* budget deficit *plus* trade surplus *minus* household savings. It is evident that policy actions successfully reducing budget deficits would *ceteris paribus* be matched by *reduced* profits by firms. But reduced profits by firms are highly unlikely to improve the sense of confidence necessary to induce private firms to invest more. As a rule, strong profits are a precondition of the investment take off. In other words, the negative *D*, as required by the Fiscal Pact, must be expected to be recessionary – the more so if at the same time the household sector attempts to accumulate more savings and the business sector does not invest enough.

Of course, recessionary adjustments could, ultimately, steer NPS into negative territory (consistent with the budgetary surpluses). That outcome, however, would feature low (falling) income and high (rising) unemployment levels. At a very low level of private savings, the requisite negative net private savings could eventually be achieved. However, even if economically imaginable, such an outcome would be unacceptable – both politically and socially. We doubt whether this is the outcome that the EU leaders actually desire. On the other hand, we deeply deplore the fact that the economic advisers to the EU heads of state apparently fail to grasp the actual consequences of the policies that they so doggedly advocate.

Notes

1 See e.g. Laski (2008).
2 Earlier years are not covered by the accessible Eurostat statistics. Most probably the budget deficits were even higher prior to 1995. In 1995 the deficit/GDP ratio for the euro area was 7.2 per cent (falling to 4.3 per cent in 1996). The lowest deficit/GDP ratio (0.1 per cent) was recorded in 2000. The average deficit/GDP ratio for the years 1995–2011 is 3.1 per cent.
3 See Wray (1998), Ch. 4.
4 The study of impacts of rising inequality on macroeconomic performance (GDP growth, current account developments, financial stability) has come to the fore of research interests recently (e.g. Rajan, 2010; Berg and Ostry, 2011). More research is on links between rising inequality, rising net private savings and the overall growth slowdown is still needed. In particular, it remains to be examined whether the relatively fast and balanced ($NPS \approx 0$, $D \approx 0$, $E \approx 0$) growth of major industrial countries in the 1950s and 1960s was not associated with rather low/falling levels of inequality then prevailing.
5 See Toporowski (2012).
6 See Council Regulation No. 1055/2005 amending the Growth and Stability Pact. *Official Journal of the European Union*, 7 July 2005, L. 174/1. The same requirement features in the recent Fiscal Compact (Article 3, point 1(a)).
7 We abstract here from another difficulty. A combination of current account surpluses with budgetary surpluses implies a shift in a country's private sector net financial wealth. To an increasing degree that wealth would consist of foreign (private or public) debt. At the same time the share/size of debt issued by that country's government would decline. It is doubtful whether the German private sector would actually be eager to substitute *bunds* for private/public Greek (or even Italian) debt.
8 See Papadimitriou and Wray (2012).
9 Giles (2011).

References

Berg, A.G. and Ostry, J.D. (2011) 'Inequality and unsustainable growth: Two sides of the same coin?' *IMF Staff Discussion Note*, SDN 11/88.

Giles, C. (2011) 'Dark humour and hard talk at IMF meetings', *Financial Times*, 25 September.

Koo, R.C. (2003) *Balance Sheet Recession: Japan's Struggle with Uncharted Economics and its Global Implications*, J. Wiley & Sons (Asia).

Krugman P. (2012) 'Death of a Fairy Tale', *New York Times*, 27 April.

IMF (2011) *Fiscal Affairs Department, Historical Public Debt Database*.

Laski, K. (2008) 'Market economy needs to run budgetary deficits', *Vienna Institute Monthly Report*, 6.

Laski, K. and Podkaminer, L. (2012) 'The basic paradigms of the EU economic policy-making need to be changed', *Cambridge Journal of Economics*, 36, 1.

Papadimtriou, D.B. and Wray, L.R. (2012) 'Fiddling in Euroland as the global meltdown nears', *Public Policy Brief* No. 122, Levy Economic Institute of Bard College.

Rajan, R.G. (2010) *Fault Lines*, Princeton University Press.

Toporowski, J. (2012) *The End of Finance: Capital Market Inflation, Financial Derivatives and Pension Fund Capitalism*, Routledge.

Wray, L.R. (1998) *Understanding Modern Money*, Edward Elgar.

10 Business investment, growth and crisis

Ana-Rosa González, Philip Arestis and Óscar Dejuán

Introduction: a broad and flexible acceleration theory of investment

The current economic crisis was accompanied by a collapse in business investment.[1] The recovery won't happen until a massive wave of investment occurs. There is nothing new in these assertions. Economic downturns and upturns coincide with the deceleration and acceleration of business investment. But, is investment the cause or the consequence of the cycle and the crisis? This is the first question addressed in this chapter. The second consists in identifying the whole set of determinants of investment. This knowledge will help us to find the best economic policies to overcome the first great recession of the twenty-first century. Our chapter is an empirical study based on post-Keynesian theories that develops the seminal ideas sowed by Kalecki and Keynes after the Great Depression of 1929 (Kalecki, 1971; Keynes, 1936).

From this theoretical standpoint the answer to the first question is "both". On the one hand, business investment depends on the expected growth of demand that may be influenced (perhaps unduly) by the current growth of output. On the other hand, since it is an important part of aggregate demand, a fall in business investment is bound to depress the current level of output and its rate of growth.

Keynes, in chapter 12 of the *General Theory*, makes clear that the main determinant of investment is the state of long-term expectations encapsulated in the *animal spirits* of the entrepreneurs. Expectations are the true independent variable of the Keynesian system (Eatwell, 1983). They refer, mainly, to the future demand of goods and services at normal prices (the difference between current and normal prices accounts for extra profits). Prediction errors result in over-using or under-using existing capacity which will speed up or slow down the investment determined by the pure accelerator mechanism that depends on the expected rate of growth and the optimal capital/output ratio.

Harrod (1939) introduced the old principle of acceleration in a Keynesian growth model. Later on, it was made flexible enough to account for capacity utilization, financial constraints and so on (Chenery, 1952). The current degree of capacity utilization plays a prominent role in Kaleckian accumulation models (Lavoie *et al.*, 2004). In our model what matters are the deviations of the current degree from the "normal" level that entrepreneurs have in mind in their desire to maximize profits in the long run (Kurz, 1986). We shall identify normal capacity with the average of boom periods that is around 0.8. This means that entrepreneurs allow for 20 per cent of spare capacity to match the peaks in demand.

Distributive variables and financial conditions are supposed to influence the level of investment and, most of all, the temporal implementation of the decisions based on the pure accelerator mechanism. Kaleckian and Marxian economists emphasize the importance of the rate of profits that can be proxied by the profit share (profits/income). A higher profit share, apart from spurring on investors, provides them with the internal funds necessary to purchase capital goods (Kalecki, 1971, 1968;[2] Bhaduri and Marglin, 1990; Alexiou, 2010).

The rate of interest is another distributive variable that indicates the cost of raising external funds. Other things equal, a fall in the real interest rate is supposed to speed up investment decisions. This justifies Keynes's suggestion, in the last chapter of the *General Theory*, to keep the interest rate as low and stable as possible. The new macroeconomic consensus distrusts such a policy because of the risk of inflation. Arestis and Sawyer (2004) show the weakness of the theory behind this conclusion and prove that in a globalized economy inflationary pressures are checked by international competition. The prices of assets (not considered in the CPI) are the only exception. Cheap credit feeds speculative movements in the stock exchange and in the real estate market that, eventually, will damage business investment. Notice that this runs against Tobin's q theory of investment (1969). In our opinion a rise in the price of shares makes external finance cheaper, but does not justify more investment. On the contrary, if people expect that the upward rally in the stock market will continue, they will sacrifice productive investment in favour of speculative purchases of assets.

Credit is part of the financial conditions. As a matter of fact, when credit is introduced in an econometric model it becomes the only explicative variable of investment. Arguably, this confirms the post-Keynesian hypothesis of the endogenity of credit-money according to which credit is more the consequence than the cause of investment booms. Remember, however, that credit implies debt and an excess of bad quality debt may cause a downturn in investment and output. Kalecki (1937) introduced the *principle of increasing risk* to explain the upwards movement in interest rates due to excessive debt and leverage ratios. Minsky (1975, 1977) introduced the *financial fragility hypothesis* that explains endogenously the deterioration of debt: booms sow the seeds of depressions because they fill the market with bad quality debt.

Entrepreneurs form their expectations of demand, prices, profits in an atmosphere of uncertainty (Demir, 2009). Post-Keynesian economists insist that we are dealing with *radical uncertainty* which rules out the probabilistic methods to deal with risk (Davidson, 1991). When uncertainty exacerbates, financial agents search for safe harbours for the savings they manage. They will invest them in real assets (like gold) and financial assets (like shares and bonds nominated in a currency free from depreciation). These harbours compete with productive investment that cannot emulate the yields of bullish asset markets (Stockhammer and Grafl, 2010). A massive deviation of savings towards them will shrink productive investment and cause a problem of effective demand that may trigger a crisis. In our chapter strong increases in the price of gold, stock exchange indexes and the exchange rate will be taken as symptoms of uncertainty that discourage business investment.

To be as rational as possible in a world of radical uncertainty, the society organizes proper "institutions" and economic agents try to rely on *conventions* (Littleboy, 1990; Runde, 1990; Crotty, 1992; Baddeley, 1999). An independent central bank, for instance, has been created to fix the inflation target and the official interest rate which is supposed to shape the whole structure of market interest rates. What matters for investment decisions is not the precise level of the interest rate, profit rate and so on, but the deviations from their conventional levels. The conventional level of these variables usually lacks a natural basis, given by technology, preferences and other factors of slow (and usually unidirectional) evolution (Dejuán, 2007). The conventional interest rate, to continue with the same example, is the one that has ruled in the recent past and people expect for the foreseeable future. A change in the official rate set by monetary authorities, if it lasts long enough, is bound to change the conventional value of the interest rate. This result demonstrates the importance of *hysteresis* in the economy. Most of the explanatory variables of investment will be treated in the same mood, i.e. deviations from the conventional level which may change from time to time.

In this chapter we try to find out the determinants of private accumulation in 12 advanced economies from 1970 to 2008. (The availability of OECD data on fixed capital has determined the territorial and temporal size of the sample.) The second section focuses on a single economy (the USA) and a shorter period of time (the years prior to the crisis, starting in 1991). It's a strategy to visualize the main relationships behind the econometric panel of data and connect them with the current crisis. Next we explain the econometric model for the whole series of data and evaluate the results. After trying several methods we have opted for the PCSE technique (Panel Corrected Standard Errors) (Beck and Katz, 1995). The use of panel data reflects the assumption that, in a globalized economy, countries share a common structure (Baltagi, 1995). Finally, we summarize the conclusions of the econometric study on accumulation and drag the policy strategies that might help to pave the way for the recovery of business investment.

A case study: the rise and fall in investment in the US during the years prior to the crisis

The last decade of the twentieth century is one of the golden epochs of American economic history. The main driving force of the economy was the ICT industry (information and communication technologies) (Gualerzi, 2010). From 1992 till 2000 the American economy increased at an annual average rate of 3.8 per cent. It created a bubble in the stock exchange which burst in 2000 causing a serious but short economic downturn. It has been called the *dot-com crisis*. The Fed reacted by cutting down the official interest rate to historical minimum (1 per cent). Residential investment became the new engine of the economy for the next five years, and through the multiplier and accelerator mechanisms, brought about a boom. From 2002 to 2007 the rate of growth approached 3 per cent which continues to be high for such an advanced economy as the US. The excessive growth of debt and the hidden risk in the financial products derived from sub-prime mortgage loans caused liquidity problems in several financial institutions. They led to the 2007–08 *debt crisis* that put the financial system and, indeed, the whole international economy, on the verge of collapse.

How did investment behave during all these years? In Figure 10.1 we can appreciate the typical pattern where productive investment replicates the evolution of output but with more pronounced turns. The share of business investment in output, which in 1991 amounted to 13.81 per cent, was above 16 per cent from 1997 to 2007. In 2009 it fell to 12.51 per cent.

Figure 10.2 shows the path of fixed capital, i.e. the accumulation rate. Let us define it as: **a** = investment/value of the capital stock. It is systematically higher than the growth of output (**g**) which implies a capital-intensive technical change and increasing technical obsolescence of capital goods. Abstracting from the level, we appreciate a common trend in both series. The third series (**u**) in the figure corresponds to the degree of capacity utilization of installed capacity. The average for the whole period is 0.8, considered the normal or optimal degree of capacity utilization. The positive deviations from normal capacity in the mid 1990s might have contributed to speed up productive investment.

The first lesson to be drawn from Figure 10.3 is that the interest rate is a monetary variable, in the sense that it may be controlled by monetary policy. Under the direction of Paul Volker, the Fed implemented a tight monetary policy

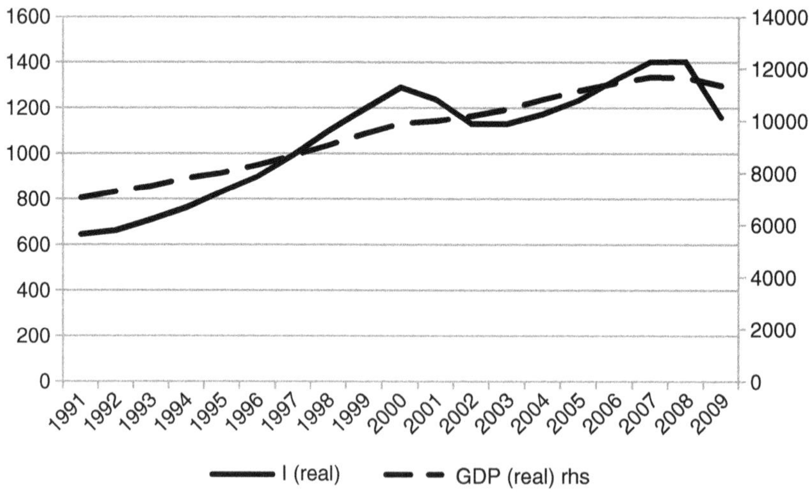

Figure 10.1 Investment and output in USA (sources: AMECO and OECD).

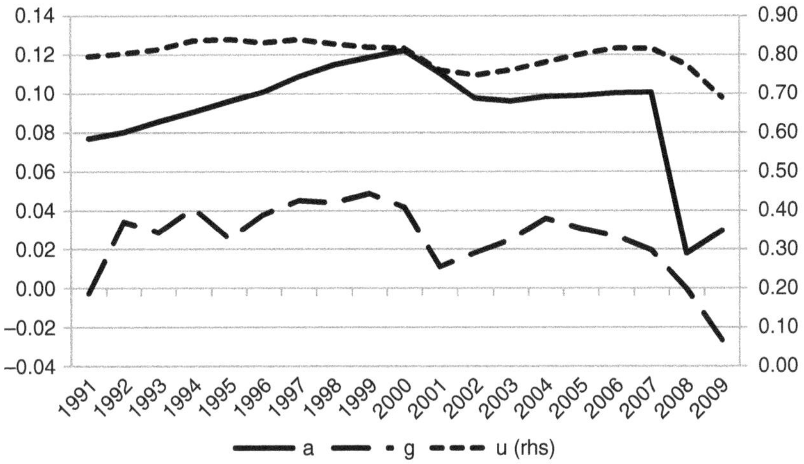

Figure 10.2 Accumulation, growth of output and degree of capacity utilization in USA (sources: AMECO and OECD).

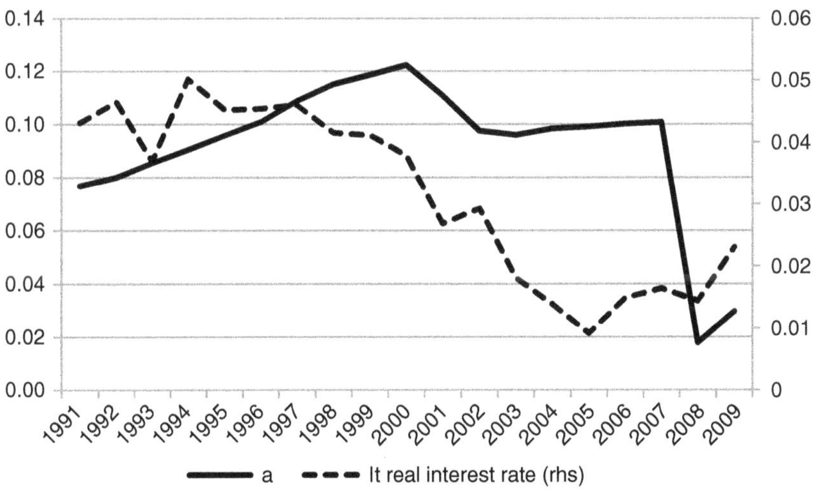

Figure 10.3 Accumulation and interest rate in USA (sources: AMECO and OECD).

resulting in high nominal and real interest rates, both for short-term and long-term loans. After the stock-market crisis in 2000, Alan Greenspan, the new chairman of the Fed, cut down the official rate to a historical minimum (1 per cent) and successfully reshaped the rate of long-term private loans. After three years of medium rates (2005–07), the official rate was cut down again to the minimum expression (almost zero). This time, the rates of long-term private loans did not fall because, in such an uncertain situation, lenders demanded risk premiums. The second lesson of Figure 10.3 is that interest rates movements had little impact on accumulation. In the 1990s investment was growing fast despite high real rates of interest. The historically minimum rates after 2003 might have helped the recovery after the dot-com bubble but the same policy failed to stimulate investment during the subsequent debt crisis.

Figure 10.4 suggests a positive correlation between the rate of accumulation and profit shares, under the leadership of the second variable. Overutilization of capacity allows the profit share to rise in boom periods, even when technology and the normal profit rate remain constant. But tensions in the labour market result in an increase in wages that check profits and herald a deceleration in investment.

The path of the stock exchange index replicates the economic path (both output and capital). But the bubbles created in the second half of these two decades might have deterred productive investment (Figure 10.5).

Figure 10.6 suggests that since the dot-com bubble financial agents perceived an increasing risk in the economy and started investing in gold to harbour wealth. The increase in the price of gold speeds up after the debt crisis without any apparent limit.

An econometric analysis of accumulation in the OECD countries

In this section we will estimate a flexible accelerator model that considers the influence on investment of real and financial variables, in an atmosphere of uncertainty. Our equation is modelled using annual data for 12 OECD countries from 1970 till 2008. The following countries are included in our panel: Australia,

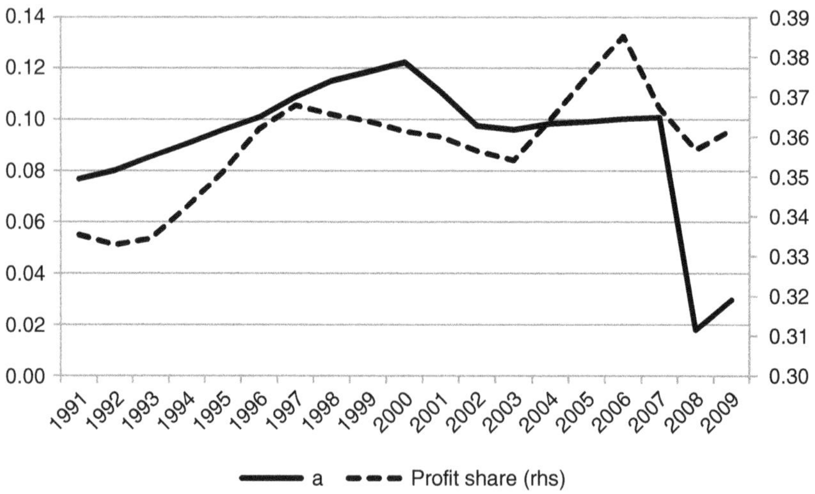

Figure 10.4 Accumulation and profit share in USA (sources: AMECO and OECD).

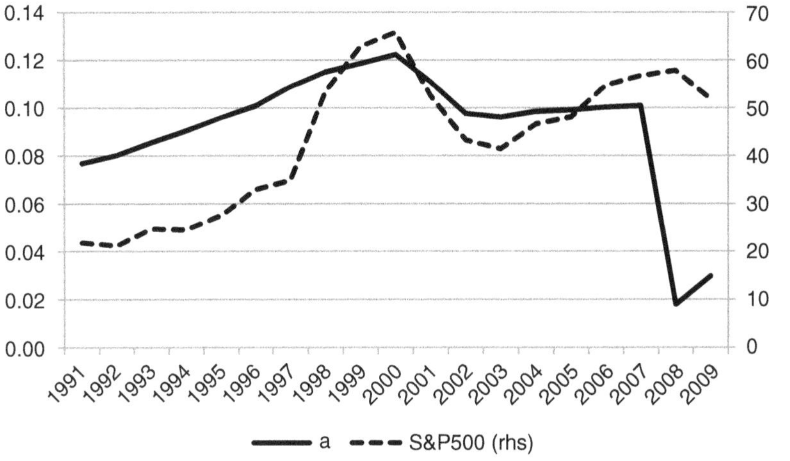

Figure 10.5 Accumulation and stock-exchange prices in USA (sources: AMECO, OECD and Standard & Poor's).

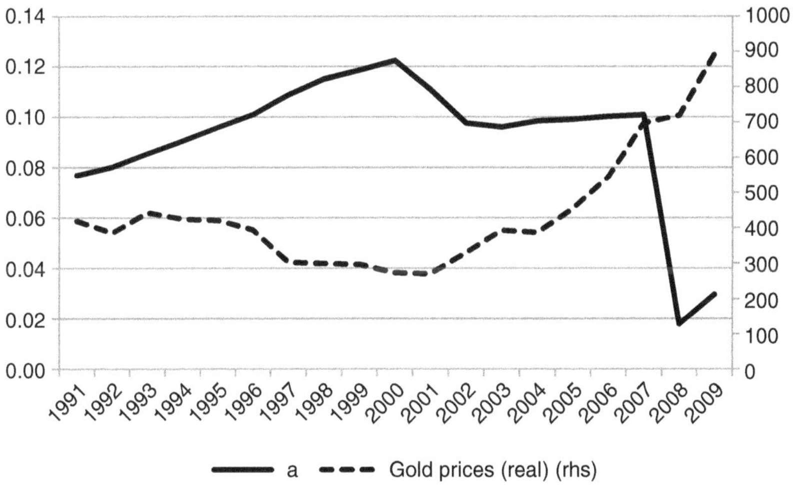

Figure 10.6 Accumulation and gold prices in USA (sources: AMECO, Kitco Metals Inc. and OECD).

Belgium, Canada, Denmark, France, Germany, Italy, Norway, New Zealand, Spain, the United Kingdom and the United States.

The independent variables included in our estimations are the rate of growth of output ($g_{i,t}$), the deviation between the effective capacity utilization and its normal level ($du_{i,t}$), the deviation of the profit share from its conventional value ($d\pi_{i,t}$), the deviation of the real long-term interest rate from its conventional rate

($di_{i,t}$), the deviation of the real current price of gold from its conventional level ($dp_{i,t}$), the deviation between a stock market index from its conventional level ($dX_{i,t}$) and the deviation of the real exchange rate from its conventional rate ($de_{i,t}$). In Appendix I we offer a precise definition of the variables and explain how the conventional levels have been figured out. The sources of data are also indicated there.

The equation to be estimated is (10.1). It shows the signs that we expect according to our post-Keynesian theory.

$$a_{i,t} = \alpha_0 + \alpha_1 g_{i,it-1} + \alpha_2 du_{i,t-1} + \alpha_3 d\pi_{i,t-1} - \alpha_4 di_{i,t-1} - \alpha_5 dp_{i,t-1} - \alpha_6 dX_{i,t-1} - \alpha_7 de_{i,t-1} + \varepsilon_{i,t} \quad (10.1)$$

α_i are the coefficients which we are going to estimate, and ε is a random error term. The dependent variable of this specification is the rate of capital accumulation in the private sector. The independent term (α_0) reflects other determinants of investment that have not been explicitly accounted for because of the difficulty in finding relevant data or because of their correlation with other variables: degree of indebtedness, liquidity preference. Add technical progress that leads to the renewal of existing capacity.

After trying different alternatives (see Appendix II) we conclude that the PCSE method is the best one to estimate the suggested model. The *Panel Corrected Standard Errors* (Beck and Katz, 1995) corrects problems of autocorrelation, heteroscedasticity and cross-sectional dependence.[3] PCSE models include country dummy variables, which collect the existence of country-specific features in the accumulation of private productive capital among different economies. These particular features collect information about diverse circumstances, for instance, the degree of indebtedness, liquidity problems, the *state of confidence* of the entrepreneur, *animal spirits*. Institutional and social differences might also be taken into account.

The regressors of equation (10.1) are lagged one period. Although, lag structures are a polemical topic in investment literature, the majority of empirical analyses find the presence of several delays in the investment process (Evans, 1969; Baddeley, 2003). They conclude that investment is related to its determinants lagged by one or more periods.

The R-square of the regression by PCSE is almost 88 per cent, way above the result obtained by alternative theories and methods (Alexiou, 2010; Bhandari and Upadhyaya, 2010). The Wald test indicates that all the explanatory variables are jointly significant (Wald Chi-square=9945.76; p=0). The specification shows us that the most relevant explanatory element is the rate of growth of GDP in the last year (0.1271). According to the theory, the deviation in the rate of capacity utilization and the deviation of the profit share have a positive impact (0.0240 and 0.0183). As usual, changes in real interest rates have a negative but almost negligible impact (–0.0007). The three variables related to uncertainty exert a negative influence on accumulation: –0.0018 for exchange rates, –0.0040

Table 10.1 Estimated coefficients for macro accumulation function (1970–2008)

Method	*Model I*
Dependent constant	*PCSE*
	a
g	0.1271*
du	0.0240*
dπ	0.0183**
di	–0.0007**
de	–0.0018**
dX	–0.0040***
dp	–0.0041*
GE	0.1064*
IT	0.0215*
AU	0.0310*
BE	0.0217*
DE	0.0791*
CA	0.0218*
NZ	0.0284*
SP	0.0266*
US	0.0257*
NO	0.0233*
UK	0.0879*
R-square	0.8788
n	440
F (or Wald Chi-square)	9945.76
p (F or W)	0.0000
ρ	0.5581
Number of covariances	78

Note
*, ** and *** indicate the statistical significance and the rejection of the null at the 1, 5 and 10% levels, respectively.

for the stock market index and –0.0041 for the gold price. All the country coefficients are significant and reflect a positive effect over accumulation. It is more intense in Germany, Denmark and the United Kingdom than in the other economies. It is possible to consider these values as an indicator that there are some economies which have an institutional framework which reinforces private productive investment. Further tests were conducted as shown in Appendix II. Specifically, we applied the augmented Dickey–Fuller (ADF) tests (Table 10.A.1), the GLS-based Dickey–Fuller (DF-GLS) tests (Table 10.A.2) and the Kwiatkowski–Phillips–Schmidt–Shin (KPSS) tests (Table 10.A.3) to each time series. We also tested the presence of unit roots in the panel data (Table 10.A.4), so we used the Im–Pesaran–Shin (IPS) tests, which assume an individual unit root process, the Breitung (B) test, the Levin, Lin and Chu (LLC) tests, which assume a common unit process, the Fisher-augmented

Dickey–Fuller (Fisher–ADF) test and the Fisher–Phillips–Perron (Fisher–PP) test. The latter were applied to the observations of each variable as a set by considering an individual unit root process. All these results clearly show that the relevant variables are stationary.[4]

Conclusions and policy implications

This chapter utilizes a flexible version of the accelerator model including deviations from the normal or conventional levels of variables such as capacity utilization, profit sharers and interest rates. Uncertainty has been proxied by the deviations from their conventional levels of three variables: the exchange rate, the Stock Exchange index and the price of gold. We have tested our macro accumulation function with panel data for the period 1970–2008. Due to the fact that the fixed effects are remarkable in the accumulation process, we have used a methodology based on the PCSE model which accounts for country specific variables. This method allows us to correct problems of autocorrelation, heteroscedasticity and cross-sectional dependence.

Our analysis shows that the key determinant of the accumulation rate is the expected rate of growth in demand, which has been approximated through the rate of growth of GDP in the last year. We find a positive influence of deviations of the rate of capacity utilization in $t-1$ and deviations of the profit share. Deviations built using the real interest rate, real exchange rate, gold prices and stock exchange indices affect accumulation in a negative way. The effect of gold prices depresses accumulation more than fluctuations of the other variables. Note that the negative impact of the stock exchange market is higher than changes in interest rates or exchange rates. The model also includes several country dummy variables which collect the presence of favourable conditions to invest in each country.

The empirical results suggest the convenience of stimulating demand growth and reducing uncertainty, as a necessary condition to resume the investment expenditure that will pave the road to economic recovery. The policy strategy should be based on the following pillars. We focus the issue from a European perspective since it constitutes the epicentre of the debt crisis after 2009.

- *Fiscal policy.* A countercyclical fiscal policy is useful to maintain the level of aggregate demand as high and stable as possible (Arestis *et al.*, 2004). A generalized austerity policy is self-defeating. It depresses not only investment and growth but also the savings and taxes necessary to reduce debt. The austerity programmes, that certain over-indebted European governments have been obliged to enforce, should be made up by an expansionary fiscal policy at the EU level.
- *Monetary policy.* Monetary policy should try to maintain interest rates as low as possible, in order to ensure a stable path of growth that goes beyond "price stability". Contrary to the postulates of the modern macroeconomic consensus, in a globalized world the IPC is quite insensible to the level of

interest rates (Arestis and Sawyer, 2004). The price of assets, on the contrary, is clearly affected by cheap credit. The resulting bubbles (in the stock exchange and in real estate) damage private investment while they are growing and when they burst. Governments should figure out the way to check loans for speculative purchases of assets without endangering loans for productive investment.

- *Institutional reforms.* Proper institutions and clever regulatory policies help to reduce economic and financial uncertainty, which is the major enemy of investment. The ECB should have the powers of a proper central bank to keep high the confidence of economic agents in the euro and in euro denominated assets. Investment banks and hedge funds should be made more accountable in order to check their proclivity to risk taking behaviour.

Appendix I: Definitions of variables

- α_0: independent term.
- α_i: estimated coefficients.
- ε_{ij}: error term.
- *a*: rate of accumulation of capital. It is the dependent variable to be estimated.

$$a_{i,t} = \frac{K_{i,t} - K_{i,t-1}}{K_{i,t-1}} = \frac{I_{i,t}}{K_{i,t-1}}$$

where *K* is stock of private productive capital and *I* is private productive investment or business investment.

Sources of data: OECD: *STAN Database for Structural Analysis.* For the US: Bureau of Economic Analysis: *National Economic Accounts, Current-Cost Net Stock of Fixed Assets and Consumer Durable Goods*

- *g*: rate of growth of GDP.

$$g_{i,t-1} = \frac{GDP_{i,t-1} - GDP_{i,t-2}}{GDP_{i,t-2}}$$

Source of data: OECD: *Annual National Accounts* and *Main Economic Indicators*

- *du*: deviations between the effective capacity utilization (*u*) and its "normal" level (*u**).

$$du_{i,t-1} = \frac{u_{i,t-1} - u^*}{u^*}$$

The "normal rate" (*u**) is the average of boom periods.

Sources of data: OECD: *Business tendency and consumer opinion surveys.* For the US: Federal Reserve; for New Zealand: New Zealand Institute of Economic Research; for Australia: Central Bank of Australia; for Spain: Ministry of Industry, Trade and Tourism.

- $d\pi$: deviations between the profit share (π) and its conventional level (π^*).

$$d\pi_{i,t-1} = \frac{\pi_{i,t-1} - \pi^*}{\pi^*}$$

The conventional profit share was calculated using the average value of the period because this variable did not suffer deep fluctuations.

Sources of data: OECD: *Annual National Accounts*; European Commission: *Annual National Accounts*; for Spain: *INE*; for Australia: Central Bank of Australia.

- *di*: deviations of the real long-term interest rate (i) from its "conventional" level (i^*).

$$di_{i,t-1} = \frac{i_{i,t-1} - i^*}{i^*}$$

In most countries we have defined three periods corresponding to three levels for the real interest rates (low, medium and high).

Sources of data: OECD: *Key short-term indicators*. For Spain: Banco de España; for Denmark: Danmarks Nationalbank; for Italy: Banco de Italia; for Norway: Norges Bank.

- *dp*: deviations of the current real price of gold (p) from its "conventional" level (p^*).

$$dp_{i,t-1} = \frac{p_{i,t-1} - p^*}{p^*}$$

We define three different sub-periods. The conventional price of gold (p^*) is the average value of each period.

Sources of data: Kitco Metals Inc.

- *de*: deviations of the real exchange rate (e) from its "conventional" level (e^*).

$$de_{i,t-1} = \frac{e_{i,t-1} - e^*}{e^*}$$

We distinguish two sub-periods and take as the conventional exchange rate (e^*) the average value of each period.

Sources of data: OECD: *Finance* and *Historical Statistics.*

- *dDAX*: deviations of the DAX Index (*DAX*) from its "conventional" level (*DAX**). (The same is done for the Standard & Poor index applied to non-European countries.)

$$dDAX_{i,t-1} = \frac{DAX_{i,t-1} - DAX^*}{DAX^*}$$

The conventional stock price is moving upwards, with sudden falls in the financial crisis. The conventional price in a given year is defined by the average level of the preceding years. We consider 24 levels for the DAX index and 19 for Standard & Poor's 500.

Sources of data: Deutsche Bundesbank and Standard & Poor's website

Appendix II: Econometric tests

Table 10.A.1 ADF tests (1970–2008)

	a	*g*	*du*	*dπ*	*di*	*de*	*dDAX*	*dSP*	*dp*
Australia	–4.560* (1)	–5.574* (1)	–5.021* (3)	–3.255* (2)	–1.743*** (0)	–3.703* (1)	–5.446* (0)	–6.465* (0)	–6.605* (1)
Belgium	–2.965** (2)	–5.844* (0)	–4.694* (0)	–1.573*** (1)	–1.694*** (0)	–4.760* (2)	–5.446* (0)	–6.465* (0)	–6.605* (1)
Canada	–2.710 (1)	–4.366* (0)	–0.077 (1)	–2.444** (0)	–1.952** (0)	–4.032* (0)	–5.446* (0)	–6.465* (0)	–6.605* (1)
Denmark	–7.082* (0)	–5.354* (0)	–4.225* (0)	–1.646*** (1)	–1.800*** (0)	–3.566* (0)	–5.446* (0)	–6.465* (0)	–6.605* (1)
France	–4.120* (1)	–2.691*** (3)	–2.855* (0)	–3.935** (3)	–2.356 (1)	–4.363* (2)	–5.446* (0)	–6.465* (0)	–6.605* (1)
Germany	–3.170** (0)	–4.141* (0)	–3.815* (1)	–2.597 (2)	–3.512*** (1)	–2.851* (0)	–5.446* (0)	–6.465* (0)	–6.605* (1)
Italy	–4.794* (0)	–5.423* (1)	–3.333* (0)	–1.494 (0)	–1.816 (1)	–2.718* (0)	–5.446* (0)	–6.465* (0)	–6.605* (1)
New Zealand	–3.796* (1)	–3.492** (0)	–2.841 (0)	–1.865*** (1)	–1.739*** (0)	–3.316* (0)	–5.446* (0)	–6.465* (0)	–6.605* (1)
Spain	–1.762 (1)	–3.671* (0)	–2.353 (0)	–3.218*** (1)	–1.956** (0)	–3.390* (0)	–5.446* (0)	–6.465* (0)	–6.605* (1)
Norway	–1.947 (0)	–3.895* (1)	–1.348 (0)	–3.766** (1)	–2.094** (0)	–3.621* (0)	–5.446* (0)	–6.465* (0)	–6.605* (1)
UK	–3.675** (3)	–5.511* (3)	–1.558 (0)	–4.003** (1)	–2.053** (2)	–3.303* (0)	–5.446* (0)	–6.465* (0)	–6.605* (1)
US	–3.021 (1)	–4.993* (0)	–2.383*** (1)	–2.460 (1)	–2.849* (1)	–5.303* (0)	–5.446* (0)	–6.465* (0)	–6.605* (1)

Note
Lags are given in parenthesis. *, ** and *** indicate the statistical significance and the rejection of the null at the 1, 5 and 10 levels, respectively.

Table 10.A.2 DF-GLS tests (1970–2008)

	a	*g*	*du*	*dπ*	*di*	*de*	*dDAX*	*dSP*	*dp*
Australia	–1.414 (0)	–3.709* (0)	–5.166* (1)	–1.152 (2)	–1.729*** (0)	–3.144* (1)	–5.480* (0)	–6.982* (0)	–4.940* (0)
Belgium	–1.644*** (1)	–5.427* (0)	–4.056* (0)	–1.626*** (1)	–1.696*** (0)	–4.217* (2)	–5.480* (0)	–6.982* (0)	–4.940* (0)
Canada	–2.788 (1)	–4.059* (0)	–1.194 (1)	–2.130 (0)	–1.943*** (0)	–3.700* (0)	–5.480* (0)	–6.982* (0)	–4.940* (0)
Denmark	–2.436** (0)	–5.322* (0)	–4.027* (0)	–1.490 (1)	–1.690*** (0)	–2.998* (0)	–5.480* (0)	–6.982* (0)	–4.940* (0)
France	–2.322** (1)	–3.353** (0)	–1.215 (0)	–3.093*** (3)	–1.957 (1)	–2.960* (0)	–5.480* (0)	–6.982* (0)	–4.940* (0)
Germany	–1.874*** (0)	–3.802* (0)	–2.148** (0)	–1.953 (1)	–3.141*** (1)	–2.790* (0)	–5.480* (0)	–6.982* (0)	–4.940* (0)
Italy	–2.486*** (0)	–4.862* (1)	–2.336** (0)	–1.628*** (0)	–1.401 (1)	–2.196** (0)	–5.480* (0)	–6.982* (0)	–4.940* (0)
New Zealand	–2.919*** (1)	–3.428* (0)	–1.959** (1)	–1.861*** (1)	–1.722*** (0)	–3.029* (0)	–5.480* (0)	–6.982* (0)	–4.940* (0)
Spain	–1.587 (1)	–2.057** (0)	–1.989** (0)	–3.221* (1)	–1.646*** (0)	–2.519** (0)	–5.480* (0)	–6.982* (0)	–4.940* (0)
Norway	–1.966** (0)	–2.700* (0)	–5.264* (0)	–3.849* (1)	–2.082** (0)	–3.023* (0)	–5.480* (0)	–6.982* (0)	–4.940* (0)
UK	–2.544** (1)	–3.911* (3)	–2.119** (0)	–3.919* (1)	–2.092** (2)	–2.777* (0)	–5.480* (0)	–6.982* (0)	–4.940* (0)
US	–2.962*** (1)	–5.060* (0)	–1.767*** (0)	–2.495 (1)	–2.707* (1)	–3.830* (0)	–5.480* (0)	–6.982* (0)	–4.940* (0)

Note

Lags are given in parenthesis. *, ** and *** indicate the statistical significance and the rejection of the null at the 1, 5 and 10% levels, respectively.

Table 10.A.3 KPSS tests (1970–2008)

	a	*g*	*du*	*dπ*	*di*	*de*	*dDAX*	*dSP*	*dp*
Australia	0.291	0.084	0.056	0.3	0.3	0.154	0.074	0.118	0.061
Belgium	0.101	0.196	0.055	0.284	0.187	0.077	0.074	0.118	0.061
Canada	0.152**	0.204	0.174	0.093	0.226	0.141	0.074	0.118	0.061
Denmark	0.134***	0.076	0.081	0.085	0.303	0.077	0.074	0.118	0.061
France	0.140***	0.423***	0.338***	0.086	0.397***	0.109	0.074	0.118	0.061
Germany	0.071	0.339	0.099	0.132***	0.144***	0.183	0.074	0.118	0.061
Italy	0.715**	0.076	0.118	0.285	0.236	0.17	0.074	0.118	0.061
New Zealand	0.276	0.117	0.286	0.106	0.150**	0.163	0.074	0.118	0.061
Spain	0.326	0.135	0.311	0.299	0.167	0.141	0.074	0.118	0.061
Norway	0.118	0.077	0.096	0.076	0.32	0.11	0.074	0.118	0.061
UK	0.096	0.061	0.299	0.085	0.133***	0.167	0.074	0.118	0.061
US	0.1	0.050**	0.117	0.104	0.189	0.104	0.074	0.118	0.061

Note
*, ** and *** indicate the statistical significance and the rejection of the null at the 1, 5 and 10% levels, respectively.

Table 10.A.4 Panel tests (1970–2008)

Panel tests	*a*	*g*	*du*	*dπ*	*di*	*de*	*dDAX*	*dSP*	*dp*
ADF	–3.853*	–13.010*	–4.106*	–3.919*	–5.109*	–6.286*	–11.672*	–4.987*	–14.151*
PP	–1.676**	–13.506*	–3.661*	–4.594*	–5.202*	–4.699*	–11.656*	–2.765*	–14.471*
IPS	–5.753*	–11.478*	–4.720*	–3.929*	–1.0187	–6.680*	–8.041*	–3.191*	–17.702*
LLC	–4.880*	–3.213*	–3.768*	–3.510*	–5.7673*	–6.602*	–12.328*	–2.817*	–18.083*
B	–1.353***	–5.051*	–2.156**	–3.407*	–3.096*	–6.083*	–16.169*	–4.786*	–4.665*

Note

*, ** and *** indicate the statistical significance and the rejection of the null at the 1, 5 and 10% levels, respectively.

Notes

1 By business investment we refer to "gross fixed capital formation", i.e. the purchase of equipment and buildings by firms. In this chapter it will also be named "productive investment", "accumulation" or, simply, "investment".
2 In 1933 (Kalecki, 1971) the Polish economist pointed to expected profitability and interest rates as the main determinants of the accumulation process. In 1968 Kalecki modified his initial view by considering investment as a function of cash flows, technical progress and profitability.
3 EViews version 7.1 and STATA version 9.2 were the software packages utilized.
4 These tests are widely available; see, for example, Mills and Patterson (2006).

References

Alexiou, C. (2010) "A Keynesian–Kaleckian model of investment determination: a panel data investigation", *Journal of Post Keynesian Economics*, 32 (3), 427–443.

Arestis, P., Dunn, S.P. and Sawyer, M. (1999) "On the coherence of Post-Keynesian economics: a comment on Walters and Young", *Scottish Journal of Political Economy*, 46 (3), 339–345.

Arestis, P. and Sawyer, M. (2004) *Re-examining Monetary and Fiscal Policies in the 21st Century*, Cheltenham: Edward Elgar.

Baddeley, M. (1999) "Keynes on rationality, expectations and investment", in C. Sardoni (ed.), *Keynes, Post-Keynesianism and Political Economy: Essays in Honour of Geoff Harcourt*, Vol. III, London: Routledge.

Baddeley, M. (2003) *Investment: Theories and Analysis*, Basingstoke: Palgrave Macmillan.

Baltagi, B.H. (1995) *Econometric Analysis of Panel Data*, Chichester: Wiley.

Beck, N. and Katz, J.N. (1995) "What to do (and not to do) with time-series cross-section data", *American Political Science Review*, 89 (3), 634–647.

Bhaduri, A. and Marglin, S. (1990) "Unemployment and the real wage: the economic basis for contesting political ideologies", *Cambridge Journal of Economics*, 14 (4), 375–393.

Bhandari, R. and Upadhyaya, K.P. (2010) "Panel data evidence of the impact of exchange rate uncertainty on private investment in south-east Asia", *Applied Economics*, 42 (1), 57–61.

Chenery, H.B. (1952) "Overcapacity and the acceleration principle", *Econometrica*, 20 (1), 1–28.

Crotty, J.R. (1992) "Neoclassical and Keynesian approaches to the theory of investment", *Journal of Post Keynesian Economics*, 14 (4), 483–496.

Davidson, P. (1991) "Is probability theory relevant for uncertainty? A post Keynesian perspective", *Journal of Economic Perspectives*, 5 (1), 19–43.

Dejuán, O. (2007) "The conventional versus the natural rate of interest: implications for central bank autonomy", *Journal of Post Keynesian Economics*, 29 (4), 645–666.

Demir, F. (2009) "Macroeconomic uncertainty and private investment in Argentina, Mexico and Turkey", *Applied Economics Letters*, 16 (6), 567–571.

Eatwell, J. (1983) "The long period theory of employment", *Cambridge Journal of Economics*, 7, 269–285.

Evans, M. (1969) *Macroeconomic Activity*, New York: Harper and Row.

Gualerzi, D. (2010) *The Coming of Age of Information Technologies and the Path of Transformational Growth: A Long-run Perspective of the Late 2000s Recession*. New York: Routledge.

Harrod, R. (1939) "An essay in dynamic theory", *Economic Journal*, 49 (193), 14–33.

Kalecki, M. (1937) "The principle of increasing risk", *Económica*, 4 (4), 440–446.

Kalecki, M. (1968) "Trend and business cycle reconsidered", *Economic Journal*, 78 (2), 263–276.

Kalecki, M. (1971) *Selected Essays in the Dynamics of the Capitalist Economy (1933–1970)*, Cambridge: Cambridge University Press.

Keynes, J.M. (1936) *The General Theory of Employment, Interest and Money*, London: Macmillan.

Kurz, H. (1986) "Normal positions and capacity utilization", *Political Economy: Studies in the Surplus Approach*, 2, 37–54.

Lavoie, M., Rodríguez, G. and Seccareccia, M. (2004) "Similitudes and discrepancies in Post-Keynesian and Marxist theories of investment: a theoretical and empirical investigation", *International Review of Applied Economics*, 18 (2), 127–149.

Littleboy, B. (1990) *On Interpreting Keynes: A Study in Reconciliation*, London: Routledge.

Mills, T.C. and Patterson, K. (2006) *Palgrave Handbook of Econometrics*, New York: Palgrave Macmillan.

Minsky, H.P. (1975) *John Maynard Keynes*, New York: Columbia University Press.

Minsky, H.P. (1977) "The financial instability hypothesis: an interpretation of Keynes and an alternative to standard theory", *Nebraska Journal of Economics and Business*, 16 (1), 59–70.

Runde, J. (1990) "Keynesian uncertainty and the weight of arguments", *Economics and Philosophy*, 6 (2), 275–292.

Stockhammer, E. and Grafl, L. (2010) "Financial uncertainty and business investment", *Review of Political Economy*, 22 (4), 551–568.

Tobin, J. (1969) "A general equilibrium approach to monetary theory", *Journal of Money Credit and Banking*, 1 (1), 15–29.

11 Does the effectiveness of fiscal stimulus depend on economic context?

Steven M. Fazzari[1]

Does the effectiveness of fiscal policy in stabilizing an economy depend on the underlying economic context in which the policy is implemented? The answer to such a broad question must certainly be yes, but I argue in this chapter that the answer differs across various dimensions of "context," three of which are considered here. First, I consider in some detail the most obvious context: the state of economic activity relative to some measure of the economy's potential. I discuss logic and evidence that implies that the presence or absence of idle resources is the key context for fiscal policy. Second, I explore whether the openness of the economy matters, especially the extent to which fiscal stimulus flows abroad by boosting imports or is financed by borrowing from abroad. While this dimension will likely affect the quantitative stimulus that a country gets from fiscal expansion, I conclude that the open-economy context is unlikely to affect the decision of a country that borrows in its own currency to undertake fiscal stimulus. Third, I look at how the level of government debt, what is sometimes called the "debt overhang," matters for the decision to undertake fiscal stimulus. While I accept that government debt can, in principle, be excessive, I discuss why concerns about the current level of debt in developed, sovereign-currency countries are likely exaggerated.

At the outset, I note that the discussion that follows is largely based on the US economy. In the absence of political incompetence of the kind demonstrated by the US Congress in debate over raising the legal debt limit in the summer of 2011, default on a sovereign debt obligation is not a concern. Why would a government default on a debt when it has the means to discharge that debt by simply creating the means of payment?[2] Creation of money to pay debt may have other consequences, but default should not ever occur for a government that borrows in its own sovereign currency. This US-based analysis extends to other countries with similar fiscal and monetary circumstances. It does not apply, however, to countries that borrow in foreign currency or to countries that must maintain a fixed exchange rate, which takes its most extreme form for countries that are part of a currency union. Thus, the substantial recent difficulties of Greece, Spain, Portugal, Ireland, and Italy are outside the context of what follows. While this limits the relevance of the discussion to some extent, the issues addressed here are of fundamental importance, and seem badly understood in much of the current discussion by journalists and policy analysts. Furthermore, I argue that to develop an effective institutional framework for a currency union like the one based on the euro, the designers must begin from the principles analyzed here.

The idle resources context

The most obvious context of significance for the macroeconomic effects of fiscal policy is the amount of slack in the economy. If government spending rises in an economy in which productive resources are fully employed, this spending must necessarily crowd out the private use of output because total output cannot exceed what the economy's resources can produce. Similarly, while tax cuts in a full-employment economy might encourage more consumption or higher investment spending, without resources available to increase total production, any new demand induced by the tax cuts will crowd out other activities. This is the world of classical economic theory. The most obvious market channel through which fiscal expansion crowds out other activities operates through higher interest rates that choke off any excess demand. The loanable funds theory of interest rates prevails.[3]

If the economy has slack productive capacity, however, the most obvious effect of fiscal expansion is higher production and employment as firms produce more to meet the rise in demand. The effect is direct: more sales lead to more production. Prices may rise, depending on the response of firms to the shift in demand, but firms may well not raise prices.[4] More important for the purposes of this chapter, there is no need for interest rates to rise despite the fact that higher government spending and/or lower taxes raise the government deficit. Yes, the government borrows more, but equilibrium in the loanable funds market for an economy operating with slack resources is established by endogenous increases in saving rather than higher interest rates. The intuition behind this result is that the multiplier process that raises income continues to operate until the sum of three variables increases to match the size of any fiscal injection: (1) domestic saving induced by the higher income, (2) imports, and therefore foreign saving, induced by higher spending, and (3) tax revenue induced by higher income. Any initial deficit created by fiscal stimulus will therefore be offset directly by somewhat higher tax revenue and what remains of the deficit will be matched by higher saving, domestic or foreign. There is no upward pressure on interest rates.[5]

This result is basic and should be uncontroversial: if there are Keynesian demand effects of fiscal stimulus and the stimulus is not so large as to push the economy up against resource bottlenecks, there is no loanable funds pressure on interest rates. Nonetheless, many policymakers, journalists, and even economists seem to fear that large fiscal deficits of recent years will push up interest rates in spite of the extreme economic slack that emerged in the wake of the Great Recession. This fear is inconsistent with the evidence: interest rates have not risen despite the massive recession-induced deficits; indeed they fell to historic lows. The link between deficits and interest rates is therefore one part of the macroeconomic impact of fiscal policy that depends fundamentally on context: with substantial economic slack, interest rates do not rise when expansionary fiscal policy increases government deficits. Instead, when the demand for funds goes up the income and import expansion that results from the Keynesian effects of the stimulus endogenously raises the supply of funds by an equivalent amount.

One might reasonably ask if this result depends on monetary policy and whether it will accommodate the fiscal expansion. In a sense, the answer is yes, but this answer is nuanced and requires some explanation. When the economy operates with slack interest rates and other asset prices are determined by the supply and demand for the stocks of assets; this is liquidity preference theory generalized to a multiple-asset world. Monetary policy is a key player in these markets, and it has the power to raise or lower interest rates independently of the state of fiscal policy. Monetary policy *could* offset the demand effects of stimulative fiscal policy to some degree by raising interest rates, but it need not do so. Indeed, it usually *does not* do so for obvious reasons: macroeconomic conditions that call forth the need for fiscal expansion usually result in expansionary monetary policy as well. The prevailing wisdom of what came to be called "new consensus" macroeconomics in recent years held that monetary policy should be the first line of defense against insufficient demand and economic slack. Therefore, as a practical matter, fiscal expansion in developed countries to address unemployment usually takes place in a context of accommodative monetary policy. But, as a theoretical matter, a neutral monetary policy in the sense of a constant interest rate target will mean that fiscal expansion neither raises nor lowers interest rates unless the economy is pushing up against resource constraints.[6]

This logic also implies that the absence of interest rate increases from fiscal expansion does not require nominal interest rates pinned at the zero bound. One could argue that if interest rates are not at the zero bound, monetary policy is the preferred tool to raise demand in the face of economic slack, rather than expansionary fiscal policy. But as a matter of theory, there is no need for fiscal expansion to raise interest rates even if monetary policy targets a positive nominal rate, as long as the economy has slack productive capacity.

Of course, the perspective that expansionary fiscal policy is effective when the economy has idle resources is highly controversial. Many prominent economists and influential policymakers do not accept this result and this contrary position has become manifest recently in calls for fiscal austerity even though it is abundantly clear that economies have substantial economic slack. What kind of evidence can we muster to support this key contextual result? The size of the fiscal multiplier has been the study of voluminous empirical work. Results are mixed, with estimated multipliers ranging between slightly negative and huge values around 4.0. Balanced surveys of this literature, however, suggest that the best evidence centers on values of about 1.5 (see Ramey, 2011, for a recent and insightful example). A value of this size supports Keynesian results and the likelihood that the benefits of fiscal expansion far exceed any costs when there are slack resources (as will be discussed in the following sections). Considering the importance of this issue, the volume of research, and the obvious implication of basic theory that the size of the multiplier should depend on the state of the economy, it is somewhat surprising that hardly any of this empirical research has explored the dependence of estimated multipliers on the context of idle resources. Parker (2011), in particular, presents a strong and coherent call for such work.

Most likely, a major reason why the empirical study of fiscal expansion has not much explored the context of idle resources is that the econometric methods employed in past research did not have a straightforward way to estimate a model that makes the size of the multiplier depend on the state of the economy. Recent innovations in time-series econometrics, however, have produced tractable "threshold models" in which the impulse-response functions can change as key state variables transit a threshold. In two innovative studies, Auerbach and Gorodnichenko (2010, 2011) estimate multipliers with threshold models that change between "recession" conditions and "expansion" conditions. They find that the multiplier is indeed higher in what they define as recessions, about 2.2, versus 0.6 in expansions. Mittnik and Semmler (2011) obtain related results, estimating higher multipliers in low-growth periods than in high-growth periods.

Fazzari *et al.* (2013) present results that provide strong support for the view that the effectiveness of fiscal stimulus depends on the amount of productive slack. We estimate impulse-response functions for an increase in government spending. The model has two regimes, defined by the level of capacity utilization relative to an estimated threshold.[7] In the "low" regime, capacity utilization is low and the economy has a greater amount of slack. In the "high" regime resource constraints are more likely to reduce the real impact of fiscal expansion. Figure 11.1 shows the estimated impulse-response functions in both regimes.

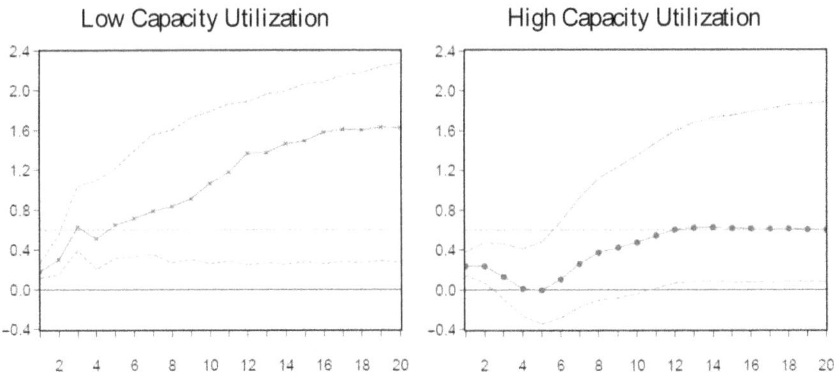

Figure 11.1 Response of output to 1% of GDP shock to government spending (source: Fazzari, Morley, and Panovska (2012, figure 3)).

Notes

The left panel shows the estimated cumulative rise in output induced by a temporary government spending shock equal to 1% of GDP when the economy begins and remains in the low capacity utilization regime. The right panel is the response of output when the economy begins and remains in the high utilization regime. Vertical axis units are percent of GDP; horizontal axis units are quarters. Dotted lines are 90% credibility intervals.

The cumulative effect of a one-time shock to government spending implies a very substantial multiplier of about 1.6 in the low regime when the economy has a lot of slack. In the high regime the multiplier is far from negligible at about 0.6, but it is less than half the value from the low regime. The data strongly prefer a nonlinear threshold model with two regimes against the typical linear model estimated in most of the relevant literature that imposes the same impulse-response function regardless of the state of the economy.[8]

Perhaps just as striking as the size difference in the multipliers, the data imply that about 60 percent of the sample observations (quarterly data from 1967 through the first quarter of 2011) fall in the "low" regime.[9] This means that the typical state of affairs for the US economy is one of substantial slack and high multipliers. In addition, the multiplier is economically and statistically significant even in the high regime. Full employment conditions that would prevent fiscal stimulus from having a strong positive effect on economic activity seems to be a rare event, even in what was, prior to the Great Recession, a relatively well functioning economy like the US.

We also studied the effect of higher government spending on other macroeconomic variables. There is no evidence whatsoever of crowding out in the low regime. Consumption responds strongly and positively to higher government spending. Investment generally rises, sometimes substantially, after a positive shock to government spending, but the credibility interval for the investment results is somewhat sensitive to the initial conditions when the shock occurs and the particular history of shocks assumed in the simulations. The investment response in the low regime is strongly positive when the simulations are run with recent histories of the data. In the high regime, consumption also responds positively to government spending, but much less than in the low regime. There is some evidence of investment crowding out in the high regime with negative impulse-responses to a positive government spending shock. But the US economy has not spent more than a few quarters in the high regime since 2000.

These results strongly support the basic Keynesian interpretation of the effect of fiscal policy. The context of idle resources has important empirical effects on how fiscal policy affects key macroeconomic variables, but most of the time there are idle resources. Under these circumstances, fiscal expansion raises output and employment. Any resulting deficits will not raise interest rates.[10]

The multiplier results discussed above might understate the empirical importance of fiscal policy for macroeconomic stability. The findings in Fazzari *et al.* (2012), and the vast majority of the related literature, are based on data drawn from an era when both automatic stabilizers and discretionary polices responded rather strongly to periods of economic weakness. Deficits increased substantially in every US recession, which the results above suggest had important effects on output and employment. These deficits contained the damage and reduced the sense of panic that could have led to a crisis of confidence and a much more severe collapse of demand and finance than actually occurred. Because our sample comes from a historical period when a catastrophic crisis did not occur, the estimated multiplier effects may be biased downward. One example of this phenomenon occurred in late 2008 and early 2009 when, following the failure of the Lehman Brothers investment bank, the US economy plummeted at rates reminiscent of the most severe declines of the early 1930s. But as automatic fiscal stabilizers kicked in and discretionary fiscal measures were anticipated (along with a healthy dose of lender-of-last-resort intervention), the economy stabilized. Most studies of the impact of fiscal stimulus introduced during this period imply that it had standard positive effects, which were substantial. But we cannot know how bad things would have got if there had been no fiscal response at all, perhaps due to binding balanced budget restrictions that many politicians and some economists seem to favor.

The open-economy context

The second dimension of context for fiscal stimulus is the fear that international financial flows will soften (or even eliminate) the punch from the basic effects of fiscal expansion discussed in the first section. Unlike the idle resource context, I argue here that open-economy considerations make little difference to the effectiveness of fiscal policy for large countries with sovereign currencies. I use the US and the dollar in the discussion below, but the analysis applies to countries like Japan and the UK. It *could* apply to the Eurozone as a whole, although the lack of a tight fiscal union among the countries using the common currency makes things more complicated.

The most obvious difference between the effect of fiscal stimulus in closed versus open economies is the likelihood that some of the private spending induced by higher incomes flows to imports rather than domestically produced output. The channel reduces the multiplier and therefore lowers the impact from fiscal stimulus.

The salient question in this context is whether the import leakage would flip the social cost–benefit calculation for a given stimulus action from favorable to unfavorable. I consider this outcome highly unlikely because even with import leakages the multiplier in periods with significant economic slack is high. Import leakages undoubtedly reduced the multiplier for the US over the estimation sample period discussed in the previous section, yet the multiplier remains large. The impact, even in the open economy, is substantial.

If some stimulus leaks abroad into imports and exports are unchanged, international debt will rise. In the US, this worry reaches its highest volume when the issue is whether China's massive purchases of US government debt will compromise the future economic security of American citizens. The conclusion often drawn is that we "can't afford" stimulus. I disagree. Consider the most extreme case when *all* of the government deficit created by fiscal stimulus is financed from abroad. Suppose that the multiplier is 1.6, as discussed previously. Then a dollar of government stimulus creates 1.6 dollars of new domestic income, which generates new tax revenue. An estimate of this new revenue is 37 percent of the rise of income.[11] If this is the case, a dollar of stimulus increases tax revenue by 37 percent times 1.6, or 59 percent of the stimulus spending. Thus, the net cost of a dollar of stimulus is just 41 cents in new foreign debt, with the extreme assumption that all of the new borrowing comes from abroad. Assuming the discount rate on foreign borrowing equals the interest rate, the present value of the cost of this debt is 41 cents compared with a benefit of new production of 1.6 dollars: a benefit–cost ratio of nearly four!

What about the fear that foreigners will decide at some point to divest their dollar debt? If they traded their debt for domestic production, domestic exports would rise, an outcome that seems desirable for any country in today's environment. If foreigners sold dollar debt for securities denominated in other currencies, the value of the dollar would fall, also stimulating exports and reducing imports. This outcome implies that Americans have less command over world production, but it also stimulates domestic demand. In the context of the results discussed above that imply that the US is operating with significant slack most of the time, a rise in demand is likely to be welcome.

Finally, if there were some fear that US debt (or Japanese debt, or British debt) were an unsound international investment, we would expect to see the fear reflected in interest rates. Instead, interest rates are at historic lows.[12] An interesting vignette proves the larger point. In the summer of 2011 the US Congress became embroiled in an entirely artificial debate about raising the legal debt ceiling limit, even threatening technical default on US Treasury obligations. During this period, bond prices for US government securities *rose*, as investors seemed more worried about financial turmoil induced by the debate than the actual ability of the US to meet its obligations.

The open economy context is unlikely to change the basic result from the first section: fiscal stimulus has substantial positive effects, which likely greatly exceed costs, in the *normal* case when the economy operates with slack resources.

The context of government debt overhang

Let us combine the messages of the discussion so far. The first section reports evidence that the government spending multiplier is consistent with the presence of substantial slack, most of the time. Even in the minority of periods when the economy operates in the "high" regime with less slack, the estimated multiplier is positive and substantial. The calculations in the second section show that when we account for the additional tax revenue generated by stimulus the benefit–cost ratio is highly favorable, even if foreigners purchase government debt issued because of the resulting deficit. Is there *any* situation, aside from rare moments when the economy approaches true full employment, in which the society would not benefit from more fiscal stimulus?

The most obvious way to answer yes would be a situation in which interest payments necessary to service government debt have got so high that they impose social costs that exceed the benefit from creating new flows of demand.[13] It is important to recognize that these payments are a *transfer*, not a net social cost. Government bonds impose a liability on future generations of taxpayers, which politicians and pundits almost universally decry as the dark side of any debt-financed fiscal stimulus. But the typical discussion of these issues almost always ignores the fact that the bonds also are an *asset* for future generations of bondholders. If transfers are lump sum with no supply-side incentive effects and there is no social cost to redistribution, the transfers would be neutral. Fiscal stimulus when resources are under-utilized would have no cost, regardless of the size of the debt overhang. But as a practical matter, taxes will not be lump sum and the distribution effects cannot be ignored.

To assess the redistribution costs of servicing government debt we must first consider the magnitude of transfers. Interest rates on government bonds in countries that borrow in their own sovereign currency are low. In the US the real interest rate measured by the yield on five-year and ten-year inflation-protected securities averaged 1.64 and 2.06 percent, respectively, from 2003 through 2007. This period was before the Great Recession when interest rates were likely more representative of long-run yields. The five- and ten-year inflation-protected yields averaged 0.56 and 1.28, respectively, from 2008 through 2011 as monetary policy responded to the economic collapse.

Consider what these figures imply about the costs of servicing US debt arising from the Great Recession. This has been a historic period of weakness in the economy when the size of deficits relative to GDP greatly exceeded the previous postwar high. It is therefore a rather extreme case study. From 2008 through 2011, the debt-to-GDP ratio increased by roughly 30 percentage points.[14] Since the recovery has gained little traction as of this writing, suppose that continued stagnation raises this ratio by another 15 points over the next several years. The interest rate projections presented in the previous paragraph imply annual debt service legacy of this once-in-two-generations event of approximately the product of a 1.5 percent interest rate and a 45 percentage point rise in debt to GDP, which equals just under 0.7 percent of GDP. This figure is hardly "unaffordable"; it seems like a modest cost to pay for the critical support that fiscal policy provided the economy during seven or more difficult years. Indeed, it is easy to imagine that this fiscal support could have prevented declines in the *level of potential output* by at least 0.7 percent in the aftermath of the Great Recession by containing negative effects on capital investment, R&D spending, and deterioration of worker skill due to unemployment. Thus, one could make a strong case that this higher debt, widely decried in political circles, *has no aggregate social cost at all* when compared with a counterfactual of some kind of balanced-budget rule for the federal government. As the economy grows over time, the debt service required by these circumstances will shrink relative to GDP. Although one hopes that it will not be necessary, there is nothing in this record to suggest that the legacy of what has happened since 2008 would make a similar intervention infeasible or even require a higher cost should it be necessary in future years.

It is important to remember that this debt service is not a net social cost, it is a transfer. Some authors have raised concerns that transfers to service government debt act as a regressive tax. Since saving rates probably increase with income, it is likely that the distribution of government bond holders is skewed toward the wealthy. But, as discussed in Cynamon and Fazzari (2013, ch. 11) the wealthy also pay a higher share of income taxes. If income taxes rise to cover higher debt service (a questionable assumption considering the relatively small size of the transfers discussed above), they *could* be raised on high-income earners to offset regressive transfers to bondholders. The critical word in the previous sentence is "could." If government debt service leads to higher taxes on the middle class, or to cuts to social safety net programs, the effect of debt-service transfers would indeed be regressive. But this outcome is a political problem, and not a necessary result of government debt overhang.

This discussion implies that the US, and other sovereign-currency, developed countries, do not now have a debt overhang problem at this time, and are unlikely to develop one from the need to pursue fiscal stimulus in the face of economic slack in the foreseeable future. That said, governments should not issue debt without bound. Suppose the debt-to-GDP ratio, rather than flirting with 100 percent, became 200 percent, or 500 percent, or 1000 percent. Even with low interest rates these figures imply transfer payments that rise from about 1.5 percent of GDP to 3.0 percent, 7.5 percent, or 15 percent, respectively. Although it's probably impossible to define a precise limit on when these transfers become too large to be accepted by the taxpayers, it seems that there is some limit on how high government debt and debt service can rise relative to the size of the economy. In the long term, government budgets should be balanced, or at least set at a level that sustains an acceptable debt-to-GDP ratio, *when the economy operates at full employment.* In the US, for example, the tax revenue base reflected in current law is inadequate to fund the current path of health care entitlements in the long run. This problem should be addressed. But it should not be used as a reason for austerity when the economy suffers from significant slack.

We also cannot ignore the role of monetary policy together with fiscal stimulus. Modern economies need large fiscal expansion when they suffer from low employment. At these times, interest rates should be low, and new government debt will be issued with low debt-service commitments. (US inflation-adjusted securities of most maturities have slightly negative real yields in 2012.) As the economy recovers, budget deficits should move toward balance, reducing the growth rate of government debt below the growth rate of the economy and leading to a decline in debt-to-GDP ratios. If monetary policy must tighten to prevent inflation in such circumstances, at least this tightening will occur when the government balance sheet is improving and tax revenues are growing quickly.

Conclusion

This chapter considers three different dimensions of the economic context that many commentators argue matter for the effectiveness if fiscal policy. The discussion above leads to the following summary conclusions:

1. The extent of *idle resources* is the most important context for fiscal policy. Basic Keynesian theory predicts that higher government spending will raise output and employment when the economy has under-utilized labor and capital, but higher government demand crowds out other activities when resource constraints bind. Recent studies that explicitly take the idle resource context into account support this prediction. Moreover, the multiplier is large which implies that higher government spending stimulates substantial private activity, again, when the economy has idle resources.
2. An *open economy* will cause some part of fiscal stimulus to leak abroad as imports. But the effects of fiscal stimulus are large enough, even in an open economy, that the import leakage is unlikely to cause a policy action that would be judged worthwhile in a closed economy to be assessed as undesirable in the open economy context. Furthermore, the accumulation of foreign debt, even if viewed as a dollar-for-dollar social cost (which is far from obvious), is very unlikely to generate enough debt service to justify curtailing fiscal stimulus that would be viewed as desirable if it were financed domestically.
3. While government debt cannot grow without bound relative to the size of the economy, I conclude that the *debt overhang* context does not constrain the effectiveness of fiscal policy for the practical circumstances faced in 2012 by developed countries that borrow in their own sovereign currency. Current ratios of debt to GDP leave substantial room for further fiscal expansion to address unemployment, even following the very severe Great Recession and its aftermath. Nonetheless, tax and spending policies should approach balance that maintains an acceptable debt-to-GDP ratio when the economy reaches full employment.

For developed countries like the US, the UK, Japan, Australia, Canada, and others, I argue that the primary context for fiscal policy should be the state of the economy. Current policy debates, in my view, reflect too much fear about the foreign debt or debt overhang contexts. Our evidence to date, even after the most severe crisis in almost eight decades, and the highest government deficits in 70 years, shows that fiscal stimulus can be an effective tool to address the social costs of under-employed resources with only very modest implications for future debt service transfers, either domestically or abroad.

Notes

1 The author thanks the Institute for New Economic Thinking for generous financial support for the research described in this chapter and he is grateful to Irina Panovska for helpful comments on an early outline for this chapter. An earlier version of this chapter was presented at the Institute for New Economic Thinking annual conference in Berlin, April 2012.

2 In the US, legal restrictions prevent the monetary authority, the Federal Reserve, from directly purchasing US debt from the Treasury, the fiscal authority. But this legal restriction can be, and is, circumvented by modern market practices. It is certainly not an economic constraint. See Wray (2011) for further discussion.

3 In some new classical models of fiscal policy the crowding out is not one-for-one. One reason could be wealth effects: higher government spending forces higher expected taxes, lowering household wealth, and encouraging more work effort that raises potential output.

4 Fazzari *et al.* (1998) argue that a model with monopolistically competitive firms with constant marginal costs and a constant markup of price over marginal cost is a realistic approximation to realistic aggregate conditions. In this model, firms will not choose to increase prices when demand rises unless money wages increase. Especially in recent years, wage increases relative to expected inflation in the US are unlikely unless the economy operates at or close to full employment.

5 See Fazzari (1995, 2009) for more detailed discussion about the operation of loanable funds markets in a Keynesian context.

6 In older textbook IS/LM analysis it would be usual to define "neutral" monetary policy as one that holds the money stock constant. In this case, fiscal expansion (an outward shift of the IS curve) would push up interest rates as higher income raised the demand for money holding the supply constant (a movement along an upward-sloping LM curve). But in the modern context of monetary policy that targets interest rates this channel is of little empirical relevance. Furthermore, there is a strong argument that it was never practical for the central bank to target the stock of money, because what serves as money is endogenous; see Wray (2011).

7 We consider a variety of threshold variables and results are quite similar to the baseline results described here.

8 The impulse-response results reported in the text assume that the economy remains within the low or high regimes for the entire simulation horizon. If we allow the threshold variable (capacity utilization) to evolve over the impulse-response simulation and average over a large number of simulated paths generated by drawing initial values and shocks from their empirically estimated distributions, the average multipliers are roughly the same.

9 The determination of the share of observations that fall in each regime from the data distinguishes our approach from the small number of studies that also estimate state-dependent multipliers. For example, Auerbach and Gorodnichenko (2011) impose that just 20 percent of the observations fall into their "recession" regime.

10 Fazzari *et al.* (2013) present a Keynesian growth model in which the usual state of the economy is one of idle resources, but the economy occasionally and momentarily bumps up against resource constraints.

11 This calculation updates the figures reported by Cynamon and Fazzari (2013, ch. 11) who discuss this approach in somewhat more detail. The 37 percent figure is the change in total government revenue divided by the change in national income, averaged over three expansions: 1991:3 to 2001:2 (36 percent), 2003:1 to 2008:1 (40 percent), and the partial expansion from 2009:1 through 2011:3 (35 percent). The revenue expansion includes state and local governments, which is appropriate considering the substantial transfers to state government units from the federal government. If one includes federal revenues only, the average increase over the same three expansions is 26 percent. In Fazzari *et al.* (2012), we estimate the effect of a government spending shock on tax revenues. The point estimate in the low utilization regime implies an even larger increase in tax revenues following a government spending shock, but the confidence intervals for this estimate are quite wide. Also note that effective stimulus will reduce spending on safety net programs like unemployment insurance and health care costs for the unemployed, which makes the trade off discussed in the text even more favorable.

12 See Irons and Bivens (2010) for further discussion and references.

13 These transfers are relevant only if fiscal stimulus ultimately results in the issue of bonds. Governments of countries with sovereign currencies could also create new money to cover fiscal stimulus spending. Although conventional thinking implies that

this action would create transfers through an inflation tax, higher inflation would not necessarily be forthcoming, especially when economic slack is substantial. See Wray (2011), for example, for further discussion. He emphasizes that the decision to issue government bonds to drain reserves created by new government spending is a "choice," not a requirement. Even though the possibility of substantial money-financed fiscal expansion is intriguing, this chapter focuses on stimulus that leads directly to higher government debt because that is the most relevant context with current institutional structures in most countries.

14 The vast majority of this increase in debt was due to automatic stabilizers rather than discretionary fiscal stimulus.

References

Auerbach, A.J. and Gorodnichenko, Y. (2010) "Measuring the Output Responses to Fiscal Policy," *NBER Working Paper*, 16311.

Auerbach, A.J. and Gorodnichenko, Y. (2011) "Fiscal Multipliers in Recession and Expansion," *NBER Working Paper*, 17447.

Cynamon, B.Z. and Fazzari, S.M. (2013) "No Need to Panic about U.S. Government Deficits," in B.Z. Cynamon, S.M. Fazzari, and M. Setterfield (eds.) *After the Great Recession: The Struggle for Economic Recovery and Growth*, New York: Cambridge University Press, ch. 11.

Fazzari, S.M. (1995) "Why Doubt the Effectiveness of Keynesian Fiscal Policy?" *Journal of Post Keynesian Economics*, 17, 231–248.

Fazzari, S.M. (2009) "Keynesian Macroeconomics as the Rejection of Classical Axioms," *Journal of Post Keynesian Economics*, 32, 3–18.

Fazzari, S.M., Ferri, P., and Greenberg, E.D. (1998) "Aggregate Demand and Micro Behavior: A New Perspective on Keynesian Macroeconomics," *Journal of Post Keynesian Economics*, 20, 527–558.

Fazzari, S.M., Ferri, P., Greenberg, E.D., and Variato, A. (2013) "Aggregate Demand, Instability, and Growth," *Review of Keynesian Economics*, 1, 1–21.

Fazzari, S.M., Morley, J., and Panovska, I. (2012) "State-Dependent Effects of Fiscal Policy," Working Paper, Research Paper 2012-27, UNSW Australian School of Business.

Irons, J. and Bivens, J. (2010) "Economic Growth: Overreaching Claims of Debt 'Threshold' Suffer from Theoretical and Empirical Flaws," *EPI Briefing Paper* #271, July 26.

Mittnik, S. and Semmler, W. (2011) "Regime Dependence of the Fiscal Multiplier," Working Paper No. 05, Center for Quantitative Risk Analysis (CEQURA), Department of Statistics, University of Munich.

Parker, J.A. (2011) "On Measuring the Effects of Fiscal Policy in Recessions," *Journal of Economic Literature*, 49, 703–718.

Ramey, V. (2011) "Can Government Purchases Stimulate the Economy?" *Journal of Economic Literature*, 49, 673–685.

Wray, L.R. (2011) *Modern Money Theory*, http://neweconomicperspectives.org/p/modern-money-primer.html.

12 Spain during the Great Recession

Teetering on the brink of collapse

Eladio Febrero and Fernando Bermejo

Introduction

In this contribution, we offer a non-orthodox interpretation of the causes that have driven the Spanish economy to a protracted state of recession. Next, we discuss what should be done in terms of economic policy to drive this economy to pre-downturn figures and review what has in fact been put in practice. We conclude that the measures adopted will neither bring prosperity to the Spanish economy (the ultimate goal), nor will they restore macroeconomic balances. In our view, the roots of the crisis are a rocketing private indebtedness and an excessively large size of the construction industry; these factors are located within the national borders and they have spilled over to the rest of the euro zone through a current account deficit and a highly negative financial investment position. The consequences of these imbalances have led to a problem of effective demand, a real estate bubble that burst and a lack of domestic credit and of funding in international markets. The institutional setting which frames the Spanish economy poses serious limits to the measures required to get out of this mess. Solving these problems would require a proactive fiscal authority, a central bank able to play the role of lender of last resort and a realignment of the real exchange rate. This we shall call the expansive option, and would require more political union than exists at the moment in the European Monetary Union (EMU onwards). There is an alternative option which consists of fiscal austerity measures, where public spending should be replaced by exports. This alternative requires prices to increase less than in neighbouring countries, something which could be attained through additional supply side reforms, particularly in the labour market. It can be implemented at the national level. And here is the dilemma: the expansive option requires the cooperation of all of the countries within the EMU and some institutional changes, pointing to more political union. But this is a slow process, and hard to achieve because of strong discrepancies (institutional, cultural, nationalistic sentiments, etc.). On the contrary, the austerity alternative can be put into practice at the national level, though its likely outcomes are stagnation and rising unemployment, because fiscal cuts and improving competitiveness to ease the balance of payments constraint will tighten domestic demand. Furthermore, the austerity option, which aims at balancing the public budget to avoid default risks as a precondition for restoring macroeconomic equilibrium, will fail to attain its target because public revenue will plummet.

The causes of the crisis in Spain: accumulated imbalances during the booming period

After having enjoyed an outstanding period of prosperity from 1997 to mid 2007, Spain officially fell into recession in the last quarter of 2008, when GDP showed a second negative quarterly rate of growth. After seven quarters with negative growth rates (between 2008:2 to 2009:4), the current GDP yearly growth ratio (fourth quarter of 2011 with respect to the same quarter of 2010) is –0.2 per cent, and the prospect for 2012 and 2013 is rather gloomy: according to the IMF (2012), it is –1.8 per cent and +0.1 per cent for GDP growth rate.

The true cause of the current state of affairs lies in the accumulation of imbalances during the booming period which, in turn, were the outcome of an unsustainable pattern of growth, driven by household indebtedness. Other factors, such as the financial turmoil caused by the debacle of the American subprime mortgages, or the sovereign debt crisis deepened the downturn aggravating these problems but they did not cause the crash.

Figure 12.1 illustrates what has happened in Spain from 1997 to mid 2007.[1]

In 1997, household borrowing (from banks) began to grow making indebtedness relative to household gross disposable income increase, particularly to fund the purchase of a house (and to a lesser extent to fund the import of consumer goods). Two main factors explain this fact. In the mid 1990s, baby boomers reached their 30s, the age at which people used to purchase a house in Spain, and the implementation of the euro, through the Maastricht criteria, led to falling interest rates and fostered

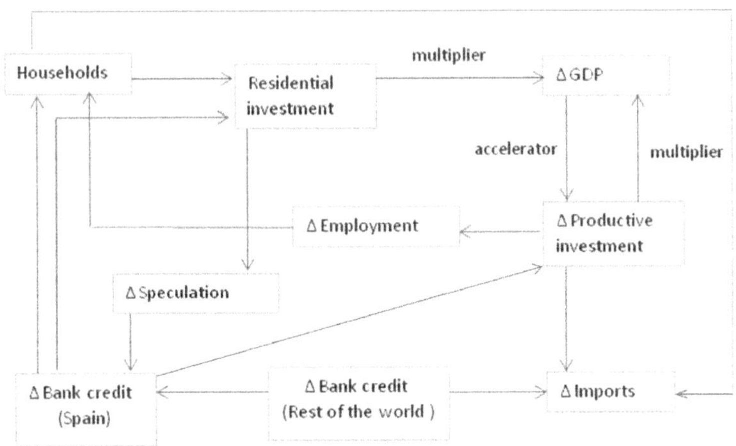

Figure 12.1 Accumulated imbalances: Spain 1997–2007.

financial capital movements within countries in the future euro zone, thus giving rise to an extraordinary expansive monetary policy for Spain.

The shift in the demand for houses led to two related reactions within the supply side: on the one hand, the number of dwellings increased hugely, making GDP and employment grow spectacularly; as a matter of fact, the multiplier in the construction sector is the largest one. On the other hand, house prices sky-rocketed, making way for speculative activities.

When GDP grows, productive investment grows, as explained by the theory of the accelerator (Baddeley, 2003, Dejuán, 2005) which, combined with the multiplier, makes GDP grow even faster. Nevertheless, more than half of the demand of productive investment was covered by imports (as the Spanish symmetric input–output tables for 1995, 2000 and 2005 show). A high growth of GDP involves a large growth in employment, chiefly when the rate of growth of productivity is low, as it is in the building sector. Growing employment further encourages households to purchase a house. And the rising prices of houses makes it profitable for developers to purchase land in the present and sell houses in the near future, making a capital gain on land, plus an ordinary profit on building, even more in a context of easy lending criteria. Although purchasing a standard house requires growing indebtedness, the low initial level does not pose any obstacle to this growth pattern. And the growing current account imbalance is offset by a huge financial capital inflow from core-EMU countries.

Therefore, Spain experienced a virtuous circle linking GDP, employment and the real estate sector which lasted for a decade or so, and also contained the seeds for what was to come next. The current meltdown is the consequence of three intertwined, accumulated imbalances during the prosperous decade:

- very high private indebtedness (non-financial corporations and households),
- the construction sector became too big,
- very large current account deficit and indebtedness to the rest of the world (especially of financial institutions).

Regarding the first imbalance, Table 12.1 offers a summary of this. Private indebtedness increases almost three times more than GDP between 1997 and 2007, with borrowing related to construction representing almost 50 per cent of total private debt in 2007.

Public indebtedness shows an inverse trend: it falls markedly when private indebtedness rises. Additionally, total debt with the rest of the world trebles during the prodigious decade, with financial assets owned by the rest of the world rounding 160 per cent GDP in 2007.

And growing general indebtedness has a single root: a strong demand for houses by households, which is amplified by the demand for land by developers, for speculative purposes.

The second imbalance, the excessive size of the construction industry, can be seen in the Table 12.2 (see also Table 12.5). The construction sector grew twice more than GDP during ten years: a pace which was difficult to maintain.

Table 12.1 Indebtedness over GDP: Spain, 1997–2011

	1997	*2000*	*2003*	*2005*	*2007*	*2011*
Households[1]	35.37%	47.18%	58.65%	73.35%	84.54%	81.73%
Non financial corporations[1,2]	47.22%	77.63%	91.82%	106.89%	133.92%	134.89%
(Construction and real estate)[1]	29.42%	40.95%	54.57%	79.87%	104.20%	98.37%
(Corporate construction and real estate)[1]	8.35%	12.34%	18.69%	29.50%	44.07%	37.05%
Total private (non-financial)[1,2]	82.59%	124.81%	150.47%	180.25%	218.46%	216.62%
Government[2]	60.41%	54.34%	46.55%	42.89%	33.74%	62.78%
Financial institutions[1,2]	8.47%	14.43%	28.65%	59.92%	97.79%	105.05%
Total	151.46%	193.58%	225.67%	283.06%	349.99%	384.45%
Held by domestic agents[1,2]	124.85%	151.41%	167.55%	197.50%	240.69%	281.68%
Held by the rest of the world[1,2]	26.62%	43.83%	58.38%	85.62%	109.96%	102.76%
Total debt held by the rest of the world[3]	57.59%	87.50%	106.97%	136.39%	160.91%	167.81%

Source: Banco de España, INE and authors' calculations.

Notes
1 Bank loans.
2 Securities other than shares.
3 Bank deposits, loans, securities other than shares, trade credit, insurance and reserves.
The row 'Construction and real estate' accounts for all credits granted by banks and used to fund operations related to construction, including household purchases of houses, developers' purchase of land or corporate disbursements to build a new house. 'Corporate construction and real estate' stands for bank lending to corporations in the real estate industry.

Table 12.2 GDP: demand side, 1997:1–2011:4

	Growth rate (% yoy)	*Accumulated change (1997:1 = 100)*	*Accumulated change (2008:2 = 100)*
	1997:1 to 2007:2	*1997:1 to 2007:2*	*2008:2 to 2011:4*
GDP	**3.85**	**46.97%**	**–4.14%**
Consumption	4.09	51.98%	–3.48%
Consumption, households	3.94	49.58%	–6.16%
Consumption Government	4.54	59.32%	4.77%
Gross fixed capital (GFK)	6.62	96.46%	–30.62%
GFK Equipment goods	7.44	112.90%	–26.50%
GFK Construction Dwellings	**7.53**	**107.43%**	**–38.03%**
GFK Other constructions	5.23	72.88%	–29.43%
GFK Other products	6.85	97.49%	–20.67%
Exports	6.47	81.27%	7.55%
Imports	9.47	152.33%	–15.53%

Source: INE and authors' calculations.

The reader will realize that the rate of growth of GDP during the prosperous decade between 1997 and 2007 reached 3.85 per cent per year, on average. In this period of time, the housing industry grew twice as much as GDP. However, the demand for houses fell dramatically in the last four years, dragging GDP.[2]

Finally, during the buoyant period the Spanish economy accumulated a huge current account imbalance.

The Spanish current account balance reached a deficit equivalent to 10 per cent GDP: the largest in percentage terms of GDP of OECD countries and the second largest one in absolute terms, after the US economy. Although its unit labour costs have increased substantially, leading to a loss of competitiveness, the main explanatory variable for the current account deficit is the rate of growth of GDP: otherwise, the share in world exports should have declined. Also, it should be noted that the rising unit labour costs took place simultaneously with a large falling labour share of almost five percentage points of GDP: prices rise faster than wages minus productivity, because of a lack of competition in goods and services markets.

As a consequence of this accumulated current account deficit, the international investment position for the Spanish economy, in net terms, is in the red, having reached a net debt to the rest of the world amounting to almost 90 per cent GDP (in gross terms, it rounds 160 per cent).

When private debts to the rest of the world, mostly held by banks, are due for payment, and creditors do not wish to refinance them, and the economy lacks a national central bank, there is a serious risk of default. This risk is even larger when the economy is running a current account deficit and the rate of non-performing loans rises, because of the burst of the real estate bubble. In this situation, if the government provides guarantees to banks (issuing public debt and then lending the collected funds to banks, aiming at keeping bank credit flowing, or simply guaranteeing deposits), then the risk of private default turns into the risk of public default. The outcome is a banking sector restricting the credit supply when the asset side of their balance sheets is shrinking and investors of the rest of the world are withdrawing funds.

If we had to choose one main factor unleashing all the aforementioned imbalances, this is, as pointed out above, the booming residential investment by households during the Golden decade between 1997 and 2007. The chief arguments affecting the purchase of so many houses are encapsulated in Table 12.4.

Table 12.4 shows that in the ten years from 1997 to 2007, the population (especially baby boomers, who reach their 30s in this period, the age at which people used to purchase a house in Spain) increases by 5.6 million people (specifically, the number of people over 25 increases more than 6.5 million). Banks grant mortgage loans at a steadily declining interest rate, with increasingly longer maturities and under much easier credit standards. This makes it possible, despite house prices almost trebling from 1997 to 2007, for the debt effort to remain almost flat until the end of 2005, and then for it to go up because the ECB raises the interest rate at the end of 2005 (due to fears of inflation because of the hike in raw material prices). This strong demand was matched with an amazing supply: between January 1997 and December 2007 almost 6.25 million dwellings were initiated. Developers

Table 12.3 Evolution of current accounts and their main determinants

	1997	*2000*	*2003*	*2005*	*2007*	*2010*
Spain						
Current account balance[1]	0.14%	–4.02%	–4.03%	–7.46%	–10.00%	–4.52%
GDP growth rate	4.70%	4%	3.20%	3.80%	3.20%	0.60%
Unit labour costs	100	101.46	111.69	118.31	124.70	137.45
Adjusted labour share	60.04%	58.87%	56.94%	55.62%	55.60%	55.75%
Share in world exports[2]	100	103.59	122.53	112.74	112.88	100.75
Net financial assets[1]	–25.66%	–32.00%	–45.24%	–55.59%	–78.13%	–89.54%
Germany						
Current account balance[1]	–0.45%	–1.63%	2.05%	5.23%	7.64%	5.06%
GDP growth rate	1.80%	3.21%	–0.22%	0.75%	2.66%	3.63%
Unit labour costs	100	101.57	104.02	102.60	100.87	107.65
Adjusted labour share	59.87%	60.56%	59.59%	57.77%	55.09%	57.27%
Share in world exports[2]	100	91.01	109.00	106.33	108.96	101.70
Net financial assets[1]	4.13%	3.27%	6.61%	21.04%	26.50%	38.41%
France						
Current account balance[1]	2.55%	1.11%	0.25%	–1.79%	–2.22%	–3.46%
GDP growth rate	2.24%	3.91%	1.09%	1.90%	2.37%	1.58%
Unit labour costs	100	106.40	116.28	123.05	132.24	137.94
Adjusted labour share	57.53%	57.29%	57.46%	57.55%	56.84%	58.66%
Share in world exports[2]	100	93.24	94.54	81.38	73.44	63.30
Net financial assets[1]	10.02%	18.51%	0.65%	1.13%	–1.48%	–9.96%
US						
Current account balance[1]	–1.69%	–4.18%	–4.66%	–5.90%	–5.06%	–3.24%
GDP growth rate	4.46%	4.14%	2.54%	3.07%	1.91%	3.03%
Unit labour costs	100	107.95	112.96	117.02	124.01	126.06
Adjusted labour share	61.31%	63.17%	62.18%	60.59%	60.57%	59.30%
Share in world exports[2]	100	101.34	85.32	77.97	75.84	78.07

Sources: AMECO, IMF, WTO, Eurostat and authors' calculations.

Notes
1 Net financial investment position, as a percentage of GDP.
2 Merchandise and services exports.

Table 12.4 Main factors affecting the demand for houses

	1997	*2000*	*2003*	*2005*	*2007*	*2010*
Interest (real, long term)	3.92%	2.01%	–0.04%	–0.91%	1.01%	3.83%
Maturity mortgage (years)	19	22	24	25	28	25
Population (thousands)	39583.4	40264.2	42717.1	44108.5	45200.7	46072.8
Unemployment	16.7%	11.1%	11.1%	9.2%	8.3%	20.1%
Ownership	–	84.54%	84.08%	86.28%	–	–
Debt effort (percentage income)	23.6%	22.7%	23.9%	27.7%	39.7%	27.2%
Price m^2 nominal (euros)	702.8	893.3	1380.3	1824.3	2085.5	1825.5
Price m^2 (real) base year: 1997	702.8	813.1	1145.4	1413.3	1514.8	1260.2

Source: Banco de España, AMECO, INE, Colegio de Registradores de la Propiedad y Mercantiles de España and authors' calculations.

Notes

The real interest rate has been deflated using the GDP deflator. The rate of ownership represents the percentage of population living in a house of their own. Debt effort accounts for the percentage of disposable income (after tax deductions) which a median household has to set aside to settle debt services caused by the purchase of a house, per year.

become indebted to purchase land and next they built houses convinced that banks would grant credit to house buyers with some lag (between 18 and 24 months) giving rise to the possibility of making a profit plus a capital gain on the buying and selling of land. Actually, the price of houses could not have risen to such an extent without the willingness of banks to grant larger mortgages, as Figure 12.2 shows.[3]

Officially the Spanish economy entered a period of recession, at the end of 2008, though prosperity ended in mid 2007, because of the end of the boom in the construction industry. The following factors are relevant.

- The ECB begins to raise interest rates at the end of 2005, because of fears of inflation caused by hikes in raw material prices, shifting from 2 per cent in November 2005 to 4.25 per cent in July 2008, for main refinancing operations.
- The real estate market had become rather saturated. In 2007, more than 400000 dwellings remain unsold, and in 2008, 200000 more dwellings are added to this stock.
- Households had become highly indebted in 2007. As Table 12.1 shows, household debt reached 84.54 per cent GDP in that year, whilst it was 35.37 per cent ten years before.
- House prices are really high in 2007. At the end of 2007 the price of one square metre of a new dwelling is 23.7 per cent more expensive than at the beginning of 2005, and 200 per cent higher than at the beginning of 1997.

When the demand for new houses stops the construction industry comes to a standstill and, through the multiplier, GDP slows down; next, through the

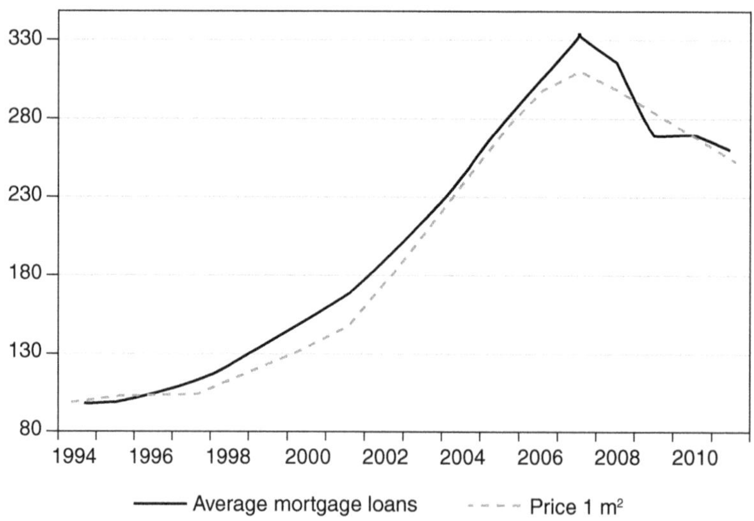

Figure 12.2 House prices and mortgage loans: Spain, 1994–2010 (index 1994=100) (source: Banco de España, Colegio de Registradores de la Propiedad y Mercantiles de España and authors' calculations).

accelerator, investment demand comes to a standstill dragging GDP down. The vicious circle closes when unemployment rises, further weakening the demand for residential investment and making the rate of non-performing loans to rise.

After the party comes the hangover: consequences of the accumulated imbalances

When the locomotive of residential investment lacks fuel, the train of the economy suddenly stops. But what is coming next? The post real estate bubble Spanish economy faces three problems:

- The skyrocketing debt accumulated in the recent past has to be settled. Debt service payments are a forced saving which will drag aggregate demand for a long period of time. Private spending, particularly household consumption, will be weak in the near future.
- The construction industry had become too big for its boots. When the bubble bursts, and the construction industry starts getting back to *normal* figures, a lot of workers become unemployed, not only in the building sector but also, through the multiplier, in other related industries. The pattern of growth should be changed.
- As output and employment fall, some borrowers cannot pay back debts to banks and the price of houses (used as collateral for loans) declines. This makes the asset side of banks' balance sheets shrink. In addition, when the financial crisis caused by the American toxic mortgages spreads all over the world, Spanish banks face increasing problems to get funds in money and interbank markets. As a result, they tighten credit standards to borrowers. Financial straits are amplified by the fact that investors (and Spanish savers) begin, in mid 2007, to shift their funds to safer harbours (especially Germany).

Lack of effective demand

We present this factor with a simple model, akin to (though not equal to) the Sraffian supermultiplier (see for instance Bortis (1997), Cesaratto *et al.* (2003) or Dejuán (2005)).

We shall assume an open economy with government and private sectors. Also we shall assume that inflation only exists in the housing market; the rest of commodities are traded at constant prices (this is only for simplicity). We assume the Keynesian principle of effective demand:

$$Y_t = AD_t \tag{12.1}$$

where Y_t is GDP and AD_t is aggregate demand. Next,

$$AD_t = C_t + I_t^R + I_t^P + G_t + NX_t \tag{12.2}$$

with C_t being consumption, I^R_t residential investment, I^P_t productive investment, G_t public spending and XN_t net exports.

Regarding consumption:

$$C_t = c(wL_{t-1} - DSP_t) \tag{12.3}$$

On the right hand side of this expression we have c as the (average) propensity to consume, w is the (average) nominal wage, L is employment and DSP accounts for debt service payments corresponding to past household borrowing.

With respect to residential investment:

$$I_t^R = p_{H_t} \Delta H_t \tag{12.4}$$

where p_H is the price of a house and ΔH is the increase in the number of houses in period t.

We shall assume that the purchase of a house is fully funded with bank borrowing. Hence:

$$\Delta D_t = p_{H_t} \Delta H_t \tag{12.5}$$

Next, concerning productive investment, we decompose it into two factors, the first one accounts for modernization of capacity, and it is treated as an independent factor, whilst the second factor depends on the accelerator, and informs about adjusting capacity to expected demand:

$$I_t^P = I_0 + v[Y_t^e - Y_{t-1}] = I_0 + v[Y_{t-1}(1+g^e) - Y_{t-1}] = I_0 + v \cdot g^e \cdot Y_{t-1} \tag{12.6}$$

where g^e stands for the expected growth rate of GDP.

G_t, for public spending, is taken as an exogenous variable and net exports, NX_t, depends on an autonomous factor, NX_0, the differential between domestic price inflation and inflation in the rest of the European Monetary Union, (EMU), $(p_t - p_t^{EMU})$, and the level of output (we assume, for the sake of simplicity, that Spain only trades with other countries within the EMU, with which it shares the same currency):

$$NX_t = NX_0 - x(p_t - p_t^{EMU}) - mY_{t-1} \tag{12.7}$$

Considering (12.1) to (12.7), and rearranging, we have:

$$Y_t = \left[c \cdot \frac{wL_{t-1}}{Y_{t-1}} + v \cdot g^e - m \right] Y_{t-1} + \left[I_0 + G_t + NX_0 - x(p_t - p_t^{EMU}) + \left\{ \frac{\Delta D_t}{p_{H_t}} - c \cdot DSP_t \right\} \right] \tag{12.8}$$

We divide new borrowing (as in expression (12.5)) by the price of houses in order to account for the output at constant prices which this new borrowing puts in motion.

We obtain a first order difference equation. If the term $[c(wL_{t-1}/Y_{t-1})+v\cdot g^e-m]$ is stable, and lower than one, the economy is driven by:[4]

$$\left[I_0 + G_t + NX_0 - x(p_t - p_t^{EMU}) + \left\{ \frac{\Delta D_t}{p_{H_t}} - c \cdot DSP_t \right\} \right]$$

Further, under the assumption that the term $[I_0+G_t+NX_0-x\ (p_t-p_t^{EMU})]$ remains stable, and the propensity to consume is close to unit, the economy is driven by the difference between new borrowing (deflated by the price of houses) and debt service payments:

$$\left\{ \frac{\Delta D_t}{p_{H_t}} - c \cdot DSP_t \right\}$$

In Figure 12.3, the solid line for new borrowing represents all new bank borrowing by households (including short-term credit, mortgage loans and other long-term loans) deflated by its corresponding deflator (short-term credit by HICP, mortgage loans by household prices and other long-term loans by the industrial price index), and divided by household gross disposable income (deflated as well, by the GDP deflator). The broken line represents debt service

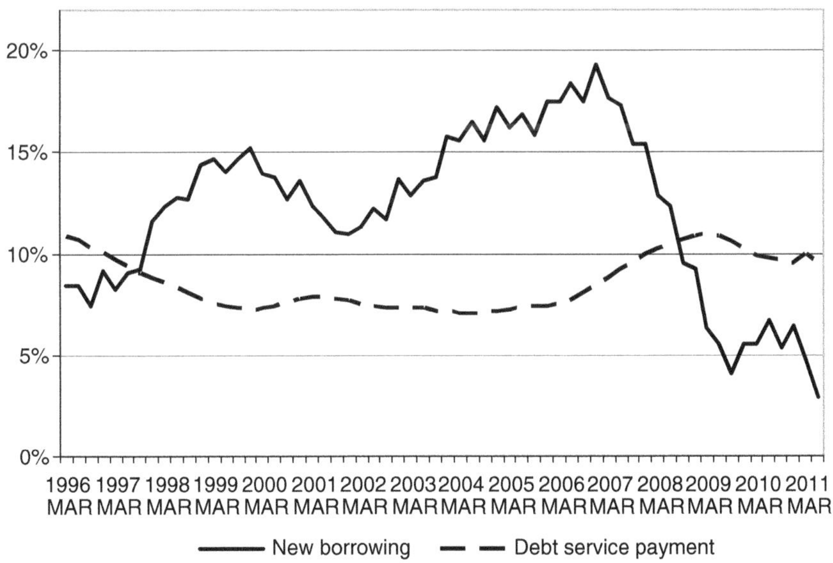

Figure 12.3 New borrowing and debt service payments over household disposable income: deflated; Spain, 1996–2011 (source: Banco de España, INE and authors' calculations).

payments by households, deflated by HICP, and also divided by the household real gross disposable income. New borrowing reaches its maximum at the end of 2006, then declines, and it crosses debt service payments in late 2008, which is when, officially, the Spanish economy enters into recession. This figure illustrates the problem of effective demand: although new borrowing has fallen to the bottom, forced saving to settle debt is going to stay for a long period of time.

If we subtract real debt service payment from real new borrowing, we obtain net (real) new borrowing, by households. This variable informs us about the difference between monetary efflux caused by borrowing and monetary reflux due to debt settlement. It measures output put in motion by households, divided by household disposable income. And it explains quite well the evolution of GDP and employment during the boom and the subsequent downturn (Figure 12.4).

However, the rebound of GDP and employment which takes place in mid 2009 is not explained by household net borrowing. Actually, it is mainly due to the timid Keynesian policy implemented from 2008 to May 2010, and also due to exports (see Table 12.2, and Figure 12.7, below).

The construction industry becomes too large

Residential investment pulled the economy during the Golden decade and the construction industry became too large. And when the real estate bubble burst, it got back to its normal level. This readjustment led to almost 50 per cent of the increase in unemployment figures (Table 12.5).

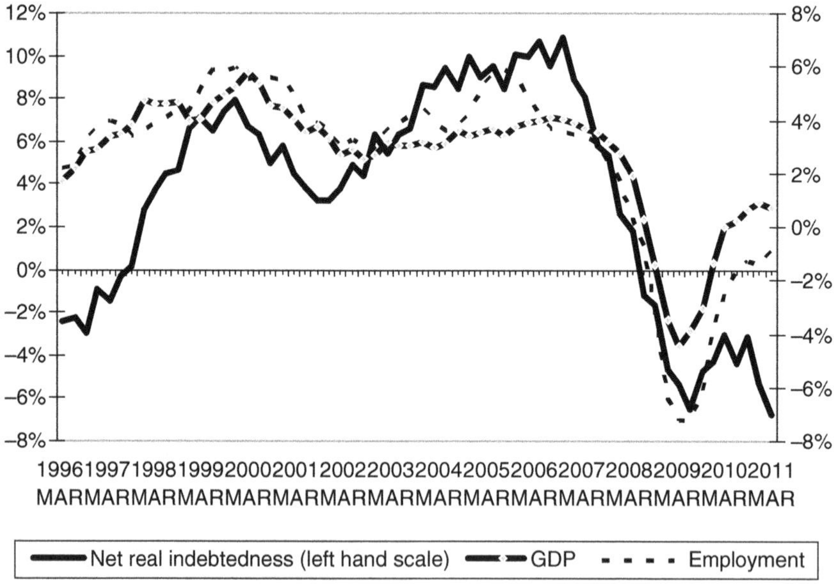

Figure 12.4 Net real borrowing, GDP and employment (source: Banco de España, INE and authors' calculations).

Table 12.5 Employment (thousands) and percentages on total employment

	Spain						*European Union*					
	1997		*2007*		*2010*		*1997*		*2007*		*2010*	
Agriculture	1068	8.04%	925	4.55%	793	4.30%	7316	4.87%	12207	5.59%	11112	5.13%
Industry	2653	19.98%	3262	16.02%	2613	14.16%	32721	21.79%	42450	19.45%	39167	18.10%
Construction	1318	9.93%	2697	13.25%	1651	8.94%	11715	7.80%	17915	8.21%	16570	7.66%
Services	8237	62.04%	13471	66.18%	13400	72.60%	98424	65.54%	145728	66.76%	149555	69.11%
Total	13276	100.%	20356	100%	18456	100%	150176	100%	218300	100%	216405	100%

Source: Eurostat and authors' calculations.

This means that one of the traditional locomotives for the Spanish economy (and not only for that economy: see Leamer, 2007) has been knocked out for a long period of time.[5]

Banks stop granting credit

The model stated in expression (12.8) provides an explanation for economic fluctuations combining a flow and a stock of debt (the latter 'generates' a flow of debt service payments: see Bhaduri, 2011). However, it leaves aside one important point: how do banks react to these fluctuations and what are the consequences of banks' reactions?

Table 12.6 provides some relevant information about the evolution of banks in Spain. In this table, we gain some interesting insights. First, from 1997 to 2007, credit grows much faster than GDP, with loans to construction (to fund the building industry, real estate services or the purchase of houses by households) growing at a very strong pace. Also, loans grow faster than deposits. The profitability of the financial corporations, measured by the return on equity (RoE) grows from 15.25 to 20.77. The rate of non-performing loans to total credit remains quite low. And the TARGET2 balance, which when it is negative indicates that the central bank[6] has to provide liquidity to financial corporations in order to make possible the cancellation of debts to other banks in the EMU,[7] remains quite low, because the huge current account deficit is compensated by a very large inflow of financial capital.[8]

Table 12.6 Financial corporations: Spain, billion euros

	1997	*2007*	*2009*	*2011*
Spanish GDP (nominal)	505	1053	1048	1070
Bank credit to households and non-financial corporations	345	1760	1837	1789
Credit to productive activities	198	943	991	951
Credit to households	145	789	813	794
Credit to construction, real estate and purchase of houses	145	1081	1108	1061
Non-performing loans	8[1]	16	93	128
Return on equity	15.25%	20.7%	8.03%	2.4%[3]
TARGET2	11[2]	–4	–34	–150
Loans/deposits	56.68%	85.31%	77.90%	77.77%
Bank liabilities owned by RoW/ total liabilities	17.36%	29.19%	27.97%	26.49%

Source: Banco de España.

Notes
1 December 1998.
2 January 1999.
3 Average of the four quarters of 2011.

However, from 2007 to the present, things worsen considerably. On the one hand, the credit supply slows down. And non-performing-loans get multiplied by eight, mostly because of developers' and builders' default. As defaults rise, the profitability of banks falls; and as the Spanish economy is not giving any signs of recovery, many agents are moving their financial investments to safer harbours. Hence the liabilities to the TARGET2 increase substantially, currently reaching 14 per cent GDP. Consequently, banks stop granting credit for two reasons: on the one hand, there is no solvent borrowing demand; household borrowing does not grow, nor does non-financial corporations' borrowing, since the prospects they face are rather gloomy. Only the government is managing to find some bank funding. On the other hand, banks cannot raise funds in bonds and money markets because they are perceived to have serious difficulties to pay back debts in the near future (it is very difficult to know how much banks are affected by the burst of the real estate bubble), and because of the absence of economic growth. In this situation, two additional factors have contributed to the fall in bank lending: the sovereign debt crisis is affecting banks' assets negatively, and the new Basel Agreements (or Basel III) which required banks to increase their equity in relation to assets.

In essence, banks' behaviour is being procyclical. Thus, to falling household spending, due to forced saving to settle bank debt, and to firms declining investment demand because of the pessimistic expectations for future effective demand, we must add falling bank lending which drags aggregate demand even further in a context of recession.

What should be done to bring the Spanish economy back to pre-downturn figures?

Spain has a problem of effective demand, in a context which requires restoring competitiveness and reducing private leverage. This means 'squaring the circle'.

According to expression (12.8) above, GDP is ruled by the Keynesian principle of effective demand, where we can single out an autonomous demand, given by:

$$\left[I_0 + G_t + NX_0 - x(p_t - p_t^{EMU}) + \left\{\frac{\Delta D_t}{p_{H_t}} - c \cdot DSP_t\right\}\right] \tag{12.9}$$

$$Y_t = \left[c \cdot \frac{wL_{t-1}}{Y_{t-1}} + v \cdot g^e - m\right] Y_{t-1} + \left[I_0 + G_t + NX_0 - x(p_t - p_t^{EMU})\right.$$

$$\left. + \left\{\frac{\Delta D_t}{p_{H_t}} - c \cdot DSP_t\right\}\right]$$

All factors are given in real terms, with ΔD_t, which accounts for household borrowing (for residential purposes).

If the root of the Great Recession in Spain is a lack of effective demand, as we defend, the recommendation of economic policy is clear; though, the accumulated imbalances, the institutional setting and the context in which the Spanish economy is embedded pose some constraints to the solutions which could be implemented.

We have set aside, from the beginning, the management of the interest rate and the exchange rate of our currency for obvious reasons.[9]

All the following measures increase demand:

- technical change, which encourages firms to invest in order to modernize capacity, as encapsulated in factor I_0;
- expansive fiscal policy, G_t;
- expansive demand policies in partner countries, thus increasing Spanish exports, NX_0;
- improving competitiveness, making domestic inflation fall relative to inflation in partner countries, in order to increase net exports, $-x(p_t - p_t^{EMU})$: it should be noted that this can be achieved either reducing p_t or, alternatively, by increasing p_t^{EMU};
- stimulating residential investment (reducing the price of houses, reducing taxes on house purchases, subsidizing house prices, etc.), increasing the factor $\Delta D_t / p_{Ht}$;
- reducing debt service payments, $c \cdot DSP_t$: reducing interest rates, increasing maturities on outstanding bank debt, and, especially, increasing domestic inflation so that there will be a redistribution in favour of borrowers at the expense of lenders.

With regard to these measures, increasing investment for the modernization of capacity and stimulating residential investment are no longer feasible options for restoring prosperity. The first one is not under the control of economic authorities in the short run and the second one is difficult to implement, once the market is saturated (almost 700000 dwellings unsold, according to official figures). Implementing expansive demand policies and increasing inflation in neighbouring countries requires cooperation from surplus countries in the euro zone. These measures would allow the Spanish economy to grow without increasing indebtedness.

The remaining ones, particularly expansive fiscal policy and increasing domestic inflation are interesting options, though difficult to put in practice by a single nation belonging to the EMU especially those with a current account deficit, and with a dubious effect on output and employment because of *secondary effects*. Fiscal policy will lead to crowding out: increasing public debt will widen the spread with German bonds, leading to more expensive funding for private corporations and households (Figure 12.5). This is because the government would have to issue debt in a currency which is not under its control (see

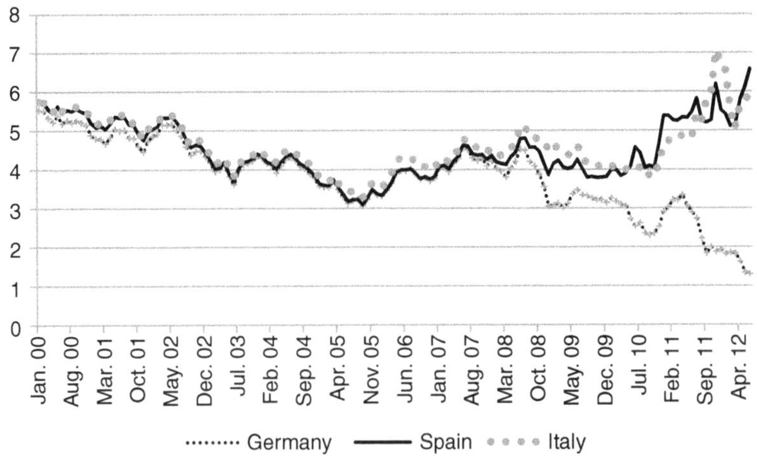

Figure 12.5 Ten-year bond yields: Germany, Italy and Spain (source: Banco de España).

De Grauwe, 2011; Kelton, 2011), and an important fraction of this debt is held by non-resident investors, despite the level of public debt over GDP in Spain is lower than in larger EMU countries.

And regarding growing domestic inflation, whilst it could reduce the burden of debt servicing on households, it would have a negative impact on the trade balance, thus requiring further borrowing in international markets. This is no longer feasible, because the Spanish economy is already heavily indebted to the rest of the world, a great deal of bank assets are not performing and, additionally, the Spanish Treasury is unable to provide support to a fund guaranteeing all bank deposits.

Therefore, it becomes aparent that expansive fiscal policies cum inflation in trade surplus countries of the core EMU plus an active ECB granting the liquidity which the interbank market is not providing are a feasible and useful option to put the wheels of the Spanish economy in motion.

Table 12.2 and Figure 12.7 (below) show that public consumption in 2008 and 2009, and exports since 2010 are the components of aggregate demand which are pulling the Spanish economy since it fell into recession, in 2008. However, it looks like being insufficient to leave the situation of low growth. Further, as most EMU countries are adopting fiscal consolidation measures, these sources of growth are no longer expected to work in the short to medium term, leading all agents to expect a new contraction of output and employment in the next two years.

And what is being done to get out of the current mess?

We can clearly distinguish two periods, regarding the economic policy put in practice by the Spanish government: before and after May 2010, when the Greek economy falls officially into crisis, then followed by Ireland (November) and Portugal (May 2011).

In 2008 and 2009, the Spanish government adopted an expansive, Keynesian fiscal policy, following recommendations of the G-20, the IMF and the European Plan for Economic Recovery, and provided some liquidity support to banks, with a view to keeping credit flowing.

Spain's government budget, which has traditionally been in the red, had enjoyed a fiscal surplus in 2005, 2006 and 2007, ranging around roughly 2 per cent GDP. However, two years later, in 2009, the fiscal deficit became 11.2 per cent GDP.

We can clearly see in Figure 12.6 and Table 12.7 two facts. First, the fiscal deficit in 2008 and onwards, is the consequence of the crisis, not its cause. Actually, revenue is greater than expenditure during the three years prior to the crisis. And second, whilst public expenditure kept on growing at a roughly stable pace until 2009, revenue fell sharply during the recession, thus leading to a loss of fiscal space in a very short period of time (there has been a ratchet effect: public spending has grown *pari passu* with revenue, driven in its turn by a booming real estate market; when the latter burst, revenues fell though public spending could not be reduced in similar proportions). The public budget shifted from a surplus of 1.9 per cent GDP to a –11.2 per cent GDP deficit, with public debt rising 17 percentage points of GDP, to 53.8 per cent GDP.

More than 50 per cent of the increase in the public deficit in 2009, in relation to 2007, is due to a fall in public revenue, mostly because of its strong dependence on real estate activities, but also due to automatic stabilizers.[10] And, in a period of strong private deleverage, falling taxes have a low

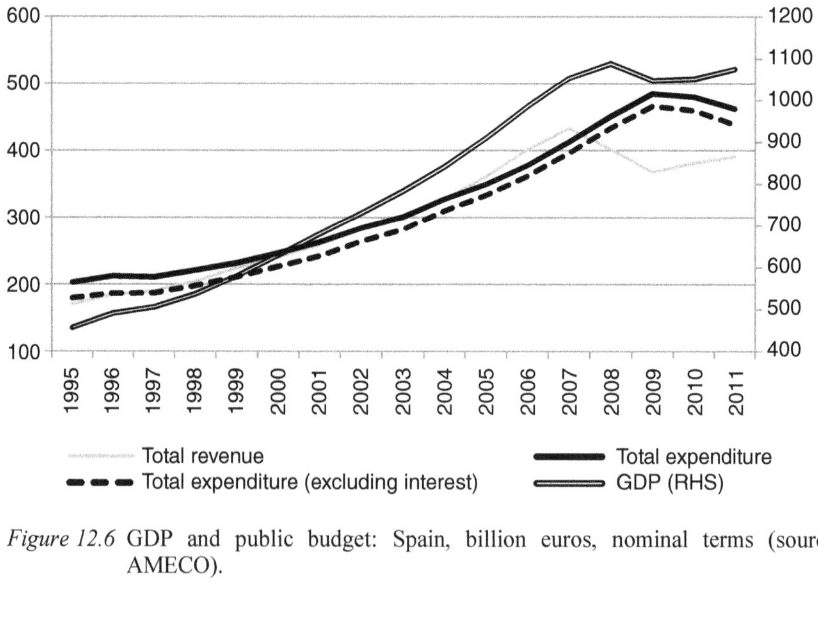

Figure 12.6 GDP and public budget: Spain, billion euros, nominal terms (source: AMECO).

Table 12.7 GDP, public budget and public debt: real terms, base year 2006

	GDP	*Public spending (% GDP)*	*Interest on debt (% GDP)*	*Public revenue (% GDP)*	*Budget deficit (% GDP)*	*Public debt (% GDP)*
2006	100	38.4	1.7	40.7	2.3%	39.6%
2007	103.5	40.6	1.7	42.5	1.9%	36.2%
2008	104.4	43.3	1.7	38.6	–4.5%	40.1%
2009	100.6	46.5	1.7	35.3	–11.1%	53.8%
2010	100.5	45.8	1.9	36.5	–9.3%	61.2%
2011	101.2	44.1	2.4	35.5	–8.5%	68.5%
Change 2009–2007	–2.83%	14.52%	3.72%	–17.02%	–13.0%	17.6%

Source: AMECO and authors' elaboration.

multiplier effect on output. Regarding expenditure, the government focused on activities related to the construction industry (mostly repairs of urban infrastructures) which had a short-term effect on employment and had little impact in terms of output.[11]

The other measure developed by the government was the provision of liquidity to troubled financial firms (especially saving banks, or *cajas*) through the *Fondo de Adquisición de Activos Financieros* (FAAF or Fund to Purchase Financial Assets) and the provision of guarantees to banks when they borrowed in financial markets, which was quantitatively low, relative to other EMU countries (see European Commission, 2009: 63).

However, since May 2010, the government, under pressure from the European Commission, made a U-turn: it continues providing support to financial institutions though, regarding fiscal policy, it shifts towards austerity, and introduces some supply side reforms (especially in the labour market) with the hope that the latter will compensate for the former in the long run.

Regarding support to financial institutions, the government changes from liquidity support to restructuring the sector with additional help to recapitalize banks and a restructuration of the sector creating the *Fondo de Restructuración Ordenada Bancaria* (FROB, or fund for restoring order in the banking sector, through mergers, reducing public control on the *Cajas*, reforming stress tests, adopting new Basel Agreements which involve higher capital ratios, increasing the provision coverage of financial assets related to the real estate market, better and greater transparency, etc. See Carbó and Maudos, 2011).

With respect to fiscal austerity and structural reforms, the Spanish government adopts the *Euro Plus Pact* and the *European Semester* (see European Commission, 2011). In essence:

- Fiscal consolidation and sustainability of public accounts in the long run:
  - reducing social expenditure, especially in health and education;
  - reducing public sector wages;

- increasing direct and indirect taxes;
- reforming the pension system, delaying the retirement age, reducing pension benefits and making it harder to retire before the legal age;
- legislative changes to prohibit *excessive* fiscal deficits.

- Reforms in the labour market, aiming at increasing competitiveness and reducing dualism (between insiders and outsiders):

  - reducing firing costs;
  - increasing the circumstances under which firms can opt out of collective wage bargaining;
  - allowing private employment agencies to operate in the labour market;
  - subsidizing the hiring of young unemployed people.

This shift in economic policy from Keynesian to austerity measures is caused by the fear of a sovereign debt default due to (i) the rapid increase in public debt in 2008 and 2009 and (ii) the risk that private debt (mostly held by banks) becomes public debt when the government provides financial support to banks in order to make credit keep flowing.

To sum up. Authorities have reacted to the Great Recession, after the onset of the Greek crisis, assuming that (i) fiscal consolidation is a necessary condition for recovery, (ii) rising unemployment can and must be solved by means of reforms in the labour market, (iii) current account imbalances are a consequence of wages growing faster than productivity and (iv) banks are not lending because of a lack of confidence in the funding markets. This appears to be in great contradiction with the thesis which we defend in this contribution: (a) the public deficit is the consequence of the recession, not its cause, and more public spending is required, (b) the Spanish economy was able to increase the amount of employment by 50 per cent between 1997 and 2007, with a given set of rules and institutions in the labour market, and it is not clear why such a labour market does not work now, (c) core European countries, with current account surpluses, are partially responsible for the imbalances at the EMU level, because of their restrictive policies since the mid 1990s (see Uxó *et al.*, 2011) and (d) banks are not lending because they cannot find solvent borrowers, and not only because they encounter problems when asking for funds in money markets (as the Bank Lending Survey for the third quarter of 2011 shows: see ECB, 2011). The economic growth of a country cannot be grounded on unlimited indebtedness, either private or public. Though, public spending should not be removed when private agents are deleveraging.

But, will austerity work?

This question raises another two. First, how cuts in public spending, plus reforms in the labour market, will affect the evolution of GDP? And second, what is the relation between GDP and the ability to settle debts when they are due for payment? According to the policy implemented by the government (ruled by the Socialist Party until November 2011 and the Conservative Party since then) the recovery in Spain is expected to occur through the following steps. First, it is assumed that fiscal consolidation will subtract aggregate demand to the whole economy, thus leading to a contraction, which should be added to the one caused by the bursting of the real estate bubble. However, this consolidation will revive confidence in financial markets if debts can be paid back as they mature, and then, the interest rate (related to long term public debt) will fall and funds will be become available, stimulating private components of aggregate demand. Second, the reforms in the labour market will bring some competitiveness as wages will become more aligned to productivity. This will add a positive contribution to output through the trade balance, and some additional reserves to pay back debt to the rest of the world. And as output begins to grow, and employment recovers, consumption will follow *pari passu* with employment. A rate of unemployment around 16 per cent is expected in 2014 (according to the Stability Programme for 2011–2014).

This account fits in well with the New Consensus or three-equations model.[12] The only alien element is the interest rate, which is not determined by a national central bank but by participants in the sovereign debt markets. Hence, confidence replaces the central bank making this interest rate fall when fiscal consolidation takes place.

There are two officially admitted related risks (IMF, 2010), within this strategy. (i) Fiscal consolidation is grounded on a rather optimistic view of the evolution of GDP. If forecasts are mistaken because a larger GDP growth was expected than actually happened, interest rates will not fall (and then public debt will crowd out private investment). (ii) If the fiscal consolidation is performed too fast and the subsequent recovery takes place slowly there is a risk of hysteresis, with output and employment stabilizing around too low a level. And another risk which is not taken into account is that the fall of GDP will make the rate of non-performing loans rise, giving rise to further problems to banks' lending.

In our view, these are not risks within a well-defined strategy, but the expected outcome of a programme unwillingly designed to keep the economy performing below socially acceptable levels of activity and employment. Fiscal consolidation has been dragging output since 2010. And a lower GDP reduces public revenue making it even harder to reach targets on the public budget balance and giving rise to a downward spiral, as Spain's recent experience is showing.[13] Actually, the stability programme for the Spanish economy from 2011 to 2014 projected a public deficit amounting to 6 per cent GDP in 2011, that has actually been 8.5 per cent GDP because of the insufficiency of effective demand needed to make GDP grow enough. And the expected lack of growth is leading rating agencies to downgrade public debt so that the spread with German *bunds* is not falling, despite the big fiscal effort (see Figure 12.5). Exports have been doing pretty well since the end of 2009 up to the present. However, they will not be able to take the relay baton of growing demand from public consumption (see Table 12.8 and expression (12.8) above), because of austerity in the rest of the EMU.

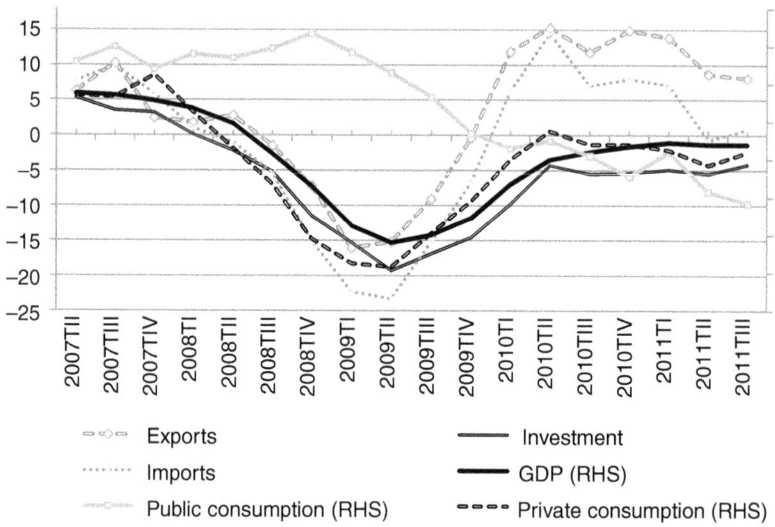

Figure 12.7 GDP, demand components, growth rates, real terms: Spain, 2007:2 to 2011:3 (source: INE and authors' calculations).

Further, when households are still heavily indebted to banks, an internal competitive devaluation aiming at stimulating exports, will do more harm than good because, as pointed out above, this will mean a redistribution in favour of creditors. Falling nominal wages, with debt servicing in nominal terms, will lead to a weaker demand for consumer goods, as household disposable income, net of debt settlements, fall (the Fisher effect). And falling inflation, when the nominal interest rate is not falling in a larger proportion (as the three-equations model holds, grounded on the Taylor's Rule) makes the real interest rate rise, further aggravating the situation.[14]

In a short period of time, the official projections about the evolution of GDP and its main components have changed dramatically, as Table 12.8 shows.

Contrary to the government's expectations, GDP did not grow at 1.3 per cent in 2011 and will not grow at 2.3 per cent in 2012, but the rate in 2011 was 0.7 per cent (0.5 percentage points lower) and it is now expected to grow at −1.7 per cent in 2012. Because of the lack of GDP growth, the target for the budget deficit could not be met (it has been 8.5 per cent GDP instead of the 6 per cent forecast). Private consumption and investment will recover neither in 2012, nor in the next year. And exports will not grow as expected in 2012, as indicated by the bottom row in Table 12.8, mostly because our neighbouring countries will implement austerity policies as well. Consequently, fiscal consolidation will shrink output, and will also shift the rate of unemployment upwards by roughly five percentage points.

And the absence of a central bank playing the role of lender of last resort, particularly providing guarantees to bank deposits, will make public debt rise as

Table 12.8 Official projections: Spanish government; stability programmes 2011–2014 and 2012–2015

	2010	*2011*	*2012*	*2013*
Spanish government's forecast April 2011				
GDP	–0.1	1.3	**2.3**	2.4
Budget balance	–9.2	**–6**	–4.4	–3
Revenue	37.7	36.7	37	37.5
Expenditure	45	42.7	41.4	40.5
Interest	1.9	2.2	2.5	2.7
Primary balance	–7.3	–3.8	–1.9	–0.3
Private consumption	1.2	0.9	1.4	1.6
Public consumption	–0.7	–1.3	–0.8	–0.6
Investment	–7	–1.3	2.7	3.7
Exports	10.3	8.3	7.9	7.2
Imports	5.4	3	4.1	4.7
Current account balance	–3.9	–3.4	–2.7	–2
Rate of unemployment	20.1	19.8	18.5	17.3
Spanish government's forecast April 2012				
GDP		0.7	**–1.7**	0.2
Private consumption		–0.1	–1.4	–1.1
Public consumption		–2.2	–8.0	–4.6
Investment		–5.1	–9.0	–0.5
Exports		9.0	3.5	6.9
Imports		–0.1	–5.1	1.3
Current account balance		–3.4	–0.9	0.8
Rate of unemployment		21.6	24.3	24.2
Budget balance		**–8.5**	–5.3	–3
Growth of Spanish exports markets		4.8	2.4	5.4

Source: Ministry of Finance.

the National Treasury assumes that role, because the rate of non-performing loans will increase *pari passu* with unemployment.

So is there any possibility of recovery? Some concluding remarks

Problems at the EMU level require solutions at the EMU level. The main problem of the Spanish economy is that of lack of effective demand, as a consequence of the aforementioned excessive private indebtedness, in a context of high (private) indebtedness to the rest of the world, when international financial markets are frozen. The Spanish authorities, forced by the European Commission, have reacted as if the cause of the crisis was the public deficit, out of control because of lack of discipline, and low competitiveness, because wages have outstripped productivity during a long period of time. Consequently, politicians have opted for fiscal austerity and competitive devaluation. In this chapter, we have argued that this economic policy will not bring Spain back to pre-downturn figures, either for output or employment. Furthermore, austerity will shrink GDP and thus public revenue, making it harder to settle debts and this will make the spread with German bonds too high.

The alternative to austerity is expansive fiscal policy. However, this Keynesian option is not free of obstacles if it is implemented at the nation state level: the possibility of default for the government is very real if public debt goes beyond a certain threshold, so that public deficit may cause crowding out; and existing competitive problems may make the economy derail if the economy returns to a path of prosperity.

So, if an expansive strategy, which appears to be what is really needed, will not work when put in practice at the level of a nation state, what about implementing it at a European level? Many authors have suggested that the chief problem in the euro zone is current account imbalances within countries sharing the euro as a single currency (see for instance Hein *et al.*, 2011; Uxó *et al.*, 2011). To this we should add that this is taking place in a context of generalized low aggregate demand. An adequate economic policy would consist of two elements. On the one hand, a proactive fiscal policy at the EMU level, managed by a true European fiscal authority – something which needs to be created – and an ECB providing financial support for public deficit. On the other hand, a realignment of the price levels within the EMU, mostly by increasing, temporarily, nominal wages above productivity in the surplus countries, something which would have two effects. First, it would lead to a functional redistribution in favour of labour in these countries and, second, it would help periphery European countries restore competitiveness without requiring deflationary policies.

A fully fledged political union would make this economic policy easier to implement. However, a fully political union appears to be unlikely, even in the long run. Although this *ideal* solution is far from achievable, some small steps may help. As De Grauwe (2011) suggests, a European Monetary Fund, Eurobonds and some coordination on fiscal and wage policies could help restore prosperity in the EMU.

If a European solution is not possible, should we not think about leaving the European project?

Notes

1 A more detailed account can be found in Dejuán and Febrero (2011).

2 The reader will also realize that since mid 2008, the only components of aggregate demand making a positive contribution to GDP are public consumption and exports. See Figure 12.7.

3 When a bank grants a mortgage loan, its amount depends on the current value of the stream of future debt service payments which are calculated as a given percentage (usually 30 per cent) of the borrower's household income. Therefore, the size of a mortgage loan directly depends on: (i) household income, which in Spain has remained stable in real terms, (ii) the loan maturity, which has increased, on average, from 19 to 28 years and inversely on (iii) the interest rate, which has declined greatly. It is these factors which led to larger mortgages and then it was these larger mortgages which drove house prices upwards, leading to capital gains on land for developers.

4 If the first factor on the right of the equality in expression (12.8),

$$c \cdot \frac{wL_{t-1}}{Y_{t-1}} + v \cdot g - m$$

is lower than one, we can write (12.8) as:

$$Y_t = \frac{1}{1 - c \cdot \frac{wL_{t-1}}{Y_{t-1}} - v \cdot g^e + m} \cdot \left[I_0 + G_t + NX_0 - xp_t + \left\{ \frac{\Delta D_t}{p_{H_t}} - c \cdot DSP_t \right\} \right]$$

5 According to the Spanish National Statistics Agency, between early 2008 and the end of 2011, employment fell in Spain by roughly 2.6 million people. More than 1.4 million people were working in the construction and related industries.

6 It is the Spanish central bank which lends to Spanish banks mostly through main financial operations. As the reader knows, in the EMU, open market operations are implemented by national central banks as we have a decentralized system of national central banks.

7 Debts from one bank to another bank may rise because of a balance of trade operation or, just because agents decide to shift their savings from a deposit within a bank in country A to another bank in country B. See for instance Bindseil and König (2011).

8 According to the endogenous money view, Spanish banks create deposits when they grant loans to resident borrowers. And part of these deposits are used later to fund the purchase of some imports. Then, Spanish banks become indebted to banks in the exporting countries. These debts are financed often through the sale of Spanish mortgage backed securities to the creditor banks. In other words: the current account deficit is offset by a surplus in the capital account balance. Therefore, the savings glut hypothesis, an international version of the loanable funds theory, should not be accepted.

9 Also, as Koo (2008) has pointed out, when an economy is heavily indebted and in a process of deleveraging, monetary policy is not effective. This notwithstanding, the ECB should play a more active, stabilizing role in the sovereign debt market, because it is part of the monetary policy transmission mechanisms.

10 Though, not all of the fall in revenue is caused by a contraction of economic activity: in 2008 there were general elections and the government introduced tax cuts as a way to get more votes.

11 In quantitative terms the fiscal stimulus programme in these two years was estimated at about 2.32 per cent GDP. For more details, see Uxó *et al.* (2010).

12 For a critical appraisal of this model see, for instance, Arestis and Sawyer (2004) especially chapter 2.

13 In the absence of a sovereign central bank, the Spanish fiscal authority will have to provide support to some troubled financial institutions. By and large, this help does not raise the public budget deficit, though it contributes to raise public debt.

14 The three-equations model, underlying the austerity option, requires the nominal interest rate to change in the same direction as inflation, though to a greater extent, for a stable solution for output and inflation. In graphical terms, this condition grants a negatively sloped aggregate demand. However, when an economy is heavily indebted, and the interest rate is given from the outside and it does not change when inflation changes, as is the case for the Spanish economy, such a stability condition does not hold. Falling inflation (because of falling nominal wages) reduces the purchasing power of households reducing consumption, as debt servicing is in nominal terms; and falling inflation for a given (and non-falling) nominal interest rate leads to a rising real interest rate. Of course, declining inflation is a competitive devaluation which

(under normal circumstances) positively affects exports. Yet, it looks like the latter will not compensate for the negative consequences of the former.

References

Arestis, P. and Sawyer, M. (2004) *Re-examining Monetary and Fiscal Policy for the 21st Century*, Cheltenham: Edward Elgar.

Baddeley, M. (2003) *Investment: Theories and Analysis*, New York: Palgrave-Macmillan.

Bhaduri, A. (2011) "A contribution to the theory of financial fragility and crisis", *Cambridge Journal of Economics*, 35 (6): 995–1014.

Bindseil, U. and König, M. (2011) "The economics of TARGET 2 balances", *SFB 649 Discussion paper* 2011-035, Humboldt-Universität zu Berlin.

Bortis, H. (1997) *Institutions, Behaviour and Economic Theory: A Contribution to Classical-Keynesian Political Economy*, Cambridge: Cambridge University Press.

Carbó, S. and Maudos, J. (2011) "Reflexiones en torno a la reestructuración el sector bancario español", *Cuadernos de Información Económica*, 221, March to April: 81–96.

Cesaratto, S., Stirati, A. and Serrano, F. (2003) "Technical change, effective demand and employment", *Review of Political Economy*, 15 (1): 33–52.

De Grauwe, P. (2011) "Managing a fragile Eurozone", *CES-Ifo Forum* 2. Available at: www.cesifo-group.de/portal/pls/portal/docs/1/1211472.PDF (retrieved: 21 February 2012).

Dejuán, Ó. (2005) "Paths of accumulation and growth: towards a Keynesian long-period theory of output", *Review of Political Economy*, 17 (2): 231–252.

Dejuán, Ó. and Febrero, E. (2011) "The aftermath of a long decade of real interest rates (Spain, 1996–2008)", in Ó. Dejuán, E. Febrero and M.C. Marcuzzo (eds) *The First Great Recession of the 21st Century: Competing Explanations*, Cheltenham: Edward Elgar.

European Central Bank (2011) *The Euro Area Bank Lending Survey*, 6 October. Available at: www.ecb.int/stats/pdf/blssurvey_201110.pdf?b3a21aab22acbb0302ec64e6316a0b8e (retrieved: 22 February 2012).

European Commission (2009) *Annual Report on the Euro Area*, Economic and Financial Affairs, Directorate-General, Luxembourg. Available at: http://ec.europa.eu/economy_finance/publications/publication15951_en.pdf (retrieved: 22 February 2012).

European Commission (2011) "The EU's comprehensive policy response to the crisis", *Quarterly Report on the Euro Area*, 10 (1): 7–14.

Hein, E., Truger, A. and van Treek, T. (2011) "The European financial and economic crisis: alternative solutions from a (Post-) Keynesian perspective", *Institute für Makroökonomie und Konjunkturforschung*, Hans Böckler Stiftung, Düsseldorf, working paper no. 9/2011, 11 July.

IMF (2010) *Spain: Staff Report for the 2010 Article IV Consultation*, Washington: Publication Services. Available at: www.imf.org/external/pubs/ft/scr/2010/cr10254.pdf (retrieved: 21 February 2012).

IMF (2012) *World Economic Outlook, April 2012: Growth Resuming, Dangers Remain.* Washington: Publication Services. Available at: www.imf.org/external/pubs/ft/weo/2012/01/pdf/text.pdf (retrieved: 28 April 2012).

Kelton, S. (2011) "Limitations of the government budget constraint: users vs. issuers of the currency", *Panoeconomicus*, 58 (1): 57–66.

Koo, R. (2008) *The Holy Grail of Macroeconomics: Lessons from Japan's Great Recession*, Hoboken, NJ: Wiley.

Leamer, E. (2007) "Housing is the business cycle", *NBER Working Paper*, no. 13428,

Spanish Ministry of Finance (2011) *Stability Programme 2011–2014*, 29 April. Available at: www.minhap.gob.es/Documentacion/STABILITY%20PROGRAMME%20SPAIN%202011-2014%20ENGLISH%20VERSION.PDF (retrieved: 21 February 2012).

Spanish Ministry of Finance (2012) *Stability Programme 2012–2015*, 29 April. Available at: http://ec.europa.eu/economy_finance/economic_governance/sgp/pdf/20_scps/2012/01_programme/es_2012-04-30_sp_es.pdf (retrieved: 30 April 2012).

Uxó, J., Paúl, J. and Salinas, F. (2010) "Análisis y valoración de las medidas discrecionales de estímulo fiscal aplicadas en España en 2009", *Presupuesto y Gasto Público*, 59 (2): 55–82.

Uxó, J., Paúl, J. and Febrero, E. (2011) "Current account imbalances in the monetary union and the great recession: causes and policies", *Panoeconomicus*, 58 (5) Special Issue: 571–592.

Index

For Product Safety Concerns and Information please contact our EU
representative GPSR@taylorandfrancis.com
Taylor & Francis Verlag GmbH, Kaufingerstraße 24, 80331 München, Germany

www.ingramcontent.com/pod-product-compliance
Ingram Content Group UK Ltd.
Pitfield, Milton Keynes, MK11 3LW, UK
UKHW022218190926
475702UK00003B/416
* 9 7 8 0 4 1 5 8 2 2 7 6 3 *